A Shaping Joy

STUDIES IN THE WRITER'S CRAFT

A Shaping Joy

STUDIES IN THE WRITER'S CRAFT

CLEANTH BROOKS

Harcourt Brace Jovanovich, Inc., New York

Permission to reprint certain material has been obtained from the following. Astor-Honor, Inc.: from "Miss Leonora When Last Seen" in *Miss Leonora When Last Seen and Fifteen Other Stories* by Peter Taylor, Copyright © 1964 by Peter Taylor. Harcourt Brace Jovanovich, Inc: from "Old Mortality" in *Pale Horse, Pale Rider* by Katherine Anne Porter, copyright © 1937, 1965 by Katherine Anne Porter. Harcourt Brace Jovanovich, Inc. and Faber and Faber Limited: from *Collected Poems 1909-1962* and *Selected Essays* by T. S. Eliot, copyright 1932, 1946, 1950 by Harcourt Brace Jovanovich, Inc., copyright © 1960, 1963, 1964 by T. S. Eliot. Harcourt Brace Jovanovich, Inc. and Russell & Volkening, Inc.: from "A Piece of News" in *A Curtain of Green and Other Stories* by Eudora Welty, copyright © 1937, 1965 by Eudora Welty. Holt, Rinehart and Winston, Inc.: from *The Poetry of Robert Frost*, edited by Edward Connery Lathem, copyright 1923, © 1969 by Holt, Rinehart and Winston, Inc., copyright 1936, 1951 by Robert Frost, copyright © 1964 by Lesley Frost Ballantine. Holt, Rinehart and Winston, Inc., The Society of Authors, and Jonathan Cape Ltd.: from *The Collected Poems of A. E. Housman*, copyright 1922 by Holt, Rinehart and Winston, Inc., copyright 1950 by Barclays Bank Ltd..; from "A Shropshire Lad"—Authorized Edition—*The Collected Poems of A. E. Housman*, copyright 1939, 1940, © 1959 by Holt, Rinehart and Winston, Inc., copyright © 1967, 1968 by Robert E. Symons. The Macmillan Company, A. P. Watt & Son, and M. B. Yeats: for quotations of William Butler Yeats from *Collected Poems*, excerpts from "A Prayer for My Daughter," copyright 1924 by The Macmillan Company, renewed 1952 by Bertha Georgie Yeats, "Ego Dominus Tuus," copyright 1918 by The Macmillan Company, renewed 1946 by Bertha Georgie Yeats, "The Fisherman," copyright 1919 by The Macmillan Company, renewed 1947 by Bertha Georgie Yeats; from *Autobiography*, copyright 1916, 1936 by The Macmillan Company, renewed 1944 by Bertha Georgie Yeats; from *Essays and Introductions*, © Mrs. W. B. Yeats, 1961; from *Explorations*, copyright © Mrs. W. B. Yeats, 1962; from *The Letters of W. B. Yeats*, edited by Alan Wade, copyright 1953, 1954 by Anne Butler Yeats; from *Mythologies*, © Mrs. W. B. Yeats, 1959; from *A Vision*, copyright 1937 by The Macmillan Company, renewed 1965 by Bertha Georgie Yeats. Oxford University Press, Inc.: "Wordsworth and Human Suffering: Notes on Two Early Poems," from *From Sensibility to Romanticism*: Essays Presented to Frederick A. Pottle, edited by Frederick W. Hilles and Harold Bloom, copyright © 1965 by Oxford University Press, Inc. Random House, Inc.: from "Balaam and the Ass" and "The Guilty Vicarage" from *The Dyer's Hand* by W. H. Auden, copyright © 1962 by W. H. Auden; from the copyrighted works of William Faulkner; from *Ulysses* by James Joyce, copyright 1914, 1918 by Margaret Caroline Anderson, renewed 1942, 1946 by Nora Joseph Joyce; from *Selected Poems* by John Crowe Ransom, copyright 1945 by Alfred A. Knopf, Inc.; from *Selected Poems New and Old 1923-1966* by Robert Penn Warren, copyright © 1958 by Robert Penn Warren. Random House, Inc. and Faber and Faber Ltd.: from *Collected Shorter Poems 1927-1957* by W. H. Auden, copyright © 1966 by W. H. Auden. Vanderbilt University Press: "Eve's Awakening" from *Essays in Honor of Walter Clyde Curry*, 1954. *Ventures*, Magazine of the Yale Graduate School: for "Edgar Allan Poe as Interior Decorator," Volume VIII, Number 2, Fall 1968. The Viking Press, Inc.: excerpts from "Clay" from *Dubliners* by James Joyce. Yale University Press: for "William Butler Yeats as a Literary Critic" from *The Disciplines of Criticism*, edited by Peter Demetz, and others, 1968.

This joy, because it must always be making and mastering, remains in the hands and in the tongue of the artist, but with his eyes he enters upon a submissive, sorrowful contemplation of the great irremediable things. . . . That shaping joy has kept the sorrow pure, as it had kept it were the emotion love or hate, for the nobleness of the arts is in the mingling of contraries, the extremity of sorrow, the extremity of joy. . . ."

W. B. YEATS Poetry and Tradition

AUTHOR'S NOTE

I have made no special attempt to alter the form in which these essays first appeared. Thus many of them will at once reveal to the attentive reader that they were originally devised as lectures. Most of such alterations as I have made have to do with omitting or explaining references made obscure by the passage of time or with deleting illustrative material that had been used in more than one essay.

Contents

Acknowledgements

The following were first given as lectures: "The Uses of Literature," Ontario Education Association, 1963; "The Modern Writer and his Community," Glasgow University, 1965; "T. S. Eliot: Thinker and Artist," University of Kent, 1965; "Poetry Since *The Waste Land,*" the Grolier Club, New York, 1964; "Poetry and Poeticality," University of Manchester, 1966; "Auden as a Literary Critic," The English Institute, 1962; "The Criticism of Fiction: The Role of Close Analysis," Georgetown University, 1959; "The American 'Innocence' in James, Fitzgerald and Faulkner," Stanford University, 1964; "The Southern Temper," The British Association for American Studies, 1965; "Southern Literature: The Wellsprings of its Vitality," College Writers' Society of Louisiana, 1962; "Faulkner's Treatment of the Racial Problem: Typical Examples," Nordic American Studies Association, Helsinki, 1967; "The Unity of Marlowe's *Doctor Faustus,*" Oxford University, 1965; and "Alfred Edward Housman," first published by the Library of Congress, 1959 (the lecture was sponsored by the Gertrude Clarke Whittall Poetry and Literature Fund, and is reprinted by permission of the Library of Congress).

"Joyce's *Ulysses*: Symbolic Poem, Biography or Novel?" appears in *Imagined Worlds,* edited by Maynard Mack and Ian Gregor, Methuen, 1968.

Introduction

Most of the essays that appear in this collection were written within the last ten years; about half, within the last five. Many of them were first delivered as lectures and I have not seriously tried to remove the flavor of oral delivery. Some were commissioned; others represent an attempt to explore a problem that I personally found interesting. Thus, the collection is quite miscellaneous as to topic, style, and the originating impulse of the various essays. Yet I hope that the reader will be able to discern an underlying unity. Each essay is an attempt to refer a certain literary work to critical principles or to explore the principles themselves through a series of concrete illustrations.

It is possible, of course, that the reader may find not too little unity but too much, and a unity of the wrong kind, nothing less than an insistence on a methodology. A hurried and cluttered age such as ours must necessarily rely on classifications and labels and, in the interest of sheer good housekeeping, has to put people into appropriate pigeonholes and keep them there. The pigeonhole assigned to me carries the label "The New Criticism". Now, it is bad enough to live under any label, but one so nearly meaningless as "The New Criticism" – it is certainly not *new* – has peculiar disadvantages. For most people it vaguely signifies an anti-historical bias and a fixation on "close reading". The New Critic would seem to be trapped in a cell without windows or door, staring through a reading glass at his literary text, effectually cut off from all the activities of the world outside – from history and science, from the other arts, and from nature and humanity itself.

There are, to be sure, instances of "close reading" scattered throughout this volume and the familiar terms occur, particularly in essays like "The Language of Poetry" or "Poetry Since the *Waste Land*" or "Milton and the New Criticism". Yet the first essay in this volume speculates on the place of literature in the human economy and the very title of the second essay,

"The Modern Writer and his Community", promises a commentary on literary creation. The reader may feel gratified at a seeming change in direction or he may feel affronted to have his expectations disappointed. In either case, he may feel that he deserves some explanation.

I am not conscious of any fundamental change in my critical principles and what follows is no palinode. Rather, it constitutes an attempt to put my conception of the critic's job into better perspective.

Let me attempt to distinguish three areas of critical emphasis. And since I am being elementary, let me call them the three R's of criticism: criticism focused on the reader, on the writing, and on the writer.[1]

The critic who concentrates upon the reader may well stress his own reactions to a poem or novel and so give us an impressionistic criticism. Or he may study the reactions of other readers in order to provide a kind of literary sociology. Thus he may comment on the fact that certain novels appeal primarily to women or to the young or to the alienated; he may try to explain why the typical nineteenth-century reader tended to admire one version of Shakespeare and the eighteenth-century reader quite another, thus giving us a chapter in the history of literary taste. Yet, whether such criticism records the reader's own personal reaction or the reactions of others, it may justly be called an affective criticism.

A second kind of critic concerns himself with the writer. He is interested in how the literary work came to be, with its genesis. He may choose to explore the background, public and private, of the man who produced it. He may concern himself with the writer's economic or social or political experience, with the psychic turmoil that he has undergone, or with various other aspects of the writer's personality. This critic views the work with an eye to what it may reveal about its creator and about the culture which produced him and it.

A third kind of critic concerns himself primarily with the writing – with the literary work as such. The critical interest

---

[1] I *am* being elementary. For detailed discussions of such distinctions, I refer the reader to the work of two of my colleagues, René Wellek and W. K. Wimsatt, Jr.

here is with the poem or play or novel as a structure of meanings, as a piece of artistic craft, as a verbal context which, as Aristotle said in the *Poetics*, has a beginning, a middle and an end. What this critic stresses is the meaning of the work as developed through its form and structure. Plot, symbol, metaphor, tone, and even diction are some of the matters which come in for special attention. What has been inaccurately named the New Criticism is to be located here. It might better be called a structural or formal criticism, on the assumption that it is through literary form that the writer mediates his meanings.

Now obviously these three kinds of criticism are interrelated. Poems are not produced by machines[1] nor do they grow like turnips, though the process of organic growth in the vegetable and animal worlds has long furnished the literary scholar with an analogy of the way in which the parts of a poem or a novel are related to one another and of the way in which they seem to take form in the author's mind. But the human brain is a very special soil indeed. Poems don't normally "grow" outside the human mind, and even within it they do not literally spring up like mushrooms.

Since literary works are written by human beings, and human beings are always qualified by the age and society in which they live, any critical reader must take into account that qualification. At the most primary level there are the very words that the writer employs, for language is itself the product of a society, living through history. Language is an amalgam of representations of reality, both abstract concepts and valuations. Not even the most "formal" critic can ignore such considerations as these.

Since the formal critic is himself a reader, it will never do for him to forget the role always played by the reader in the process of realizing as an experience the words that appear on the page.

---

[1] Of course, the laws of chance are such that conceivably a good poem could be written by random distribution of words. If throughout eternity one filled bowls with alphabet soup, it is just possible that the "Ode on a Grecian Urn" might turn up, line by line through successive bowls, though of course only people who read English and know how to read a poem would recognize it when it appeared. Computers (because of human tampering, programming, that is) might be expected to do somewhat better.

If he is honest, he recognizes that he has his own blindsides and his own preferences and prejudices.

Yet having made all these admissions – I was once unwary enough to suppose that they could be taken for granted – there may be a great deal to say for criticism that puts its heaviest stresses on the writing itself. The most important thing about Shakespeare, for example, is the fact that he was a great dramatist. For better or worse, we know very little about his personality and most of the little that we do know is gained by inference from his plays and poems. Moreover, important as it may be to know the history of Shakespeare's time and his intellectual and social background, this background material is not the meaning of the plays, even though a knowledge of it may be a necessary requirement for a reader's comprehension of the meaning. The shape that Shakespeare has given the materials that he used – the form in which he has presented them – is the difference: the form makes his work something much more special and concentrated than a compendium or digest of the history and philosophy of his time.

The distinctions that I have made between emphasis on the reader, the writing, and the writer are, of course, arbitrary, just as are the political boundaries marked down on maps. Such distinctions have their use, but I do not suggest that they should be allowed to act as tariff barriers. I believe in free trade – nowhere more so than among the various areas of literary interest. I envisage the literary critic and scholar as constantly passing from one area to another. But it is important not to confuse one interest with another – the genesis of a work, for example, with its meaning or its value. To take the author's intent – as gleaned, say, from a letter or from his reported conversation with a friend – for the accomplished work is naïve. (This error is the intentional fallacy.)

One must also be wary of judging the value of a work by its effects – such as the intensity of its impact on the reader or the fact that it achieves great popularity, or its influence, say, in the realm of politics. (This error is the affective fallacy.) Every one of us has had the experience of admiring excessively – because of some personal or specially charged association – a poem or song which, in our more detached and judicious moments, we know to be of little value.

To sum up: though experience is ultimately a seamless garment and everything is related to everything else, the form of the achieved work is properly distinguished from the process that went into its making and from the effects that it produces on a particular reader or company of readers. Studies of the creative process and socio-psychological reports on reader response do have their own interest and they are valid literary studies. But it is the examination of the work itself that seems to me to have the best claim to be called a specifically "literary" criticism.

It may be useful at this point to offer an illustration. How might the three critical emphases that I have described be applied to Robert Frost's familiar poem "Stopping by Woods on a Snowy Evening"?

> Whose woods these are I think I know.
> His house is in the village though;
> He will not see me stopping here
> To watch his woods fill up with snow.
>
> My little horse must think it queer
> To stop without a farmhouse near
> Between the woods and frozen lake
> The darkest evening of the year.
>
> He gives his harness bells a shake
> To ask if there is some mistake.
> The only other sound's the sweep
> Of easy wind and downy flake.
>
> The woods are lovely, dark and deep,
> But I have promises to keep,
> And miles to go before I sleep,
> And miles to go before I sleep.

On the surface, the poem is casual enough. There is nothing portentous about this particular evening or this particular stretch of woodland or about anything that has happened to the man who is stopping by the woods. But the poem, though not in the least solemn, is rich and has a depth of meaning. It would be nonsense to regard it as merely a charming vignette which pays a half-whimsical tribute to the beauty of a winter landscape.

One notices in the first place that in the very beginning of the poem the speaker is aware that he is doing something that others might regard as curious – even suspicious. Why should anyone stop on this darkest evening of the year unless perhaps to speculate on some kind of business deal, calculating how he can buy this property at less than its value? The implication is that it may be just as well that the owner of the woods can't see him looking so intently at his trees.

In the next stanza the speaker says "My little horse must think it queer / To stop without a farmhouse near. . . ." The horse will be happy enough to get into his warm stall and to his dinner of oats. He gives the harness bells a shake and the man in the sleigh, half playfully, interprets the action as an intimation from the animal that they ought to drive on.

Why indeed *is* the man pausing by the woods? I have a friend who once wrote a charming and quite persuasive parody of a Freudian interpretation of the poem. In the parody he argued that the man in the sleigh was indulging in the Freudian death-wish – the yearning to sink back into the dark lovely depths of nature, to give over the human struggle, and to rest from the strain of living. Frost might have been amused had he read this interpretation, though I think he would have resented anyone's taking it seriously. Be that as it may, there is a fascination in regarding the way in which nature, tirelessly and instinctively and effortlessly, goes through its ineluctable processes. Such contemplation always involves separating oneself from the purely instinctual on the one hand and the merely calculating on the other, and thus requires some kind of quiescent state that might tempt one to call it a wish for death. At any rate, what the man in the sleigh is doing is indulging in an activity that is peculiar to man.

The horse cannot understand his master's motive in stopping nor could a purely practical man, the man who owns the woods. The man in the sleigh, then, is poised somewhere between the tyranny of instinct and the tyranny of reason – between blind animal impulse and pure rational calculation. Man

– when he is fully man, when he is truly human – is the aesthetic animal: he can appreciate in detachment from his wants. But man is also the ethical animal: he can remember his obligations, honor his promises, and drive on.

Or we can put matters in a slightly different way: man, unlike the horse, is not absorbed into nature: man is not at the mercy of his instincts, but is able to *know* what he is enjoying. Yet, if man is not submerged in nature, neither is he detached from nature, cut off from it as is the man who sees the woods as only so many board feet of lumber that will bring a certain price.

In trying to suggest that the poem involves a definition of man, I have risked burdening it – making it out to be more philosophical than it is. This would be a mistake, for the charm of the poem, and indeed its very value as a poem, comes from the fact that it does not spell out its meaning in some kind of message or commentary, but is content to suggest it through the drama of the incident, merely to hint at the deeper meanings, and to keep the tone of the poem dry, half-whimsical, half-ironic.

But couldn't we fortify our interpretation of the poem by appealing to Frost's letters or to friends' memories of his conversations? Yes, I suppose that we could. My memories of Frost the man make this poem seem thoroughly characteristic, not only of the depths but of the play of his mind. But one does not need to appeal to Frost's habit of talk in order to establish the meaning of the poem. The best evidence to attest the artistic choice and arrangement of the elements of this experience lies in the poem itself.

Someone recently told me a story that bears on this poem. There is in a Canadian cabin, carved on an interior wall with a jack-knife, a doggerel poem that ends: "But I have some promises to keep." Could Frost possibly have seen this poem? Or heard of it? Did he perhaps borrow from it for the last stanza of his own poem. We don't know.

Yet, suppose that a scholar finds that Frost did in fact borrow from this anonymous poet. What will that fact tell us? A good deal about the origins of the poem – about how Frost sometimes gathered his materials; but to the meaning of the poem it will add little if anything.

Thus far I have not considered in relation to this poem a criticism oriented to the reader. As for the background of the poem, the average reader requires little help: even if he lives in a climate without snow and though for him horse-drawn sleighs belong to a remote past, the movies, television, and Currier and Ives prints have supplied him with all the background material that he needs.

As for my own reactions, I prefer to leave them to be inferred from my account of the structure and meaning of the poem. But it may be well to say something here about the way in which "Stopping by Woods" has affected a generation of readers. Most of them have enjoyed it as a simple and warm-hearted human document without benefit of close examination or "explication" – to use the currently fashionable term. Some readers of a romantic cast of mind may even refuse to look at the text as carefully as we have done, for fear of destroying its charm and grace – that is, for fear of complicating their unthinking appreciation of it.

A reply to them might take this form: No one ought to recommend explication for explication's sake, anymore than one ought to ask the person who is enjoying a good dinner to chew the food strenuously just for the sake of giving it a thorough chewing. Yet there are people who think that they have got the meaning of this poem but who quite clearly have not got it – people who proceed to gulp the poem down without any chewing at all, as if it were a dab of ice-cream or a fluff of cotton candy. In doing so, they miss a true pleasure which they might otherwise have. The reputation of Frost's poetry was for a time injured by well-meaning friends who portrayed him as a kind of cracker-barrel philosopher, sitting on the porch of a Vermont general store, full of whimsical sententiousness and countrified wisdom. But Frost has much more to give us than simple countrified wisdom. He is an artist, and we have to take into account his use of the artistic medium if we are fully and truly to understand what he has to tell us. It is not enough to regard his poems merely as the expressions of a charming personality or as statements embodying some of the wisdom which we associate with his thought. The special character of the wisdom is mediated through the particular artistic form in which Frost has chosen to embody it.

If the artistic form, the dramatic structure of the poem, defines, fortifies, and validates what the poet has to say – if the poet speaks more meaningfully when he speaks as artist through the medium of his poetic form, then we will do well to take into account the niceties of that form if we want to know precisely what he has to tell us. Because this is true, one feels justified in emphasizing what I have called a formal or structural criticism.

What kind of critical emphasis is to be found in this collection? Various kinds. Yet emphasis on the work rather than on the reader or the writer is the staple of the criticism offered in these pages. Such is clearly the character of essays like "The Criticism of Fiction" but also even of those that make modest gestures toward literary history, like "The Southern Temper" or give an account of a poet's mind like that on Poe.

My concern in this introduction has been to try to mitigate the effects of an overshadowing generalization – not to offer further generalizations in an effort to justify the essays that follow. I would be happy if the reader came to them without special preconceptions and read them with as much openness and innocence as he could manage. For unless they can say something to him at this level, it will hardly be worth his trouble to try to establish the point of view from which they derive or the body of literary theory that they may be thought to support.

Cleanth Brooks
1970

1

The Uses of Literature

The uses of literature are obviously many. They range from the most serious to the most frivolous. Someone, once remarked in *The Partisan Review* that his reason for reading novels was to keep up with the latest trends in fashions in human conduct. What he sought in fiction, he was frank to say, was really a kind of ‚ossip, though of a somewhat higher order than that to which most gossip belongs. Other readers use literature, not to keep up with the ways of the world but to get away from them. This too is a time-honoured use, and though movies and television have tended to take over much of this function, many people still use literature to get away from boring monotony and find release in a strange, exciting, and wonderful world. I have mentioned two not very exalted uses, but there are dozens that might be named and I suppose that there is literally no end of naming them.

Before proceeding any further, I think that I should take notice of the fact that a large and vocal group of students and teachers today are asking for a moratorium on this naming and classifying the uses of literature. They argue that we are nowadays entirely too self-conscious about literature. Ours, so the word goes, is an age of criticism, and those who call it such, on the whole, deplore the fact. Perhaps the most witty and convincing writer who has taken this line is my good friend, the distinguished poet, Randall Jarrell. I admire his poetry, and I am bound to take seriously anything that he says on the subject of poetry. But in this instance, I have my disagreements with him, though I share his dismay at the mechanization of criticism which we have witnessed in the last decades and the perversions of criticism, especially that which I should call "symbol-mongering".

The person who deplores the self-consciousness of an age of criticism may well be a person who reads sensitively and easily and takes an obvious delight in his reading. Like the girl in the early lyric by William Butler Yeats who bade her lover "take love easy, as the leaves grow on the tree", such an amateur of literature would counsel that we take our literature easy. Easy does it. Just give yourself up to it. Read what you enjoy and read for enjoyment. Such counsels as these are winning in their simplicity, but I think that they are really counsels of perfection. I am not at all convinced that they will serve for a generation which has never been taught to read, or worse still, which perhaps has been systematically mistaught. In any case, our generation inherits a language that has lost its hold on concrete reality, that is slack and imprecise, and that reflects a culture that lacks any commonly accepted value-system. The symbols that the average reader knows are not disciplined by traditional and concrete rituals. They are often the emanations of a popular vulgarized Freudianism. The only discipline that they know is that of current journalism and best-selling fiction. I am speaking, of course, of the situation in the United States, but Canadians too may know some of these ills, and if you do not have your own home-grown viruses, contaminations do reach you nevertheless, I am told, across our celebrated unfortified common border.

I too wish that we could become less self-conscious about our reading, but I reflect that the ills that beset our culture do not stem merely from our literary self-consciousness. They have a deeper source in the underlying culture. Instead of simply forgetting about critical methods and doing what comes naturally to the healthy spirit, we shall be forced to use good method in order to drive out bad method, and sound procedures in order to correct unsound procedures.

What I have just been saying accounts for the fact that in talking about the uses of literature, I shall have little to say about the pleasure that it provides, for the modern deprecation of definition and classification of literary effects usually goes hand in hand with an admonition to read literature for pleasure. I enjoy literature, but I would prefer not to make pleasure the end by which literature is defined, but rather to take the view that any healthy use of literature is bound to be pleasurable. In an age of criticism, there are doubtless students of literature who gloomily swat up their assignments in a thoroughly joyless fashion, but this sad state of affairs is not confined to literature. It crops up in other places in our civilization. I know some tennis players, for example, who play the game not for fun but in a spirit of grim, close-lipped competition, and there are indeed some dark stories about some American university football teams that train so assiduously, what with sessions with the tackling dummy and skull practice around the blackboard, charting formations and learning plays, that the players come to hate the game. But in any case, one cannot hope to mend matters by a simple reversal of procedures. The casual, thoughtless reading of literature will not automatically make reading a pleasure. Besides, the joys of ignorance are nearly always bought at a rather high price. In any case, my experience tells me that delight in an activity tends to accompany intensity of application. The young men who really love automobiles literally can't leave them alone. They are continually tinkering with their jalopies and hotrods, equipping them with cut-outs, experimenting with special kinds of carburetors, endlessly taking them to pieces and putting them back together again. These are the true amateurs of automobiles – not the lady who says to her chauffeur, "Home, James" and whose concern is only with the upholstery of the seat on which she sits, and not the business man who never looks under the hood of his car and does not care to look provided the car continues to get him to his office on time. With this analogy in mind, I can find it in my heart to forgive a good deal of the endless tinkering with literature that goes on in some far-fetched and often silly analyses in which young instructors in English literature attempt to install in Keats's "Ode to a Nightingale" a Freudian manifold with which the designer obviously did not equip it, or attach a two-tailed symbolic exhaust as a kind of postlude to William Wordsworth's *Prelude*.

Since we are not now in a state of literary innocence, and are not likely to be so again for a long time, I can see no harm in reflecting upon what we may hope to derive from literature and in trying to distinguish between the central and essential and the peripheral and adventitious uses of literature. But the spirit in which I address you is not dogmatic, and though I shall point to one particular use as the essential use of literature, I am far from denying that other uses exist or that they may have their importance. Perhaps a homely illustration will serve to make my point. A yardstick is a handy thing to have around the house. One may use it to tap on the window to attract the attention of a passerby, or to knock down a cobweb too high to reach in one of the corners of the ceiling, or to start a stuck curtain ring moving on its rod, or as a stick to threaten a dog that is about to jump on the sofa. But it does no harm to remind ourselves that the specific function of a yardstick is to measure whatever needs to be measured. Moreover, to remind ourselves of the fact will not keep us from snatching up the yardstick to threaten the dog or using it as a pointer when we are teaching a child his figures from some blackboard that we have set up in the room. In short, my wish is not to add one more specialization to a modern man who is already woefully over-specialized. He will doubtless continue to get out of his reading the various things that literature provides, and let us hope that among them he will get the essential things.

That essential thing has seemed to many thinkers in the past to be self-expression, and the need to express ourselves may possess a peculiar urgency in our own day. Some of you in the audience may be surprised, therefore, if I do not choose this as the prime and significant use of literature.

Expression does have a definite therapeutic value, not only for the author, but possibly also vicariously for his reader. But whatever may have been the value to the author in getting the perilous stuff out of his system, in making a clean breast of it, or to go, as Aristotle's metaphor directs us, to another part of the human anatomy, in achieving a *katharsis*, whatever the value of these purgatives, the experience of a good novel or a powerful poem is not precisely the same thing as having it out on the psycho-analyst's couch.

Doubtless an expressive theory can be so qualified as to take into account some of these peculiar and special effects of literature, but a great deal of qualification is needed unless we are willing to settle for a vague and general account.

If we can show that a poem or a novel is no mere blowing off of steam, no mere releasing of emotions that have been bottled up, we will be on the way to defining literature as a species of knowledge. For that reason, I prefer to begin by considering a kind of knowledge. But I would be disingenuous if I did not concede that a knowledge theory requires qualification, too. For if literature yields knowledge, it is surely of a special and peculiar kind. It is not, for example, either philosophical or historical knowledge as such, though literature may incidentally involve such knowledge. The peculiar kind of knowledge that literature gives us is concrete – not a generalization about facts but a special kind of focusing upon the facts themselves – not the remedy for a problem but the special presentation of the problem itself. In short, we oversimplify the way in which literature offers its characteristic knowledge if we see the form of literature as merely rhetorical and its method merely didactic.

In his "The Social Function of Poetry" T. S. Eliot makes this point – or at least a closely related point – in his own terms. He writes that Dante in his *Divine Comedy*, Lucretius in his *De Rerum Natura* and Virgil in his *Georgics* wrote poems that "were not designed to persuade the readers to an intellectual assent, but to convey an emotional equivalent for the ideas. What Lucretius and Dante teach you, in fact, is *what it feels like* to hold certain beliefs; what Virgil teaches you, is to feel yourself inside the agrarian life."[1] Eliot, to be sure, is here demonstrating his favourite point, that poets had better not attempt to invent philosophies but ought to make use of philosophies and value systems that are already in existence. Nevertheless, and perhaps all the more powerfully, Eliot strikes a direct blow at the didactic theory when he holds that even a Lucretius or a Dante is not primarily teaching us certain beliefs.

Let me attempt to illustrate this general point from some of the classics of our western literature. If we look closely at the

---

[1] I am quoting here from the 1945 text.

great works we shall find that they turn out to be, not generalizations about life, but dramatizations of concrete problems – not remedies designed to solve these problems but rather diagnoses in which the problems are defined and realized for what they are.

A formula can be learned and applied, but the full, concrete, appropriate response to a situation can only be experienced. Literature is thus incurably concrete – not abstract. That fact sometimes distresses the man who has a programme to be carried out. It sometimes, for instance, disturbs the forward-looking liberal who thinks that surely there are certain rules that human kind can learn, once and for all, and so avoid *that* problem again.

Some years ago I finished a public lecture upon one of the great meditative lyrics in English literature, Andrew Marvell's "The Garden". I was interested in having my audience understand the richness and fulness of the poem. I took if for granted that the poem constituted one of the great exercises of the human spirit. But when questions were asked for, one young university teacher in the audience indicated his distress at the formal emptiness of my discussion of the poem. My account of the poem had told him nothing about how to handle the problem of the atomic bomb. The young man was earnest; he was concerned. He pointed out that we lived in parlous times – as indeed we do – and that if the English teacher was simply going to fiddle with nuances of meaning and niceties of technique, then that was a waste of precious time when the great peril was already upon us. He gave me to understand that my fiddling with the poem was almost as bad as Nero's fiddling while Rome went up in smoke. I had not set the city on fire but I was clearly not putting my own shoulder to the hose-cart – worse still, I was beguiling others to imitate my irresponsibility.

It was not enough to assure the young man that the task of the English teacher was an important one even if it could provide no defense against the atomic bomb – that the effects of the teaching of literature were at best long-term effects and pervasive effects, not direct and immediate effects – that the task of keeping the imagination alive and the methods of communication unblocked was in the long run an indispensable task and one that was rendered more important rather than less important by the fact of the bomb. The young man wanted direct action and he wanted it promptly. Whether or not he knew it, he was actually insisting that literature be a powerful propaganda instrument, at the service, of course, of a true ethic or the correct political programme, if only, alas, we could agree upon what the true ethic or the correct political programme is. But many of us who teach English share in some less flagrant form my young friend's misapprehension of what literature is and of what it can do. And the root of the misapprehension, let me say again, is in our assumption that the themes of literature are generalizations to be affirmed rather than situations to be explored.

One of the most important themes to be met with in literature is that of the difficult choice. There is, for example, the choice between evils or the choice between goods. Huckleberry Finn has to face the problem with reference to his companion on the raft, the runaway slave Jim. He can act in accordance with the social pressures of his community and turn Jim over to the authorities, or he can act in accordance with his human sympathies and help him escape. Here the choice will seem to us perfectly obvious, yet Mark Twain has tried to make it a difficult choice for Huck, one that goes against the grain of his upbringing and one that is achieved only after some agony of will. The choice that Sophocles' Antigone makes is more clearly and obviously – even to a modern reader – a choice between rival goods. She may choose to obey the law of the state and refuse to bury the body of her brother who has been slain in his rebellion against the state. Or she may honour the claims of blood kinship and defy the state. In our day Antigone's choice has actually been rewritten as a defiance of the claims of the tyrannical Fascist state, and the difficulty of Antigone's choice as Sophocles conceived it has been obscured. But in any case the modern reader probably has some difficulty in resisting a tendency to think of Antigone's choice as one that certainly required bravery but no special moral discrimination. Yet there is every indication that for the Greek audience her choice was a difficult one, for if the necessity for burying one's kinsman was fraught with the highest religious import, so was the Greek citizen's conception of his debt to the *polis*.

For a modern reader the choice that Shakespeare's Isabella is forced to make in the play *Measure for Measure* may seem a more obvious instance of the choice between goods or the choice between evils. Isabella, you will remember, is told by the ruler of the city that if she will yield her body to his lust he will pardon her brother who faces execution for having begot a bastard. In effect, Angelo tells Isabella that if she feels her brother's offense to be so slight, perhaps she will think it no great matter, to risk his begetting a child upon her. The Elizabethan audience certainly would have regarded Isabella's dilemma as a cruel one, no matter which action she finally took. The play actually suggests that it is a defect in Isabella that she found the choice too easy.

As one looks back over these three examples of excruciating choice, several observations seem in order. One of them is this: that the historian of morals and manners could use them to show how much the notions of what is right and what is wrong have shifted through the course of the ages. But though such a use would be perfectly valid, it seems to be just as evident that what the author in each case wanted to do was to present the experience of the agony of will. In short, what is really common to all three cases is not a set of specific moral judgments – the Greeks regarded slavery in a different fashion from the way in which we regard it and we attach a different significance to the importance of burial rites – the common elements inhere, not in specific judgments, but in the fact that human beings throughout the ages have been faced with the moral responsibility of choosing even when there could be no simple, clear, and just choice. Even when we seem to move away from the dramatization of particular problems, from the question of what is the truth about this matter to the quest for knowledge itself, the general considerations that I have urged seem to hold. We get a concrete testing of the quest rather than a recipe for the acquisition of knowledge – a criticism of the search and what it entails rather than a mere incitement to it. Consider, for example, the story of Doctor Faustus as Christopher Marlowe tells it. Faustus values knowledge so much that he sells his soul to the devil in order to obtain the arcane knowledge that he covets. But the play makes plain why it is a bad bargain, and insists upon the ironic fact that the only knowledge that Faustus ultimately obtains is a knowledge of his own limitations as a moral being. Faustus could say with Milton's Adam:

> . . . our Eyes
> Op'nd we find indeed, and find we know
> Both Good and Evil, Good lost and Evil got,
> Bad fruit of knowledge, if this be to know . . .

In Marlowe's play the search for knowledge is open and evident, but the theme can be found in many another work in which it is not explicitly declared. For example, the subplot of Shakespeare's *King Lear* yields a fine example. Gloucester does not know that he is embarking on a search of this sort when we first meet him in the play. He thinks that he knows both his sons, the legitimate son Edgar and the illegitimate son Edmund. But as events prove, he does not know which is the true son and which the false, and learns about them and about himself only after terrible mistakes and terrible suffering. Indeed before he can see the truth he must forfeit his own eyesight. As he puts it, in response to the remonstrance that "You cannot see your way",

> I have no way, and therefore want no eyes;
> I stumbled when I saw.

It may seem perverse to argue that the story of Gloucester may be interpreted as a search for knowledge, particularly in view of the fact that the Gloucester whom we meet at the beginning of the tragedy is a sufficiently complacent and jolly courtier, one who is obviously not searching for anything. Yet I know no other way in which to regard the whole story of Gloucester except as a search for knowledge, a search begun unwittingly, no doubt, but one which has meaning for Gloucester himself and for us as readers only as it culminates in a series of disclosures in which the truth about himself and about his world is eventually revealed to the sufferer. One could go on, of course, to the main plot of this great play, and see it as also embodying the theme of self-discovery. For the story of Lear (which the story of Gloucester echoes in minor key) is the story of a search for knowledge, again unwittingly embarked upon by the aged king, but accepted, and followed through, and eventually culminating in the precious truth about his daughters, and about the nature of filial love, and about the nature of himself.

There is another great play that echoes, or rather anticipates, Gloucester's story even in specific happenings. Gloucester loses his eyes before he can truly see, and so does Sophocles' great protagonist, Oedipus, in the play of *Oedipus the King*.

Unlike Faustus, Oedipus is not embarking upon a quest for self-knowledge or knowledge in any general sense. His plague-stricken people are appealing to him for help and he speedily finds that in order to render help he must discover the murderer of Laius, the former king. The knowledge he seeks is *ad hoc* knowledge, knowledge as specific and limited as that sought by the detective hero in a current who-done-it. But imperceptibly this search for specific knowledge turns into self-knowledge and becomes precisely that in the great climactic scene in which Oedipus does finally see who the murderer is and who *he* is, and in the agony of that knowledge, tears out his own eyes.

I can see no other way in which to teach *Oedipus the King* except as a search for knowledge. If it is Oedipus' disaster that he should attain to the knowledge to which he finally wins, it is also his glory that, once he is embarked upon his quest, he allows absolutely nothing to deter him from it. In this matter, Oedipus seems to me as fine an example of questing Faustian man as is Faustus himself. The times of the atomic bomb, far from making Sophocles' play remote and peripheral, have succeeded in bringing it into the sharpest focus once again. I find in the *Oedipus the King*, therefore, a wise and penetrating critique of the claims of rationality. But I find in it also a parable about the kind of knowledge that literature yields.

The knowledge that literature gives us is specifically a knowledge of ourselves: *Oedipus the King* is indeed quite typical. The knowledge vouchsafed is never merely of outside forces or situ-

tions but of ourselves in relation to them. We usually learn that
we are involved and what it feels like to be involved. The
knowledge that literature gives, we might say, is always knowledge of a value-structured world, not the abstract world of the
mathematician or the physicist but a world conceived in human
terms, which means conceived dramatically.

If it is this kind of human world – a world ordered with reference to human values – you may well ask what is so very
special about such knowledge. Is it not available to any human
being simply by virtue of his being a human being? Is it not
available to the aboriginal savage? To the child who believes in
his fairy stories and practices his own fantasies? Such questions,
I concede, are quite in order and there is a very real sense in
which a savage or a child does seem closer to this kind of knowledge than the man of the twentieth century or the sophisticated
adult. But in spite of an essential connection between poetry and
the childlike or preliterate imagination, the knowledge that the
great dramas and the great fiction and great poetry give is not
childish and is not simple. Moreover, it may be that the work
of the artist is most important in a civilization like our own,
simply because our civilization is abstract and complicated.
Eliseo Vivas has put the matter very well in his essay *Literature
and Knowledge*. He writes that "there is a superior reality sym-
bolized in the work of art – but it is superior, not to the reality
of the world of physics, but to the alleged reality of our physical
world, that is, of the cliché-cluttered, hastily grasped, by-pas-
sion-blurred world in which we daily live". Thus Vivas makes
plain that the knowledge given by the artist does not compete
with scientific knowledge; it is not a matter of claiming that it is
superior to, or truer than, such knowledge. What it is superior to
is the pseudo-scientific, pseudo-artistic, blurred and smudged
world in which most of us conduct our desperate lives.

I want to stress Vivas's term "cliché-cluttered", for falsity and
distortion are involved in these second and third-hand impressions of the world. All of us are aware that the artist tries to
remove "the film of familiarity" – Coleridge's phrase – to get
past the stereotypes – to restore a fresh and immediate and thus

true vision of reality. This is why a Wordsworth found truth in the child's view of nature or why a Herder found a vital poetry in the savage's awed vision of a numinous world.

I should like, however, to turn to one of the classics of our time, James Joyce's *Ulysses*, for an illustration of this prime function of literature. I grant that at this date it is perhaps rash to venture still another suggestion as to the meaning of that curious and wonderful book, but I shall make the venture anyway. I suggest that *Ulysses* is, among other things, about the breakup of modern civilization and the plight of our present culture. I know that the critical consensus at the moment is that the novel tells how Stephen Dedalus completed his education as an artist by learning the importance of the commonplace. Doubtless it was very important for Stephen Dedalus, the arrogant young artist, to learn about charity and to come to respect the dignity of the common man – though I do not find any evidence in *Ulysses* itself that Stephen Dedalus ever did come to this kind of knowledge. But in any event, the city through which Stephen and Leopold Bloom walk is a community which has fallen to pieces, a world ending not with a bang but a whimper. A tell-tale sign of this is the way in which the whole novel is loaded with clichés – clichés wittily used and masterfully used to show the hardening of the arteries of thought and feeling in this culture which has slipped back towards the barbarism of civilization. Joyce has a great deal of fun with his clichés: most of the comedy of the book arises from his manipulation of them, but I suggest that there is serious import as well. Consider, for example, the mind of Gerty MacDowell as she sits on the beach and lets her sensibility play in daydreams about the dark stranger, Leopold Bloom, seated not too far away from her. "The waxen pallor of her face was almost spiritual in its ivory-like purity though her rosebud mouth was a genuine Cupid's bow, Greekly perfect. Her hands were of finely veined alabaster with tapering fingers and as white as lemon juice and queen of ointments could make them though it was not true that she used to wear kid gloves in bed or take a milk foot bath either. Bertha Supple told that once to Edy Boardman, a deliberate lie, when she was black out at daggers drawn with Gerty (the girl chums had of course their little tiffs from time to time like the rest of mortals) and she told her not to let on whatever she did that it was her who told her or she'd never speak to her again. No. Honour where honour is due. There was an innate refinement, a languid queenly *hauteur* about Gerty which was unmistakably evidenced in her delicate hands and higharched instep. Had kind fate but willed her to be born a gentlewoman of high degree in her own right and had she only received the benefit of a good education, Gerty MacDowell might easily have held her own beside any lady in the land and have seen herself exquisitely gowned with jewels on her brow and patrician suitors at her feet vying with one another to pay their devoirs to her."

Now Joyce is not making fun of Gerty. He is not breaking this tawdry little butterfly on the wheel. Gerty is, let us grant, more sinned against than sinning. But Joyce is exposing her little corrupted soul. Her mind – or what passes for her mind – is made up of stereotypes from the cheaper fashion magazines, third-rate fiction, and the nasty-niceness of a sentimental art.

Here for example is Gerty's womanliness as she imagines what she could do for the dark stranger seated across from her on the beach. "She would care for him with creature comforts too for Gerty was womanly wise and knew that a mere man liked that feeling of hominess. Her griddlecakes done to a goldenbrown hue and queen Ann's pudding of delightful creaminess had won golden opinions from all because she had a lucky hand also for lighting a fire, dredge in the fine selfraising flour and always stir in the same direction then cream the milk and sugar and whisk well the whites of eggs though she didn't like the eating part when there were any people that made her shy and often she wondered why you couldn't eat something poetical like violets or roses and they would have a beautifully appointed drawing-room with pictures and engravings – and the photograph of grandpapa Giltrap's lovely dog Garryowen that almost talked, it was so human, and chintz covers for the chairs and that silver toastrack in Cleary's summer jumble sales like they have in rich houses."

But can the sleazy, shop-worn fabrics that made up the rag-bag of Gerty's little soul be of any importance? Is it worth revealing the quality of such a soul? I think that it is of the highest importance. When the very means for registering value are as coarsened and corrupted as are Gerty's, how can one hope for honesty, decency, charity, or any of the other virtues on which any healthy civilization is founded? Gerty's values have been imbibed, if not with her mother's milk, at least from the dugs of a corrupt civilization and so she, herself, is tainted. Even her chlorotic virtue and her strained attenuations of refinement testify to her corruption.

What Joyce is saying here about Gerty MacDowell is, of course, only one aspect of what he is saying about twentieth-century man in his great novel. The clichés that make up the stuff of Gerty's mind constitute only one particular bundle of the clichés exposed by Joyce in other chapters. But wherever we want to look in this novel, we shall find the same close union between the state of language and the state of the mind, and to peel off the dead skin and callosities from the language – even if this seems to be done simply for the fun in it – is not merely to remove dead tissue. It could mean exposing once more the living fibres of the imagination so that men might once again see who they are and where they are.

I should like to draw my concluding illustration, however, from another source, on the supposition that it might carry greater weight. For one of our most powerful falsifying stereotypes is the notion that literature cannot really have very much to say about life unless it does convey an explicit message. My illustration comes from the trial of Adolph Eichmann. Miss Hannah Arendt commented effectively upon the importance of stereotypes in her discussion of the Eichmann trial in the *New Yorker*, Miss Arendt gives the following description of Eichmann's execution. After the guards had tied his ankles and knees, they offered him the black hood, which he refused with the statement "I don't need that". Miss Arendt writes that "He was in complete command of himself. Nay, he was more; he was completely himself. Nothing could have demonstrated this more convincingly than the grotesque silliness of his last words. In these last words, at the foot of the gallows, after having declared himself a *Gottglaübiger* – a Nazi expression for those who have abandoned their Christian faith in a personal God and life after death – he addressed the group that witnessed the execution as follows: 'After a short while, gentlemen, *we shall all meet again.* Such is the fate of all men. Long live Germany, long live Argentina, long live Austria. *I shall not forget them.*' In the face of death, he had found the cliché used in funeral oratory, but his memory had played him one last trick: he had forgotten that he was no Christian and that this was his own funeral. It was as though in those last minutes he was summing up the lesson that this long course in human wickedness had taught us – the lesson of the fearsome word-and-thought-defying *banality of evil.*"

But Miss Arendt's point about the banality of evil may not, to those of you who have not read her other articles, be altogether evident, and I shall beg your indulgence as I spell out in a little more detail what I think she means to say. Let me try to put it in my own words: the most terrible aspect of the Nazi executions was the frivolousness with which they were ordered and carried out. The murderers could not really take in what they were doing. They simply could not respond with sensitivity. They might have been killing pigs instead of human beings. When evil becomes banal, then almost any monstrous thing can happen. When the soul becomes so calloused, so insensitive, so much a mass of worn and almost automatic responses, then the human being, having lost his sensitivity, is capable of almost anything. I think that I recall that the poet W. H. Auden has spoken of this same banality with which the Nazis beat up and killed Jews, simply out of boredom – for want of having anything more interesting to do. People who are sensitive and fully aware of what they are doing and whose responses to the world about them, including their responses to other human beings, are fresh and individual, are simply incapable of this kind of wickedness. (I do not deny that they are capable of evil, but they are not capable of this kind of dehumanized wickedness.)

Miss Arendt then is quite right in seizing upon the fact that Eichmann, in his last speeches, is making use of clichés: phrases so worn that they have ceased to have very much meaning, and which, therefore, do not jostle against each other in the mind of the speaker even though they are inconsistent with each other and with the speaker's own professed beliefs. Thus Eichmann could say "We shall all meet again" though he did not believe in an afterlife, and though on the verge of death, he could assert, with a straight face, "I shall not forget them."

It would, of course, be nonsense to say that the man whose metaphors are dead and whose speeches are automatic and whose mind is a basket of deadened phrases and odds and ends of rhetorical junk is necessarily a human butcher. I have no intention of trying to turn the tired business man (or for that matter, the tired teacher marking freshman themes) into a monster. But the death of language is serious. The dying flesh of language may produce a spiritual gangrene. One of the uses of literature is to keep our language alive – to keep the blood circulating through the tissues of the body politic. There can scarcely be a more vital function.

2

The Modern Writer and his Community

For whom does the poet or the novelist or the dramatist write? To please himself, most writers would say. This is what they do say in a recently published series of interviews with modern British and American authors, entitled *Counterpoint*.[1] A writer like Peter De Vries tells us that a writer best discharges his obligation to the public "by honouring his obligation to himself". Doris Lessing observes that "You should write, first of all, to please yourself. You shouldn't care a damn about anybody else at all". Irwin Shaw holds that "the writer has only one obligation – to stay alive and try to please himself". These sentiments are typical – and, as far as they go, perfectly sound. How else can a writer function? With dozens of problems of selection and emphasis and articulation to make on every page that he writes, he cannot be always looking back over his shoulder to to try to catch the changing expressions on the faces of a hypothetical public.

He must try to please himself first of all, but in our civilization a crucial problem may be that of discovering the self that he ought to please. The difficulty of identifying and realizing one's true self is a *leitmotiv* of another recently published series of interviews, entitled *Under Pressure*, edited by A. Alvarez.[2] The identity of the self becomes problematical because of the nature of modern society – because of the relation of the writer to his community – or more properly, because for him there may be no real community. The modern writer is alienated from society – a point that the writers interviewed in *Under Pressure*

---

[1] Ed. by Roy Newquist, London: George Allen & Unwin, Ltd, 1965.
[2] London: Penguin Books, Ltd, 1965.

make over and over, though some of them rejoice rather than lament that this should be true.

The importance of the community to the writer, then, may show itself most powerfully in the lack of a community; and the very self-consciousness of the contemporary writer may spring from the disappearance of any strongly felt relation to the society about him.

The alienation of the writer from his society was not, of course, discovered yesterday. In the early Wordsworth there are clear references to such a lesion. But I would like to take up the matter at a point much nearer our own time and to choose for my principal texts some comments by two of the great literary masters of our century, T. S. Eliot and W. B. Yeats, both of whom were aware of the problem of alienation and both of whom had thought long and hard about it. In 1940 Eliot had this to say about the writer's relation to an actual community:

> We write for our friends – most of whom are also writers – or for our pupils – most of whom are going to be writers; or we aim at a hypothetical popular audience which we do not know and which perhaps does not exist. The result in any case is apt to be a refined provincial crudity[1]

Eliot would doubtless agree that we write to please ourselves, but he is too much the realist to leave it at that: one writes to please the other writers that one knows – most probably those closest in sympathies and aims. The risk is that the author limits himself to a clique, and yet if he attempts to write for a general audience, he finds himself, in our times at least, writing for an audience that he does not know and at whose sensibilities he can only guess. In sum, as Eliot puts it, "the more serious authors have a limited, and even provincial audience, and the more popular write for an illiterate and uncritical mob."[2] The last phrase may seem ungenerous, and yet anyone who has been forced to take a hard look at current best-sellers, magazines of mass circulation, and popular journalism, will concede that the statement is literally true. If the words *illiterate, uncritical,* and

---

[1] *The Idea of a Christian Society*, London: Faber & Faber, 1939; New York: Harcourt, Brace & Co, 1940, p. 38.
[2] Ibid., p. 40.

mob seem too much charged with emotion, then let us risk jargon by revising the phrase to read: the more popular writer addresses a mass audience, largely innocent of literary training, without critical standards, and, in David Riesman's phrase, "other-directed" – the others who supply the directions often being the advertisers.

Hasn't this, however, always been the essential situation? Has there ever been a time in which the writer, in writing to please himself and those people whose minds he knows best, could also write – without condescension – for a general audience?

I think there has been such a time. In an earlier age the writer was evidently less sharply detached from society, had the support of a community, and consequently escaped much of our modern self-consciousness. Eliot obviously sees the modern situation as relatively new and a change for the worse. This also is the basic supposition of W. B. Yeats, nearly all of whose critical writing is suffused with an awareness of the difference between the modern writer's situation and that of a Shakespeare or a Chaucer.

In that brilliant little thumbnail sketch of English literature which Yeats borrowed from his friend William Magee ("John Eglinton")[1] – and improved upon – the history of English literature since the Middle Ages is described as essentially a movement from unity of culture to the isolation of the individual. Yeats arrives at our present day by imagining "Chaucer's personages" to have disengaged themselves from "Chaucer's crowd" through having forgot their "common goal and shrine" and after "sundry magnifications [to have become] each in turn the center of some Elizabethan play", and then, finally, through having split into their elements, to have "given birth to romantic poetry". When men experience a weakening of the common values that make them one people and when, as a consequence, they become more and more interested in themselves, they gain dramatic intensity; but as the process of disintegration goes on, eventually they become isolated monads, each

[1] Thomas R. Whitaker, *Swan and Shadow* (Chapel Hill: University of North Carolina Press, 1964), p. 30.

man limited to his own subjective values and dreaming his own individual dream.[1]

I am not concerned here with Yeats's question, put to himself as a modern writer, as to whether he ought to try to run the film back the other way and thus reverse the course of literary history, turning modern men back once more into a group of pilgrims who shared a common dream and were moving once more toward some common shrine. What I would stress here is the neatness and concision with which Yeats has related, in a meaningful series, Chaucer, the Elizabethan playwrights, and the Romantic poets of the early nineteenth century. Yeats sees Chaucer as a writer who participates in the unity of culture characteristic of the high Middle Ages, a unity so authentic that he could present with objectivity, and yet with animation and zest, the whole society in its characteristic activity – its folk-lore and its science, its religion, its entertainment, and even its bawdry, all fitting into a coherent schema. Next, Yeats sees in Elizabethan drama a partial fragmentation of medieval society, the writer's attention now focused upon the individual and his relationship to his fellows. But in the Elizabethan period, of course, the general community of values still held, and because it did, this concentration on the individual could yield a tremendous gain in dramatic power. Lastly, Yeats sees the Romantic period as the result of a further fragmentation of society. The Romantic poet is cut off from the values and beliefs held by his fellows, alienated from his society, filled with his own dreams and visions like Coleridge's Ancient Mariner or like the ecstatic visionary depicted in "Kubla Khan", whose awful holiness must appear to the crowd gathered about him a kind of derangement and madness:

> Weave a circle round him thrice,
> And close your eyes with holy dread,
> For he on honey-dew hath fed,
> And drunk the milk of Paradise.

By the time that Coleridge and his fellow Romantic poets

---

[1] *Autobiography*, London: Macmillan 1955; New York: Macmillan, 1953, 'The Trembling of the Veil', Book I, Sec. 23. The English edition is entitled *Autobiographies*.

were writing, the industrial revolution had already occurred, Blake's dark satanic mills had arisen in England's green and pleasant land, and society had lost much of the common dream that had given the medieval community its basic unity.

In a later section of his *Autobiography*, Yeats recurs to the notion that the great Elizabethan period was the result of an incipient disintegration of the medieval culture. He writes:

> Somewhere about 1450 . . . men attained to personality in great numbers, [to] "Unity of Being", and became like "a perfectly proportioned human body", and as men so fashioned held places of power, their nations had it too, prince and ploughman sharing that thought and feeling. . . . Then the scattering came, the seeding of the poppy, bursting of peapod, and for a time personality seemed but the stronger for it. Shakespeare's people make all things serve their passion, and that passion is for the moment the whole energy of their being – birds, beasts, men, women, landscape, society, are but symbols and metaphors, nothing is studied in itself, the mind is a dark well, no surface, depth only.[1]

But if the unity of culture which is like "a perfectly proportioned human body" showed itself as such in the men of the early Renaissance, in men of a later age a growing abstraction is revealed. Yeats illustrates the point by holding up to contrast a portrait of some nameless Venetian gentleman painted by Strozzi and the portrait of President Woodrow Wilson executed by John Singer Sargent.

> Whatever thought broods in the dark eyes of that Venetian gentleman has drawn its life from his whole body; it feeds upon it as the flame feeds upon the candle – and should that thought be changed, his pose would change, his very cloak would rustle, for his whole body thinks. [On the contrary] President Wilson lives only in the eyes, which are steady and intent; the flesh about the mouth is dead, and the hands are dead, and the clothes suggest no movement of his body, nor any movement but that of the valet, who has brushed and folded in mechanical routine. There [in the painting of the Venetian gentleman], all was an energy flowing outward from the nature itself; here, all is the anxious study and slight deflection

[1] Ibid., "The Trembling of the Veil", Book IV, Sec. 3.

of external force; there man's mind and body were predominantly subjective; here all is objective. . . .[1]

How seriously are we to take this comparison? Is it nonsense? Gorgeous, but nonsense nevertheless? How much of the difference between the portraits lies in Yeats's own eye? How much of it lies in Sargent's eye? For that matter, how representative of the modern world is Woodrow Wilson? We have a whole group of variables here, and too few constants. Yet even if we take the passage at the lowest discount, it can tell us a great deal about Yeats and Yeats's notion of the problems of the artist in the modern world, and specifically his own problems as he himself saw them.

For Yeats, there descended upon Europe and upon the life of the West, somewhere toward the seventeenth century, a decisive change:

> . . . popular, typical men have grown more ugly and more argumentative; the face that Van Dyck called a fatal face has faded before Cromwell's warty opinionated head.[2]

In this wonderfully eloquent sentence Yeats has managed to express his dislike of Cromwell, to associate violence with Cromwell, the image-smasher, to allude to the anecdote in which Cromwell insists that he wants the wart depicted in his portrait, and to imply that one of the disasters of the modern world is its loss of any common ideas, a loss which leaves it at the mercy of contentious and violent opinions. Henceforth, Yeats goes on to observe, "no mind made like 'a perfectly proportioned human body' shall sway the public, for great men must live in a portion of themselves, [Yeats means in *only* a portion of themselves, and must] become professional and abstract. . . ."[3]

Yeats pays George Bernard Shaw the dubious compliment of considering him a man congenial to his times. Shaw was conscious of no war between his inner nature and the external world of affairs. In fact Yeats discovers in Shaw's writings and in his public speech the very "civilization that Sargent's picture [of Woodrow Wilson had] explored."[4]

---

[1] Ibid., p. 175. [2] Ibid., p. 175.
[3] Ibid., p. 175. [4] Ibid., p. 176.

One cannot appreciate the force of Yeats's thrust at Shaw unless one takes into account Yeats's belief that the true artist can create only through meditation and that his basic insights come to him through a process of revelation.

> I know now that revelation is . . . from that age-long memoried self, that shapes the elaborate shell of the mollusc and the child in the womb, that teaches the birds to make their nest; and that genius is a crisis that joins that buried self for certain moments to our trivial daily mind.[1]

This observation, in a day in which all literary people have gone to school to the depth psychologists, has perhaps become a commonplace. Most of them would remove from it Yeats's special kind of mythology and rephrase it in terms of Jung's mythology. But when Yeats put it to paper forty years ago the observation was scarcely commonplace. In any event – Yeats's terms and his mythology aside – what is it that Yeats has to tell us, if anything, about this union of the poet's daily trivial mind to that of his age-long memoried self?

In civilizations which possess a true spiritual unity, civilizations in which men are united in virtue of sharing a common dream, a man could afford to be solitary and to cultivate his thoughts from his inmost self, for he could take for granted that on the larger issues he was united with his fellows and so could go on to explore his own individuality. Indeed, in such a case it may be rather easy, if it is in fact ever easy, for the poet to unite his daily mind with the mind of the buried self, for the descent into the well of the self is not perilous, and that buried self is not radically separated from the daily and day-lit mind. But when the common dream has been dissipated, and the world of objective sanctions and values has been lost, then a man is forced either to find his unity with his fellows through some abstract system, consciously worked out, or else be driven back into his own nature, forced to content himself with subjective and private values. Yeats's sardonic comment on George Bernard Shaw's complacent exchange of Narcissus and his pool for the signal-box at a railway junction is thoroughly relevant to the argument.

[1] Ibid., "The Trembling of the Veil", Book III, Sec. 9.

I suggest that Chaucer – at least the man that Yeats conceived Chaucer to be – was never confronted with such a choice. If the Canterbury pilgrims on their way to the shrine of the holy blissful martyr found that their road never crossed over a line of steel rails along which locomotives passed, neither did it lead them by the margin of the pool over which brooded Narcissus, obsessed with his own image mirrored therein. Chaucer knew about Narcissus, but only as an interesting story culled from the wreck of the classic world – certainly not as an obsessive symbol for his own plight. In short, a morbid inwardness occurs only when the self finds its solitude threatened by the rumbling traffic of actions and ideas, and is confronted with the possibility – and perhaps the necessity – of making a choice between the world of action and his inward dream.

Yeats sees the twentieth-century poet as appreciably worse off than his brothers of the nineteenth century. They had the support of a traditional doctrine: Matthew Arnold had his faith in what he described as the best thought of his generation. Tennyson had his "moral values that were not [merely] aesthetic values".[1] But for our modern writers, most of whom are finally bereft of traditional doctrine of any sort, believing in no values which are "out there" in the outside world, their art must be everything to them, amounting to a religion. Moreover, when the artist has become, to use Joyce's now celebrated phrase, "a priest of the imagination", and when there is no religion that the artist can serve apart from his own imagination, then, if his personal vision becomes intolerable, there is no escape for him.

In that curious poem entitled "Ego Dominus Tuus" Yeats puts the question:

> What portion in the world can the artist have,
> Who has awakened from the common dream
> But dissipation and despair?[2]

The common dream is that which binds a culture into unity – that which gave Chaucer's pilgrims their "common goal and

[1] Ibid., "The Trembling of the Veil", Book IV, Sec. 9.
[2] *Collected Poems*, London: Macmillan, 1950; New York: Macmillan, 1951.

shrine"; the reference to "dissipation and despair" is applied here, I suspect, particularly to Ernest Dowson and Lionel Johnson as a way of explaining their lives. But what Yeats says here is prophetic. How much more sharply do his lines apply to some of the writers of our own day. How intense is their sense of outrage against the world! Moreover, in writers like Norman Mailer and William Burroughs, for instance, there is a violent oscillation between the abstract and the intensely subjective. The writer may champion a cause in almost complete abstraction, or, again, he may turn inward and acknowledge no values except his own right to express his own emotions as they move him. Yeats's analysis made forty years ago seems to be thoroughly vindicated by what has occurred since.

The plight of the poet is for Yeats a kind of measuring stick for the health of the civilization – indeed, one of the most important measurements that we have. The fact that the modern poet tends to be either Narcissus or Thersites measures the break-up of the civilization. In an earlier day, it was possible to have an epic poet telling the life of a hero and in telling that life, recounting the values of a total civilization. If, as Yeats maintains, this is no longer possible, then society has lost its character as a spiritual community and indeed can be united only as a bundle of sticks can be united – by being faggotted together with a piece of cord.

Yeats's description of the modern world is very close to Eliot's. If Yeats sees the modern world as far gone in abstraction, mechanization, and materialism, Eliot sees it in much the same terms: "a state secularized, a community turned into a mob, and a clericy [Eliot takes over the term from Coleridge] disintegrated."[1] Yeats's choice between the pool of Narcissus and the signal-box in the marshalling yards of opinion becomes for Eliot a related choice: "the more serious authors have a limited, and even provincial audience, and the more popular write for an illiterate and uncritical mob."

In spite of their sombre views of the modern writer's plight, neither Eliot nor Yeats quit writing. Each man went on to write some of his greatest poetry. But the greatness of the poetry does

[1] *The Idea of a Christian Society*, p. 42.

not argue the falsity of the analysis of the modern writer's relation to his world. If we conclude that it does, we show that we have failed to understand the analysis. What, then, did an Eliot or a Yeats do? Each faced his problem honestly and made a virtue out of the very necessities that threatened to cripple him. Eliot attempted to reclaim his Christian heritage, though thoroughly aware that the Christian communion, in the English-speaking world and especially among its intellectuals, represents a minority. His community is the remnant of the Christian community in a post-Christian world. His poetry – including his specifically religious poetry – consistently addresses itself to the "gentiles" – takes into account the reader's agnosticism.

Yeats made up his own religion, or, as he proudly puts it in *A Vision,* he set out to restore to the philosopher the myths that the philosopher had unphilosophically discarded. But behind this attempt – providing the ground for, and justification of, it – is a vision of traditional Ireland, of a people still linked to the past and still rooted in a visible landscape.

Actually, Yeats has put his problem of audience in quite concrete terms. In a poem written a year before "Ego Dominus Tuus" and entitled "The Fisherman", he gives a bitter description of the modern world:

> The craven man in his seat,
> The insolent unreproved,
> And no knave brought to book
> Who has won a drunken cheer,
> The witty man and his joke
> Aimed at the commonest ear,
> The clever man who cries
> The catch-cries of the clown.
> The beating down of the wise
> And great Art beaten down.[1]

In scorn of an audience of this kind, Yeats turns to one of a very different sort: to the fisherman, a wise and simple man, dressed in "grey Connemara clothes", casting at dawn his flies into the stream. Though so vividly present to his imagination, the poet

[1] *Collected Poems.*

concedes that this man for whom he now means to write, "does not exist" – is "A man who is but a dream. . . ."

Perhaps someone will exclaim: But to choose an audience such as this is, after all, to turn inward, to fall back upon one's own resources, and to write simply to please oneself. In some sense this is true. But to write for what Yeats called his "anti-self" is something very different from writing the "confessional" poetry that is so much in repute today. To write for the anti-self – to try to realize one's mirror image – is to do something more than to gaze into the pool of self in Narcissistic absorption. Yeats's fisherman casts his flies into a pool of a quite different sort, and Yeats, in undertaking to write for the fisherman a poem "maybe as cold / And passionate as the dawn", is attempting something more than an outpouring of personal emotion.

I am not forgetting that Yeats was a man who celebrated personality and indeed cultivated his own personality, deliberately imposing a certain style upon his personal life, even dressing the part, down to flowing necktie and theatrical cape. But Yeats's conception of art as something more than an expression of personal emotion is deep and central in his work. In his *Autobiography* he asks:

> Does not all art come when a nature, that never ceases to judge itself, exhausts personal emotion in action or desire so completely that something impersonal, something that has nothing to do with action or desire, suddenly starts into its place, something which is as unforeseen, as completely organised, even as unique, as the images that pass before the mind between sleeping and waking?[1]

To say this is to insist upon an impersonal art as emphatically as Eliot did when he wrote that "Poetry is not a turning loose of emotion, but an escape from emotion: it is not the expression of personality, but an escape from personality".[2]

In "Ego Dominus Tuus", Yeats develops this point further. In the dialogue that constitutes the poem, one of the two voices

[1] *Autobiography*, "The Trembling of the Veil", Book IV, Sec. 16.
[2] *Selected Essays, 1917–1932*, London: Faber & Faber 1932 New York: Harcourt, Brace & Co., 1932, "Tradition and the Individual Talent".

announces that he wishes to find himself and not an image. This is the wish expressed over and over by the Americans quoted by Alvarez in *Under Pressure*. And they go still further: they feel not merely the necessity to find themselves but, as one of them puts it, "We are obligated to create ourselves."[1] Alvarez remarks that this "responsibility of the artist to himself, the feeling that he has to create his whole world – his moral order, his style and his tradition – for himself and from scratch, seems to be a belief shared by almost every American writer I've ever met".[2]

But if the American writer does feel – mark you, I have my reservations about so sweeping a generalization – if the American writer does feel the need to define himself, "to find [himself] and not an image", Yeats's own notion is clearly very different. The other voice in his poem remarks that this wish to find oneself

> . . . is our modern hope, and by its light
> We have lit upon the gentle, sensitive mind
> And lost the old nonchalance of the hand. . . .
> We are but critics, or but half create,
> Timid, entangled, empty and abashed,
> Lacking the countenance of our friends.[3]

I am tempted to interpret the last line, "Lacking the countenance of our friends," as a reference to the loss of community, but I do not wish to strain for this point, and I am indeed far from certain that I understand Yeats's meaning here. I am confident, however, that I do understand what he means by *entangled* – he will say a few lines later that those artists who are deluded into the search for themselves in fact imitate "The struggle of the fly in marmalade" – and I also believe that I understand why Yeats accuses such deluded artists of confusing art with action, turning their art into a practical instrument. The second voice in the poem tells us that

> . . . those that love the world serve it in action,
> Grow rich, popular and full of influence,
> And should they paint or write, still it is action:
> The struggle of the fly in marmalade.

[1] *Under Pressure*, p. 162.   [2] Ibid., p. 160.   [3] *Collected Poems*.

> The rhetorician would deceive his neighbours,
> The sentimentalist himself; while art
> Is but a vision of reality.[1]

It is amusing to put beside this description of those who, loving the world and serving it in action, "Grow rich, popular and full of influence," the plight of the modern writer. Diana Trilling observes that

> A writer becomes fashionable and glamorous so terribly fast these days. Once he's become a public personality, once he lets himself become *too* public a personality so that he's busy all the time being on radio panels and television programs and having his picture in the fashion magazines, he's straying from his job and he's bound to be engaging in things that are destructive to time and talent and development.[2]

The struggle of the fly in marmalade indeed, an embarrassment of sweets, the poet mired down in *la dolce vita*!

Saul Bellow told Alvarez that today

> A man may write a protest novel, a novel about the poor and, find himself, having done so, a millionaire. . . . There isn't a writer in the United States who doesn't feel proud of his rebellious record. The only trouble is that his rebellion doesn't have a great deal of content, and I sometimes wonder whether this is because American society doesn't relegate all its critics to a sort of infantile or childish situation.[3]

Yet before weeping for the embarrassed and frustrated writer, one should like to know what he did with the million dollars with which society rewarded him for his protest. Having discovered that the novel wasn't an effective way to make his protest, did the writer then spend part of that million for bill-board advertising or to buy time on the radio to put his protest more effectively? For the moment, however, I am interested not in the writer's convictions but in Yeats's point about writing regarded as a piece of action and the writer's consequent entanglement with the world. In this matter, Yeats would seem to have proved a true prophet.

There is another way in which the modern writer is tempted

[1] Ibid.,   [2] *Counterpoint*, p. 601.   [3] *Under Pressure*, pp. 140–41.

to become the man of action. Diana Trilling's comments on Norman Mailer are pertinent. She says:

> I have an extraordinarily high regard for Norman Mailer, perhaps more for that which is intended than for that which is yet accomplished; I think the intention is a major one, but I'm afraid that he's mythologized himself so much that people are judging the personality more than they are the work.[1]

Her judgment is a sound one. The very titles of Mailer's last three books suggest such an emphasis: *The Presidential Papers, Advertisements for Myself,* and *An American Dream,* the last a novel. The mythologizing of which Diana Trilling speaks amounts to the artist's using his art in order to enhance the impact of his personality on society, rather than using his powers as an artist in order to create and embody the vision of reality in a novel. The man competes with his art.

Something of this sort apparently happened to Ernest Hemingway. The early Hemingway, the rather shy young man who worshipped bravery, celebrated in his stories and novels the bravery of his various heroes. Undoubtedly Hemingway put much of himself into his Robert Jordans and Lieutenant Henrys, but these characters are not mere projections of Hemingway's yearnings. In his best work Hemingway was willing to put into his fictional characters only so much of his own experience as could be deemed relevant by a creative intelligence that never – to use Yeats's fine phrase – ceased to judge itself and that, accordingly, permitted nothing to go into the created characters that could not be absorbed and reshaped and given a new life by the imagination.

Toward the end of his literary career, however, Hemingway the artist began to close the distance between the shy admirer of bravery and the valiant characters of his fiction, to act out in his personal life the role of the admired character, and, what was more damaging, to put too much of himself into the fictional character. Something of this sort seems to have happened in his disastrous short novel *Across the River and into the Trees.* The difference between the earlier Hemingway and the later might be

---

[1] *Counterpoint,* p. 600.

put in this fashion: the earlier created from his anti-self; the later tended to express himself.

The temptation to make an impact upon the public has, of course, presented itself to the writer for a long time. In an age of advertising and press-agentry, the temptation may become overpowering – especially in so far as the public seems to be an inert mass of *other* people who may have to be prodded and even shocked into any proper response. Yeats's argument that those writers who turn their writing into action do so because they love the world does not imply a love for the reading public. As for contemporary American writers, the passages quoted from them by Alvarez suggest that they feel even more remote from the anonymous reading public, and that they fear and loathe the "absorbtive society" of the contemporary world. In such a society, the writer is accepted too easily. He finds it harder and harder to get a rise out of the reading public, even when he uses shock methods. Richard Hofstadter says that "What used to be quite marginal and on the border-lines of pornography . . . is now to be had on practically any American news-stand."[1] Elizabeth Hardwick complains that the public "accept everything. . . . They cannot really afford to ignore anything, everything is absorbed and accepted. There isn't an *avant-garde*."[2] The note here is almost plaintive: it must indeed be frustrating to live in a society where the *avant-garde* walks in daily fear of being run down by the rear ranks who, in their desire to be in the mode, forget their place and threaten to trample their cultural betters.

Alvarez sums up such complaints by saying that "the writers want to be against the *status quo*, but it can't be done. The *status quo* changes too quickly for them. And in changing it buys them off: it salves their wounds with money; it stuffs those cultural gaps with hard cash."[3]

I'm not sure that I understand what is being said here. No one is bought off who will not accept the cash. And if the *status quo* changes so rapidly that the writer can't hope to keep on the wrong side of it, why should it need to buy him off? I am even

---

[1] *Under Pressure*, p. 140.   [2] Ibid., p. 140.
[3] Ibid., p. 140.

more puzzled by this description of the writer's antics. Why is it worth keeping on the side opposite to an Establishment that perpetually changes? If you really believe that your position is correct, why is it so anguishing to have society agree with you? Does one's own identity have to depend so completely on one's opposition to society? If it does, then the writer has become the dullest of conformists – a "no-man" rather than a yes-man, automatically denying whatever it is that society affirms.

But there is no need to press Alvarez's statement too hard. I dare say that here he is writing hastily and a little off-guard. What I would stress in this and related passages of his book is the sense of the contemporary writer's disquietude. The fact that the writers represented are American and that most of them live in New York City is highly pertinent. Their relation to society will on the whole represent the furthest extreme from Yeats's notion of what Chaucer's was. The community – at least in the old sense – has disappeared, and in its stead there is the literary clique or the literary cult. The disappearance of the community will account for the writer's sense of alienation, his interest in his own psychic disturbances (which may seem to him the most real thing about him), and his belief that an unsatisfactory society needs to be reconstituted and in the process radically reshaped. If modern man wears the day-time face of Prometheus, his night-time face is that of Narcissus, and the modern writer usually shares in both experiences and may indeed feel torn apart by them.

These last comments are not meant to imply that modern writers, including some of those from whom I have quoted, are unable to produce first-rate literary works. One should never put his judgment of a particular literary work at the mercy of a theory of composition. Writers work in various ways and sometimes the most unpromising theories of what a work ought to be or the most grudging circumstances under which it has to be written will not prevent its turning out to be quite excellent. The proof of the pudding is the eating thereof, nowhere more so than in the world of literature. But though the difficulty of the times and the lack of unity in the culture will not prevent the production of good works of art, they may account for some of the failures, and they may also have a part in determining what kinds of excellence are now possible.

Can one draw any conclusions, however tentative, about what is the best situation for the writer in the twentieth century? I would hazard these. Yeats derived great strength from what he called his "company of friends" – people like John Synge and Lady Gregory; but these were more than a clique. They participated, as Yeats himself did, in the larger community of Ireland, one comprehending not only artists and intellectuals but all levels of a society. Even so, Yeats was acutely aware of the hiatus that existed between the writer and the sources of power in his culture; the fact of the hiatus and its consequences becomes a major theme in his poetry.

As for T. S. Eliot: one could argue with some plausibility that his whole life was an attempt to discover his true community – even if that attempt involved the rather desperate expedient of trying to put down roots in the culture of an island that his ancestors had left some three hundred years before. He did not merely theorize about the issues, but made the attempt in concrete personal terms. Moreover, though Eliot's deep concern for religion was not self-serving, something undertaken because he thought it would help his poetry, his return to the Church had as one of its consequences a deepening and strengthening of his ties with a community, though a community of a very special kind.

Two more instances from the recent past, those of Robert Frost and William Faulkner, are simpler but may prove no less instructive. Robert Frost was intensely interested in the modern world and in the more recent transformations of modern man, but he found a *point d'appui* in the New England culture which had shaped his boyhood. That older culture of farm and village was disappearing and the coastal regions had already become heavily industrialized, had been filled with people of different racial stocks and different cultures, and yet, nevertheless, Frost found in what was left of the older New England a kind of spiritual community. It provided a means for defining himself without magnifying his differences from his fellows. Frost doubtless

idealized the older New England culture, but he did not senti-
mentalize it, and he never deluded himself into thinking that it
provided any final refuge from what he hated in the modern
world.

Though in moving from northern New England to the deep
South we change cultural worlds, what has been said about
Frost proves to be essentially true of William Faulkner. The
older culture in which he and his forebears had been rooted and
which he counted as in some sense a part of himself, gave him
the necessary spiritual community. The little town of Oxford,
Mississippi, had, to be sure, not much to offer in the way of
literary associates – though it had at least one, and for Faulkner
an important one; and the people of Oxford for a long time
were hostile to, rather than complacent about, what their
fellow townsman was writing. But there were plenty of fishermen about, wearing the Mississippi equivalent of grey Connemara clothes, and plenty of hunters with a fund of traditional
stories about the wilderness, about pioneer days when the
Chickasaw Indians were still in the land, about the countryside invaded during the War between the States, and about
the relations between the white man and the Negro through
some one hundred and fifty years. Most of all, there was a community in being – to be accepted or rejected – to be loved
or hated – but in any case there, with its specific shape and
character.

But does the community still exist any longer? Is there any
community available for such writers as those interviewed by
Alvarez, for example? Perhaps not – though I think that the
Jewish writers of New York and the Negro writers of New York
– groups that figure so prominently in *Under Pressure* – depend
far more upon their Jewish culture and their Negro experience
than the comments in *Under Pressure* would suggest. Indeed, it
may be the fact of these special "communities" of the so-called
minority groups that has enabled the Jewish and the Negro
writer in the last decades to find himself and to define his
world with so much power. This is mere speculation, however,
and I do not propose to develop it here. But there is one further
topic that I must mention before I conclude.

The alienation of the writer is a fact of the literary life, widely acknowledged in the western world. Since Wordsworth's day the writer has been increasingly aware of it, and one may be forgiven for thinking that this is about all that the writers in *Under Pressure* – at least as quoted by Alvarez – want to talk about. But I suggest that though the writer of the twentieth century is bound to be aware of the problem, too much self-consciousness may do more harm than good. It may be better for the writer to take, like William Faulkner, a relatively naïve view of the matter than to think upon the issue too narrowly and too continually, for this kind of self-consciousness can become morbid unless it is informed with a really deep knowledge of history and unless one preserves a modicum of detachment. In an Eliot or a Yeats the consciousness of self does become deep enough and wide enough to transcend mere self-consciousness. But theirs is a heroic regimen and requires abilities and energies that I think are beyond most people. Those who cannot go this far in their thinking will be fortunate if they have inherited a community that can divert them from too much preoccupation with themselves.

If the writer lacks such a community, he is scarcely to be blamed for a situation that is not of his own making. The born writer is going to continue writing. It would be silly as well as unfair to try to serve on him an order to cease and desist. But even the born writer might well heed some such word as this: to become a member of a literary clique or to find oneself the object of a cult of readers and followers is not the same thing as to be part of a community. The clique is too close to one's professional life and perhaps too complacent of one's faults; the cult is too remote and too much given to unthinking adulation.

Moreover, the cult points toward the "priesthood of the imagination". Such a conception of the literary profession is exalted, but it has its perils. It is not always healthy for the writer to feel that he is primarily responsible for the good health of his society. Man is one, and the writer's problems are in some ultimate sense the problems of society. But a certain hubris is involved in the assumption that the solutions of the problems of mankind, including economic and political problems, can be obtained through one's own privileged insights, or that one's own psychic disturbances are somehow continuous with the disturbances of society at large. A more modest conception of his role might be in the interests of everybody, including the writer himself.

3

T. S. Eliot: Thinker and Artist

In a reasonably brief lecture, how can one deal adequately with an influence so powerful and pervasive as that which T. S. Eliot has exerted upon the last half-century? Truly one is confronted with an embarrassment of riches: the poet, the dramatist, the critic, the editor, the student of culture – all invite attention, and two of Eliot's roles, those of poet and critic, demand it. My task is made somewhat easier, to be sure, by the fact that Eliot's career is no loose bundle of unrelated activities but possesses an essential unity. Indeed, once discovered, this unity of purpose becomes increasingly evident. Few literary men in our history have so consistently related all their activities to a coherent set of principles. And the consistency of his various writings reflects the quality of the man. In a time of disorder, Eliot moved toward a restoration of order .

Thus, Eliot's fundamental reassessment of the twentieth-century literary – and cultural – situation was *not* expressed in his poetry alone. The poetry arose out of a mental and spiritual activity that necessarily showed itself in literary and social criticism – in his brilliant essays on the Elizabethan dramatists, for example, but also in a work like *Notes towards the Definition of Culture*.

Yet even this aspect of Eliot's achievement is too large for adequate comment in one lecture. In any case, I would like to find a more concrete way in which to deal with it. When one discusses literature, few things are so deadly as the recital of abstract statements and wide generalizations. Moreover, it seems impertinent to treat a poet in this fashion, especially a poet who succeeded so brilliantly in giving his ideas concrete embodiment

and who devoted so much of his discursive prose to this very
split in the modern mind – this dissociation of sensibility –
in which Eliot saw not only the distemper of literature but a
symptom of a more general disease. Let me try to illustrate, then,
as much as I can, the essential unity of Eliot's work from his
handling of a single topic.

I should like to examine Eliot's treatment of the urban scene.
In an essay entitled "What Dante Means to Me", he tells us
how he discovered that the urban scene was proper material for
poetry, and specifically the proper material for his own poetry.
The passage that I mean to quote begins with some observations
on literary influences and on what a poet can learn from earlier
poets.

> Then, among influences, there are the poets from whom one
> has learned some one thing, perhaps of capital importance to
> oneself, though not necessarily the greatest contribution these
> poets have made. I think that from Baudelaire I learned first, a
> precedent for the poetical possibilities, never developed by any
> poet writing in my own language, of the more sordid aspects of
> the modern metropolis, of the possibility of fusion between
> the sordidly realistic and the phantasmagoric, the possibility of
> the juxtaposition of the matter-of-fact and the fantastic. From
> him, as from Laforgue, I learned that the sort of material that
> I had, the sort of experience that an adolescent had had, in an
> industrial city of America, could be the material for poetry; and
> that the source of new poetry might be found, in what had been
> regarded hitherto as the impossible, the sterile, the intractably
> unpoetic. That, in fact, the business of the poet was to make
> poetry out of the unexplored resources of the unpoetical; that
> the poet, in fact, was committed by his profession to turn the
> unpoetical into poetry. A great poet can give a younger poet
> everything that he has to give him in a very few lines. It may be
> that I am indebted to Baudelaire chiefly for half a dozen lines out
> of the whole of *Fleurs du Mal*; and that his significance for me is
> summed up in the lines:
>
> > Fourmillante cité, cité, pleine de rêves,
> > Où le spectre en plein jour raccroche le passant. . . .

What is shocking is that the presence of the spectre can be felt on
crowded streets and in an environment of brick and stone

Wordsworth also knew of a spot where "ghostly shapes" might "meet at noontide". But their meeting place was in the "pillared shade" close by the four great yew trees at Borrowdale in Cumberland, in a spot so quiet that from it one could hear the mountain flood "murmuring from Glaramara's inmost caves". With Baudelaire's spectre domiciled in the city, we cross a kind of watershed of the sensibility.

But I must go back to the quotation from Eliot, which I did not quite finish. After citing the passage from Baudelaire, Eliot goes on to say:

> I knew what *that* meant, because I had lived it before I knew that I wanted to turn it into verse on my own account.

About what it meant to Eliot, I shall have something to say a little later on. At the moment, I want to consider further Eliot's notion that the poet, by his very profession, is committed "to turn the unpoetical into poetry", and I want to consider further Eliot's idea that poetry is a fusion of opposites – in this instance, a fusion of "the sordidly realistic and the phantasmagoric", of "the matter-of-fact and the fantastic".

Poetry is evidently not to be thought of as a bouquet of "poetic" objects. The implication is that the materials the poet uses are not in themselves poetic. To be agreeable or pleasant or charming is not the same thing as being poetic. Poetic value is a quality of a different order. It is not a *property* of objects but a relationship among them, a relationship discovered and established by the poet. Moreover, that relationship may be a tensional one in which the materials pull against each other and resist any easy reconciliation. In this instance it is the sordidly realistic and the phantasmagoric that may seem intractable, or the matter-of-fact and the fantastic.

All of this Eliot has said before, and because he had said it before, in this rather late essay from which I have been quoting, he could afford to touch upon it lightly. But when he first enunciated this tensional view of poetry, it very much needed saying – or at least needed re-saying. And Eliot's statement of this conception, together with the poems that embodied it, inspired the literary revolution that is sometimes given Eliot's name.

At this point it may be useful to call your attention to another passage in which Eliot discusses the poet's use of what the Victorians sometimes regarded as hopelessly unpromising materials for poetry. The Victorian in this instance is Matthew Arnold commenting upon the ugliness of the world of Robert Burns. After quoting Arnold's rather prim observation to the effect that "no one can deny that it is of advantage to a poet to deal with a beautiful world", Eliot suddenly rounds on the nineteenth-century critic and quite flatly denies his basic assumption. The essential advantage for a poet, Eliot remarks, is *not* that of having a beautiful world with which to deal, but rather "to be able to see beneath both beauty and ugliness; to see the boredom, and the horror, and the glory. The vision of the horror and the glory", he rather acidly concludes, "was denied to Arnold, but he knew something of the boredom".

This is excellent polemics: the hard backhand drive that rifles across the court and just dusts the opponent's back line. Yet the reader may wonder at the energy – here as often elsewhere – with which Eliot rejects Arnold. He may wonder too at what may seem an almost gratuitous reference to "boredom", not, surely, an obvious member of a cluster that would include "horror" and "glory". But references to boredom often come into Eliot's account of urban life, and we have in his passage mention of concerns central to his poetry.

They are indeed central to his experience of the modern metropolis where so many people find themselves caught in a world of monotonous repetition, an aimless circling without end or purpose. Eliot's early poetry is full of it:

> The morning comes to consciousness
> Of faint stale smells of beer
> From the sawdust-trampled street
> With all its muddy feet that press
> To early coffee-stands.
> With the other masquerades
> That time resumes,
> One thinks of all the hands
> That are raising dingy shades
> In a thousand furnished rooms.

They are rattling breakfast plates in basement kitchens,
And along the trampled edges of the street
I am aware of the damp souls of housemaids
Sprouting despondently at area gates.

At the violet hour, the evening hour that strives
Homeward, and brings the sailor home from sea,
The typist home at teatime, clears her breakfast, lights
Her stove, and lays out food in tins.

Let us go, through certain half-deserted streets,
The muttering retreats
Of restless nights in one-night cheap hotels
And sawdust restaurants with oyster-shells:
Streets that follow like a tedious argument
Of insidious intent. . . .

The wanderer moving through the deserted city streets long
past midnight walks through a genuine nightmare in which

> the floors of memory
> And all its clear relations,
> Its divisions and precisions

are dissolved, a fantastic world in which every street lamp that
one passes

> Beats like a fatalistic drum.

Yet when the wanderer turns to his own door, he steps out of one
horror into a worse horror:

> The lamp said,
> "Four o'clock,
> Here is the number on the door.
> Memory!
> You have the key,
> The little lamp spreads a ring on the stair.
> Mount.
> The bed is open; the tooth-brush hangs on the wall,
> Put your shoes at the door, sleep, prepare for life."
> The last twist of the knife.

The wound in which this knife is twisted is modern man's loss
of meaning and purpose. When the life to which one expects to
rise after sleep – a daylight world of clear plans and purposes –
turns out to be simply a kind of automatism, as absurd as the

bizarre world of the nightmare streets, the knife in the wound is given a final agonizing twist.

At this point it may be useful to remind the reader – especially the reader who finds that Eliot's Anglo-Catholicism sticks in his craw and prevents his swallowing the poetry – that in passages of the sort that I have been quoting, we are not getting sermonizing, but bits of drama, not generalizations about facts but responses to situations, not statements about what ought to be but renditions of what is.

Eliot once remarked that prose has to do with ideals; poetry, with reality. The statement has proved puzzling to many a reader who has been brought up on just the opposite set of notions, but Eliot's observation seems to be profoundly true. Discursive prose is the medium for carrying on arguments, drawing conclusions, offering solutions. Poetry is the medium *par excellence* for rendering a total situation – for letting us know what it feels like to take a particular action or hold a particular belief or simply to look at something with imaginative sympathy.

Here are some presentations of reality. An urban vignette: a winter evening in the city:

> The winter evening settles down
> With smell of steaks in passageways.
> Six o'clock.
> The burnt-out ends of smoky days.
> And now a gusty shower wraps
> The grimy scraps
> Of withered leaves about your feet
> And newspapers from vacant lots;
> The showers beat
> On broken blinds and chimney-pots,
> And at the corner of the street
> A lonely cab-horse steams and stamps.
> And then the lighting of the lamps.

The songs of the three Thames-daughters:

> "Trams and dusty trees.
> Highbury bore me. Richmond and Kew
> Undid me. By Richmond I raised my knees
> Supine on the floor of a narrow canoe."

> "My feet are at Moorgate, and my heart
> Under my feet. After the event
> He wept. He promised 'a new start'.
> I made no comment. What should I resent?"

> "On Margate Sands.
> I can connect
> Nothing with nothing.
> The broken fingernails of dirty hands.
> My people humble people who expect
> Nothing."
>   la la

Even the raffish Sweeney's recital of his philosophy – a view of life held, incidentally, by many of Sweeney's betters – is a bit of reality too; for it is a dramatic projection of a man, not an abstract formulation. Its very rhythms testify to a personality and an attitude.

> Birth, and copulation, and death.
> That's all the facts when you come to brass tacks:
> Birth, and copulation, and death.
> I've been born, and once is enough.

Readers have responded powerfully to such passages – readers who hold very different conceptions of what the world ought to be – for what is primarily at stake in all these passages is not the reader's approval or rejection of a statement, but his response to authentic reality. The only compulsion to respond is that exerted by the authority of the imagination. Perhaps the poet can never do more than exert such authority; but in any case he cannot afford to do less.

This matter of the reader's response has another and more special aspect. Eliot suggests that many of those who live in the modern world have been drugged and numbed by it. One task of the poet is to penetrate their torpor, to awaken them to full consciousness of their condition, to let them see where they are. The theme recurs throughout Eliot's poetry from the earliest poems to the latest.

The people who inhabit *The Waste Land* cling to their partial oblivion. They say:

> Winter kept us warm, covering
> Earth in forgetful snow, feeding
> A little life with dried tubers.

Or like the old women of Canterbury, they may say:

> We do not wish anything to happen,
> Seven years we have lived quietly,
> Succeeded in avoiding notice,
> Living and partly living.

The trivial daily actions, they point out, at least marked

> a limit to our suffering.
> Every horror had its definition,
> Every sorrow had a kind of end. . . .

What they dread now is the "disturbance" of the seasons, the decisive break in the numbing routine that will wake them out of their half-life.

But the partially numbed creatures may be, and usually are, people of the contemporary world. They may, for example, be like the characters in *The Family Renunion* who do not want anything to rumple their rather carefully arranged lives – who wants things to be "normal" – and who cannot see that – to use their nephew's words – the event that they call normal "Is merely the unreal and unimportant".

They may be like certain well-bred inhabitants of Boston, Massachussetts:

> . . . evening quickens faintly in the street,
> Wakening the appetites of life in some
> And to others bringing the *Boston Evening Transcript* . . .

Or they may be the bored drawing-room characters in "The Love Song of J. Alfred Prufrock" whom Prufrock would like to confront with the truth about themselves. He would like to say to them:

> "I am Lazarus, come from the dead,
> Come back to tell you all, I shall tell you all."

But he well knows that these overcivilized and desiccated people would not be impressed by the Lazarus of the New Testament, much less by a self-conscious man "with a bald spot in the middle of [his] hair", a man aware of the fact that he wears a "necktie rich and modest, but asserted by a simple pin". In any case, these people would not understand the talk of a man who had experienced real death – or real life.

The themes that run through so much of Eliot's poetry – life that is only a half-life because it cannot come to terms with death – the liberation into true living that comes from the acceptance of death – the ecstatic moment that partakes of both life and death:

> I could not
> Speak, and my eyes failed, I was neither
> Living nor dead, and I knew nothing,
> Looking into the heart of light, the silence –

these and the other themes that recur in Eliot's poetry bear the closest relation to his concern with the boredom and the horror and the glory that he finds in our contemporary metropolitan life. They also bear the closest relationship to the sense of unreality that pervades a world that has lost the rhythm of the seasons, has lost any sense of community, and most of all, has lost a sense of purpose. Such a world *is* unreal: the sordid and the matter-of-fact do not erase the phantasmagoric but accentuate it. The spectre does indeed in broad daylight reach out to grasp the passer-by. London, "Under the brown fog of a winter noon" as well as "Under the brown fog of a winter dawn", is seen as an "Unreal City", and the crowds flowing across London Bridge might be in Dante's Hell:

> I had not thought death had undone so many.
> Sighs, short and infrequent, were exhaled,
> And each man fixed his eyes before his feet.

The echo of the *Divine Comedy* is not merely a highfalutin flourish or an attempt to touch up the modern scene by giving it literary overtones. What connects the modern scene with Dante's *Inferno* is the poet's insight into the nature of hell. The man who sees the crowds flowing over London Bridge as damned souls, if challenged at putting them thus into hell, might justify his observation by paraphrasing a line from Christopher Marlowe: "Why this is hell, nor are they out of it."

In view of the complaint that Eliot sighs after vanished glories, sentimentalizes the past, and hates the present, one must insist on Eliot's ability to dramatize the urban reality with honesty and sensitivity. If the world about which he must write has lost the rhythm of the seasons, then the poet must be open to the new rhythms so that he can relate them to the old. Eliot once wrote that the poet must be able to use the rhythms of the gasoline engine – and Eliot has:

> At the violet hour, when the eyes and back
> Turn upward from the desk, when the human engine waits
> Like a taxi throbbing waiting. . . .

If the modern world has lost its sense of community, the poet must present that loss not as a generalization, but as a dramatic rendition, not as observed from the outside but as felt from the inside. He has done so not only in the nightmare passages of *The Waste Land*:

> There is not even solitude in the mountains
> But red sullen faces sneer and snarl
> From doors of mudcracked houses –

but also in the realistic passages:

> "My nerves are bad to-night. Yes, bad. Stay with me.
> "Speak to me. Why do you never speak. Speak.
> "What are you thinking of? What thinking? What?
> "I never know what you are thinking. Think."

But, he has also on occasion rendered the sense of community in positive terms – not as something lost but as a present reality:

> O City, city, I can sometimes hear
> Besides a public bar in Lower Thames Street,
> The pleasant whining of a mandoline
> And a clatter and a chatter from within
> Where fishmen lounge at noon. . . .

As for the sense of loss of purpose, that loss is never merely asserted but always rendered concretely. It occurs so frequently in Eliot's poetry that it hardly needs illustration. Indeed, it may be best in this instance to take the illustration from Joseph Conrad's *Heart of Darkness*, a story that lies behind so much of Eliot's early poetry. Marlow, the character who relates the story, finds many of his experiences tinged with unreality. As he makes his way to the African coast and then on up the Congo to try to locate Kurtz, his sense of unreality is magnified – not merely because the jungle seems fantastic, but because the civilized characters that he meets are disoriented, obsessed, and thus absurd. One object stands out sharply from this miasma of unreality. Marlow finds in an abandoned hut "an old tattered book, entitled *An Inquiry into Some Points of Seamanship*, by a man Tower, Towson – some such name . . . Not a very enthralling book; but at the first glance you could see there a singleness of intention . . . which made these humble pages . . . luminous with another than a professional light . . . . [The book] made me forget the jungle and the [ivory-seeking] pilgrims in a delicious sensation of having come upon something unmistakeably real". It seems so because it is instinct with purpose – because, to use Marlow's words, you could see in it "an honest concern for the right way of going to work". This is why the book shines with the light of reality.

The sense of unreality is also associated with the vision of a world that is disintegrating. In *The Waste Land*, the cities of a disintegrating civilization seem unreal as if they were part of a mirage. The parched traveller asks:

> What is the city over the mountains
> Cracks and reforms and bursts in the violet air
> Falling towers

– but these cities are also like a mirage in that they are inverted, are seen as upside down; and the passage that follows shows everything turned topsy-turvy:

> . . . bats with baby faces in the violet light
> Whistled, and beat their wings
> And crawled head downward down a blackened wall
> And upside down in air were towers
> Tolling reminiscent bells, that kept the hours
> And voices singing out of empty cisterns and exhausted wells.

Eliot also uses the empty whirl in order to suggest the break-up of civilization. Towards the end of "Gerontion" we have such a vision, people whose surnames suggest that the disintegration is international and world-wide: De Bailhache, Fresca, and Mrs Cammel are whirled

> Beyond the circuit of the shuddering Bear
> In fractured atoms.

Though "Gerontion" was written long before the explosion of the first atom bomb, I suppose there is some temptation nowadays to read into the passage our present unease and to regard the fractured atoms into which human kind has been vaporized as the debris of an atomic war. But I doubt that Mr Eliot ever changed his opinion about the way in which the world ends.

"The Hollow Men", who know in their hollow hearts that they are not really "lost / Violent souls", but only "stuffed men", sing

> This is the way the world ends
> This is the way the world ends
> This is the way the world ends
> Not with a bang but a whimper.

The vortex in which De Bailhache, Fresca, and Mrs Cammel are caught is essentially that later described in "Burnt Norton":

> Men and bits of paper, whirled by the cold wind
> That blows before and after time. . . .

With the empty whirl, the purposeless moving in a circle, we are back once more to the theme of boredom, and there is a good deal of evidence that Eliot did indeed see in such torpor and apathy the real dying out of a civilization. In 1934, for example, he wrote: "Without religion the whole human race would die, as according to W. H. R. Rivers, some Melanesian tribes have died, solely of boredom". This is a polemical passage out of a polemical essay, but we need not discount the idea merely for that reason. It is an integral part of Eliot's thinking. It is to be found everywhere in his prose and poetry – even in a poem like *Sweeney Agonistes*, where we have the following spoof

on the cinematic stereotype of the golden age, life on a South
Sea island:

> Where the Gauguin maids
> In the banyan shades
> Wear palmleaf drapery
> Under the bam
> Under the boo
> Under the bamboo tree.
>
> Tell me in what part of the wood
> Do you want to flirt with me?
> Under the breadfruit, banyan, palmleaf
> Or under the bamboo tree?
> Any old tree will do for me
> Any old wood is just as good
> Any old isle is just my style
> Any fresh egg
> Any fresh egg
> And the sound of the coral sea.

Doris protests that she doesn't like eggs and doesn't like life on
"your crocodile isle". And when the singers renew their account
of the delights of such a life, Doris replies:

> That's not life, that's no life
> Why I'd just as soon be dead.

Doris is a young woman who is clearly no better than she should
be, but in this essential matter, she shows a great deal more
discernment than J. Alfred Prufrock's companions, the ladies
who "come and go, / Talking of Michelangelo".

I have tried to suggest how the themes and images of Eliot's
poetry are related to his convictions about the nature of our
present-day civilization. But I shall have badly confused matters if in doing so I have seemed to reduce his poetry to a kind of
thin and brittle propaganda for a particular world view. As I
said earlier in this paper, the primary role of poetry is to give us
an account of reality, not to argue means for re-shaping it. To
be more specific: if a culture is sick, the poet's primary task is to
provide us with a diagnosis, not to prescribe a specific remedy.
For all of his intense interest in the problems of our culture, and
in spite of the fact that he himself was deeply committed to a

doctrinal religion, Eliot was careful never to confuse poetry with politics or with religion. The loss of a sense of purpose – the conviction that one is simply going round in a circle – this is an experience that many of the readers of Eliot's poetry have recognized as their own; but in their decisions as to what to do about it, such readers have differed as much as the Christian differs from the atheistic existentialist – as much as the rather prim university don from the deliberately disheveled Beatnik. To get out of the circle, to find one's proper end and begin to walk toward it – this is a matter of the highest importance, work for the statesman, the sage, and the saint; but Eliot was too modest ever to claim any of these roles for himself, and he was as well aware as anyone of the confusion of tongues that makes it difficult for men of our century to agree on what the proper goal is. At any rate, he argued the case for what he took to be the true goal, not in his poetry, but in his prose.

At the beginning of this lecture, I remarked that, in a time of grave disorder, Eliot had moved toward a restoration of order. Not the least important part of this work of restoration has been to clarify the role of poetry, not claiming so much for it that it is transformed into prophecy, or Promethean politics, or an ersatz religion; but at the same time pointing out its unique and irreplaceable function and defending its proper autonomy.

Genuine poetry, seen in its proper role, performing for us what only it can perform, does contribute to the health of a culture. A first step toward the recovery of the health of our culture may well be the writing of a poetry that tells us the truth about ourselves in our present situation – a poetry which is capable of dealing with the present world – a poetry that does not have to dismiss the boredom and the horror of our world in the attempt to discern its true glory. More modestly still, a poetry that can deal with the clutter of language in an age of advertising and propaganda restores to that degree the health of language.

Eliot was well aware of this problem. Advertising and propaganda were for him instruments for "influencing . . . masses of men" by means other than "their intelligence". And he once went so far as to say: "You have only to examine the mass of newspaper leading articles, the mass of political exhortation, to appreciate the fact that good prose cannot be written by a people without convictions".

The difficulty of writing good prose in our era extends to other kinds of writing, including poetry. Of this, too, Eliot was aware. In *The Rock*, he has the chorus assert that "the soul of men must quicken to creation" – not only to create new forms, colours, and music, but so that

> Out of the slimy mud of words, out of the sleet and hail of verbal imprecisions,
> Approximate thoughts and feelings, words that have taken the place of thoughts and feelings,
> . . . [may] spring the perfect order of speech, and the beauty of incantation.

In a later and finer poem, he puts this ideal of style more precisely and more memorably still, and he makes this ideal structuring of the language a model of that thing that men must try to accomplish in their lives. The passage has been much admired and much quoted, but I shall not apologise for quoting it once more. It is Eliot's description of the relation that obtains among the words that make up a passage luminous with meaning. In it,

> every word is at home,
> Taking its place to support the others,
> The word neither diffident nor ostentatious,
> An easy commerce of the old and the new.
> The common word exact without vulgarity,
> The formal word precise but not pedantic,
> The complete consort dancing together. . . .

These beautiful lines celebrate the poet's victory over disorder, the peculiar triumph possible to a master of language. They describe what Eliot actually achieved again and again in his own poetry. But they provide an emblem of the kind of harmony that ought to obtain in wider realms – in the just society and in the true community.

4

Poetry Since The Waste Land

At the end of *The Waste Land*, the agonized wanderer has not been able to make his way out of this spiritual desert. In our last glimpse of him, he is still fishing, "with the arid plain behind [him]," and though he has heard the eloquent peals of thunder, no rain has fallen. But he has, one assumes, penetrated to the secret of the fisher-king's malady. He has at least asked the right questions, and the secret of life has been intimated to him. If the poem itself closes with a confusion of tongues, we are not to assume that they are, at least to this dogged pilgrim, a meaningless babble. But what happens to him? To put this question is comparable to tracing the design of a picture on out past the picture frame. The picture space stops – the poem ends. But we can ask, of course, what happened to the creator of the poem. Mr Eliot, at any rate, evidently did manage to make his way out of the waste land, or at least managed to find within the desert of modern civilization, the garden, the "garden within the desert", with its twin yew trees that whisper of eternity.

Two or three other modern poets have retraced Eliot's journey, but I hardly need to emphasize that it has been only two or three. What have been some of the courses taken by other poets? Some have denied that the desert ever existed, regarding it as simply a hallucination conjured up in Mr Eliot's own fevered brain. Others have conceded that the desert does exist, but have gone on to propose special ways of dealing with it – the building of aqueducts or the boring of artesian wells, or even the performance of magical rain-making, with ritual dances analogous to those of the Hopi Indians. (You see I'm not forgetting the poets of the myth school.) Still others, though conceding the drought in the great world cities, have pointed out that, in an earlier, and still rural, America, streams still flow and fountains still bubble up with their healing waters. For example, Robert Frost in one of his last big poems invited us to find in some lost township in the Vermont hills a broken goblet which we could dip into the immemorial stream and thus "drink and be whole again beyond confusion".

But whatever the various courses taken, the modern poet has, in general, tended to find in the individual's own imagination the healing waters which will redeem a world of drab mediocrity and spiritual despair. This appeal to the individual as against the civilization which surrounds him in itself involves several possibilities. The appeal may amount to something as deep and meaningful as Plato's act of anamnesis which discovers reality in the profound depths of the human soul, or, on the other hand, it may be as shallow as the recommendation to indulge in wish-fulfillment. For surely it is one thing to penetrate specious appearances in order to discover the garden within the desert of drought; it is quite another to get out of the desert by taking a firm hold on one's spiritual bootstraps and giving a strong tug. Eliot himself would have been the first to say that, like the kingdom of heaven, the waste land is within you, can be perceived only through an effort of the imagination, and can be escaped, if at all, only through a facing of the truth about one's relation to reality.

But I do not mean to argue that modern poetry is still stuck in the waste land, seeing bats with baby faces in the violet light and hearing spectral voices singing out of exhausted wells, or, on the other hand, that it has moved on to the green pastures and pleasant waters of the perfectly solid and bracing post-Christian world that one glimpses in some of the poetry of Wallace Stevens.

I shall be content to remark that since 1922 we have had some amazingly fine poetry, quite magnificent in its range, embracing everything from the apocalyptic exaltations of Hart Crane to the radiantly quiet world of Robert Frost. Honesty compels me to add that we have also had an enormous lot of second- and third-rate poetry, dull and lack-lustre, not to mention a great deal of trash – silly, pretentious, and whining. But I shall try to avoid assigning goodness to poetry having one philosophical content and dullness and badness to poetry having another. The case is far more complicated than that.

On consideration, then, I think that I shall abandon any attempt to deal with the poetry of the last four decades in terms of waste-land analogies. Such an examination would almost inevitably lead into a discussion of the philosophical content of modern poetry, and on into a discussion of philosophy itself. That might prove to be a fascinating topic if I were competent to deal with it – and philosophy surely has its relevance to modern poetry. Indeed, I must confess my suspicion that the decisive issue lying beneath the kinds of modern poetry has to do with that cloudy and difficult topic, religion. Yet if my surmise is correct, all the more reason – since I have no theological credentials either – to try to organize my remarks about modern poetry in a very different fashion.

In any case, let us begin with T. S. Eliot. A concise way to describe his achievement is to say that he discovered a fundamental likeness between the poetry of the English metaphysical poets of the seventeenth century and that of the French symbolists of the nineteenth century, and that his own poetry adapts to the sensibility of our own age what these poetries have in common. Thus Eliot's poetry bears to that of Donne and Laforgue a relationship comparable to that which William Wordsworth's poetry bears to the medieval folk ballad and to the Miltonizing descriptive poetry of the eighteenth century. A large body of Anglo-American verse has indeed been influenced by the revolution which Eliot brought about, and one could find throughout the poetry of such men as MacLeish, Auden, Jarrell, and Warren plenty of instances of this strain of witty, intellectual verse, which makes emphatic use of the verbal medium, including complicated metaphor and involved symbolism. But pervasive as the influence of Eliot has been, it has not been the sole modern influence, and the tide that turned against it some years ago is now at full flood. One searches, therefore, for modes more general than those associated with the Eliot revolution – modes indeed general enough to reveal themselves in the poetry of William Carlos Williams and even that of the Beatniks.

In looking for such modes, I mean, then, to go back earlier than Eliot – indeed, as far back as the Romantic Revolt. Suppose we take a look at Wordsworth's Lucy poems. These seem, goodness knows, innocent enough; and indeed after Wordsworth's own contemporaries got over their shock at what they felt to be their silliness and inanity, nobody since has ever felt them to be very strange or very revolutionary. Yet they present problems, not the least of which is their lack of logical structure; and simple and easy as most of us think they are, they have sometimes proved bafflingly obscure. Indeed, they continue to baffle.

Consider, for example, "She dwelt among the untrodden ways." The second stanza describes Lucy as follows:

> A violet by a mossy stone
> Half hidden from the eye!
> Fair as a star, when only one
> Is shining in the sky.

Wordsworth has simply set down the comparisons side by side, with not an "and" or a "but" or a "therefore" or a "nevertheless" to relate one to the other. Are they related? Or do they cancel each other out? For if Lucy's loveliness is indeed scarcely visible, half hidden from the eye, how can she be as prominent as the evening star? The answer is simple; but for the sake of my general argument, I should like to spell it out. Though Lucy, to the great world, is as obscure as the violet, to her lover she is as fair as Venus, the first star of evening. It is this contrast between her utter inconsequence to the world and her overwhelming importance to him that constitutes the theme that runs through the three stanzas. Indeed, the second stanza anticipates the third. Lucy's descent into her grave is, for the world, no more than the wilting of an obscure flower, though for the lover it is the winking out of the one luminary in his heaven.

I have said that the answer is very simple, but it is not so

simple as to have been obvious to everybody. At least one unwary scholar of our own generation – in spite of what the violet-
star comparison might have told him – has discovered that
Lucy was neurotic: her shyness concealed "an unpleasant
rejection of other people". For he takes the lines, "A maid whom
there were none to praise / And very few to love," to mean that
few people loved her, and of those who did, none could honestly
say a good word in her behalf!

The same sort of apparently contradictory and unexplained
juxtapositions, with their threat to trip the unwary reader,
occur in Wordsworth's famous little poem "A slumber did
my spirit seal" – and, of late, our modern critics have been
stumbling over all sorts of difficulties in it. For instance, Laura
Riding and Robert Graves – themselves distinguished poets –
once complained that the details of this poem "are even more
illogical than the main argument. Apparently what Wordsworth had in mind," they think, is this: "'I thought once that
she was non-human in a spiritual sense, but now she is dead I
find her non-human in the very opposite sense.' But," they
insist, "all the words have got misplaced. 'Spirit' has got attached to Wordsworth when it should go with Lucy; 'no human'
likewise. . . . 'Thing' should not qualify the first Lucy, but
should be with the second Lucy among the rocks and stones.
As a [completely logical poem]," they claim, "it would run . . .
something like this":

> A slumber sealed my *human fears*
> For her mortality:
> Methought *her spirit* could withstand
> The touch of earthly years.
>
> Yet now her spirit fails, she is
> Less sentient than a *tree*,
> Rolled round in earth's diurnal course
> With rocks and stones and *things*.

The logical scrubbing administered to this little poem may very
well leave you aghast. I rather hope that it has done so. For I am
not recommending the Riding and Graves rewritten version;
nor do Riding and Graves themselves recommend it. They

admire the violations of logic that occur in the original and go on to praise what they call its "supra-logical harmony". Other modern commentators like Florence Marsh and F. W. Bateson, though they would read the poem in quite different ways, nevertheless would agree with Riding and Graves as to the apparent contradictions to be found in it. Miss Marsh refers to its "dual vision", and Bateson, to its "two contrasting moods", which somehow at the end give the impression of "a single mood".

As for myself, I would stress the fact that Wordsworth here manages a series of paradoxes worthy of John Donne, but – and this is my point – Wordsworth presents them in a completely un-Donne-like way. Donne might have pointed up the paradoxes thus: if a slumber had sealed the lover's spirit, a slumber, immersed in which he had thought it impossible that his loved one could perish, now a very different kind of a slumber has sealed *her* spirit. If it had seemed to the lover impossible that a creature so evidently divine and immortal could ever feel "the touch of earthly years", he now knows that she feels that touch indeed, for like the "rocks and stones", she feels nothing at all. But Wordsworth leaves us to find the paradoxes as, and if, we can. He has been content with the simple juxtapositions that first disturbed and, on second thought, gratified Riding and Graves.

This device of direct confrontation and juxtaposition came into being, one supposes, as an almost instinctive attempt on the part of Wordsworth and his brother poets to circumvent what had seemed to them the numbing effects of misapplied reason. These poets will forgo the logical structure dear to a Pope or a Dryden. Wordsworth tended to strip away even more: he abjures formal rhetoric, including elaborate analogies and complicated metaphors. He will make scenes from actual life rise up before us and trust that if he has chosen the right scenes and presented them in the right order, that very presentation will generate directly any proper commentary and interpretation. The notion is not unlike that of the late Ernest Hemingway: render detail faithfully enough and your writing will attain a kind of fifth dimension.

In putting it thus, I overstate the case and I make Wordsworth a great deal more self-conscious than he actually was: but there *is* in Wordsworth a certain anti-rhetorical tendency, nor can it be completely an accident that Wordsworth's simplest poems, when thrown on the screen of the twentieth-century sensibility, light up in a special way. They reveal gaps in logic that the reader is forced to cross with a leap of the imagination – they hint at analogies that cry out to be completed – and yet which can only be completed by the reader himself.

In a very general sense, this structure of simple and un-analyzed juxtapositions is the groundwork of a great deal of modern poetry – not least in that of Eliot. In Section II of *The Waste Land*, for instance, there is the bored neurasthenic woman sitting in the rich room talking to her husband (or is it her para-mour?) and then without warning, this scene is sharply juxta-posed with one of completely different complexion in which we find two cockney women talking in a pub. No more than Wordsworth has Eliot spelled out the relationship of one scene to the other, or the purpose that he has in making the contrast. He has thrown this burden upon the reader himself, demanding that he relate the two scenes in his own imagination.

The Waste Land is full of such juxtapositions, offered drama-tically and sometimes even crashingly, without comment by the author. Thus, the short lyric Section IV, "Death by Water", is flung up in stark contrast against Sections III and V. Within the sections themselves, the smaller elements jostle with each other like the bits of material mounted upon a canvas in an audacious montage. Consider Section I. Cruel April and com-fortable winter; sunlight in the Hofgarten, two children sledding in the mountains; the luxury hotel in some city like Naples; stony rubbish and a heap of broken images; a scrap of song from *Tristan und Isolde*, the remembered hyacinth garden, and another scrap from *Tristan*; the hyacinth girl in her dew-laden innocence played off against Madame Sosostris with her bad cold, her greasy pack of cards, and her mumbled prophecies.

I grant that Eliot brings to his poetry also the resources of a rich analogical tradition. We are all aware of his essays on Andrew Marvell and on the metaphysical poets, and of his own experiments in adapting their conceits to the modern situation, but we must also note that he grafted the metaphysical mode onto a poetry of very different structure: Donne's logic onto Wordsworth's lack of logic.

The general point that I am making here is closely related to one made a number of years ago by W. H. Auden. Indeed, my point was initially derived from his. In his introduction to Volume IV of the *Poets of the English Language*, Auden remarked that "the real novelty in Romantic poetry is not its diction but its structure. If the Romantic poets," he says, "after rejecting Pope and Dryden, did not rediscover Donne and the metaphysical poets, this was because the latter, no less than the former, organized their poems *logically*." And he points out that this is precisely what the Romantic poets did not do.

Now I am inclined to think that the matter of diction was more important than Auden is willing to concede, and I am not satisfied with his illustration – he cites Keats's "Ode to a Nightingale" – of the a-logical structure of Romantic poetry. Wordsworth's Lucy poems, I believe, provide simpler as well as clearer instances. For the distinctive element – or at least what was to become the distinctive element in modern poetry – is the stark confrontation, the juxtaposition without explanation or rhetorical accommodation.

One has to concede that the continuity of this device from the Romantics to the moderns is far from clear. The Victorian poets, who of course built upon Romantic foundations, tended to muffle and conceal this aspect of their poetry by embedding these crucial scenes in a continuous narrative, or by providing explicit commentary and rumination upon them. (The a-logical juxtapositions do peep out in some of the early poetry of Tennyson or later in his "Maud, a Monodrama".) But Victorian poetry has rarely raised eyebrows through any seeming lack of coherent structure. When the wit and logic of the metaphysicals was brought back into the poetry in our time, the old-fashioned reader regarded it as supererogatory – an impertinent intrusion.

Yet the revival of this witty rhetoric, with its paradoxes and occasionally elaborate analogies, certainly did not mean a return to the discursive structure of Dryden and Pope. Auden is one of the very few poets of the twentieth century who has been able to adopt, or has cared to adopt, the urbane ratiocination of the eighteenth century. Consider the following lines from his "New Year Letter":

> I see it now: The intellect
> That parts the Cause from the Effect
> And thinks in terms of Space and Time
> Commits a legalistic crime,
> For such an unreal severance
> Must falsify experience.

Auden does this sort of thing very well, but even for Auden, it is a *tour de force*, and remains a special case. The characteristic structure of modern poetry is of quite another sort.

This structure of unanalyzed juxtapositions shows itself even in a poet as comfortably coherent as Robert Frost. One does not usually think of Frost as a difficult poet. Indeed, Frost's status as a great modern artist was for a time obscured by the well-intentioned plaudits of some of his friends who, as I have remarked earlier, in insisting upon his humanity and his wisdom, portrayed him as a kind of cracker-barrel philosopher, sitting on the porch of some Vermont general store, full of folksy sententiousness. But Frost refused to fritter his poems away in talk or to explain the connections. He deliberately left much to his reader's imagination. A poem like "Stopping by Woods on a Snowy Evening" shows that he knew what to leave out. The poem maintains a note of whimsy; it doesn't talk itself out to the reader: it is a dramatization – a confrontation – not a rimed disquisition.

This, I take it, is the point that MacLeish had in mind in his poem "Ars Poetica", where he states categorically that a poem should "not mean but be". "Ars Poetica" is itself no mere statement but a poem and its rhythms and its images will tell the sensitive reader how it is to be understood. That reader will interpret his final line as a denial of overt messages, not as a denial of meaning as such. What MacLeish demands for a poem is that being and meaning coalesce, the meaning absorbed by, and continuous with, the very structure of the poem.

Speaking of MacLeish, one might cite several fine examples of his own use of juxtaposition and confrontation: there is "You, Andrew Marvell", in which the meaning of the passage of time is dramatized for us without a word of philosophical commentary on time; or "Memorial Rain", in which the public speech of the ambassador dedicating the cemetery is played off against the private thoughts of the grieved listener whose brother's body lies in one of the graves of that cemetery. Incidentally, I prefer, on the whole, MacLeish's private speech to his public speech. His "public" poems sometimes become abstract, preachy and argumentative, whereas his private poems at their best are not merely private but yield a public and negotiable meaning, yet one that has been sharpened and focused by having entered our consciousness through the narrow door of the particular.

The general structure of which we have been speaking is ubiquitous in modern poetry. It is hardly necessary, however, to multiply examples. It is the staple of the deliberately flattened vignettes of American life to be found in the poems of William Carlos Williams. It determines the structure of whole cantos of Ezra Pound. William Butler Yeats used it over and over again, especially in some of his more laconic late poems. For example, in "Long-Legged Fly", Caesar in his tent, looking at the battle maps, is set over against a girlish Helen of Troy, musing and practising a shuffling dance step, and she, in turn, is set over against a Michelangelo, paint brush in hand, lying on a scaffolding under the ceiling of the Sistine Chapel. The way in which the mind of each is like the long-legged fly upon the stream is left to the reader's imagination. I grant that it will be a dull reader whose imagination, when confronted with this little masterpiece, cannot rise to the occasion. But the point is that the inter-connections *are* left to the reader's imagination, and I have known some graduate students who failed to make them out.

Wallace Stevens will, of course, show this structure almost anywhere: "The Emperor of Ice-Cream" and "The Sense of the Sleight-of-Hand Man" are good examples. Robert Lowell began very strongly in the tradition of wit as one would expect, remembering that his early mentors were John Crowe Ransom

and Allen Tate, and he has never wholly discarded intricate
analogies and brilliantly ironic effects, but his later poems –
particularly the poems of *Life Studies* – demand that the reader
make sense of what may seem no more than a brilliant hap-
hazardry. Look at "Sailing Home from Rapallo", which sets
the sub-zero graveyard in New Hampshire over against the
bubbling water of the "Golfo di Genova", and which begins
with the author's tears as he talks to the Italian nurse who
watched over his mother's last hour and ends with a reference
to her corpse, "wrapped like *panetone* in Italian tinfoil"; or look
at the brilliant poem entitled "Skunk Hour" and see what you
make of its somber and terrifying juxtapositions.

W. H. Auden and Robert Penn Warren, in my opinion the
two most powerful poets of their generation, are sufficiently
versatile to illustrate nearly any kind of modern structure, and
they will abundantly illustrate that with which I am concerned
here. Warren's "Original Sin", for example, finds its resolving
images in the old horse turned out to grass, and the old mother
searching the darkened house, long past midnight, for a childhood picture. But these images are slipped into the poem almost
surreptitiously, almost as an afterthought. They are masterfully
placed, I hasten to say, but their effectiveness turns upon what
may seem at first glance their almost meaningless and casual
inconsequence. A last example, this time from Auden: his
"Fall of Rome" gives us a series of witty, brilliant scenes, illus-
trating the breakup of a civilization. But these scenes culminate
in an image that must have seemed to some readers, and
momentarily at least to most readers, to constitute an imagistic
non-sequitur:

> Altogether elsewhere, vast
> Herds of reindeer move across
> Miles and miles of golden moss,
> Silently and very fast.

The current reaction against Eliot and the modern school of
wit is essentially a reaction against overt analogy and overt
logic. The poets of this reaction hope, as Blake once hoped, to
write so ecstatically as to project a personal vision, or else, as

perhaps Wordsworth had hoped, to write with such naked austerity as to make the poem rise spontaneously, like an exhalation, from the minutely observed particulars. It is the latter notion that seems to underlie Donald Hall's Introduction to the Penguin edition of *Contemporary American Poetry*. He discovers in our most recent poetry something genuinely new. He writes that

"In lines like Robert Bly's

> In small towns the houses are built right on the ground;
> The lamplight falls on all fours in the grass

or Louis Simpson's

> These houses built of wood sustain
> Colossal snows,
> The light above the street is sick to death

a new kind of imagination seems to be working. The vocabulary is mostly colloquial, but the special quality of the lines has nothing to do with an area of diction; it is a quality learned neither from T. S. Eliot nor William Carlos Williams. This imagination is irrational yet the poem is usually quiet and the language simple; there is no straining for apocalypse and no conscious pursuit of the unconscious. There is an inwardness to these images, a profound subjectivity. Yet they are not subjective in the autobiographical manner of [Robert Lowell's] *Life Studies* or [William Snodgrass's] *Heart's Needle*, which are confessional and particular. The new imagination reveals through images a subjective life which is *general*, and which corresponds to an old objective life of shared experience and knowledge."

But how new is this new imagination? Its character reveals itself in the way in which it restructures experience and that, in turn, in the structure of the poem. But the structure of the two poems cited by Hall looks to me as old as that of Wordsworth's Lucy poems. The poet juxtaposes two images and hopes that the steel of the first will strike a spark from the flint of the second, and thus kindle the reader's imagination. But my metaphor actually overstates the technique, for there is nothing in this poetry so violent as the striking of sparks. What is to happen is more nearly analogous to spontaneous combustion: the poet does no more than put one substance beside the other and leave the combustion to occur, or not to occur, in the reader's imagination.

Perhaps the passages quoted by Hall do ignite into quiet flame. But much poetry of this general sort does not. I would have to say this of some of the poetry of William Carlos Williams, for example. His "Red Wheelbarrow" – to cite a famous short "objective" poem – remains for some of us quite inert. I see the white chickens and the raindrops glazing the red paint, but I have to take on faith the author's statement that "so much depends" on this scene.

Wordsworth also, it ought to be conceded, sometimes wrote "private" poems of this sort – poems based on experiences that evidently meant much to him, but which, for many a reader, do not so much tease him out of thought as simply tease him with a blank uncomprehending stare.

I have preferred in this discussion to talk about the form of modern poetry rather than its content and its beliefs and that is also what Mr Hall has on the whole preferred to talk about. But his remarks about a "subjective" life that is "general" and corresponds to an "old objective life of shared experience" that had presumably somehow become lost but that is now being recovered remind me of Wordsworth's own terms. In any case, Mr Hall's last statement seems to make a large claim. Genuine poetry has always united men by bringing them into a shared experience, but if Mr Hall means more than this, if he finds in recent poetry something truly new, if he means for us to take his statements literally, then we are apparently about to witness a shift in our whole cultural situation. For it was the split between the subjective and the objective – the chasm between the life of the emotions and attitudes within the poet and the universe outside him – that so much troubled the Romantic poets. The poetry of Wordsworth and the criticism of Coleridge are dominated by the attempt to bridge this chasm. It would be tidings indeed to learn that the American poets of the 1950's had finally spanned it.

Such tidings might signal an end to the waste-land experience, for if men could now find in their own subjective life something that corresponds to what Mr Hall calls the "old objective life of shared experience", then they would have reestablished a rapport with nature and restored the community of values, the loss of which wasted the land. The quickening rain for which the protagonist in *The Waste Land* yearned would at last have begun to fall. The prospect is exciting, but I remain skeptical. I am not sure that poetry can solve our problems, though I think that it can throw light upon them by helping us to understand ourselves. At any rate, it seems certain that poetry will continue for a long time to revolve around the matter of man's consciousness – the consciousness which separates him from the other animals and alienates him from nature but which at the same time is the very power that allows him to *see* nature, as it were, from the outside and to see himself in the very act of seeing it.

5

Joyce's Ulysses: *Symbolic Poem, Biography or Novel?*

Is James Joyce's *Ulysses* a novel – interpret the term with as much latitude as you like? Or is it a kind of ragbag of Joyce's personal memories, inspired doodlings, speculations, private jokes, and scattered observations on Dublin life as it was lived in the early nineteen hundreds? Some of Joyce's Dublin acquaintances and friends, like Oliver St John Gogarty (transmogrified in the novel into Buck Mulligan) have contended that to look for any consistent or over-all meaning is silly. Those that do so are "victims of a gigantic hoax, of one of the most enormous leg-pulls in history". But the general view has been quite otherwise. In that view, *Ulysses* is an ordered and intricately organized masterpiece. Indeed it is usually accorded the treatment given to a sacred book. A painfully careful exegesis is regarded as appropriate to these Joycean scriptures, which have been diligently searched in order to discover proof texts, to recover hidden meanings, to unravel cryptic allusions, and, more ambitiously, to develop a systematic symbolism.

The appearance of Robert M. Adams's *Surface and Symbol* a few years ago raised a good many questions about the consistency of the symbolism of *Ulysses*. As Richard Ellmann has said, after Adams's exploration of the relation of fact and fiction in this work, "everyone will have to reconsider his position about *Ulysses*".

What Adams shows is that "there is no proper fictional reason for some of the things that are said and done" in *Ulysses*. Some of the items are found to lack any symbolic import whatever. For example, the winners in the bicycle race that is held on Bloom's Day are mentioned by name and some commentators have tried to find special meanings in the names that Joyce chose for them. Is, for example, the name of the winner, J. A. Jackson, an "enigmatic allusion" to the author himself, viz. James Augustine Joyce, the son of Jack Joyce? Such an interpretation has been proposed. But Adams shows that Joyce copied the names from a newspaper account of a race that actually took place in Dublin on 16 June 1904. Adams is able indeed to prove that the newspaper that Joyce used was the *Irish Independent*, for the name of one of the riders, J. B. Jones, as printed in that paper, looks – probably because the type was dirty – "remarkably like 'Jeffs'", the name that Joyce uses in *Ulysses*. In this instance, the symbol-hunter would be very much in the plight of the fabled cornet-player who was unfortunate enough to mistake a fly speck on his score for a musical note.

Usually, however, Joyce did not slavishly follow his sources but reworked the materials he derived from them very freely indeed. Yet the motive determining his alterations and transpositions is not always easy to discern. Often there seems to be no "fictional reason" served by the changes. There may be personal reasons: occasionally Joyce seems to be simply venting his dislike of a Dublin acquaintance as when, for example, he calls a priest whom he knew, and whom Adams is able to identify, "Father Purdon", assigning to him "deliberately, the name of a street in the red-light district of Dublin". In other instances the alterations serve to develop a private joke, and often a joke so private that only a Dubliner of the time and in the know would find it comprehensible. Adams, it should be said, is not particularly worried by Joyce's propensity to insert his signature thus into odd corners of his canvas or to work into it his little private ceremonies and rituals. Yet Adams does question, and properly, "a general principle of construction not very economical of the general reader's time, and not very neat so far as the economy of forces within the novel is concerned".

It is the latter point, of course, that is finally important. Conceivably the scholars some day may have succeeded in annotating all the private allusions and in solving all the riddles, but in so far as such material cannot be related to the import of the novel – in so far as it has no "fictional reason" behind it – then so much the worse for *Ulysses* as a work of fiction.

Because the prime critical sin of our day – certainly the currently fashionable sin – is "symbol-mongering", and because critics too often seize upon any item that seems invitingly "symbolic" or that evokes something remembered from *The Golden Bough*, we have had a proliferation of *Ulysses* "symbols", some of them clearly possessing no genuine relation to the work. Against this kind of reading, *Surface and Symbol* serves as a powerful counter-blast. Adams has shown that some of the matter in *Ulysses* is mere connective tissue, some of it is not even healthy connective tissue. This or that suspicious lump, under his probing, turns out to be simply an excrescence, a wart, or, if deeper below the surface, a mere tumour, serving no function even though it may be harmless and benign. Such elements in *Ulysses* may represent bits of the author's private life, elements that he has not been able – or perhaps has not taken the trouble – to transmute into the fictional fabric. Or, to change the metaphor, such elements may be regarded as odd pieces of scaffolding, necessary perhaps for Joyce's rather peculiar method of composition, but once composition has been completed, serving no function, constituting no part of the total architecture, though still firmly attached to the permanent structure.

But the reader may ask, are you sure that you really understand Joyce's architecture? Isn't it possible that someone whose head was filled with preconceived notions about what a novel ought to be might mistake for bits of leftover scaffolding what are actually essential parts of the building? That indeed is the question. How does one determine what is integral and what is not? What is the organizing principle of *Ulysses*? Mr Adams's essential contribution is to show that odd bits of scaffolding do remain – i.e. J. B. Jeffs for J. B. Jones – that some parts of *Ulysses* are merely surface and have no symbolic reference. Mr Adams has also thrown suspicion on a still larger number of allegedly symbolic items by showing that the symbolic patterns they seem to suggest either peter out to nothing when one explores them further, or else require so much elaboration and so many esoteric references that the law of diminishing returns sets in.

On the more positive side, however, Adams is less helpful. He fails to discern some of the symbolic patterns that are really there. The section of *Surface and Symbol* entitled "Dog-God" is an instance. Adams begins this part of his book by referring to Joyce's well-known fear and hatred of dogs. He goes on to sum up what is known about the real life antecedents of the Citizen's dog Garryowen. The incident on the beach, recounted in the third chapter, in which Stephen sees the live dog sniff at the body of the dead dog is referred to Mulligan's earlier characterization of Stephen as a "dogsbody". Furthermore, Adams sees that the various references to dogs in *Ulysses* are connected in some way with spelling "God" backwards when the black mass is celebrated in the Circe chapter. The general inversion of the sacred rites converts "God" into "dog" – a matter most apposite to the pattern of Stephen's thoughts as developed in the earlier chapters of *Ulysses*.

In Adams's view, however, no really meaningful pattern emerges from the references to dogs; he finds the mention of them in *Ulysses* to be "surely random". The distant bark of a dog that is heard at the end of the Circe chapter may be read, Adams tells us, "if one wishes, as a pathetic picture of God in the modern world, where truth cries out in the streets and no man regards it". But Adams quite properly sees little point in pressing this particular notion. Even the fact that Rudy's conception is occasioned by Molly's sexual stimulation at seeing two dogs copulating doesn't seem to him to have any "crucial symbolic significance". If it does have, it is "buried in an oddly out-of-the-way corner of the book structure".

In his attempt to discover whether the references to dogs mean anything in particular in this novel, Adams considers the associations of Odysseus with the dog and with other animals, the pig and the fox. He is also driven back into speculations about what books on the subject Joyce might have read, including quite remarkable lexicons such as Selig Korn's *Etymologisch-symbolisch-mythologisches Real-Wörterbuch zum Handgebrauche für*

Bibelforscher, Archäologen und bildende Künstler (Stuttgart, 1843)
and Oskar Seyffert's *Lexikon der klassischen Alterthumskunde.*
Adams's conclusion is cautiously, but rather disappointingly,
inconclusive. Joyce, he finds, digs up various traditional properties for Odysseus and Telemachus. For these he sometimes
found "brilliant applications – parodic, serious, symbolic,
superficial . . . but sometimes he did not. Quite sensibly he
continued to use them anyway, whether or no; and left the
reader to find or neglect the application, according to his
temperament."

But surely Joyce's reference to dogs is more significant than
Adams has found it to be. One can show that the development
of symbols and the interrelating of them are more coherent and
even more traditional than a good deal of Joyce criticism would
lead us to believe.

Though it is interesting to know that Joyce himself, like
Stephen Dedalus, hated and feared dogs, the reader does not
need to have this information in order to discover Stephen's
attitude. The opening chapters of *Ulysses* reveal what the dog
has come to stand for in Stephen's sensibility. Stephen's experience on Sandymount Beach (in the Proteus chapter) with the
live dog and the dead dog is intimately related to his feelings
about Buck Mulligan, to the recent death of his mother, and to
his own sense of the importance of his vocation as an artist.

These are matters that are touched on in the very opening
pages of *Ulysses.* And by beginning with them, we begin at the
beginning, with the obvious, and not with the esoteric. For
Stephen, who distrusts Buck Mulligan and who resents his having invited Haines to the tower, "dogsbody" and "beastly"
are loaded terms to which Stephen overreacts. That his reaction
is in excess of the occasion is plain enough if we are willing to
read *Ulysses* "straight" – that is, as we might read any other
novel. The reason for Stephen's sensitivity and bitterness also
becomes plain enough, if, again, we read the first chapter with
sufficient care to see that Stephen, in spite of his pose of
callousness, has been powerfully affected by his mother's death.
(Buck is quite right in seeing that Stephen is brooding over this
hurt.)

Buck's merry travesty of the mass as he shaves also has its relevance to Stephen's mood. Holding up the bowl of lather, Buck intones "*Introibo ad altare Dei*" and then calls out to Stephen: "Come up, Kinch. Come up, you fearful Jesuit." But Stephen is not amused. We are told that Stephen is "displeased and sleepy" and looks "coldly" on Buck's antics.

When Buck, a few moments later, addresses Stephen as "poor dogsbody", even though Buck speaks in a kind voice, the word *dogsbody* bears a meaning that for Stephen is edged. But before turning to inquire what the word conveyed to Stephen, we ought to determine what the term means in itself. Adams senses that "the overtones [of this epithet] are more important than the literal meaning", but he has not grasped the literal meaning. He writes that "the only recognized public meanings of the epithet, first applied to Stephen by Mulligan, are ludicrously irrelevant – midshipman or pease pudding. Even if we suppose it used loosely and in derision, the epithet in this sense has very little point." But "dogsbody" as currently used in Great Britain signifies a flunky of all work, a person on whom any kind of task can be imposed.

Midshipman, indeed, is or was one of the meanings of the word, but a midshipman is also called a "snottie". An illustrative quotation printed in the Supplement to the *Oxford English Dictionary* reads: "A midshipman is known . . . in the service as a 'snottie' . . . If he is a junior midshipman he is also a 'dog's body'." Joyce was evidently aware of the relation of "dogsbody" to "snottie", for when Buck, "thrusting a hand into Stephen's upper pocket", borrows his handkerchief, Joyce has him say: "lend us a loan of your noserag to wipe my razor . . . The bard's noserag. A new art colour for our Irish poets: snotgreen." The association would be "snotrag" – "snottie" – "dogsbody".

Stephen evidently understands the term to mean someone of no standing who can be saddled with any onerous or humiliating task, for a little later, noticing Buck's abandoned bowl of lather, Stephen observes to himself: "So I carried the boat of incense then at Clongowes. I am another now and yet the same. A servant too. A server of a servant." The Pope's proud title is the servant of the servants of God. It is in an ironically different sense that Stephen sees that he is the server of a servant. The man whom Stephen serves is in Stephen's embittered imagination himself a servant, truckling to and fawning over Haines, the Englishman. Stephen views himself as a dogsbody indeed.

The element "dog" in "dogsbody" has its own special and bitter meaning for Stephen on this morning. *Beast* and *beastliness* are very much on his mind, and the dog is perhaps the most familiar and least exalted example of the beasts. Doubtless this is why the common term of contempt is "son of a bitch" rather than son of a mare or son of a cow or son of a cat. When Buck Mulligan exclaimed to his mother some days earlier that his visitor was "only Dedalus whose mother is beastly dead", he was, of course, using *beastly* as a loose intensive. But when, challenged by Stephen, he undertakes to explain what he meant by the word, *beastly* takes on specific meaning: "You saw only your mother die. I see them pop off every day . . . and cut into tripes in the dissecting room . . . To me it's all a mockery and beastly. Her cerebral lobes are not functioning".

Yet what Buck Mulligan can accept with equanimity is to Stephen agonizing. Part of the agony stems, of course, from Stephen's own personal involvement: his mother's recent death. Of much greater importance is the fact that Stephen is keenly aware of the full consequences of the changed view of man that is implied. He knows what he has lost; he cannot accept palliatives and compromises. When Haines asks Stephen whether he is a believer, "I mean, a believer in the narrow sense of the word", Stephen replies: "There's only one sense of the word, it seems to me." Haines's "Yes, of course" assumes a community of feeling that is not there. He hastens to add: "Either you believe or you don't, isn't it. Personally I couldn't stomach the idea of a personal God. You don't stand for that, I suppose?" Stephen drily observes, "with grim displeasure", that Haines beholds in him "a horrible example of free thought".

If man is only a beast, then all priests of whatever religions are really "medicine men", and Buck, the medical student, who is preparing to be a genuine medicine man with effective medicaments, can see himself as the only true priest of the twentieth century. His mockery of the Mass asserts a claim which, even if made humorously by Buck, has to be taken seriously by Stephen. Stephen reacts to this assertion with active hostility, for Stephen himself claims to be the true priest of the modern world: the artist, the priest of the eternal imagination. Later on, in the middle of the library chapter, Best observes that "the sense of beauty leads us astray", John Eglinton replies: "The doctor can tell us what those words mean." The doctor in the group is, of course, Buck Mulligan. Stephen's comment to himself a propos of Eglinton's deference to science is: "Sayest thou so? Will they [the medical men] wrest from us [the artists], from me the palm of beauty?" Stephen is hypersensitive on this issue and allows his resentment of Buck to colour his whole notion of the relation of science to art, but that fact is scarcely the point here. To a very considerable extent *Ulysses* is "about" Stephen and his relationship to his world. At any rate, Stephen here plainly means to generalize the issue. His bitter remark to himself is not "Will Buck wrest from me the palm of beauty", but will "they" wrest it?

The collapse of religion has left science and poetry quarrelling over the spoils and jostling each other for place. It is thoroughly appropriate, therefore, that early in the first chapter Matthew Arnold should come into Stephen's thoughts. He has a vision of the neat quadrangle of an Oxford college, and in it, pushing his mower, "a deaf gardener . . . masked with Matthew Arnold's face". If Buck's proposal to "Hellenize" Ireland, and his playful hint of an Oxford-style debagging to be executed on the Oxonian Haines – if Haines misbehaves in the future – provide the immediate stimulus to this absurd vision, the relevance of Arnold to the general situation is nevertheless thoroughly appropriate. On the assumption that science had destroyed the "fact" to which religion was unfortunately attached, Arnold had prophesied that literature would assume the burden of promoting and dispensing values. Literature was fortunately not attached to the fact, was thus invulnerable to the corrosions of science, and for that reason "the future of poetry was immense". The point is not that Stephen's speculations necessarily duplicate those of Matthew Arnold. But the basic problem that faces

him is that which Arnold had earlier faced, and Stephen at the
end of the *Portrait*, just before setting out for Paris, had proclaimed himself a "priest of the eternal imagination", an
Arnoldian solution of the problem.

On this morning, art is very much on Stephen's mind. He tells
Buck that the "symbol of Irish art" is the "cracked looking-
glass of a servant". A moment later he says to himself that
Buck "fears the lancet of my art as I fear that of his". Stephen
opposes to the surgeon's lancet the artist's "cold steelpen".
As we have already observed, Stephen is distrustful of and
irritated by Buck, not merely as a person, but for what Buck
represents.

It is in this general context that the colloquy about "beastly
dead" occurs. As we have seen, Buck has referred to Stephen as
"poor dogsbody", and Stephen, a moment later looking at
himself in the mirror, has asked himself. "Who chose this face
for me? This dogsbody to rid of vermin." In this instance,
"dogsbody" insists upon the "dog" element: viz. this "beastly"
body – this contemptibly animal organism. The specific occasion for Stephen's irritation at Buck is, of course, Buck's relation
to Haines. Stephen not only resents the presence of Haines and
regards him as a "usurper", but has been badly frightened by
Haines's conduct during the night before. Haines, caught up in
a nightmare about a "black panther", had seized his rifle and
fired a shot in the room. Stephen's first words to Buck on the
next morning are an inquiry as to how long Haines is going to
stay in the tower. Stephen tells Buck: "If he stays on here I am
off." It is a threat which Buck does not take seriously, but which
Stephen is to make good.

The black panther has its connections also with the theme of
man as mere beast. In using the term *panther* Joyce may have
had in mind the fanciful etymology (Greek *pan* meaning *all*
plus *ther* meaning *beast*) which intimates that the nature of this
animal includes somehow all the beasts. Perhaps so, perhaps
not. If Stephen was familiar with the eytmology, that fact
might help account for the celebrated passage in the Proteus
chapter where to Stephen's eye the dog on the beach imitates in
his actions the whole animal kingdom – bounding like a hare,

skimming like a gull, tripping like a buck, halting with stiff "forehooves". A little later, the dog rears up on his master with "mute bearish fawning", then lopes off "at a calf's gallop", sniffs at the carcass of a dead dog, then, ordered away by his master, runs down the beach and starts digging in the sand. Stephen watches the dog scraping "up the sand again with a fury of his claws, soon ceasing, a pard, a panther, got in spouse-breach, vulturing the dead".

Stephen's way of seeing the dog's action here is of course an amalgam of his own thoughts and associations. It is these associations that make the dog melt into a panther and then finally take on the attributes of a bird ("vulturing" the dead). They also account for Stephen's curious observation that this monster was "got in spouse-breach".[1]

Stephen's notion that man is a mere animal, beastly born and later to be beastly dead, gives point to – as well as receives illumination from – the various references in the early chapters to panther, fox, and dog. These three animals have rather differing associations. The black panther is the terror of nightmare, but in Stephen's mind it associates itself with British colonialism – with the colonel who has served in India perhaps – and Stephen in applying the epithet to Haines thinks of him as a "panthersahib" who demands that others fawn on him. But we are not dealing with a rigid symbolism. When Stephen scornfully asks himself whether he is pining for "the bark of *their* applause", Buck and Haines are both dogs. The fox is peculiarly a type of Stephen himself, having to live by Stephen's credo of silence, cunning, and exile. He provides an analogue for Stephen's own apparent callousness toward his mother: "and on a heath beneath winking stars a fox, red reek of rapine in his fur, with merciless bright eyes scraped in the earth, listened".

[1] The *Oxford English Dictionary* does quote from a medieval writer, Trevisa, the following incidence of the word: "Leopardus is a cruel beeste and is gendred in spowsebreche of a parde and of a lionas." The usage is so odd and the quotation is so apt to this passage in *Ulysses* that one finds it hard to believe that Joyce had not read this very passage in the *Oxford English Dictionary*. I suppose that he had, and that his having done so probably accounts for his choice of this particular word here. But if Trevisa has extended the meaning of *spouse-breach* to include monstrous and unnatural union, its primary meaning of adultery is still present: etymology sees to that.

But Stephen is a dog too: he had called himself "poor dogs-body" as he gazed on his own face in the mirror, and now on the beach he applies the same term to the dead dog, the "one great goal" to which the live dog Tatters, "sniffing . . . eyes on the ground", moves. Mr Deasy, an hour or so before, had remarked to Stephen that all "history moves towards one great goal, the manifestation of God". That great goal to which history leads, the manifestation of God, turns out to be the rotting mammalian flesh: "Here lies poor dogsbody's body."

Stephen, watching the dog digging in the sand of the beach, describes him as a "panther, got in spouse-breach". Stephen knows that in the kingdom of the animals, as in heaven, there is no marrying or giving in marriage, and that among the beasts, there can hardly be adultery. Is it not a bit highfalutin to make the dog Tatters the bastard offspring of an adulterous union? Why, in his reverie, does Stephen do so? Because in some way the theme of adultery is tied in with man's mere bestiality and the emptying of any belief in the Christian story.

This is the primary stress when the theme of adultery first makes its appearance with Buck's rendition of "The Ballad of Joking Jesus". The Jesus who is the "I" of the ballad guarantees his divinity by claiming a divine father, a bird, the dove of the Holy Spirit. Joseph the Joiner is not his father, but in this poem which Buck chants in a "quiet happy foolish voice", this "queerest young fellow" is clearly a fraud, and the true story is not one of miraculous birth in which the divine becomes incarnate in human flesh, but a rather sordid account of adultery in which Joseph the Joiner has been deceived by his wife.

Stephen's Nestor, Mr Deasy, touches the theme again. "A woman brought sin into the world. For a woman who was no better than she should be, Helen, the runaway wife of Menelaus, ten years the Greeks made war on Troy. A faithless wife first brought the strangers to our shore here. MacMurrough's wife and her leman O'Rourke, prince of Breffni. A woman too brought Parnell low." References to Helen of Troy and to Jesus as touching on spouse-breach occur throughout *Ulysses* – most notably in the Circe chapter where Virag asserts that the real father of Jesus was a Roman centurion named Panther!

Stephen thinks of Shakespeare, type of the artist, as a man deceived and cuckolded. Leopold Bloom is a cuckold and throughout the day remains uneasily conscious of Blazes Boylan's assignation with his wife. But at this point I am less concerned with Bloom and the later chapters in general than with seeing whether a pattern does begin to emerge in the opening pages of the novel.

Adultery, as we have seen, is associated in Stephen's mind with the disappearance of any supernatural claim and man's reduction to the status of beast. But it also has for him another powerful association. Doubtful paternity emphasizes the link between mother and child as the only certainty. In the second chapter, Stephen's meditations as he helps one of his students with his arithmetic problem enforces the point. As Stephen looks at the boy before him, "ugly and futile: lean neck and tangled hair and a stain of ink, a snail's bed", he reflects that "someone had loved him, borne him in her arms and in her heart . . . had loved his weak watery blood drained from her own. Was that then real? The only true thing in life?" These thoughts, of course, are tangled with his thoughts about his mother. Stephen says to himself: "Like him was I, these sloping shoulders, this gracelessness." Stephen's sight of the old midwives on the beach reinforces the same thought: "One of her sisterhood," he reflects, "lugged me squealing into life. Creation from nothing. What has she in her bag? A misbirth with a trailing navelcord, hushed in ruddy wool. The cords of all link back, strandentwining cable of all flesh." Then after a brief interval comes the thought: "Wombed in sin darkness I was too, made not begotten." In the Nicene creed Christ was "begotten, not made, being of one substance with the Father". But Stephen ruefully assigns to his own creation only a biological making – made by "the man with my voice and my eyes and a ghost woman with ashes on her breath. They clasped and sundered, did the coupler's will."

Motherhood for Stephen is associated with the biological, and woman herself is the prime instance of the mammal: the creature that suckles its young. Fatherhood, on the other hand, is a mystical estate. As Stephen is to put it later on in the Library chapter, "fatherhood, in the sense of conscious begetting, is unknown to man. It is a mystical estate, an apostolic succession, from only begetter to only begotten. On that mystery and not on the madonna which the cunning Italian intellect flung to the mob of Europe the church is founded and founded irremovably because founded, like the world, macro- and microcosm, upon the void. Upon incertitude, upon unlikelihood. *Amor matris* . . . may be the only true thing in life. Paternity may be a legal fiction." For Stephen, Jesus as the son of God has become merely a fiction, though Stephen can still believe in a god of art, and view himself as standing in the apostolic succession of the priests of the imagination.

We do not, however, have to wait until the Library chapter for Stephen's full statement of the matter. The groundwork for this distinction is laid in the early pages of the novel. For example, in the Proteus chapter, as Stephen watches the cocklepickers on the beach, he thinks of woman as the "hand-maiden of the moon". The phrase echoes St Luke's account of the Annunciation, where Mary replies to the Angel: "Behold the handmaid of the Lord; be it unto me according to Thy word." Woman now has to be regarded as the handmaiden of the moon, subject to the biological process and bound to the the cycle of menstruation and gestation measured off in lunar months. A moment later, Stephen thinks of her as one summoned to "Bridebed, childbed, bed of death, ghostcandled. *Omnis caro ad te veniet*". The Latin sentence ("All flesh shall come to thee") is from Psalm 65. There the psalmist declares that all flesh shall come to Jehovah, but in the context of Stephen's present thoughts the deity to whom all flesh shall come is the vampire of death, "his bat sails bloodying the sea, mouth to her mouth's kiss". In a later chapter that deity will be seen as neither the dove of the Holy Spirit nor as the bat-winged vampire, but as "the reverent Carrion Crow", as Stephen now envisages "the third person of the Blessed Trinity".

In some respects, the most brilliant instances of the reduction of the divine to the merely animal occur in the Circe chapter. The Black Mass in which the voices of all the damned utter "dog", reversing the syllable "God" uttered by the voices of the blessed, has been referred to. The other instance is that in which Stephen appears as the "Primate of all Ireland". When Stephen conjures one of the whores to "beware Antisthenes, the dog sage, and the last end of Arius Heresiarchus", Lynch observes: "All one and the same God to her." This exchange prompts Florry to say to Stephen: "I'm sure you are a spoiled priest. Or a monk." Lynch chimes in: "He is. A Cardinal's son." Stephen's comment, "Cardinal sin. Monks of the screw," calls up a vision of "His Eminence, Simon Stephen Cardinal Dedalus, Primate of all Ireland". He "appears in the doorway, dressed in red soutane, sandals and socks. Seven dwarf simian acolytes, also in red, cardinal sins, uphold his train, peeping under it . . . Round his neck hangs a rosary of corks ending on his breast in a cork-screw cross." Joyce (and perhaps Stephen too) is making use of the Elizabethan pun that turned on the fact that "cardinal" had come to be pronounced as "carnal". The word *monks* pro-duces the "dwarf simian acolytes". They are seven presumably because of the number of the deadly sins, though here they are simply called "cardinal sins".

As we have observed earlier, "dog" is not used in *Ulysses* as a kind of mechanical counter: it is only one of the several sym-bols of the beastly. For the present instance Joyce has chosen the most nearly man-like of the animals, an anthropoid species, belonging to the highest order of the Mammalia. Stephen is doubly a primate: as the wisest of the beasts and as one of the highpriests of the eternal imagination, among clergy of that ilk, an archbishop and cardinal.

So much for the principal dog references as they concern Stephen. But does the dog really have any particular significance elsewhere in the novel? And specifically, what of its relation to Bloom? It is used significantly if only as helping to stress the polar contrasts between Bloom and Stephen. Bloom does not hate and fear dogs, but rather likes them, though not all dogs like him. He is chased by the Citizen's dog, Garryowen.

Bloom is perfectly content to belong to the highest order of mammals, not in the least dismayed to find man reduced to the naturalistic level. That the conception of his beloved little son Rudy was associated with the copulating of two dogs outside the Blooms' window does not trouble him. His memory of the event elicits from him no more than an elegiac sigh: "How life begins." There may be pathos and sadness in much of human life, but for Bloom the matter of concern is not that man is beastly born and will some day be beastly dead.

The appearance to Bloom of Paddy Dignam as a beagle, now that he is beastly dead and buried, makes good sense. But I must confess that I see little special meaning in the successive metamorphoses of the dog that Bloom meets in Dublin's night town. The fact that the dog is a retriever and then turns into wolf dog, setter, etc. accords with the general atmosphere of hallucination that hangs over this whole chapter. Perhaps nothing more is to be inferred. At any rate, Bloom is not terrified of the dog, whatever the breed he assumes. Bloom opposes cruelty to animals, loves doing good to others (including gulls, horses, and dogs), and readily gives the dog the tidbit that he bought to eat himself.

The distant bark of the dog in the Circe chapter certainly does not suggest "a pathetic picture of God in the modern world, where truth cries out in the streets and no man regards it". Adams has been quite right to reject this view of the matter. If God is, as Stephen earlier that morning told Mr Deasy, simply a noise in the street, then the distant bark of the dog at this point in the novel makes good enough symbolic sense. But one need not insist on extracting a symbolic meaning; most of us will be willing to accept it as an incidental item in the description of the night scene.

The question put some pages earlier was whether *Ulysses* can be read as a novel. The reader's answer will depend upon whether he can discern a pattern of meaning that grows out of the thoughts and actions of the various characters. The first chapters, as I have tried to show, do yield a pattern of meaning, and one which, if it does demand a sensitive and careful reading, and if it does require that the reader should know something about the Mass, and that he have at least a bowing acquaintance with such historical figures as Matthew Arnold, Pyrrhus, Oscar Wilde, and Bishop Berkeley, does not require any encyclopedic scholarship. More important still, it does not require that the reader have the key or code to a private and esoteric set of "symbols".

Stephen's irritation at Buck and his resentment of Haines are indeed unreasonable, though understandable. The author has made it plain that we are not asked to agree with Stephen or to give him more than "dramatic" sympathy. Moreover, Stephen's gloomy thoughts and his bitter speculations are related to a more general state of affairs: they have relevance to the culture of our age, and they are used to throw light upon a climate of opinion that characterizes modern civilization.

The opening chapters of *Ulysses* give us a brilliant dramatization of, among other things, the alienation of the sensitive artist in our day. Stephen's case is, of course, special. It is related to his personal circumstances: his education by the Jesuits, his bitterness at his poverty, and his hurt at the recent death of his mother. But his case, special as it is, is related to general and universal problems including the relation of science, poetry, and religion seen in the post-Arnoldian world. Stephen has won a Pyrrhic victory. He has decided not to join Buck and Haines at The Ship at half-past noon and he has resolved not to return to the Tower that evening. He will break off his connection with Buck Mulligan. If this will cost him a place to sleep, so be it.

How is this pattern of meaning developed in the subsequent chapters? How is Stephen related to Bloom and what part does Bloom play in this emerging pattern of meanings? What finally is the total meaning of the novel? In a short essay, one can only sketch very general directions. Moreover, *Ulysses* is such a rich novel that one does not want to risk oversimplifying it or reducing it to an abstract theme. Perhaps the most concise way to indicate the pattern of meaning that develops in the novel is to make some comments upon the meaning of Stephen and Bloom. What occurs when these polar extremes are connected? What currents leap across from one to the other? Or does anything leap across! In my own view, no transaction takes place. The total meaning of the novel, so it seems to me, has to be one that accepts this obvious fact.

In spite of the many attempts to show that Stephen and

Bloom achieve some sort of real communication, I think that the case is not proved. On this point I would agree with Harry Levin's early and excellent introductory study (*James Joyce*, 1941) and with Adams in his *Surface and Symbol*. There is no real communication between the two men. How could there be? Stephen and Bloom speak different languages. Indeed, these polar, antithetical men come closest to a meeting of minds in an incident that occurs in the Circe chapter. When Bloom and Stephen both look into the mirror in Mrs Cohen's establishment, each sees not his own face but the face of Shakespeare, "beardless . . . rigid in facial paralysis, crowned by the reflection of the reindeer antlered hatrack." If one can accept the fact that they are "seeing things" in this chapter of hallucinations, there is perfectly good reason to account for their seeing this face. Stephen can see himself reflected in Shakespeare because for him Shakespeare is the type of the artist. Stephen conceives that Shakespeare, like himself, lacked appreciation, was betrayed, and had to live by Stephen's own code of silence, cunning, and exile. As for Bloom, Shakespeare, like himself, was a cuckold and a kind of commercial traveller.

The vision of Shakespeare that unites Stephen and Bloom has welled up, as it were, out of the subconscious, bypassing the medium of words. Yet the shared perception hardly amounts to communication, for presumably neither man knows that the perception is shared – that his opposite is seeing Shakespeare too.

Why is it that so many commentators have felt that Stephen and Bloom simply must have something to say to each other, something that will alter the lives of both? The demand has arisen from the very fact of polarity. Stephen and Bloom so completely divide the world of man between themselves that each obviously needs the other: either standing alone is incomplete. Yet the reader's sense that the two men ought to join forces or become atoned one with the other does not mean that they do. To argue that since an atonement is desirable it must occur takes the intent for the deed. In fact, it does more: it makes an assumption about the author's intent that cannot be supported by the author's text.

A complicating factor has been the prominence given in *Ulysses* to the theme of paternity. It has been argued that Bloom, throughout the day, is the only person who takes a fatherly interest in Stephen. Indeed, according to this argument Bloom proves himself to be Stephen's spiritual father. Yet it is a very obtuse special pleading that can make the argument that Bloom is the only person who is kind to Stephen during the day. Miles Crawford, the newspaper editor, Professor McHugh, Mr Deasy the schoolmaster – all of them recognize Stephen's talent and express a wish to help him. Even Buck Mulligan, it is plain, thinks of him as a kind of genius and wishes him well.

Stephen does indeed need a father, but the father whom he has already chosen for himself is his namesake, Dedalus, the fabulous artificer. In any case, Bloom's efforts to engage Stephen's interests do not get very far. Stephen, tired and bored, rejects them politely, and finally, when Bloom suggests that Stephen spend the night with him, Stephen again politely but firmly rejects the invitation.

For the sake of argument, however, let us assume that the meeting of Stephen and Bloom is productive of something. What did it produce? Is there any evidence that Bloom's life has been changed by the meeting? It is true that in the Oxen of the Sun chapter, we are told that one of the dreams that Bloom has had argues that he is in for a change. But the only change that he finds when he returns home is a rearrangement of the furniture. He bumps into a walnut sideboard which is not in its accustomed place, thanks to Molly's altered notions of where it and other pieces of furniture should be. But apparently this is all that has been altered in the Bloom household. Bloom does request Molly to make breakfast for him the next morning, and several commentators have rather desperately interpreted this modest request as betokening that Bloom will become from now on master in his own house. It would be nice to think that the worm has finally turned, but the logic of the book would indicate that no real change in his relation to Molly has occurred or can occur.

Yet so insistent has been the urge to endow the meeting of

Bloom and Stephen with significance that various expedients have been used to get over the obvious fact that they have nothing to say to each other and that nothing happens. One stratagem has been to point to "symbolic" communion or communication. In the kitchen of Bloom's house Stephen and Bloom have a cup of cocoa together. Since Joyce refers to the cocoa as "Epps's massproduct", it is evident to some readers that what really is being celebrated in the kitchen is a symbolic equivalent of the Mass, a rite of communion.

To take another instance: stepping out of the kitchen, Stephen and Bloom urinate in the garden, an act that is said to symbolize fertility. As they do so, they gaze upward and see the lighted window of Molly's bedroom. She is a kind of fertility goddess who presides over the scene. Stephen has found his true Muse and will become the writer that he ought to be. Thus, what does not occur in the thoughts and actions of the characters may still occur symbolically, and what occurs symbolically must be true.

A second strategy for proving that something does come out of the meeting of Stephen and Bloom is to make Stephen Dedalus and James Joyce interchangeable. The argument runs this way: since Stephen is an expression of Joyce as a young man, anything that happened to or was true of Joyce can be attributed to Stephen.

When Stephen leaves Bloom, after declining Bloom's offer of hospitality, where does he go? He has resolved not to return to the Tower. Where did he sleep that night? What happened to him? We are not told. The novel does not take his career any further. On the other hand, we know that James Joyce did indeed survive his experiences in Ireland, went to live on the Continent, and wrote *Ulysses*. Joyce did develop, was turned into a man by his marriage to Nora, and put away the rather brittle aestheticism of Stephen Dedalus. By a kind of illicit transfer from the realm of biography to that of fiction, various things that are true of Joyce can be attributed to Stephen Dedalus. W. Y. Tindall puts the matter quite explicitly in *James Joyce: His Way of Interpreting the Modern World*. He writes: "The encounter with Bloom has changed Stephen's inhumanity to humanity. The egotist has discovered charity, the greatest of virtues, and compassion for mankind . . . 'Pity', Stephen says in *A Portrait of the Artist,* 'is the feeling which arrests the mind in the presence of whatsoever is grave and constant in human suffering and unites it with the human sufferer.' He now discovers what this means, and leaving Bloom, he goes away to write *Ulysses.*" But the "he" who left Bloom with *"Liliata rutilantium"* still ringing in his head was Stephen, and that "he" who wrote *Ulysses* was James Joyce. For all we know, Stephen Dedalus never wrote any fiction at all.

What, then, is one to say about *Ulysses* as a novel? When one reviews the various attempts to elucidate the meaning of *Ulysses* it quickly becomes apparent that the red herring lying across the path is Joyce's own biography together with his own incidental comments about *Ulysses.* It is this material that has put most of the hounds off the true scent. One readily grants that *Ulysses* bears a very special relationship to Joyce's biography, and further that all sorts of parallels exist between Joyce and Stephen and between Joyce and Bloom, for that matter. I think also that one has to accept the fact that the structure is intricate, and that there are levels of meaning which will elude readers who are not in possession of certain specialized bodies of knowledge. Thus, in the earlier chapters the various heresies concerning the doctrine of the Trinity are used to comment upon Buck and Stephen and on the modern world generally. Averroes and Moses Maimonides, "flashing in their mocking mirrors the obscure soul of the world, a darkness shining in brightness which brightness could not comprehend", reverse St John's account of the Logos, as a "light shining in the darkness" which the darkness could not comprehend.

Most readers will not be able or willing to pursue these more delicate ramifications. And they need not: the general import of the novel will come through even though the reader has to regard Aquinas, Averroes, and Aristotle as simply part of the equipment of Stephen's mind and thus dramatically appropriate to his brooding meditations. Furthermore, one has to concede the fact that *Ulysses* is a kind of private logbook and spiritual diary containing Joyce's own personal revenges on particular people, his private jokes, and allusions to incidents and happenings that had some particular meaning for him. On this general point, Adams's book has been decisive.

Yet when all is said and done, *Ulysses* is not simply a catchall into which Joyce stuffed such materials. Nor is it merely or even primarily a Joycean riddle. It is a novel, and yields, in spite of its special difficulties, the sort of knowledge about ourselves and about our world that any other authentic novel does yield.

Among other things, *Ulysses* is a novel about the rift in modern civilization – as reflected in the attitudes of an intransigent and sensitive and brilliant young artist, of a good-natured, rather bumbling, bourgeois citizen, and of a sceptical, practical, "nature" female like Molly Bloom, who is fascinated by men but who is also amused by them, and in some sense rather contemptuous of them and the elaborate intellectual structures that they insist upon raising. There is a great deal of comedy in *Ulysses*, though it does not bar out pathos. There is some very brilliant and searching satire.

The fabric of the book is intricate. The tone is of an equivalent complexity. Commentators, in their anxiety to find a happy ending, have insisted on the book's compassion and on its final optimism, have oversimplified and probably distorted its meaning. In any case, whatever conclusions about the meaning of this novel we are to draw will require testing against the fictional structure – will have to be matched with what can actually be found in the novel. Too often the commentator has argued in effect that the meaning of *Ulysses* is the development of James Joyce, and if we venture to ask why it is so important to learn about the artistic development of James Joyce, we are told that this is important because James Joyce was able to write *Ulysses*. The hopelessly circular nature of this argument needs no comment.

6

Poetry and Poeticality

For a long time poets have observed that it is much easier to write of hell than of heaven. John Milton found it so in his *Paradise Lost* – or at least most of his readers have found it so. The gorgeous infernal tapestries of the first two books and Lucifer's showy histrionics have so dazzled their eyes that the later books have often seemed pale and commonplace, a falling off from the epic splendour. Yet even if one makes all the proper discounts for the average reader's love of the spectacular and of the obviously dramatic, one has to concede in the end that Milton's hell is more interesting than his heaven, and that the human pair after the fall are more thoroughly credible than when they dwelt in the Happy Garden. By implication, Milton himself endorses this view. Milton tries very hard to give Adam and Eve a vocation and a meaningful life before the Fall. He provides them with an occupation, social and religious interests, and opportunities for intellectual converse, including specula-tion about the nature of the universe. Their garden life was not empty, and it is with sorrowful reluctance that they give it up to go out into the world where they must confront all the evils of sickness, age, and death, and to foresee in the world of their descendants, anger, violence, and hate. And yet, no less an authority than the archangel Michael promises Adam, just before he and Eve are hurried outside the gates of paradise, that he has it within him to attain "A paradise . . . happier far" than that which he is leaving.

Does Milton, in his anxiety to provide the human pair with some hope as they go out to confront the world of pain and death, have Michael speak words of comfort that are in fact excessive? Could this not be an inadvertence on Milton's part? One might think so, except that it is unwise to assume that

Milton is ever inadvertent. Apparently Milton means quite literally what is said here: that the inward paradise, possessed in the spirit, is a more beautiful and satisfactory paradise than that from which the human pair are now being expelled, and that the joy which becomes possible through redemption and the bringing of good out of evil is greater than that known in the pristine innocence of Eden.

The notion that the happiness possible to man after the Fall surpasses that found in the Garden is reinforced by another of St Michael's utterances. He unfolds for Adam the course of human history until the Second Coming of Christ and says that then the earth "Shall all be Paradise", a "far happier place / Than this of *Eden*. . . ."

Adam's ecstatic comment at this account of the redemption of the Elect has tempted some unwary readers to conclude that Milton subscribes to the notion that God's plan required man to sin, and that it is well that he did sin in order that grace might abound. Adam's outburst of joy does indeed seem subversive of orthodox doctrine, for he exclaims to the warrior Archangel:

> Full of doubt I stand,
> Whether I should repent me now of sin
> By me done and occasioned, or rejoice
> Much more, that much more good thereof shall spring. . . .

Professor Arthur Lovejoy has shown that this paradox of the fortunate fall is not new in Christian tradition, but has a long and honourable place in the liturgy and the early hymns of the church. On this issue Milton's theological orthodoxy needs no special defence. I am not in fact at all concerned with it here, but with a different – though I dare say a related – consideration. It is this: that Milton's *poetry* requires for its fullness the mortal world, the "fallen" world, the world of loss and defect and ugliness, and that indeed all poetry requires such a soil for its growth.

In his "Hound of Heaven" Francis Thompson expostulated with his God, asking Him why He needs must dung His fields with rotten death. Whatever the theological answer, the answer for poetry is quite clear. Such dreadful fertilization is needed.

Poetry is no airplant. Even the most heavenly blossoms draw their beauty from roots that go down into the soil of mortality.

The point that I have in mind is something rather different from Shelley's statement that our sweetest songs are those that tell of saddest thought. In saying so, Shelley was contrasting the songs made by human beings with the ethereal music made by the skylark, a music which seemed to arise from ecstatic joy. It is the skylark's gladness that Shelley wishes that he might learn – not a deeper sorrowfulness. Much of Shelley's own poetry aspires to the unearthly disembodied intensity of the skylark's music. But are our sweetest songs in fact those that tell of saddest thought? I am not sure that they are, but in any case, a pleasing melancholy is not the special quality that I would ascribe to our most intense poetry.

Nor do I mean to suggest that there lurks at the heart of every fine poem, like the fragment of grit embedded in the center of every pearl, some incident of disappointment and loss, the irritant that scarred the poet's soul and generated the poem. There is an argument to this effect – the Freudian belief that all art is rooted in neurosis – but whatever its merits, I have no special concern with it here. My interest is not in the origins of poems but in their structure – not in how they come to be, but in the kind of ingredients that they contain. I mean to put to you the suggestion that the vitality and energy of a poem is dependent on its use of the disparate and even the contradictory, and that no poem can seem authentic unless it reflects in its own makeup the contradictions of the world that we actually know through experience.

I have mentioned Milton and Shelley. Let me now invoke a poet of a rather different order, W. S. Gilbert, who supplied the words for the operetta *Patience*. The anti-hero of this work, Reginald Bunthorne, the fleshly poet, is meant to be an absurd man, but he has some very sensible things to say on the subject of poeticality. One remembers his song "Oh hollow, hollow, hollow". Bunthorne explains to the bevy of twenty lovesick maidens who follow him about that his song is "the wail of the poet's heart on discovering that everything is commonplace". How can the poet, the first stanza inquires – how can the poet paint the woes of "the lithe-limbed", "writhing maid", when he knows very well that she is not suffering from some divine discontent and that what is really wrong with her can be set right with calomel? The last stanza of his song puts the question in universal terms:

> Is it, and can it be,
> Nature hath this decree,
> 　　*Nothing* poetic in the world shall dwell?
> Or that in *all* her works
> Something poetic lurks,
> Even in colocynth and calomel?
> 　　I cannot tell.

"I cannot tell": so Bunthorne says, but obviously he can. Set a thief to catch a thief – set a self-confessed aesthetic sham to detect aesthetic pretentiousness. The very terms of Bunthorne's poem expose the absurdity of assuming that the objects of the world of our experience can be sorted out into poetic things on the one hand and commonplace things on the other. Poets do not form poems by selecting intrinsically poetic materials and arranging them tastefully. A poem is not a bouquet of poetic objects. It is the poet's imagination that makes them poetic and not they themselves. Hence, the poet must regard everything in experience as potentially poetic, even "colocynth and calomel".

Two generations later, T. S. Eliot was to provide an emphatic twentieth-century answer to Bunthorne's question. "Those who object to the 'artificiality' of Milton or Dryden sometimes tell us," Eliot observes, "to 'look into our hearts and write'. But that is not," he remarks, "looking deep enough; Racine or Donne looked into a good deal more than the heart. One must look into the cerebral cortex, the nervous system, and the digestive tracts."

I said a moment ago that the poet properly regards everything in experience as potentially poetic, but this does not mean, of course, that there are no differences, and that since a poet may conceivably put anything into a poem, it doesn't matter therefore, what he puts into it. Such a notion is as absurd as to say that because the painter has a right to use any pigment in his picture, chrome yellow is equivalent in color value to cobalt blue, or that it is a matter of indifference as to whether he covers a particular part of his canvas with burnt umber or with lamp-black. Though the painter has a right to use any hue that he needs, he must still justify it in relation to the total pattern.

A moment ago I also quoted with approval Eliot's statement that a poet needs to look into the digestive tracts as well as into the heart. But to give primary attention to the intestines is merely to invert (and thus retain) the false distinction between the poetic and the unpoetic. For looking merely into the digestive tracts – or into the genito-urinary system – may yield as foreshortened and distorted a view of reality as looking merely and exclusively into the heart.

If the poet's materials are not in themselves poetic, if the quality of poetry is conferred on them by the poet through his own vision, through his perception of a pattern of unity and order, perhaps not hitherto discerned, then the differences among the materials with which the poet works become as important as the similarities. Our interest in patterns and the nature of our experience as human beings make the same demand. No diversity, no pattern. If all is sweetness, our taste-buds can stand only so much: the sweetness will either lose intensity and become cloying and finally insipid, or, if it does retain full intensity, it will become unbearably painful. It cannot remain simply pleasurably sweet. Or again, if all is light, then light and darkness become in effect the same, and we cease to see a world of separate objects.

Something of this kind happens in the hyacinth garden passage of Eliot's *Waste Land*. The protagonist recalls an event of beauty and significance. He remembers the girl's having said

> "You gave me hyacinths first a year ago;
> They called me the hyacinth girl"

and he remembers his reply:

> – Yet when we came back, late from the Hyacinth garden
> Your arms full, and your hair wet, I could not
> Speak, and my eyes failed, I was neither
> Living nor dead, and I knew nothing,
> Looking into the heart of light, the silence.

Intensity of vision eliminates vision, the power of the ecstatic experience takes one out of life altogether. Looking into the heart of light, one finds there is nothing that he can see.

The passage that I have just been quoting seems to me brilliantly successful. The poem demands that at this point, having been shown the world as a place of dryness and sterility, as a waste land, we be given a glimpse of the hyacinth garden – that the monotony of a world that is neither truly dead nor truly alive should find its emphatic contrast in a vision of genuine life, life experienced with such intensity that it merges with and includes death. Like life and death, light and darkness also, in the intensity of the experience, become the same thing. The failure of sight here is climactic and suggests the meaning of the poem.

The usual task of poetry, however, is not to blind us with light but to make us see, to give us the special kind of knowledge that only poetry can give, to make us more fully conscious of ourselves in relation to our world. That world is a world of failure and compromise as well as of occasional victory and triumph; it is a world in which sickness and death are to be found side by side with health and life. The curious matter is that apparently we can experience one only through the other. For a world of pure vitality, pure health, pure harmony – a world of pure undimmed light – would, because it lacked any shadows, appear to us a mere blank radiance.

Long ago, Samuel Taylor Coleridge warned us against entering any act of uniformity against the poet. I do not mean to disregard his warning here. The house of poetry has many mansions and I would not suggest that we ought to abide only and always in the most magnificently austere of these. In the house of poetry, comedy has its place as well as tragedy. Generous provision is also made for the joyous celebration of life and for the simple and charming lyric. One must be careful not to imply that the only poetry worth the reading represents some strenuous exercise of the spirit. But though our world would indeed be diminished without the simple lyric, in practice, even the simplest lyric turns out to be less simple than we may suppose. It too is a mixture of elements. The childhood rime told us that though little boys were made of snips and snails and puppydog tails, little girls were made of sugar and spice and everything nice. Thank goodness such are not the actual ingredients of little girls, and such are not the ingredients of the lyrics that we cherish in our tradition. Shakespeare's charming spring song of *Love's Labour's Lost* is ostensibly a bouquet of spring flowers, made up of daisies pied and violets blue, of "lady-smocks all silver-white" and "cuckoo buds of yellow hue". But the poem also makes a good deal of the fact that just when such flowers "paint the meadows with delight", the cuckoo bird sings

> "Cuckoo cuckoo"; O, word of fear,
> Unpleasing to a married ear!

And the second stanza, which notices the merry piping of shepherds, the love-making of the birds, and maidens making their own preparations for courtship as they bleach their summer smocks, also ends on this ominous portent of infidelity and cuckoldry.

To take another example: William Blake, in writing his poem "The Lamb", balanced this celebration of innocence with an evocation of terrible power in "The Tiger". But even in "The Lamb" itself, taken as a separate poem, there is something more than a child's joy in the lamb's "clothing of delight" and in the lamb's tender voice that makes "all the vales rejoice". The reference to the Creator of the universe as one who "became a little child" and called himself a lamb establishes a new dimension. It does not matter whether the child is fully conscious of the implications of this reference to the Lamb of God. The poem is probably more movingly poignant if the child is not aware of them. But the reader is aware of them – or ought to be – of verses like those from the fifty-fourth chapter of Isaiah: "He was oppressed, and he was afflicted, yet he opened not his mouth; like a lamb is led to the slaughter, and like a sheep that before its shearers is dumb."

One of the most purely lyrical poems of the recent past is E. E. Cummings's "Chansons Innocentes". The poet rejoices in spring – in what he calls "just-spring", – that is, spring pure and simple, springtime in its essence. But the scene is described firmly within a world that he knows, the "puddle-wonderful" and "mud-luscious" world in which little boys play at being pirates and little girls at hopscotch. The separate scenes of the poem are linked by references to the little old lame balloon seller whose whistle, "far and wee", becomes a kind of refrain. The balloon man's lameness – a little later he is to be called "goat-footed" – is the realistic detail that particularizes him. It sets him off from the children whose lightfooted running dominates the poem. It may even have a bearing on his way of making a living – that is, his having to peddle children's playthings on this spring day when other men are plowing or building houses. But it also adds, for those who care to see it, another dimension to the poem: the reference to the goat-foot hints that the balloon man is an embodiment of Pan, the god of nature, the only one of the old classical hierarchy who still lives on and is now walking through the streets of a twentieth-century American suburb.

We should not think it strange that "simple" lyrics such as these turn out not to be simple – that they are made up, not of homogeneous, but of heterogeneous materials, and that their unity has been achieved through a harmonizing of the disparate and the discordant. Metaphor itself exhibits such a structure. The poet does not assert that A is A but that A is B – or, to use well-worn examples, not that a rose is a rose but that his love is a rose, or that the minds of true lovers are like parallel lines, or that their souls are like the legs of a compass. If the terms of the metaphor are identical, or even substantially the same, we have no metaphor at all. Even the poorest and most trivial metaphor, if it is really metaphorical, involves a transfer – implies likeness discerned amid heterogeneity.

Such discernment – such an insight – characterizes the kind of truth with which the poet provides us. His truth does not have to do with the physical laws of the universe. The relations he asserts are not definitions such as "a straight line is the shortest distance between two points" or formulae of structure like H_2SO_4. The poet is not properly concerned with the space-time continuum in which man lives but with man's characteristic apprehensions of it and his characteristic reactions to it. But man's apprehension of his world has to be constantly freshened, redeemed from staleness – sometimes even rediscovered. Because this is true, we so often apply to poetry adjectives like *surprising*, *fresh, original,* and *wonderful.* The great Romantics, Wordsworth and Coleridge, stressed surprise and wonder as proper to all poetry, and described their own aims in the *Lyrical Ballads* as an attempt either to give substance to the marvellous or to render the ordinary and commonplace, fresh and new. But freshness, surprise, and originality are also the distinguishing notes of the poetry of John Donne. Donne is constantly making us see the discrepancy between reality and its specious appearance. Though most of us are disposed to think that Donne usually views the discrepancy with irony rather than with wonder, yet wonder is not absent from his poetry. One remembers lines like "I wonder by my troth what thou and I / Did till we loved" or his ecstatic address to his mistress – "O my America, my new found land."

One way in which to account for the new discovery, the fresh apprehension that poetry gives, is to regard it as a widening of the context in which a person or event or object is commonly seen. Shakespeare's spring song puts the joys of youthful love in a context that acknowledges the nether side of springtime love-making, the possibility of unfaithfulness and unhappiness. E. E. Cummings, by making his little balloon seller lame, widens the context of his mud-luscious spring world of childhood to include an older and less carefree world, and to include the world of pagan Greece as well as that of twentieth-century America.

I think that I should point out that the effect of the larger context amounts to something more than a judicious balancing of accounts – as between happiness and unhappiness or youth and age. The delights of the spring season, indeed, far from being toned down, are actually rendered more intense by the hints of the mortal world, a world that includes winter and heartbreak.

I. A. Richards makes this matter of contexts the very essence of metaphor. In one of the best books that he ever wrote, *The Philosophy of Rhetoric*, he defines metaphor as a transaction between contexts. The notion is a fruitful one: it suggests why metaphor is so important in literature, and it may help us to see what a given metaphor actually accomplishes in a particular poem. Donne's comparison of the souls of the lovers to the legs of a compass weaves together contexts that may seem very different indeed – that of romantic love and that of mathematics, tender passion and meticulous accuracy. Burns, on the other hand, in saying that his love is like a rose that's newly blown in June, brings together rather similar and easily assimilated contexts, for roses have long been associated with love, and June is the traditional month of brides. But even in the Burns simile, there is a decisive difference between the contexts. Here again a reference to the hero of Gilbert and Sullivan's *Patience* will prove useful. The lover who speaks Burns's lyric is not like Reginald Bunthorne, cultivating "a sentimental passion of a vegetable fashion for a not-too-French French bean" and the essential difference between the two men is not that a rose *is* a poetical love-object whereas Bunthorne's "not-too-French French bean" is *not*. Bunthorne, walking down Piccadilly with a lily (or with a rose, for that matter) in his medieval hand, is absurd because he has reduced to literalism something that makes sense only as a metaphor.

If metaphors are transactions between contexts, and if bold metaphors link shockingly different contexts, then one can see the more easily why contrasts to be harmonized and differences to be reconciled constitute the very stuff of poetry. But perhaps one can put this point best by considering briefly two kinds of poetry that depend upon rather narrow contexts, since a widening of the context would destroy them. The first is sentimental poetry, verse in which the author, in his anxiety to produce a certain effect on the reader, has omitted everything calculated to contradict the primary effect at which he aims. If it is a sentimental love poem, the realistic and everyday are made to give way to perfumed flowers and gleaming stars and whispering breezes. If the mood is to be one of tender melancholy, then everything that might be regarded as tough-minded or humorous is carefully excluded. The world of such a poem is bathed in a special light, and the reader is forced to view the scene from a prescribed vantage point. The reason is simple: if the reader were allowed to walk all around the object, he would realize that he was not looking at a portion of the real world but at a kind of hollow sham, and that what appeared to be rocks and trees were only two-dimensional stage props. Deliberate falsification of this sort belongs, of course, not to poetry proper but to instrumental rhetoric – to the practical rhetoric that is used in politics or in advertising. Much sentimental literature, of course, is not a deliberate falsification: the writer is himself involved, may be deeply moved, and sometimes blubbers over the death scene quite as audibly as do his more susceptible readers.

Propaganda art too makes use of a narrowed and specialized context. It has a thesis to urge: it plays upon the reader's emotions so as to induce him to adopt a certain attitude and in some instances to act upon it. In propaganda art, then, we are dealing with rhetoric used to implement a cause. If the cause is a good one, and if the action is justified, then I grant that the rhetoric that induced the reader to take the action is also justified. In the far from satisfactory world in which we live, there are ills to be remedied and abuses to be reformed. But a useful tract or an effective political speech are not necessarily works of art. An effective piece of rhetoric sometimes, to be sure, outlasts the particular situation which gave rise to it and may endure as a permanent contribution to literature. Swift's *Modest Proposal* would be an instance. But a great deal of rhetoric designed to secure a particular result has little or nothing to say to posterity. I suspect that what finally determines in this matter is the relative narrowness or breadth of the context that is incorporated – that is, whether or not the work concerns itself with universal issues and perennial problems.

W. B. Yeats has a good deal to say about sentimentality and propaganda and their relation to true poetry. Rhetoric is made out of the poet's "quarrel with others". Poetry comes out of our "quarrel with ourselves". It may seem odd that a poet, and a great lyric poet at that, should think of poetry as issuing from a quarrel of any kind. The fact that he does so affords one an opportunity to underline the notion that poetry is not a bouquet of poetic flowers, but a harmonizing of the disparate and the contradictory. Be that as it may, if we grant that the quarrel analogy has any validity, then surely Yeats is right in making the relevant quarrel not a contention with others but a deep-seated struggle within the self. It is part of a process of self-discovery and self-realization.

After writing that poetry is made "of the quarrel with our-selves", Yeats goes on, in his next sentence, to observe that "unlike the rhetoricians, who get a confident voice from remembering the crowd that they have won or may win, we [poets] sing amid our uncertainty". Why "amid our uncertainty"? Because the poet is not implementing a program but exploring his own nature, not recommending a cause, but trying to discover the nature of reality itself. If I may invoke the term "context" once more: in the quarrel with ourselves, out of which Yeats says that genuine poetry comes, the context is a wide one – much wider than the context appropriate to the practical rhetorician with his special cause to recommend or the sentimentalist obsessed with his one dominant emotion.

A vision of reality rather than a manipulation of reality – thus Yeats puts matters in his poem "Ego Dominus Tuus", but elsewhere in his writings, Yeats has made his distinction in somewhat different terms – as between truth and falsity. The genuine poet will be truthful in recording the defect, the evil, that is involved in reality. For example, in one of his letters Yeats quotes Mabel Beardsley's statement that her brother Aubrey "hated the people who denied the existence of evil, and so being young he filled his pictures with evil. He had a passion for reality." Having a passion for reality evidently meant for Yeats the ability to discern the existence of evil and the honesty to record it. In his *Autobiographies* Yeats ascribes such a passion to Dante and Villon. Yeats argues that "had they cherished any species of optimism, they could have but found a false beauty". And again in his *Autobiographies*, Yeats writes that "Donne could be as metaphysical as he pleased, and yet never seem unhuman and hysterical as Shelley often does, because he could be as physical as he pleased; and besides who will thirst for the metaphysical, who have a parched tongue, if we cannot recover the Vision of Evil". The apparent *non-sequitur* – for what has the Vision of Evil to do with our thirst for the metaphysical – is cleared up when we remember that Yeats considered the ability to discern evil as an essential part of the poet's ability to apprehend reality.

The choice of Shelley as the antithesis of Donne is, by the

way, a shrewd one. Shelley – at least the youthful Shelley – with his utopian optimism and his zeal to reform the world, becomes in Yeats's notion "unhuman and hysterical". Just because Donne knew the body and its limitations, clung to the body, refused to take off from the earth in ethereal skylark flights, and could not conceivably have apostrophized the skylark with the words, "*Bird* thou never wert" – because of all this, Donne could be as metaphysical as he pleased.

But is Yeats right about the nature of reality? Does evil exist? Is not Yeats, because of his involvement with the past, too pessimistic? May not the citizen of the twentieth-century world think that on this point the youthful Shelley was actually the wiser man? The problem is essentially a metaphysical one, one hardly to be decided by statistical research. But whatever the correct answer, the question does have an important bearing upon the future of poetry.

I think that I can illustrate this bearing from an article published a few years ago in *The New Statesman*. The writer praised certain contemporary American poets because they had become "the dissident conscience of a nation". Rather wistfully he concluded by writing: "As for the English poet, he may find himself wishing that the acute but muffled tensions between himself and his society might build up to the point of strain where he too might be able, without stridency or falseness, to speak for the honour of his nation." But if it has been necessary for American society to become, in order to produce first-rate poetry, "explosive and tormented as never before in this century", should the contemporary English poet then wish that his own society might be wracked with the same torment? If his hope is that he may himself become more sensitive to the tensions already present in his society, that is one thing. But if he finds himself envying those lucky American poets who are fortunate enough to live where all hell is breaking loose and where they can't help being swept up into poetry, isn't he really yearning for more social violence in order that more first-rate poetry may be written? And if so, isn't this a variant of the heretical dogma that it is good to sin so that grace may abound the more? One need not in this instance press the issue: if the English poet, presumably a thoroughly decent young man, finds himself wishing that the "tensions between himself and his society might build up to the point of strain", he surely will be able to find a better justification for his wish than the self-serving one that it will help him with his writing. Let us hope that his justification would be that an increase of tension was a necessary stage in the elimination of social evil – like the bringing of a boil to a head, or the discharge of pus.

There is, however, one aspect of this problem that I *would* like to press. It is one on which the writer of *The New Statesman* article does not touch. If pain, cruelty, and evil are in some sense necessary to the creation of poetry, and if we succeed in eliminating them from the world, shall we not have also eliminated the possibility of poetry? The problem is intensified in so far as we believe that the greatness of poetry is related in some way to the sharpness of its protest against evil and its effectiveness in eradicating it. Suppose that the Utopians could indeed eliminate evil and give us a perfect world. What would they sing about? Yeats evidently thought that they would not sing at all.

Yeats, of course, believed that in fact poets would continue to sing, but then Yeats, as we have seen, was no utopian activist. He foresaw no millennium and believed that the task of any civilization was a ceaseless "struggle to keep self-control". He expressed rather caustically his lack of belief in progress, which he called the sole religious myth of modern man.

Someone like myself, whose topic is literature, who makes no pretence to being a philosopher, and who is confident that no one could ever take him to be a social scientist, had better avoid any prophecies about the disappearance of evil. What one can confidently say, however, is that up to our time at least all great poetry reflects a mixed world, a world of good and evil, and that the good which it celebrates can be seen in full perspective only by means of the shadows that the good itself casts. Though as decent men we are committed to try as hard as we can to make this a better world, some of us are disposed to think that the struggle with evil, in one form or another, is probably destined to go on for a very long time. When evil ceases to exist – that is, if it ever does – then the world will be so different from our own as to be incomprehensible – whether as the New Jerusalem of St John's vision in the Book of Revelation, or as a kind of sanitary hell of robots and computers. We can try to imagine what such a world will be like, but only by using analogies taken from the defective world that we know. It is just as difficult to imagine what the songs of utopia (or the hymns of heaven) will be like, for the poetry of the past, as we have seen, is rooted in no celestial soil. The great poetry of the past, and not merely comedy and tragedy, involves in its own structure the overcoming of – and therefore necessarily involves references to – the ugly, the realistic, the disappointing, and the evil. In spite of its happy ending, comedy obviously does so. Unless the comedy is brainless farce or thoroughly insipid sentimentality, it involves a series of victories over frustration and disorder and usually brings us in the end to a higher vantage point from which we attain a perspective wider than that with which we began. So it is also with tragedy. Tragedy obviously involves loss, frustration, and evil, but it too represents a kind of triumph of the spirit, and with it a higher vantage point and a clearer perspective. Without going into the vexed question of precisely what Aristotle meant by catharsis in his *Poetics*, a plausible interpretation sees it as a triumph over disorder. Milton, who was an excellent classical scholar as well as a great poet, probably conceived of catharsis in these terms. At any rate, the great passage with which *Samson Agonistes* closes will sustain such an interpretation. We are dismissed by the poet with these words:

> [God's] servants he with new acquist
> Of true experience from this great event
> With peace and consolation hath dismist,
> And calm of mind all passion spent.

The purging away of passion alluded to here is evidently more than a mere discharge of peccant humors. It is evidently part of a process by which the spectator's *vision* is also purged and cleared, and his mind is elevated and calmed, calmed because it has been vouchsafed authentic truth – "true experience", Milton says – about man and his fate.

7

W. B. Yeats as a Literary Critic

William Butler Yeats was obviously a brilliant literary critic. His incidental comments on poets and poems are often exciting, sometimes profound. To be sure, Yeats was often cranky and perverse. His *Oxford Book of Modern Verse* is a kind of monument to an arbitrary taste. He had his blind sides; he could be unfair; he made no bones about his prejudices and partialities. Yet it is a pleasure to reread his prose and it is rewarding to do so. All of his writing abounds in provocative comments, perceptive summations, revealing insights, often apparently tossed off as asides. Even *A Vision* is rich in this kind of material: see, for example, his accounts of the poets and artists used as illustrations of his twenty-six types of men. Walt Whitman "makes catalogues of all that has moved him, or amused his eye, that he may grow more poetical. Experience is all-absorbing, subordinating observed fact, drowning even truth itself, if truth is conceived of as something apart from impulse and instinct."[1] Even the devoted Whitmanian will find it difficult to cavil at this account of the basic stance of his hero though he would want, of course, to claim for Whitman much more than Yeats allows him here.

Yeats tells us that "in the poetry of Keats there is, though little sexual passion, an exaggerated sensuousness that compels us to remember the pepper on the tongue as though that were his symbol. Thought is disappearing into image."[2] This is a one-sided view, and the story that Keats put cayenne pepper into his mouth in order to relish all the more the taste of cold claret has

[1] *A Vision* (London: Macmillan, 1937), p. 114.
[2] Ibid., p. 134.

apparently now been given up. Even so, Yeats has fastened on a point worth exploring: he has noted the qualities in Keats's poetry that make the story of the pepper seem plausible. Yeats's account of Synge – he had known Synge personally – is brilliant. For Yeats, Synge was the artist who must discover his true vision not by striving for it – that, he must avoid – but by letting himself become absorbed in the technical problems of expression. He must "fill many notebooks, clap his ear to that hole in the ceiling"[1] to listen to the talk of the Aran Island girls so that he may catch the exact cadence of their speech. He must not breathe his own spirit into the scene that he is describing, for that will simply blur and distort. As Yeats puts it in a beautifully precise figure: when Synge discovers his true art, he is like a man who "wipes his breath from the window-pane, and laughs in his delight at all the varied scene"[2] which the now transparent glass reveals to him.

Yeats's letters also are filled with insights of this sort. Byron is for him a "great English poet", though, he tells us, "one can hardly call him great except in purpose and manhood".[3] Doubtless Yeats was too severe on Poe and yet how much of what has been said later he anticipates in a letter written as early as 1899. There he confesses that Poe's

> fame always puzzles me. I have to acknowledge that even after one allows for the difficulties of a critic who speaks a foreign language, a writer who has had so much influence on Baudelaire and Villiers de L'Isle Adam has some great merit. I admire a few lyrics of his extremely and a few pages of his prose, chiefly in his critical essays, which are sometimes profound. The rest of him seems to me vulgar and commonplace and the Pit and the Pendulum and the Raven do not seem to me to have permanent literary value of any kind. Analyze the Raven and you find that its subject is a commonplace and its execution a rhythmical trick.[4]

Yeats always shows some antipathy toward Wordsworth and finds it difficult to be just to him. But how neatly – and up to a

---

[1] Ibid., p. 166.   [2] Ibid., p. 165.

[3] *The Letters of W. B. Yeats*, ed. Allan Wade (London: Hart-Davis 1954; New York: Macmillan, 1955), p. 710.

[4] Ibid., p. 325.

point, I think, accurately – he assesses Wordsworth's characteristic weaknesses. He remarks in his "Anima Hominis" that
Wordsworth, great poet "though he be, is so often flat and
heavy partly because his moral sense, being a discipline he had
not created, a mere obedience, has no theatrical element. This
increases his popularity with the better kind of journalists and
politicians who have written books."[1] Whatever the justice of
this comment on Wordsworth, it at least tries to account for
what the "two voices" theory merely describes; and it is at least
a valid judgment on the typical nineteenth-century Wordsworthian.

The force and the truth of comments of this sort will be conceded by most readers – though most of us, of course, will want
to make our own choices from Yeats's critical sallies and literary
observations, discarding those that we feel are really outrage-
ous, cherishing those that we feel have merit. But that Yeats's
criticism attains to any real coherency and that it reveals any
kind of systematic relationship among its parts will not be so
readily granted.

I shall not claim that Yeats's criticism is entirely self-consistent or that it provides a complete view of poetry. But Yeats
did value system, as his labours on *A Vision* show, and his basic
conception of poetry and of the role of the poet does make a
pattern. To work out this pattern in detail would be a project
much too ambitious for this short essay. Mine is a more modest
undertaking: to show that Yeats had a very clear notion of what
poetry was and specifically that he conceived of it as providing a
special kind of truth and therefore distinguished it, on the one
hand, from mere self-expression and, on the other hand, from
propaganda for a cause. (Yeats was throughout his life a man of
causes, but he denied the title of poetry even to propaganda for
causes that he thought were noble and in which as a man he
deeply believed.)

Any account of Yeats's critical theory properly begins with his
conception of the creative process. How a poet created was a
matter of primary consequence to him, though as we shall presently see, his criticism did not remain fixated on it. Yeats's key

[1] *Mythologies* (London: Macmillan, 1958 New York: Macmillan, 1959), p. 334.

concept is that "No mind can engender till divided into two."[1] Poetry is created through a dialectical process. But Yeats, in developing his celebrated notions of creation from an anti-self, had much more in mind than a compositional trick – a gimmick by which the poet could evade the superficial and topical aspects of his mind in order to get down to the layers beneath immediate consciousness. The dialectic through which the poem is produced gives its own impress to the poem. The tension developed in the play between opposites is built into the poem.

For Yeats, penetration into the depths of the mind was indeed necessary. He describes poetic genius as "a crisis that joins [the] buried self for certain moments to our trivial daily mind" (p. 272, 164). Art is for him a special kind of knowledge, a revelation, and all revelation, he tells us, "is . . . from that age-long memoried self, that shapes the elaborate shell of the mollusc and the child in the womb, that teaches the birds to make their nest" (p. 272, 164).

Stated less gaudily – translated into the terms of current depth psychology – this conception of the process of poetic composition is now commonplace, though we ought to remember that it was scarcely so when Yeats wrote his essay entitled "Hodos Chameliontos" in 1917. The difficulties encountered in peering into the depths of the self and the possibilities of self-deception in trying to do so are matters of which Yeats was fully aware. I shall return to them a little later. At this point, however, I want to stress his belief that the process of making a poem is not one of simple self-expression. Nor does it have anything to do with the manipulation of reality so as to secure something that the poet desires for himself or for his society. Yeats is quite explicit on this point. In "The Tragic Generation", he puts the question:

> Does not all art come when a nature, that never ceases to judge itself, exhausts personal emotion in action or desire so completely

---

[1] *Autobiographies* (London: Macmillan, 1955; *Autobiography* (so titled in the American edition, New York: Macmillan, 1953) p. 345, 208. All subsequent page references to this work will be found in parentheses in the text. The first number in each case refers to the London edition; the second to the New York.

that something impersonal, something that has nothing to do with action or desire, suddenly starts into its place, something which is as unforeseen, as completely organized, even as unique, as the images that pass before the mind between sleeping and waking? (p. 332, 200).

It is interesting to see how he applied this principle to the poetry of Shelley. Shelley had been the idol of the young Yeats; yet Yeats finally had to deny that Shelley had ever made this necessary severance of art from desire. In 1932 he wrote: "Shelley was not a mystic, his system of thought was constructed by his logical faculty to satisfy desire, not a symbolical revelation received after the suspension of all desire. He could neither say with Dante, "His will is our peace,' nor with Finn in the Irish story, 'The best music is what happens.'"[1]

Yeats's poem "Ego Dominus Tuus" will show why he felt that the poet had to exclude from art personal emotion that was "unexhausted" – that is, emotion that was still alive and pushing toward expression in action or desire. In "Ego Dominus Tuus"[2] Yeats has, by the way, split his own mind into two in order to make his point. The poem is a debate between two antagonists, Hic and Ille – that is, "this one" and "that one", both of them presumably aspects of man's mind and specifically of Yeats's own mind.

Hic voices an expressive theory of art: the poet puts himself into his work, and the reader will expect to find the man who created the poem within the poem that he has created. Ille, however, denies that poetry is expressive – at least, that it is so in this simple fashion – and asserts that Dante, for example, created his poetry, not from what he was, but from all that he was not. Hic quite properly interprets this conflict between what a man is and what he is not as a "tragic war" and asks rather pointedly whether there are not at least some poets whose art comes, not out of such a conflict, but out of their love of life. Among the poets surely there are, Hic argues,

[1] *Essays and Introductions* (London: Macmillan, 1961; New York: Macmillan, 1961), pp. 421–2.
[2] *The Collected Poems of W. B. Yeats* (London: Macmillan, 1950; New York: Macmillan, 1951).

> Impulsive men that look for happiness
> And sing when they have found it.

Ille's answer categorically denies such a possibility. Those who are lovers of life and who have found their happiness in it do not sing at all, and Ille points out the reason: "those that love the world serve it in action". As happy, successful lovers of the world, they

> Grow rich· popular and full of influence,
> And should they paint or write, still it is action:
> The struggle of the fly in marmalade.

(Yeats may be remembering here the rueful comment that Paul Verlaine once made to him when, pointing to his bandaged leg, he remarked that he knew Paris all too well. In fact Paris had scorched his leg. He had lived in Paris "like a fly in a pot of marmalade" [p. 341, 206].)

In the lines that follow, Ille mentions two kinds of pseudo-artists: they are the rhetorician (the propagandist) and the sentimentalist.

Whereas the rhetorician deliberately deceives his fellows, the sentimentalist is self-deceived, the victim of his own illusions about the world. Both kinds of deception are sharply set off from the revelation of truth accomplished by authentic art.

Art, Yeats insists, "is *but* a vision of reality". I stress the adversative, for Yeats is here clearly emphasizing the sense of detachment from action and from desire. Unlike the rhetorician and sentimentalist who involve themselves in the world and whose work is consciously or unconsciously a form of action, the artist stands back from the world so that he may see it the more clearly.

The passage from "Ego Dominus Tuus" (written in December 1915) on which I have just been commenting obviously comes out of the same matrix as Yeats's often-quoted remark that "We make out of the quarrel with others, rhetoric, but of the quarrel with ourselves, poetry" (written in February 1917).[1] It may seem odd that a poet, and a great lyric poet at that, should think of poetry as issuing from a quarrel of any sort.

[1] *Mythologies*, p. 331.

But if one is willing to grant any validity to the notion that poetry issues from a quarrel, then surely Yeats is right in making the relevant quarrel, not a contention with others, but a deep-seated struggle within the self. For this quarrel is part of a process of self-discovery and self-realization.

One may sum up at this point by saying that Yeats's conception of poetry is closely linked to his conception of reality: the function of poetry is not to express man's desires or to change the world in which he lives, bringing it closer to his own desires, but to reveal reality. Yet so summary an account of Yeats's position leaves many loose ends to be tied up and many subsidiary questions to be answered. For instance, if the poet must create from his opposite – if he must, as Yeats so often puts the matter, assume a mask and consciously play a part – may not such role-playing tempt the artist to fall into insincerity and to become a rhetorician indeed? Or, to notice a related problem, is there not a danger that Yeats's conception of art throws the poet too much back onto himself and thus risks committing him to a morbid subjectivity? How does one reconcile Yeats's stress upon meditation and solitude with his celebration of poets like Chaucer, who seemed to live in the sunlight and to speak for a whole society? And how does one reconcile the emphasis upon meditation with Yeats's own lifelong preoccupation with the unity of culture – with his praise of the robust spiritual health of some of the great civilizations of the past? Again, what is the specific force of Yeats's reiterated attacks upon abstraction? Yeats constantly treats abstraction as the inveterate enemy of art. Etymologically, abstraction is a *drawing away*, but in Yeats's meaning of the term, a drawing away from what? In disparaging an "external art", is not Yeats asking that the artist withdraw from the world and thus condemning him to a form of abstraction?

These are some of the possible self-contradictions that reveal themselves when one reads Yeats's criticism. The reader has a right to ask whether they can be reconciled with Yeats's basic position, and if so, how; but he may at this point feel himself bemused by abstractions of another sort, for few things are so difficult as abstract discussions of poetry. Shouldn't we here produce particulars – illustrations of the genuine artist, the confused artist, and the sham artist, as Yeats conceives them with reference to his rather austere conception of art?

Yeats actually provides abundant illustrations. He had in mind, for example, two specific artists when he wrote

> while art
> Is but a vision of reality

and continued with the lines

> What portion in the world can the artist have
> Who has awakened from the common dream
> But dissipation and despair?

In "Anima Hominis", Yeats observes that

> no fine poet, no matter how disordered his life, has ever, even in his mere life, had pleasure for his end. Johnson and Dowson . . . were *dissipated* men . . . and yet they had the gravity of men who had found life out and were *awakening from the dream*. . . . Nor has any poet I have read of or heard of or met with been a sentimentalist. The other self, the anti-self . . . comes but to those who are no longer deceived, whose passion is reality. [*italics mine*][1]

Yeats constantly associates the artist with the hero and the saint. The hero and the saint also live their lives in terms of an anti-self, the hero modeling himself on some great figure of the past, the saint carrying out an *imitatio Christi*; but the material with which the hero and the saint work is their own flesh and blood whereas the material used by the poet is "paper or parchment". But the activity, Yeats insists, is an analogous one: he tells us that in "all great poetical styles there is saint or hero," even though, "when it is all over Dante can return to his chambering"[2] – in "Ego Dominus Tuus" we are told that though Dante found in his poetry "The most exalted lady loved by man," he was mocked by "Guido for his lecherous life" – and Shakespeare, after his great verse, can return "to his pottle-pot. [Dante and Shakespeare can do so because they] sought no impossible perfection [except when] they handled paper or parchment."[3]

In the capsule definition of art that we have quoted from

---

[1] *Mythologies*, p. 331.   [2] Ibid., p. 333.   [3] Ibid.

"Ego Dominus Tuus", Yeats treats the rhetorician as a conscious manipulator and implies that he has an ulterior purpose:
he means to "deceive his neighbours". But Yeats was well
aware that in practice few literary rhetoricians were so clearly
and consciously propagandistic as this. The typical case, both
as to methods and motives, was far more complicated. A particular example will help make this point clear. Yeats says in so
many words that Shelley lacked the vision of evil to which poets
like Dante and Villon had attained, and he is willing to associate Shelley with a naïve propagandizing for vague utopias,
but he is far from denying that Shelley was a poet, and certainly
he does not think that Shelley consciously tried to gull his
neighbours. Yeats does, on occasion, chide Shelley for having
dissipated his poetic energies in quarrels with his neighbours, but
that is a very different matter, though it remains a sufficient
indictment in view of Yeats's celebrated text that it is out of our
"quarrel with others" that we make "rhetoric", and only out of
"the quarrel with ourselves" that we make poetry.

That celebrated text – the case of Shelley quite aside – is
worth a little elaboration. One is encouraged to quarrel with
others if he thinks that all problems are soluble and that only the
stupidity or the villainy of other men prevents our solving the
world's problems. One is also encouraged to quarrel with others
in proportion as he knows himself imperfectly and is thus
inclined to be too easily impressed with his own virtue and his
own good intentions. Yet surely Yeats does not delude himself
into thinking that self-knowledge ever came easily, and he has
acknowledged that his own essential nature was in fact very
much like Shelley's.[1] Yeats describes himself as by nature political, gregarious, quarrelsome, full of schemes for the improvement of Irish culture and the liberation of the Irish spirit, and
not disposed to suffer gladly either the knaves or fools who stood
in the way of those schemes (see pp. 101–4).

Most important of all, in Yeats's view of things, man is not a
completely free agent. He feels the pressure of his own time and

---

[1] Yeats regarded Shelley as a man of "Phase Seventeen" (see *A Vision*, p. 141),
and there is abundant evidence that Yeats saw himself as belonging to the same
phase.

it imposes its limitations on him. Thus, when an artist fails to do what Yeats believes authentic art demands, it is rarely simply a matter of the artist's blindness or headstrong folly. One has to take into account the nature of the time and the state of the civilization in which the artist has been born. It was one of Yeats's deepest beliefs that some periods of a civilization had been propitious for the arts and that others had not been.

As we have already noted, Yeats wrote himself down as a man for whom unity of being was of supreme importance. The great ages for him were those in which a high degree of cultural unity was attained. The burden of his various accounts of literary history is the inevitable falling away from these periods of great and rich unity – the descent into mechanization, division, and abstraction.

Yeats tells us in his *Autobiography* that he "thought that the enemy of [the desired cultural] unity was abstraction, meaning by abstraction not the distinction but the isolation of occupation, or class or faculty" (p. 190, 117). But this process of isolation and specialization, of course, ultimately involves things far more deeply rooted in men's lives than even their occupations or their social classes. What occurs is an alteration in the very way in which men apprehend the world about them. In his attack on the mathematicians and the philosophers who begot the modern world, Yeats is not content to repeat the well-worn statement that Descartes had cut the throat of poetry. He writes that "Descartes, Locke, and Newton took away the world and gave us its excrement instead."[1] Yeats made it the glory of Berkeley that he "restored the world ... that only exists because it shines and sounds".[2] But though Yeats in this passage hails Berkeley as a world-restorer, it is plain from his other writings that he knew that the world had not been restored and that for most men it remained simply the draff and dregs of what had been the complete and solid world of earlier ages.

The theme of cultural disintegration through growing abstraction is one to which Yeats returned again and again.

---

[1] "Pages from a Diary in 1930", *Explorations* (London: Macmillan, 1962; New York: Macmillan, 1962), p. 325.
[2] Ibid.

One of his more striking ways of locating the beginning of the
mischief is his remark that the "morning when Descartes discovered that he could think better in his bed than out of it"
(p. 192, 118) was a significant day in our cultural history. Why
in bed? Presumably because Descartes discovered that thought
could be divorced from action. When thought is separated from
action, including liturgical action, and from symbolism generally, it has become truly abstract – and thus more efficient.
Yeats sees very clearly the connection between such abstract
thinking and the industrial revolution. In one of his mocking
short poems, John Locke becomes the new Adam. The "garden" dies at the moment that God takes out of Locke's side the
new Eve, the spinning jenny, the first mass-production machine.[1] Yeats says that, as a student of William Morris, he had no
difficulty in discovering that "machinery had not separated
from handicraft wholly for the world's good" (p. 192, 118). The
increasing specialization in a world that had undergone an
industrial revolution had grave social consequences as well.
Yeats notes that by Morris's time "the distinction of classes had
become their isolation" (p. 192, 118).

To spell out the implied argument: as long as a culture
does share common values and makes its pilgrimage, like
Chaucer's Canterbury pilgrims, to a common shrine, men's ultimate values do not have to be argued out afresh on every new
occasion, and the poet, rather than employing abstract arguments at all, can make use of images. With the breakup of the
culture, there are fewer and fewer values which can be taken for
granted. Less and less can the poet rely on images and so will be
tempted to establish his values by argument. Yeats is careful
not to oversimplify: he does not deny that a kind of national
unity is still possible in the modern world. He points out that
even today a "powerful class by terror, rhetoric, and organized
sentimentality may drive their people to war" (p. 195, 120). This
statement perhaps constitutes a prophecy of Nazism, but Yeats,
of course, was making use of much more general terms of refer
ence. The collocation of "terror, rhetoric, and organized sentimentality" is in itself interesting and throws a good deal of light

[1] *Collected Poems*, p. 211.

on Yeats's conception of the artist's true role. The artist reveals reality; he does not try to manipulate men's passions. He does not try to win his reader by fraudulent argument or seduce him by playing on his affections or compel him by the threat of force.

If Yeats felt out of place in his own time, a fellow Irishman, George Bernard Shaw, seemed to him to be very much at home in it and certainly his affairs prospered in that world. Another contemporary Irishman, Oscar Wilde, was not at home in the contemporary world and, though full of literary talent and a brilliant conversationalist, he eventually came to disaster. Perhaps Yeats's comments on Wilde and Shaw can furnish specific illustrations of what he meant by such terms as "personality", "abstraction", and the "anti-self". They may also show why Yeats believed that the artist needed to assume a mask (with its implication of a histrionic role) and yet also believed that the artist needed solitude. His comments on Shaw and Wilde may also reveal his notion of the close relationship between the essential nature of the sentimentalist and the rhetorician and the sharp differences that separated both of them from the genuine poet.

Shaw obviously did not belong to "the tragic generation", those artists to whom the age denied a life in which body and mind, flesh and intellect, emotion and idea could be united in a symbol (pp. 291–5, 174–76). In a brilliant phrase, Yeats remarks that Shaw was "quite content to exchange Narcissus and his Pool for the signal-box at a railway junction, where goods and travellers pass perpetually upon their logical glittering road" (p. 294, 176). Yet in spite of Shaw's contempt for solitude and the complacency with which he adopted the "inorganic, logical straightness" of steel rails, Yeats was forced to admire his energy and his ability to cope with the Philistines. Yeats says that he "delighted in Shaw, the formidable man. He could hit my enemies and the enemies of all I loved, as I could never hit" (p. 283,169).

Shaw frankly used his writing to state, and to argue for, his ideas. Yeats refers to the "street-corner socialist eloquence" (p. 294, 176) that Shaw had carried onto the stage. But one supposes that it was not so much Shaw's ideas that repelled Yeats as his notion that Pegasus should be put to the plough or turned into a dray horse. On this subject, Yeats could be downright savage. He declares that he could find not only in Shaw's "writing and his public speech", but even in "his clothes and in his stiff joints" (p. 294, 176) the quality of a civilization that was abstract, mechanical, and therefore, for Yeats, brutal. Yeats once had a nightmare in which Shaw appeared as "a sewing machine, that clicked and shone, but the incredible thing was that the machine smiled, smiled perpetually" (p. 283, 169).

Curiously enough, though Shaw, as a man who loved the world and served it in action, fits neatly Yeats's definition of the rhetorician, Yeats was unwilling to concede that Shaw possessed the art of rhetoric. On the contrary, Shaw had demonstrated, like his master Samuel Butler before him, "that it is possible to write with great effect without music, without style, either good or bad" (p. 169). (But perhaps no more is involved here than that "rhetorician" was for Yeats a term much more pejorative than "rhetoric", for Yeats conceded that even his beloved Elizabethans had rhetoric – by which he apparently meant nothing worse than an elaborate style, consciously embroidered. A "rhetorician", on the other hand, was evidently something worse than a person who made use of rhetoric.)

Wilde, to Yeats, presented a much more complicated case than did Shaw, and as a person Wilde was much more interesting and attractive. The catastrophe that befell him apparently affected Yeats deeply. He devotes a great deal of space to it in his *Autobiography*. He had known the Wilde family, and its most brilliant member was evidently something of a hero to the younger man. Yet in spite of Yeats's high regard for Wilde's literary gifts, at the end he came to see Wilde as "essentially a man of action" (p. 285, 170). Indeed, Yeats makes the remarkable assertion that Wilde would have been more important as soldier or politician, and that he was "a writer by perversity and accident" (p. 285, 170).

Yeats never directly accuses Wilde of insincerity. He explains Wilde's misuse of his gifts in terms of his psychic make-up. He was, Yeats writes, of "the nineteenth Phase, as my symbolism has it" (p. 293, 176). In the symbolism of *A Vision* the nineteenth phase is described as the "beginning of the artificial, the abstract, the fragmentary, and the dramatic",[1] and Wilde's degradation of his art into a means for action was fated and thus enforced – though not entirely so. According to *A Vision*, the true mask of Phase Nineteen is "conviction", but Phase Nineteen offers a false mask as well, and the false mask is "domination".[2] Yeats recalls Wilde's boast that he "who can dominate a London dinner-table can dominate the world" (p. 294, 176). There is always more room for freedom of the will in Yeats's system than a casual acquaintance with it might suggest. Wilde's moon did not dictate the whole course of his life. It did not ensure that he would come to grief. His moon offered him a true mask as well as a false one.

Yet the pressures on Wilde were formidable. Yeats theorizes that Wilde felt a compulsion to

> project himself before the eyes of others, and, having great ambition, before some great crowd of eyes; but there [was] no longer any great crowd that [cared] for his true thought. [Consequently, he] must humor and cajole and pose, take worn-out stage situations, for he knows that he may be as romantic as he please, so long as he does not believe in his romance, and all that he may get their ears for a few strokes of contemptuous wit in which he does believe. (pp. 293–4, 176)

So Yeats writes in his *Autobiography* and thus credits Wilde with a full awareness of his plight. In fact, Yeats says quite explicitly that Wilde "understood his weakness, true personality was impossible, for this is born in solitude" (p. 293, 176). Wilde's failure was not, then, self-deception, the failure with which Yeats taxes the sentimentalist in "Ego Dominus Tuus".

The matter at issue here, of course, is not whether Yeats has made a just estimate of Wilde's motives. His estimate of Wilde is important to my argument only insofar as it may tell us something about what Yeats considered the proper role of the poet to be. The fact that Yeats uses the phrase "true personality" (compare his reference to the "true" mask) implies that there is a sort

---

[1] *A Vision*, p. 148.   [2] Ibid., p. 147.

that is false. True personality "is born in solitude". It comes out of the depths of a man or, to use Yeats's own phrasing, out of the dark well of the self. A man's true personality is not something that he adopts with a view to impressing others. Nor can it be remodeled to fit a particular situation or chosen with an eye to the appeal that it may have for a particular group.

It is evident that drama and the dramatic meant a great deal to Yeats. Yet his willingness to associate the dramatic (as he does in his account of Phase Nineteen) with the artificial, the abstract and the fragmentary calls for clarification. In the first place one must note that the conscious adoption of a dramatic role – the assumption of a mask – is required of all men, not merely those who are poets or playwrights. In fact, in his "Estrangement" Yeats makes it a necessary condition of all "arduous full life" and of all "active virtue" as distinguished from "the passive acceptance of a current code". Yeats finds in "very active natures a tendency to pose". He tells us that one "notices this in [the characters described in] Plutarch's *Lives*" (p. 469, 285). A conscious dramatization of life is therefore demanded, not merely of the artist and the poet, but of the man of action too. It is no accident that in the part of "The Tragic Generation" in which Yeats describes Wilde's psychic make-up as essentially that of a man of action, he should mention a statesman like Woodrow Wilson – he does so twice – and that he should suggest that Wilson's failure, like Wilde's, was occasioned by the fact that he too lived in a period of increasing fragmentation and abstraction.

The theatrical element, then, applies to the whole of life, and the exercise of it is not simply a means to produce a work of art. In fact, exercised in the wrong fashion and for the wrong ends, it may damage any work of art that is attempted. Yet it is essential to any vital work of art. It is in this general context that one is to place Yeats's characterization of Wordsworth's poetry as often "flat and heavy" because his "moral sense [had] no theatrical element" (p. 470, 285). But the proper use of this theatrical element is to discipline oneself in the modes of reality – not to initiate or control action, for, as we have already seen, in Yeats's austere view the kingdom of the artist is not of this world. Those who love the world and who serve it in action are not true artists.

In his "Anima Hominis" Yeats sets up a contrast between mirror and mask and tells us that the saint and the hero make themselves "overmastering, creative persons by turning from the mirror to meditation upon a mask".[1] Throughout Yeats's prose works there are references to what he regards as a false view of art which defines it as Stendhal did: a "mirror dawdling down a lane".[2] If the artist is content to mirror the world passively, he will reproduce mere mechanism. Yeats, by the way, connects this notion with what he calls the "mechanical philosophy of the eighteenth century" and supports his position here with Coleridge's judgment that such a philosophy had had the effect of turning "the human mind into the quick-silver at the back of a mirror" (p. 358, 214).

It may be useful here to come to Yeats's basic point in another way: Authentic poetry is a form of knowledge, and yet one can truly know only what one has himself made. It is on some such reasoning that Yeats can declare that "the world knows nothing because it has made nothing, we [that is, the artists] know everything because we have made everything".[3] Yeats must have held that when Shakespeare spoke of the poet's holding the mirror up to nature, he did less than justice to his own noble art, for elsewhere he writes, obviously with Shakespeare in mind, that the truly great literary artist "is Lear, Romeo, Oedipus, Tiresias; [Shakespeare] has stepped out of a play, and even the woman he loves is Rosalind, Cleopatra, never The Dark Lady. He is part of his own phantasmagoria and we adore him because nature has grown intelligible, and by so doing a part of our creative power."[4]

Yeats chides Shaw for so jauntily exchanging "Narcissus and his Pool for the signal-box at a railway junction", but the reader would be mistaken if he concluded that the pool of Narcissus is the proper alternative to the signal-box. Yeats did not account it so. Indeed, the setting up of such alternatives – objective logic against morbid subjectivity – is part of the process of abstraction that has split apart and parcelled up the world. If

[1] *Mythologies*, pp. 333–4. [2] *Essays*, p. 404. [3] Ibid., p. 510. [4] Ibid. p. 509.

the pool into which the poet stares turns out to be a mirror in which he regards his own features and forgets the world about him, then it is no better than that other mirror that dawdles down a lane. To become absorbed in one's own image would be simply another instance of the passivity against which Yeats inveighs. The pool of self that Yeats recommends has depths. It is neither the mirror of self-love nor, like that other shallow reflector, the "Utopian dream", which causes its bemused victims to "spread abstraction ever further till thought is but a film, and there is no dark depth any more, surface only" (p. 293, 175). For the artist, mere subjectivity is not enough. Indeed, Yeats writes specifically of the withering despair that overwhelms the poet who has nothing but his own spiritual innards to feed upon. In his attack on such self-regarding subjectivity, Yeats, like Matthew Arnold before him, invokes Jonathan Swift's parable of the spider and the bee:

> Only where the mind partakes of a pure activity can art or life attain swiftness, volume, unity; that contemplation lost, we picture some slow-moving event, turn the mind's eye from everything else that we may experience to the full our own passivity, our personal tragedy; or like the spider in Swift's parable mistake for great possessions what we spin out of our guts and deride the bee that has nothing but its hum and its wings, its wax and its honey, its sweetness and light.[1]

More remarkable still is Yeats's assertion that his Irish ancestors "never accepted the anarchic subjectivity of the nineteenth century"![2] The context makes it plain that he is thinking here of the "romantic movement with its turbulent heroism, its self-assertion".[3] That movement, Yeats writes, is now over, but the reaction to it is a "new naturalism that leaves man helpless before the contents of his own mind".[4] In 1931, Yeats was willing to call down a plague on both movement and counter-movement – on anarchic subjectivity and the naturalistic recoil from it. Never having accepted such subjectivity in the first place, he feels no need to react against it now. "Why," he asks, "should men's heads ache that never drank?"[5]

Yeats is thoroughly aware that the spider-like plight of the

---

[1] Ibid., p. 409.   [2] Ibid., p. 407.   [3] Ibid., p. 405.
[4] Ibid.,   [5] Ibid., p. 407.

modern artist, forced to spin everything out of his guts, is novel
in the history of Western man. Heretofore the poet has always
had some "traditional doctrine to give [him] companionship
with [his] fellows". Thus Arnold had his faith in "the best
thought of his generation"; so with the other great Victorians:
Browning had "his psychological curiosity, Tennyson, as before
him Shelley and Wordsworth, moral values that were not
[merely] aesthetic values" (p. 313, 188). But to the poet today,
the poet who has lost all intellectual unity with his fellows, Yeats
asks, what "can the Christian confessor say?" What can the
confessor say "to those who more and more must make all out
of the privacy of their thought, calling up perpetual images of
desire, for he cannot say, 'Cease to be artist, cease to be poet,'
where the whole life is art and poetry, nor can he bid men leave
the world, who suffer from the terrors that pass before shut eyes"
(p. 314, 188). This is one of Yeats's more sombre comments upon
poetry's having become all in all.

Thus, in spite of Yeats's insistence upon the importance of
personality and in spite of his recognition of the poet's ineradicable subjectivity, the artist is no Narcissus. Contemplation, solitude, wrestling with the dark angel of one's anti-self, all of these
were for Yeats ways of getting back to ultimate reality. Doubtless
this is why certain concepts were very dear to him, concepts
like that of a vast world memory through which individual
minds could participate in the funded experience of all mankind and through which they could draw upon traditional wisdom. The trouble with Narcissus was that he did not quarrel
with himself. Instead, he fell in love with himself – which for the
poets, since it is only out of the "quarrel with ourselves" that
we make poetry, is disastrous.

We may summarize as follows: Shaw, a man who was quite
in tune with his own age, knew how to deal with it, how to
please it, how to manipulate it, and how to use it for his own
ends, but in doing so gave up poetry and perhaps art itself,
and out of his quarrel with others made rhetoric, though a very
effective rhetoric. Wilde, though he was not in accord with the
age into which he was born, nevertheless did comply with it, for
he was determined to dominate it and used his brilliant literary

talent to that end. Like Wilde, Yeats too was out of tune with his own age, but he took another course. He eschewed rhetoric. He sought solitude and forged his poetry out of the quarrel with himself. Yeats, of course, does not spell out the contrast between himself and Wilde; he was above such self-congratulatory comparisons. But his own poetry implies clearly enough his notion of the proper course for the poet of our time – even of a highly subjective poet, a member of that same tragic generation to which he said Wilde belonged.

The tragedy of such poets had to be accepted as irremediable. Yeats came to see "the dream of my early manhood, that a modern nation can return to Unity of Culture, [was] false". It could be achieved in his day only "for some small circle of men and women". All the rest of us would have to wait until "the moon bring round its century" (p. 295, 176). This is the view of the matter reflected in all of Yeats's later poetry: it is, of course, a basic theme of that poetry. The position taken here is not really very different from that of the protagonist at the end of *The Waste Land*: Yeats's idiom is different and his tone is different, and yet what he asserts in his own way is what the pilgrim at the end of Eliot's poem asserts:

> Shall I at least set my lands in order? . . . .
> These fragments I have shored against my ruins.

As the child of the romantic tradition, Yeats had to ask, as Wordsworth long before had had to ask, whether it was possible any longer to write poetry at all and, if it was, what manner of man the authentic poet would have to be. Yeats sees the poet as essentially a maker. He is not a poet in virtue of his possessing a certain kind of personality or a special sensitivity or because he is capable of passion. He is a poet by virtue of his ability to create poems. Even when Yeats talks, as he does from time to time, about the poet's turning his own life into a work of art, the dominant term in the analogy invoked is the art work, the structure formed, the lofty rhyme that has actually been built. The man who has made of his life a work of art is the man who has succeeded in giving to his own life the formed intelligibility, the unity and the stylization that one finds in a poem.

In a late essay, the "General Introduction for My Work", the introduction which Yeats wrote for the complete edition of his works that was never produced, he makes very clear this crucial distinction between the man and the artist. He tells us that though a "poet writes always of his personal life, in his finest work [he writes] out of its tragedy, whatever it may be, remorse, lost love, or mere loneliness". Then Yeats fixes the point in a decisive image. He remarks that the poet "is never the bundle of accident and incoherence that sits down to breakfast; he has been reborn as an idea, something intended, complete".[1] This new creature, the thing that has been reborn, incorporating in its own substance the disordered and incoherent fragments of its creator's life, is the poem, and the voice that speaks through this poem, because it is now truly articulate, is not for a moment to be confused with the voice of Willy Yeats, grumbling over the leader in *The Times* as he munches his toast.

William Wordsworth in a celebrated passage described poetry as the overflow of powerful emotions recollected in tranquillity. But Yeats, in a passage quoted on an earlier page of this essay, has gone far beyond any mere process of recollecting emotions. (Presumably Wordsworth as artist went beyond it too, but Yeats has taken the trouble here to spell out what he thinks occurs when recollection is deepened into meditation.) When the personal emotion of the man has been exhausted completely, "something that has nothing to do with action or desire, suddenly starts into its place, something which is as unforeseen, as completely organized, even as unique, as the images that pass before the mind between sleeping and waking" (p. 332, 200).

The conception of art adumbrated here is again curiously like Eliot's: it is an impersonal art. It may be interesting to compare the two poets on this point. In an essay written in 1917, at just about the time that Yeats was writing "Ego Dominus Tuus" and "Anima Hominis", Eliot wrote: "Poetry is not a turning loose of emotion, but an escape from emotion; it is not the expression of personality, but an escape from personality. But, of course, only those who have personality and emotions know

[1] Ibid., p. 509.

what it means to want to escape from these things."[1] A little later in the same essay, Eliot describes the kind of emotion that is significant for art. It is, he writes, an "emotion which has its life in the poem and not in the history of the poet. The emotion of art is impersonal. And the poet cannot reach this impersonality without surrendering himself wholly to the work to be done."[2] The passages are remarkably similar, and startlingly so when one remembers the differences in personality and in background of the poets who penned them.

In a letter that Yeats wrote to Sean O'Casey in 1938, he puts very forcibly his insistence on the total unity that any work of art must have. The immediate subject of the letter is a play, but what is said applies in full measure to poetry: "Dramatic action is a fire which must burn up everything but itself; there should be no room in a play for anything that does not belong to it. . . . Among the things that dramatic action must burn up are the author's opinions; while he is writing he has no business to know anything that is not a portion of that action."[3] In this letter Yeats also makes it very clear how the process of composition itself, when it is successful, discovers and authenticates the truth it embodies. (Incidentally, what Yeats says in this passage about the artist's anti-self – his Daimon – will be particularly helpful to those readers who are repelled by his more mystical descriptions of that ghostly entity.) Yeats goes on to ask O'Casey:

> Do you suppose for one moment that Shakespeare educated Hamlet and King Lear by telling them what he thought and believed? As I see it, Hamlet and Lear educated Shakespeare, and I have no doubt that in the process of that education [Shakespeare] found out that he was an altogether different man to what he thought himself, and had altogether different beliefs. A dramatist can help his characters to educate him by thinking and studying everything that gives them the language they are groping for through his hands and eyes, but the control must be theirs, and that is why the ancient philosophers thought a poet or dramatist Daimon-possessed.[4]

---

[1] "Tradition and the Individual Talent", *Selected Essays* (London: Faber & Faber 1932; New York: Harcourt, Brace, 1932).
[2] Ibid., p. 11.　　　　[3] *Letters*, p. 741.　　　　[4] Ibid.

Yeats often used the adjective "cold" to describe the quality that he sought to attain in his own poetry. He tells us that he "once boasted, copying the phrase from a letter of [his] Father's, that [he] would write a poem 'cold and passionate as the dawn'."[1] But the coldness of such art could never come from a numbed spirit and cold-stiffened fingers. The energy that produced poems that were cold and passionate as the dawn was best described as a kind of fire. So Yeats did describe it in the central passage of his "Poetry and Tradition".

The passage begins with an approving citation of Sainte-Beuve's remark that the only thing immortal in literature is style; and style, Yeats tells us, is "a still unexpended energy, after all that the argument or the story needs, a still unbroken pleasure after the immediate end has been accomplished – and builds this up into a most personal and wilful fire, transfiguring words and sounds and events".[2] But though Yeats calls it a "most personal" fire, the context makes it plain that the flame is applied strictly to anneal and glaze the work of art. In the sentence that follows, Yeats shifts his terms once more and now calls this unexpended energy a "playing of strength when the day's work is done, a secret between a craftsman and his craft, and is so inseparate in his nature that he has it most of all amid overwhelming emotion".[3] (In this last sentence Yeats may possibly be remembering Coleridge's celebrated definition of the imagination with its reference to "a more than usual state of emotion, with more than usual order". Yeats's general indebtedness to Coleridge is large, though most of his explicit references to him come in the essays written in the 1930s.)

This "playing" of the craftsman's "strength" shows most "amid overwhelming emotion", and Yeats goes on to make a curious addition – "and in the face of death".[4] Though his next sentence hardly absolves him of syntactic confusion, it does make quite clear what he has in mind. It is not the dying artist who most of all manifests this graceful play of more-than-needful strength, but his characters, the characters that he has created, as they look into the face of death. The unconscious shift from

---

[1] *Essays*, p. 523.   [2] Ibid., p. 254.
[3] Ibid.   [4] Ibid.

the artist to his characters is characteristic of Yeats, particularly the earlier Yeats. So also is his appeal to Shakespeare for illustrations of this tragic joy. "Shakespeare's persons, when the last darkness has gathered about them, speak out of an ecstasy that is one-half the self-surrender of sorrow, and one-half the last playing and mockery of the victorious sword before the defeated world."[1]

Style, as the play of unexpended artistic energy – as a fine excess, to borrow Keats's phrase – shows itself—

> in the arrangements of events as in the words, and in that touch of extravagance, of irony, of surprise, which is set there after the desire of logic has been satisfied and all that is merely necessary established, and that leaves one, not in the circling necessity, but caught up in the freedom of self-delight. . . . This [self-delight, this] joy, because it must be always making and mastering, remains in the hands and in the tongue of the artist, but with his eyes he enters upon a submissive, sorrowful contemplation of the great irremediable things, and he is known from other men by making all he handles like himself, and yet by the unlikeness to himself of all that comes before him in a pure contemplation.[2]

What prompted the poem, what set the poet dreaming, may have been any of a hundred things – his enemy or his love or his political cause – but these incitations do not ultimately matter. The verses that he writes "may make his mistress famous as Helen or give a victory to his cause", but men will not honor him because he has been a devoted servant to his mistress or served well his cause. They will do so only because they "delight to honour and to remember all that have served contemplation".[3] As the passage continues, Yeats shifts once more from the artist himself to the characters that his imagination has created and, in particular, to Shakespeare's tragic characters. Yeats writes that "Timon of Athens contemplates his own end, and orders his tomb by the beached verge of the salt flood, and Cleopatra sets the asp to her bosom, and their words move us because their sorrow is not their own at tomb or asp, but for all men's fate." They are not obsessed with their own sorrow. They are not sentimental and self-regarding. The artist's "shaping joy has

---

[1] Ibid.   [2] Ibid., pp. 254–5.   [3] Ibid., p. 255.

kept the sorrow pure, as it had kept it were the emotion love or hate, for the nobleness of the arts is in the mingling of contraries, the extremity of sorrow, the extremity of joy, perfection of personality, the perfection of its surrender, overflowing turbulent energy, and marmorean stillness".[1]

[1] Ibid.

8

Auden as a Literary Critic

Auden is pre-eminently the poet of civilization. He loves land-scapes, to be sure, and confesses that his favourite is the rather austere landscape of the north of England, but over and over he has told us that the prime task of our time is to rebuild the *city*, to restore community, to help re-establish the just society. Even a cursory glance over his poetry confirms this view. Who else would have written on Voltaire, E. M. Forster, Matthew Arnold, Pascal, Montaigne, Henry James, Melville, and Sigmund Freud? On any one of them, yes, any poet might. But only a poet of civilization would write poems about them all. If one looks through the reviews and the criticism that he has published during the last thirty years, the case for calling Auden the poet of civilization becomes abundantly clear.

A great deal of this criticism is non-literary or only partially literary. Characteristically, it has to do with the problems of modern man seen in an economic or sociological or psychological context. Auden is everywhere interested in the relation of the individual to society, in the metaphysical assumptions implied by the various societies that have existed in history, and in the claims of history and of nature as they exert themselves upon the human being. What constitutes a society and what holds it together? What is an individual and how is he related to society? What makes a hero and from what does his authority over his fellows derive? How do the differences between Greek tragedy and Elizabethan tragedy reflect differences in the civilization that produced them? What basic changes of sensibility have occurred during the history of Western civilization?

To his interest in cultural patterns and to basic psychological patterns, Auden brings a real zest for classification. In view of such interests and aptitudes, it is not surprising that much of his criticism deals with genres. He devotes a great deal of attention to such topics as the theory of comedy or the kinds of tragedy or the modes of the romantic hero. "Notes on the Comic", an essay published in 1952 in *Thought*, is typical. The tone and general arrangement of the essay remind one a little of the *Poetics* – but Auden is not consciously trudging after either the Stagirite himself or the critics of the Chicago School. He is simply very much interested in his subject, there is a great deal that he wants to make clear to the reader, and he prefers to work systematically.

Genre criticism is closely related to the explorations of the psychological categories of character and action. In this area, Auden has done some of his most brilliant work. A masterpiece of this kind of criticism is his elaborate discussion of the master-servant relationship in literature. The title of the essay is "Balaam and the Ass". It was published in 1954 in *Thought*. Auden begins by defining the master-servant relationship in almost pedantically exact terms. It is not a relationship given by nature but comes into being through an act of conscious volition. It is not an erotic relationship. It is a contractual relationship. (Auden even takes care to tell his reader precisely what a contract is.) Finally, the master-servant relationship is a relation between real persons. (The employees of a factory, for example, are not servants because the master they serve is the factory, a fictitious and not a real person.)

And what, we may ask, has all of this to do with literature? Because the soliloquy, useful though it is, is not enough. In order to present "artistically a human personality in its full depth", we need dialogue and the requisite dialogue demands a special pair. The two people must be similar in certain respects, but in others polar opposites. They must be inseparable – that is, the relationship must not be the kind that is affected by the passage of time or the fluctuations of passion. There is, Auden tells us, "only one relationship which satisfies all those conditions, that between master and personal servant."

The neat click of the logic here may remind us of Edgar Allan Poe, in his "Philosophy of Composition", reasoning his way to the most poetic of all possible topics, the death of a beautiful woman. The apparatus assembled by Auden is, in all conscience, formidable, so much so as to create some anxiety in the reader as to what of value the writer can possibly say after such a prologue. What follows, however, fully vindicates him.

The essay is too long and too richly packed for me to do more than suggest some of the matters treated. There is a very interesting account of the master-servant relationship between lovers, with observations on chivalrous service for the sake of the master-mistress of one's passion. There is a very interesting discussion of Faust and Mephistopheles, and of Don Giovanni, and of Tristan and Isolde. How does the master-servant relation bear upon these characters? Because Don Giovanni's pleasure in seducing women is not sensual but arithmetical. He simply wants to make his list as long as possible, and, since his servant Leporello keeps the list, Leporello in effect becomes the master.

Auden goes on to say that "Just as . . . Don Giovanni might have chosen to collect stamps instead of women, so . . . Tristan and Isolde might have fallen in love with two other people; they are so indifferent to each other as persons . . . that they might just as well – and this is one significance of the love potion – have drawn each other's names out of a hat." A romantic idolatry can be maintained through a lifetime only if the romance is one-sided and one party plays the Cruel Fair. In spite of their declarations of love for each other, Tristan and Isolde in fact "both play the Cruel Fair and withhold themselves". Their passion is not for each other – here Auden is in basic agreement with Denis de Rougemont – but for the Nirvana that each hopes to obtain by means of the other. They do not know each other *as persons* at all; they are really insubstantial, and it is the servants, Kurvenal and Brangaene, who make their decisions and finally control the action.

The next two sections of "Balaam and the Ass" deal with Shakespearian plays, *King Lear* and *The Tempest*. Lear as master and the Fool as servant provide the occasion for some familiar observations upon their relationship but also for much fresh and exciting commentary. A hint of its quality is given in Auden's comment that in an ideal stage production "Lear and the fool should be of the same physical type; they should be athletic mesomorphs. The difference should be in their respective sizes. Lear should be as huge as possible, the fool as tiny." Shakespeare's *Tempest* apparently exercises a peculiar fascination upon Auden. He has discussed it on a number of occasions. His *The Sea and the Mirror* carries as its subtitle "A Commentary on Shakespeare's *The Tempest*", and its long prose third section, spoken by Caliban to the Audience, has to do with the nature of art and its function in the human economy.

In "Balaam and the Ass", Auden says of *The Tempest* that he frankly finds it "a disquieting work". Auden cannot really approve of Prospero, who is guilty of – though Auden does not use the term – what would be called today colonialism. Caliban loses much more than he gains under Prospero's domination of the island. If Prospero is master and Ariel a servant who is under proper contractual relation, Caliban is simply a slave. Auden sums up his sense of disquiet by saying that "*The Tempest* is overpessimistic and manichean". On the other hand, *The Magic Flute*, one of Auden's favourite works of art, is, he concedes, "overoptimistic and pelagian".

The most orthodox, as well as the greatest of the spirit-nature pairs in the master-servant relation is that of Don Quixote and Sancho Panza. "Unlike Prospero and Caliban," Auden observes, "their relationship is harmonious and happy; unlike [that of] Tamino and Papageno [in *The Magic Flute*], it is dialectical; each affects the other." But Don Quixote is one of Auden's favourite characters and of him he always writes *con amore*.

The concluding section of this highly interesting and highly speculative essay has to do with the master-servant relationship in Jules Verne's *Around the World in Eighty Days* and in the novels of P. G. Wodehouse. At the opening of Verne's novel Mr Fogg, Auden tells us, is a kind of stoic and his servant Passepartout a kind of mercurial spirit. But, as the novel goes on, man and master transcend the merely contractual relationship: each ceases to be impersonal to the other, and finally each is willing to sacrifice himself for the other.

In the final paragraph of "Balaam and the Ass" the discussion is connected with another one of Auden's favourite themes, that of the quest and the actions of the quest hero. Wodehouse's Bertie Wooster becomes a kind of inverted quest hero. Through the voices of Bertie Wooster and his incomparable servant, the godlike Jeeves, Auden is able to hear, in spite of their comic intonations, "the voice of Agapé, of Holy Love".

The last comment is calculated to leave the reader gasping. Even the reader sympathetic with Auden's religious position may feel that this essay contains more stimulation than nourishment and constitutes a diet much too rich for his blood. But I shall not say this for myself. With particular aspects of the discussion, I have my own quarrels. I am at odds with Auden's reading of *The Tempest*, for example. I have certain reservations about the kind of criticism exhibited in "Balaam and the Ass". Discussion of ideas and psychological patterns, I would observe, always tends to move away from specifically *literary* criticism. It seems to me significant that Auden can illustrate some of the relationships that interest him most from second- and third-rate artists like Verne and Wodehouse as well as from first-rate artists like Shakespeare and Cervantes. But I go on to reflect that such observations need not, and would not, disconcert Auden. On the whole, I must say that I find "Balaam and the Ass" a remarkable document: the author is sensitive, intelligent, resourceful, quick to discern analogies and linkages where most of us, left to our own devices, would see nothing at all.

In view of his general interest in psychology and the recurrent psychological patterns that underlie the literary genres, it is apparent that Auden is also to be regarded as an archetypal critic. It is true, of course, that he does not often use the term *archetype*. I recall only one instance of it in my recent reading of his critical essays and reviews. In his first volume of criticism, *The Enchafèd Flood*, he usually employs the term "symbol" or "symbolic cluster", but his discussion of the images used by the Romantics – the desert and the sea, the paradisaical island and the magical garden, the stone and the shell carried by the Arab in Wordsworth's vision – constitutes what is frequently called archetypal criticism. His interest in symbolic clusters, especially in those that relate to recurrent psychological situations, goes far back in his literary career. That interest was well developed as early as 1940 when he published "The Quest". The psychological situations dramatized in these sonnets receive a full-scale elaboration in the essay titled "K's Quest", which was published in *The Kafka Problem* in 1946. There Auden distinguishes seven kinds of quest, beginning with the fairy story which typically has for its goal "either some sacred object which endows its possessor with magical powers . . . or marriage with a beautiful princess, or both. . . ." One of the more curious versions of the quest is the one that Auden calls the "quest for innocence". It is exemplified in the typical detective story.

In the typical detective story one finds, according to Auden, "a group of people . . . living in what appears to be a state of innocence and grace, where there is no law since there is no need for it. A corpse is found under conditions which make it certain that one of the group must be the murderer, i.e. that state of innocence is lost and the law enters. All fall under suspicion but the hero-detective who identifies and arrests the guilty one and innocence is restored to the rest. . . ."

To apply terms like "state of innocence and grace" to the detective story will seem to many addicts pretentious; but a year or two later in "The Guilty Vicarage: Notes on the Detective Story, by an Addict", Auden was to take the whole thing up another notch. There, for example, he writes: "There are three classes of crime: (a) offences against God and one's neighbor or neighbors; (b) offences against God and society; (c) offences against God."

Now Auden becomes very specific: "Murder," he writes, "is a member and the only member of Class B. The character common to all crimes in Class A is that it is possible, at least theoretically, either that restitution can be made to the injured party . . . or that the injured party can forgive the criminal . . . Consequently, society as a whole is only indirectly involved; directly, its representatives (the police, etc.) act in the interests of the injured party. Murder is unique in that it abolishes the party it injures, so that society has to take the place of the victim and on his behalf demand restitution or grant forgiveness; it is the one crime in which society has a direct interest." But this is so legalistic, so hairsplittingly precise, that to many readers it will sound like an embarrassing self-parody. People who are bored by detective stories and resent Auden's Christianity will see in this essay Auden at his weakest and most absurd. I should prefer to regard portions of "The Guilty Vicarage" as representing Auden at his most special, limited, and eccentric.

Where is he at his best as a critic? I have already praised the quality of discussion in "Balaam and the Ass" and in *The Enchafèd Flood*. If asked for a shorter example and one more directly concerned with literature as such, I think that I should suggest Auden's introduction to *A Selection from the Poems of Alfred, Lord Tennyson* (1947). It is brief – about 4000 words – but very much to the point, distinctly a professional job, the work of a practicing man of letters. In the first place, it is characteristic of Auden in its systematic arrangement. Auden defines three kinds of bad poetry. The poet "may be bored or in a hurry and write work which is technically slipshod or carelessly expressed. From this fault, of which Shakespeare is not infrequently guilty, Tennyson is quite free." Secondly, he may produce passages which are, at a serious moment, unintentionally funny. Here Tennyson is guilty and Auden submits examples. Thirdly, a poet may write bad poetry which is not "accidental", like the first two kinds, but which is rooted in some inner corruption of his own consciousness. The poet "means" the badness and cannot be convinced that it is a fault. Tennyson is guilty here and Auden submits some telling examples. There follows an interesting speculation as to the root of this third fault – with special references to Tennyson's case. The reader will be convinced or not convinced, but he will feel the point worth making and at the least will learn something about Tennyson's sensibility.

Next Auden lists – system again, though useful in this brief note – five elements that are found over and over again in Tennyson's poetry. He comments that "In no other English poet of comparable rank does the bulk of his work seem so clearly to be inspired by some single and probably very early experience." Then comes the shocker: "If Wordsworth is the great English poet of Nature, then Tennyson is the great English poet of the Nursery . . . i.e. his poems deal with human emotions in their most primitive states, uncomplicated by conscious sexuality or intellectual rationalization." Here again the reader may or may not be convinced, but he will find Auden's judgement plausible, at least partially true, and, in any case, one that will force him to consider from a new angle Tennyson's special preoccupation with numbed sadness.

In order to "place" Tennyson in his cultural scene, Auden invokes Nietzsche's description of Wagner, Kierkegaard on the subject of his own childhood, a passage from Saint Augustine's *Confessions*, and some quotations from Baudelaire – the reflections, as Auden terms them, of a "cosmopolitan satanic dandy". The range of reference is, again, characteristic of Auden's criticism. The allusion to Baudelaire develops into an extended series of parallels and contrasts with Tennyson, a series which occupies the last several pages of the introduction. Auden concedes the dissimilarities between the poets, but points out that both men "felt themselves to be exiles from a lost paradise, desert dwellers . . . both shared the same nostalgia for the Happy Isles . . . both imagine Eden in the same Rousseauistic terms; i.e. as a place of natural innocence rather than supernatural illumination."

Baudelaire is obviously the greater poet but not, according to Auden, because he had a keener sensibility – rather because "he developed a first-rate critical intelligence which prevented him from writing an epic about Roland . . . to escape from his vision of the abyss. On the other hand, it led him into an error which Tennyson escaped – the error of making a religion of the aesthetic." Auden says that Baudelaire "was right in seeing that art is beyond good and evil", and that "Tennyson was a fool to try to write a poetry which would teach the Ideal"; but Auden goes on to observe that "Tennyson was right in seeing that an art which is beyond good and evil is a game of secondary importance, and Baudelaire was the victim of his own pride in persuading himself that a mere game was '*le meilleur témoignage | que nous puissions donner de notre dignité*'."

I find these parallels and contrasts highly interesting. It is, in the best sense, an act of the imagination to relate two such poets so as to make each reflect light upon the other. But the confrontation is not arbitrary and mechanical: the perception of a meaningful relation between them derives from a coherent theory of poetry, including the limitations of poetry as well as its powers, together with specific notions about the function of the poet and his proper role in a society. To see this, one need only extract from the concluding pages of Auden's introduction such suggestive phrases as "a first-rate critical intelligence" as a prime resource of a poet, "the error of making a religion of the aesthetic" as a modern misconception of the poet's role, the lack of any "sense of a historical relation between individuals" – this said of Tennyson – and, finally, the attempt (Auden regards it as a mistaken one) "to evade the need for a religious faith by finding some form of magical certainty".

"The error of making a religion of the aesthetic" constitutes much of the substance of Caliban's speech to the audience in Auden's *The Sea and the Mirror*. Auden takes this error very seriously, but he is in no sense a didactic poet who demands that poetry should propagandize for Christianity or any other faith. Indeed, for a man so deeply engrossed in the political problems of our day, for a person who is so serious a moralist and so keen a psychologist, Auden's conception of poetry may seem startling in the limited role which he assigns it. What that role is, what the structure of poetry is, and what the relation of poetry to truth is in Auden's account – these are matters which will occupy most of the space remaining to me in this paper.

The indirect relation of poetry to the world of fact and action is not an idea which came to Auden rather late in his career. It occurs in the well-known and often anthologized poem, "In Memory of W. B. Yeats", where the poet says,

> For poetry makes nothing happen: it survives
> In the valley of its saying where executives
> Would never want to tamper. . . .

But though poetry makes nothing happen, the poet evidently has a role of some importance and a duty, for he is urged, in the perilous times of 1939 when the poem appeared, to make a vineyard "of the curse" and, though he must sing of human unsuccess "in a rapture of distress", he should "teach the free man how to praise".

Auden's essay "The Public vs. the Late Mr William Butler Yeats" (1939) constitutes a kind of gloss on the poem. In the course of that essay Auden writes: "I am not trying to suggest that art exists independently of society. The relation between the two is . . . intimate and important. . . ." But you simply can't grade a poet up for proper political opinions, and down for improper. "Art is a product of history, not a cause" – and so Auden can echo his poem in saying that the case against Yeats "rests upon the fallacious belief that art ever makes anything happen, whereas the honest truth . . . is that, if not a poem had been written, not a picture painted, not a bar of music composed, the history of man would be materially unchanged".

The first of Auden's essays that reveals his fully developed theory of poetry is "Squares and Oblongs". Though it appears to be no more than a collection of scattered observations on the poet and poetry and his audience, a very coherent and self-consistent pattern emerges. For example, Auden's earlier observation that the poet is a man of action in one field only, that of language, here becomes the statement that the poet is "before anything else, a person who is passionately in love with language". And Auden illustrates this notion by proposing a test: Ask a young man why he wants to write poetry; if his answer is, "I have important things I want to say," one can conclude that he is not a poet. But if he answers, "I like hanging around words listening to what they say," then maybe he is going to be a poet. So much for the stigmata of the poet. Now for a concise definition of poetry: there are, Auden says, "two theories of poetry. Poetry as a magical means for inducing desirable emotions and repelling undesirable emotions in oneself and others, or Poetry as a game of knowledge, a bringing to consciousness, by naming them, of emotions and their hidden relationships. "The first view was held by the Greeks and is now," Auden remarks, "held by MGM, Agit-Prop, and the collective public of the world. They are wrong."

Auden's characterization of poetry "as a magical means for inducing desirable emotions and repelling undesirable emotions in oneself and others" is derived from R. G. Collingwood's *Principles of Art*, a book published in 1938. In his chapter titled "Art as Magic", Collingwood argues that the primary function of all magical acts is "to generate in the agent or agents certain emotions that are considered necessary or useful. . . ." Magic usually works through artistic or quasi-artistic means, but its aim is not that of art: magic works up the emotions to release them for the sake of a particular practical act.

In "Henry James and the Artist in America" (1948), Auden writes about the temptation to the artist to become "an official magician, who uses his talents to arouse in the inert masses the passions which the authorities consider socially desirable and necessary". But the artist, Auden says, must never have "any truck with magic, whether in its politer forms like diplomatic cultural missions, or in its more virulent varieties. . . ." This is not, however, because art is of sacred importance but on the contrary because it is, as Auden puts it, "in the profoundest sense, frivolous. For one thing, and one thing only is serious: loving one's neighbor as one's self."

Collingwood also makes a sharp distinction between magic and religion, and between art and religion. Here the influence of Collingwood – if I am right in supposing that it is behind much of Auden's theory – would corroborate the much more powerful and pervasive influence of Kierkegaard. Art, Auden tells us in "Squares and Oblongs", is not a religion. He has to concede that the Greeks did produce some great works of art in spite of the fact that they "confused art with religion". This could happen, Auden tells us – rather consciously riding his high horse here – because the Greeks were, "in reality, like all pagans . . . frivolous people who took nothing seriously".

Auden is willing to follow this anti-emotive view of poetry right on through. He rejects, for example, in Aristotle's *Poetics* the one main deviation into emotive theory, saying that if he understands what Aristotle means when he speaks of "catharsis, [he] can only say he is wrong". You do get a purgation of the emotions from witnessing a bullfight or a professional football match, but not from a work of art. Moreover, poetry is not prophecy. Shelley's claim for the poets that they are "the unacknowledged legislators of the world" is, says Auden, "the silliest remark ever made about poets. . . ."

That the present state of the world is parlous, Auden agrees. Indeed, that state of the world is "so miserable and degraded that if anyone were to say to the poet: 'For God's sake, stop humming and put the kettle on or fetch bandages. The patient's dying,' I do not know how he could justifiably refuse." Unfortunately, no one ever asks the poet to carry out some useful and practical action. What the self-appointed, unqualified Nurse typically says to the poet is this: "Stop humming this instant and sing the Patient a song which will make him fall in love with me. In return I'll give you extra ration-cards and a passport"; and the poor delirious patient cries (out to the poet): "Please stop humming and sing me a song which will make me believe I am free from pain and perfectly well." But the poet, though he ought to be willing to mop the floor or carry bedpans or do any other useful task, must have the courage to deny all such requests and the bribes that go with them.

Does the poet, then, have no responsibility to society? Auden would, I believe, answer that he does, but he would insist that the poet cannot allow a Stalin or a Goebbels or even a President Hoover – I believe I remember Hoover's asking in 1931 for the production of a good poem that would restore our confidence and end the depression – to tell him how to discharge that responsibility, nor can the poet allow the public to tell him how to discharge it. If he has a specific responsibility *as poet*, that responsibility can be discharged only through his being the best poet that he knows how to be.

In "Nature, History, and Poetry" (1950) appeared Auden's most fully matured statement of his conception of poetry. As the title would suggest, nature and history are the co-ordinates for a whole series of definitions and observations about man and his experience. Auden distinguishes, for example, between natural events, which are related by the principle of Identity, and historical events, which are related by the principle of Analogy. He also distinguishes between laws that apply to natural events and those that apply to historical events, "laws-of" and "laws-for". As for man's social life, there are crowds, societies, and communities – among which Auden draws a very careful distinction. Crowds are simply happen-so; societies have a definitive size and specific structure. (Elsewhere, Auden tells us a "society is a group of rational beings united by a common function".) A community, on the other hand, is bound together by a common love. "It is only in history that one can speak of communities as well as societies. . . ."

Man exists "as a unity in tension of four modes of being, Soul, Body, Mind and Spirit. . . . As body and mind, man is a natural creature; as soul and spirit, an historical creature." Auden then works out the implications of this dual position for man's consciousness of himself in relation to the world about him.

Nature and history provide the distinction between science and art. The subject matter of the natural scientist "is a crowd of natural events at all times. He assumes this crowd to be not real but apparent and attempts to discover the true system concealed under its appearances. The subject matter of the poet is a crowd of historic occasions of feeling in the past. He accepts this crowd as real and attempts to transform it into a community. . . ." The implications for poetry of this last comment are immense. Because the subject matter of the poet consists of occasions of *past* feeling, in poetry "desire is seen, as it were, in a mirror, detached from its roots in appetite and passion. . . ." Auden agrees heartily with Wordsworth in thinking that in poetry the emotion must indeed be "recollected in tranquillity". Language, to be sure, can be used to introduce "emotion into the present", for example in propaganda or pornography; but, Auden says, "such use is magical, not poetical". Elsewhere in this essay he defines propaganda as "the employment of magic by those who do not believe in it over against those who do".

In order to define a poem, Auden invokes an analogy from the social context in which men live. A poem, he says, is a linguistic society or verbal system. But a poem differs from many other "verbal societies" in that "meaning and being are identical". Thus, it is not quite accurate to say that "a poem should not mean but be". On the other hand, a poem differs from a human society in the fact that it has natural being and not historical being. "Like an image in the mirror, a poem might be called a pseudo person"; that is, the poem has "uniqueness and addresses the reader as person to person but like all natural beings and unlike historical persons, it cannot lie".

Auden thus makes Philip Sidney's famous point very adroitly but in his own way. He writes that "it is not possible to say of a poem that it is true or false [,] for one does not have to go to anything except [the poem] itself to discover whether or not it is in fact . . . a community of feelings truly embodied in a verbal society. If it is not, if unfreedom or disorder is present, the poem itself reveals this on inspection." That is, if I may be allowed to make my own comment here, the problem is not one of discovering whether some proposition made by the poem is true or false; it is rather that of discovering whether the poem is truly unified or chaotic, whether its parts are related or unrelated, whether it embodies order or is rent apart by disorder.

How does the poet go about transforming the two "crowds" at his disposal – the words in his vocabulary and the feelings of past occasions that he can recall – into a verbal society in which the feelings form a community? Through a dialectical struggle. For the verbal system is "actively coercive upon the feelings it is attempting to embody" and, Auden admits, what it "cannot embody truthfully it excludes". On the other hand, "the feelings are passively resistant to all claims of the system to embody them [all claims, that is] which they do not recognize as just. . . ."

This recognition of resistances to be overcome, as feeling competes with feeling, and as word exerts its pressure on feeling and feeling exerts its pressure on the choice of word, is reminiscent of a considerable body of critical opinion in our day. I am thinking of Yeats, Nietzsche, I. A. Richards, John Crowe Ransom, and others; but I am not concerned here to trace Auden to a particular set of sources or to impugn his originality. In discussing the resistances to be adjusted and the conflicting claims to be reconciled, Auden writes that "every feeling competes with every other demanding inclusion and a dominant position to which they are not necessarily entitled, and every word

demands that the system shall modify itself in its case. . . ." Like
a human society, the poem embodies tensions and achieves its
unity, when it achieves it, through tensions. Since this is the
way in which a poem is organized, it may fail in either of two
ways: it may exclude too much and thus fall into banality, or
it may "attempt to embody more than one community at once"
and thus fall into disorder.

Naturally, my own ears perk up at Auden's use of terms like
"inclusion" and phrases like "exclude too much". Let me
attempt, then, my own summary of what Auden is saying in
this highly condensed essay. Throughout the essay, Auden sees
the basic poetic problem as the problem of securing unity. He
takes into account the resistances which any poet must acknowledge and reconcile if his poem is to become a poem at all –
resistances which he cannot deny if he is to hope to produce a
mature and an honest poem. In any poem unity is secured by
means of two basic principles. The first involves trimming off
the contradictions and irrelevances – that is, *excluding* what
cannot be honestly embodied in the poem. The second involves
a procession of *inclusion* in which the disparate and recalcitrant
are fitted into the poem by a deepening and widening of the
imaginative context. The poem which is overambitious in its
attempt to include the jarring and the difficult may, of course,
fail to achieve unity and remain incoherent. But too much reli-
ance on exclusion carries its risks, too: the poem may be robbed
of depth and richness.

Auden concludes his essay with a series of analogies drawn
from Christianity. Every poet, he writes, consciously or unconsciously holds the following "absolute presuppositions, as the
dogmas of his art: (1) An historical world exists, a world of
unique events and unique persons. . . . (2) The historical world
is a fallen world. . . . (3) The historical world is a redeemable
world. The unfreedom and disorder of the past can be reconciled in the future." That is, any poet at work on a poem finds
himself trying to put in order, and thus into meaningful relationship, experiences which demand to be redeemed in knowledge.

As he pursues this analogy, Auden may be said to present a

parallel to Eliot's view of the impersonality of art: "In poetry as in other matters," Auden says, "the law holds good that he who would save his life must lose it; unless the poet sacrifices his feelings completely to the poem, so that they are no longer his but the poem's, he fails." Whether borrowed from Eliot or not, the basic conception is the same: the poem is not primarily the poet's expression of personal feelings; it is not the expression of the poet that counts but the organization of the thing that he is making. The poem, then, according to Auden, is "beautiful or ugly to the degree that it succeeds or fails in reconciling *contradictory* feelings in an order of mutual propriety".

Why contradictory, someone will ask; and Auden's implied answer surely would run something like this: because the material with which he works involves unfreedom and disorder. Poetry which systematically ignores contradiction and disorder and evil is banal, if not lying. In the end, I suppose that Auden would finally simply appeal to the facts. The great poems, not merely the great tragedies but even lyrics that possess depth and resonance, are not really "simple" but exhibit in their very make-up a triumph won over confusion, disharmony, and disorder. Auden continues his comment by saying that "Every beautiful poem presents an analogy to the forgiveness of sins, an analogy, not an imitation, because it is not evil intentions which are repented of and pardoned but contradictory feelings which the poet surrenders to the poem in which they are reconciled."

Auden obviously values his analogy and presumably would be reluctant to surrender it. But to people who are ruffled by the Christian association, Auden could, without giving up his essential point, offer the testimony of Nietzsche. I am thinking of such of Nietzsche's statements as "contrasts are . . . the highest sign of [artistic] power . . . manifesting itself in the conquest of opposites"; or his remark that the greatest artists are those "who make harmony ring out of every discord". The genuine artist does not narrow his poetry to express one or the other of the contradictory feelings. He fashions a poem in which they are reconciled and unified.

That Auden, the poet of civilization, the student of cultural history, the serious moralist, should hold what amounts to a formalist conception of poetry may come as a shock. Yet it is plainly a fact, and a little reflection will indicate that no contradiction is involved. Auden's position may disturb some of our conventional notions and habitual associations, but the conventional notions of most of us usually profit from being shaken up. The assumption that poetry must be either an escape from life or else the blueprint for a better life is obviously oversimple.

I shall not, however, be content to argue that Auden's critical position is self-consistent and tenable for a man who is deeply concerned with the problems of civilization. I propose that Auden's special position is a positive source of strength. It has enabled him to avoid most of the traps laid for the historical critic, the moralistic critic, and the archetypal critic. Auden's respect for the autonomy of art has forbidden him to consider it as merely the handmaiden of a religion or of a political party. On the other hand, his sense of the limitations of art – he is willing to call it in final terms *frivolous* – prevents his turning it into a kind of *ersatz* religion.

Auden is not only aware of the relation of art to religion and to science. He knows how the various kinds of criticism are related to the literary work and to each other. Indeed, he practices several kinds of criticism with equal competence – not, surely, as a virtuoso display and not because one kind of criticism is as good as another or because any old criticism will do, but rather because an expert craftsman possesses specialized tools and knows what each is good for.

Auden's virtues as a critic obviously spring from his intelligence, sensitivity, power of imagination, and depth of insight. These qualities are primary: no literary theory could possibly provide a substitute for them. But a sound theory does allow the critic to make the best use of his natural endowment, and his possession of a coherent and responsible theory accounts for Auden's having become one of the soundest as well as one of the most exciting critics of our day.

9

The Criticism of Fiction:
The Role of Close Analysis

One of the questions that came up in the discussion yesterday was whether the criticism of the sort that I had been talking about was applicable to fiction. I said that it was. I argued that the critic, in moving from poetry to fiction, did not need to make basic changes in his methods, in the kind of questions that he asked, or in the way in which he approached the work. There obviously might be great differences in scope and scale between one's treatment of a lyric and of a novel. But the differences were not radical.

I want to address myself more particularly to that question this morning. I have announced in advance the titles of three pieces of fiction so that you who are interested might have a chance to read or reread them. Suppose I begin with Faulkner's "An Odor of Verbena". This is an excellent story, but one which raises a good many questions about current critical procedures. The basic mistakes in reading the story, if I may judge by what has been written, and more directly by what has happened in my graduate classes at Yale, are of two kinds: the reader loses the intrinsic meaning of the story by overstressing the historical background, or he disintegrates the story into wildly improbable "symbols". If we turn "An Odor of Verbena" into a kind of moralized sociology, it becomes a story of the depraved and repulsive post-Civil War South. The society has gone to pieces, and typical of its deterioration is its adherence to a wicked and terrible code of vengeance. Of course, there's just enough truth in this view to make emphasis upon it thoroughly misleading; for the nature of the hero, the difficulty of the decision he makes, his own commitment to the community and its moral codes – all of these get well distorted in such a simplified view. A modern student so bemused may wonder how Bayard (or any other right-thinking young man) could have had any problem at all in doing what he did. Bayard's action becomes, in this oversimplified view, an act of simple rejection. The story, thus shorn of its moral complications, becomes not much more than a rubberneck-bus tour through what the reader feels he has every reason to consider a moral slum. The other typical misreading of "An Odor of Verbena" involves what I have called "symbol mongering". Perhaps this fault originates as an overcorrection of the tendency just described. But the symbol-mongering that I speak of is a grotesque parody of anything like an adequate "close reading". It magnifies details quite irresponsibly; it feverishly prospects for possible symbolic meanings and then forces them beyond the needs of the story. For example, Drusilla, the young step-mother of the hero, is likened in one of the brilliant scenes to a "Greek amphora priestess". Evidently what Faulkner has in mind is a special kind of Greek vase, an amphora with red figure or black figure designs on it, in this instance, one that depicts a priestess celebrating a rite. The comparison is perhaps a kind of rhetorical flourish. But clearly Faulkner means to associate Drusilla with the devoted, rapt, hieratical woman such as might be suggested by one of the highly formalized figures on a Greek vase. But I have seen students seize upon the term *amphora*, go back into the original Greek meaning, and dredge up all sorts of curious significances which they tried to apply to Faulkner's character. I hardly need to say that no light is shed upon Drusilla by the fact that an amphora was two-handled, or that it was often used to hold oil or wine.

One is inclined to say that to look for subtleties of meaning is a "good" fault – that the reader ought to expect the author to be rich and complicated – to assume that it is we who are lacking if we fail immediately to understand a text. But the student can rummage about too innocently and too much at random. He can even trust his author too much. This very story supplies a nice instance of too much trust. In setting the time and the mood of the story, Faulkner talks about the long dry season and about the fact that though it was already October, the equinox had not occurred. I have had students accept the passage quite solemnly, and when I reminded them that the equinox was a particular time in the sun's seasonal progression and that the autumnal equinox could not occur later than September 23rd, they were really taken aback. They had difficulty in accepting the fact that Faulkner could fail to know the meaning of a word. This confidence in the author – when it *is* that and not mere laziness – is healthy; but it is also healthy for a class to learn that a very great author can sometimes be mistaken about the precise meaning of a word and that the reader does no compliment to his author by lapsing into blind trust.

"An Odor of Verbena" is a very rich and subtle story. In some respects it is as finely textured as a poem. It is filled with brilliant description and the description is not mere external decoration, but has its part in shaping the total meaning. Much of the action is internal action, mental action. Even particular metaphors are invested with special meaning. But I find that in teaching the story I have to start with the old-fashioned questions: What "happens" in this story? What is the story "about"? What is the character of Bayard? What is the character of Drusilla? Is she mad or not? Is she in love with her step-son? But I don't see that such questions as these imply a different view of criticism from that implied by the questions that I asked about the poem we were talking about yesterday. In order to answer them, one may eventually have to take into account the symbols, metaphors, and even verbal rhythms of the story.

The old-fashioned questions that have to do with motivation and action may, for a very different reason, however, seem inapplicable to a Faulkner story. Faulkner does not often dramatize the agony of choice – the process by which the character actually arrives at his decision – and some readers have consequently assumed that Faulkner's characters make no decisions at all and are merely driven and determined creatures, adrift on the tides of circumstance. André Gide has said something to this effect. He is only one of many. But this view is nonsensical. Faulkner, as a matter of fact, does sometimes depict the character who chooses and accepts the consequences of his choice; but he usually prefers, as in the story with which we are concerned, to dramatize the character's sustaining of a choice – Bayard's maintaining his decision against every pressure – rather than to give us the stages by which Bayard arrived at the decision. Here, then, "close reading" justifies itself. Or to put it otherwise, the critic who maintains that Faulkner's characters are mere automata has clearly not read closely enough.

I hope all of this doesn't seem too elementary to you. I would not insist upon such considerations except that I have been teaching Faulkner for some twelve years to graduate students who are intelligent, sensitive, and well trained. I know how much difficulty some of them have with this very story. Now if the difficulty were finally the fault of the author – if, for example, at the end, after they had tussled with the story, they said to me, "The story still seems to me incoherent and confused," I should hold my peace. But what they usually say after some discussion and perhaps some "close reading", is this: "This story is significant and it is coherent. But it is a story to which I came ill prepared, filled with the wrong kinds of preconceptions."

Perhaps it would save time if I simply interrupted myself at this point and asked some of you whether there were any particular problems in the story about which you would like to ask me, or which you think deserve comment.

Question: "What is the boy's attitude toward his father? How does his attitude bear upon his decision not to avenge his father's death?"

That is a very interesting question and the answer to it is not simple. A proper answer will illustrate very well the problems that one comes up against in the story. In a sense, the boy is breaking the pattern set by his father. Though he still loves his father, he knows that his father has become a ruthless, preoccupied man. The father has gone so far that when Bayard, the dutiful son, tells him that the young stepmother has kissed him, the father doesn't take in what he has said. The elder man, abstracted and indifferent, hardly hears what his son is saying: he is occupied with other things. So in some very important regards, Bayard is breaking with the father, the father who in his determination to get his railroad built and running, has acted ruthlessly – even to the point of killing his opponents.

Yet in refusing to avenge his father by shooting the assassin, it can be argued that Bayard is actually following his father's example. Two months earlier his father had told him: "... I I shall do a little moral housecleaning. I am tired of killing men, no matter what the necessity or end." In any case, Bayard evidently loved his father: the intense scene in which he views his father's dead body is sufficient testimony to that. If the scene also testifies to Bayard's candid admission to himself that his father has been fiercely intolerant and ruthless in his life, that fact but stresses the complexity of his relation to his father. His decision to refuse to kill his father's assassin stems not at all from any rejection of his father, but rather from a love for, and understanding of, him.

Bayard's attitude toward his father is analogous, in its duality, to his attitude toward the community. Here again the student may easily misread the story by underestimating the claims of the community upon Bayard's loyalty or by regarding these claims as simply a baleful and degrading inertia. Thus, the modern student may feel that it is so obviously a terrible thing to kill a man that he wonders that the decision to refrain from shooting Redmond cost Bayard anything at all. (Curiously enough, this same student will usually have no trouble with the revenge code in *Hamlet*.)

In teaching this story, therefore, one may need to call attention to the many ways in which the community exerts its pressure on Bayard to avenge his father's death. There is, of course, the feverishly wrought-up Drusilla. But there is also Professor Wilkins, a good man and a compassionate man. If we are not surprised that the rough and positive soldier, George Wyatt, will urge the action, and of course we are not, we may overlook the fact that Wyatt too is far from being the thoughtless incendiary. He is dispassionate enough to criticize his friend's conduct toward Redmond. George Wyatt says to Bayard:

"Right or wrong, us boys and most of the other folks in this county know John's right. But he ought to let Redmond alone. I know what's wrong: he's had to kill too many folks, and that's bad for a man. We all know Colonel's brave as a lion, but Redmond ain't no coward either and there ain't any use in making a brave man that made one mistake eat crow all the time. Can't you talk to him?"

If the student (by a reading sufficiently "close") can be led to see Bayard's relation to the community and to sense the weight of its various pressures upon him, he will interpret Bayard's action not as a rejection of a wrong-headed code, but as the transcendence of that code in a complex action that everywhere acknowledges the community's claim that he should call his father's assassin to account, but that also acknowledges the higher law embodied in "Thou shalt not kill". Bayard, who fears the imputation of cowardice, has done a braver thing than the code demanded: he has gone to the assassin's office, thus honouring the code, but has transcended the code by having determined, at the risk of his own death, that he would not shoot Redmond.

Question: "How much comment on, and analysis of, particular passages would you make use of in teaching a story like 'An Odor of Verbena'?"

Well, I think that it is not easy to generalize. I wish that I had time to illustrate by taking some samples. But I may say that when I teach the story I do read certain passages – for example, the fine conversation between George Wyatt and Bayard when he first returns home, or that equally fine one in which George advises him about the pistols, or that wonderful scene in which Drusilla, her voice "silvery" and "ecstatic", presents the duelling pistols to Bayard, or, perhaps best of all, Bayard's confrontation with the assassin – beginning with Bayard's mounting the "wooden steps scuffed by the heavy bewildered boots of countrymen approaching litigation and stained by tobacco spit. . . ."

These passages, because they are finely wrought and because they are integral parts of a coherent structure, can be used to show the way in which Faulkner focuses our attention upon the basic issues or illuminates the conflicting impulses in Bayard's mind or dramatizes for us the state of Bayard's heightened sensibility. Sometimes one can show how the very make-up of the sentences and their characteristic rhythms contribute to the meaning of the story. But how much attention one pays to this kind of "close reading" will depend upon a great many things – how much time one has and what the needs of the class are. There is certainly no point in making such close reading an end in itself: but if the reader misses what is necessary for comprehension and appreciation, then I see no alternative to helping him come to see what he has missed.

In teaching Joyce's story "Clay", I have had something of the same general experience that I have had in teaching "An Odor of Verbena". Because "Clay" is so closely wrought, because the point of the story is presented so quietly, I have found that many students, including some who are otherwise quite perceptive, simply miss the point. Let me take up first, however, the problem of symbol-mongering which comes up with this story. The heroine of "Clay", Maria, is the little old maid who works in the Dublin by Lamplight Laundry. On All Hallows Eve she pays a visit to the house of a friend – or is it a relative? At any rate, the story begins with Maria's preparations for her visit. It describes her journey to Joe's house, tells what happens there on that evening, and that is all. A very flat little story, apparently, in which nothing "happens". But the modern student, since he knows he is reading Joyce, is certain that a great deal must happen; and frequently he goes about extracting the meaning with all the ruthlessness of the dedicated symbol-monger. The fact that the story has to do with Halloween, and that Maria is described as a person with a nose which almost meets her chin has made not only students, but critics and commentators think that she is a witch.[1] (But they never

---

[1] See, for example, Richard Carpenter and Daniel Leary, "The Witch Maria", *The James Joyce Review*, III, 3–7, and William York Tindall, *A Reader's Guide to James Joyce* (New York, 1959), pp. 29–31). Joyce, by the way, had originally intended to call the story "Christmas Eve" (see Richard Ellmann, *James Joyce*, New York, 1959, p. 196). Had Joyce kept to his original Christmas Eve setting, one suspects that even Maria's peculiar nose would not have given her away to the modern witch-hunters.

manage to show what her being a witch contributes to the meaning of the story.) Some writers, their eye lighting up at the fact that the heroine is named "Maria", try to run some elaborate and (it seems to me) completely misplaced and meaningless analogies with the Virgin Mary. What this analogical relationship would add to the meaning of the story, again they do not make clear. (The commentators who connect her with the Virgin are, it should be said, the same ones who find her to be a witch!)

Actually, "Clay" seems to me to be, in its plot line, a very simple story, though it is also a very subtle story, in which the control of tone is quite perfect. Joyce is able to reveal Maria's plight with terrible power yet with no trace of sentimental indulgence – no sense of special pleading. But again, to indicate how poorly many of us read, I have seen many graduate students read this story without ever realizing that what Maria really wants is a husband and children of her own. The matter is made perfectly clear in the story itself: there are all sorts of hints and clues – Maria's eyes sparkling "with disappointed shyness", the coarse Ginger Mooney's teasing her about getting the ring, Maria looking with "quaint affection" at her "diminutive body" and finding it "in spite of its years" a "nice tidy little body", the incident in which the "stylish young lady behind the counter" asks her whether it was "wedding cake she wanted to buy", the encounter with the "colonel-looking gentleman" on the tram, who shows that he is a gentleman even though "he has a drop taken", and flusters her with his polite civilities. The hints are all there; one would not want more. Once one sees what Maria really wants – though presumably she herself does not know how bitterly deep her yearning is – he is able to see how powerfully, if unostentatiously, the story makes its point.

Now let me take a few instances of the kind of problem that typically comes up in this story. What, for example, is the relation of Maria to Joe, in whose home she is visiting this evening? I'll read a short passage from the story:

> She would be there before eight. She took out her purse with the silver clasps and read again the words *A present from Belfast*. She

was very fond of that purse because Joe had brought it to her five years before when he and Alphy had gone to Belfast on a Whit-Monday trip. In the purse were two half-crowns and some coppers. She would have five shillings clear after paying tram fare. What a nice evening they would have, all the children singing! Only she hoped that Joe wouldn't come in drunk. He was different when he took any drink.

Often he had wanted her to go and live with them; but she would have felt herself in the way (though Joe's wife was ever so nice with her) and she had become accustomed to the life of the laundry. [Of course, as the story unfolds we are shown, quietly but convincingly, just how nice Joe's wife is with her, and how much actually was in this invitation for her to live with them.] Joe was a good fellow. She had nursed him and Alphy too; and Joe used often say: "Mama is Mama, but Maria is my proper mother. . . ."

And so on. What is the relationship? It seems to me that Maria is an older sister. Her mother had evidently died early and she has, perhaps at thirteen or fourteen, taken care of the younger brothers, Joe and Alphy, and now Joe obviously is not taking very good care of her. True, he and Alphy have got her this good job in the Dublin by Lamplight Laundry, and evidently he allows her to come to visit his home once in a while.

Maria is obviously not going to marry. She is not getting any younger. She has no home of her own. It may be that her getting the prayer-book in the Hallow Eve game, something that Joe's wife interprets as meaning that she will enter a convent before the year is out, has significance after all. Maria's entering a convent would certainly free Joe from the last vestiges of his shabbily maintained responsibility for her. But we need not speculate upon whether Joe and his wife have this actually in mind or whether Maria ever does enter a convent: the meaning of the story does not depend upon that in the least. Joyce is content to render for us Maria's situation in its essential pathos.

The pathos is kept pure, without a hint of sentimentality. Joyce has effected this in large part by refusing to allow Maria to feel sorry for herself. Indeed, there is no indication that Maria is aware of what has happened to her; but we, the readers, are aware – or ought to be if we have followed the story with sufficient care. Throughout the story we have been allowed to follow the play of Maria's mind as she moves from one event to another. The scenes through which she passes are shaped by her sensibility and described in her very words and phrases – "He was very nice with her, and when she was getting out at the Canal Bridge she thanked him, and bowed," "Maria had never seen Joe so nice to her as he was that night, so full of pleasant talk" – but the reader is allowed to see beyond what Maria sees. This is why at the end of the story Maria's singing of "I Dreamt that I Dwelt" in her "tiny quavering voice" registers with maximum impact. For her yearning for love as she sings the words of Balfe's romantic song is expressed nakedly though quite unconsciously. Maria makes no bid for our sympathy, and is unaware that she is a figure of pathos, but in the context that Joyce has established the final incident is one of intense pathos. Even beery old Joe was "very much moved . . . and his eyes filled up so much with tears that he could not find what he was looking for and in the end had to ask his wife to tell him where the corkscrew was".

With reference to my general argument, however, it must be conceded that Joyce's "Clay" is a very special case. It is richly and delicately organized. Its verbal texture approaches so nearly to the density of lyric poetry that the reading that it requires is more intense than that which is adequate for the staple of fictional prose. If I am to make a convincing case for a close reading of fiction, I ought to try to show its relevance to fiction of a less "poetic" kind. Would a novel like *Huckleberry Finn* profit from such a reading. We think of *Huckleberry Finn* as a big, episodic novel, full of exaggeration, full of melodramatic scenes of colourful violence. Does this novel have the requisite closeness of grain, the fineness of texture, the attention to the detail of the pattern that go with the arrangement of more subtle effects? I think that it does, but I hope that this answer is not obvious, for mine is something of an *a fortiori* argument. If I can make my case for such a reading of *Huckleberry Finn* I would hope that you would regard the argument proved for all those novels which in closeness of texture are on the hither side of *Huckleberry Finn*.

In emphasizing the richness and coherence of this book, as I shall do, I do not forget the fact that it is loose-jointed and even slap-dash. Incidentally, I think that one will do well to meet with perfect candour the student who is alert to, and troubled by, these issues. I find some of the coincidences preposterous, and certain episodes unconvincing. I doubt capitally that Huck Finn would dress himself up as a girl in order to spy out the land and get information, and granting that he would do so, it is difficult to think that when he became uneasy at the questioning he would do what he is made to tell us he does: 'I had to do something with my hands; so I took up a needle off of the table and went to threading it." A real-life Huck would not have done this and the author's motive in forcing his character to do so is transparent: Mark Twain is arranging matters so that Mrs Judith Loftus, with whom Huck is talking, will be able to score her point about women holding the needle still and poking the thread at it, whereas men hold the thread still and fetch the needle up to it.

Again, in indicating the possibilities of an intensive reading of *Huckleberry Finn*, I do not mean to slight more extensive treatments. Indeed, I must ask you to allow me to take a great deal for granted. For example, I assume that anyone teaching this novel will undertake to see that the class understands the larger elements of plot and the twin themes of Jim's search for freedom and Huck's moral development. Huck's moral development is, of course, something that is not sought after consciously by Huck. The boy, like Jim, is searching for freedom too, first and immediately from his father's drunken tyranny, and secondly from the constricting refinements of genteel society. How Huck's joining forces with the other fugitive, Jim, contributes to his moral development is obviously the matter of the book. I do not see how anyone could teach this novel without constant reference to it. But what I am going to say in this necessarily brief paper must take that emphasis for granted. Again, some of the larger problems that have to do with the plot must come into consideration of any teaching of *Huckleberry Finn*, but I can do no more than mention them here. For example, there is the function of the river in providing the constantly changing highway down which our two fugitives flee. There is the generally picaresque character of the action as our hero meets with charlatans and knaves, the good, the strong, and the pathetically weak. Again there is the melodramatic cast of the narrative with scenes of violent action and coincidence, some of them wildly improbable.

We may agree then that Huck's moral development is a central element of the book. The student must be brought to see it, but there are ways *and* ways of accomplishing this. If we do it clumsily the student will miss something very important in the book. Managing it ineptly, we may even distort the book. Let me illustrate. Mr Lionel Trilling in his attractive introduction to the Rinehart edition of *Huckleberry Finn* seems to me to risk just such a distortion. He refers to Huck and Jim on the raft as constituting a "community of saints". Now I think that I see what Mr Trilling means. Huck and Jim lack the kind of pride which distorts vision and dries up human sympathies. But it would certainly embarrass Huck to be thought a saint, and the student, on this point, is probably still closer to Huck Finn than he is to Lionel Trilling. The phrase "community of saints" will simply confuse the student. In any case, Huck's progress down the Mississippi on his raft is something more – and less – than a Pilgrim's Progress from the city of destruction to the heavenly city – even if we translate it into such terms as progress from the parochialism of the small slaveholding community to a wholehearted belief in the community of man. And even if Huck's voyage did in summary constitute such a progress, we would still have to vindicate it in detail. For it is the concrete detail of the story that renders it a work of art. It is this that brings us back to the book again and again as to something that is ultimately inexhaustible. No bare bones of a moral allegory protrude from this story. Such, then, would be one justification for the intensive reading of certain passages – to help the student to see in the very handling of the concrete detail of the story some of the specific workings out of the moral development that occurs in Huck.

But not only does Huck himself develop, as the novel goes on. He is the means through which the author's own moral judgements are mediated. For it is Huck who tells the story and it is what Huck says, and sometimes what Huck in his naïveté fails to say, that gives us the author's vision. The quality of Huck's vision is then all important. It is the matter which T. S. Eliot stresses in his introduction to the novel. He writes: "Huck has not imagination, in the sense in which Tom [Sawyer] has it: he has, instead, vision. He sees the real world; and he does not judge it – he allows it to judge itself."

Eliot's observation is central. From the quality of Huck's vision we can work outward to Huck's moral development. What Huck sees helps determine his moral development, and what he sees in turn measures that development for us. But the quality of Huck's vision also gives us our necessary point of reference for examining the sights and scenes and happenings that make up the novel; for, since Huck tells the story, his consciousness is its organizing principle. The way in which Huck sees, then, relates to both the formal properties of the novel and to the theme of moral development.

The quality of Huck's vision is central, but how shall we go about making the *student* see this? We cannot simply tell him about it. We shall have to suggest it to him concretely and dramatically. Something like an intensive reading seems to be in order. For only some such mode of reading can furnish the student with the concrete particulars that he will require.

This kind of examination can, of course, be applied to any part of the novel. But I shall limit myself to one section of the novel, that beginning with the Grangerford episode and ending with Huck's visit to the circus. It is a very rich section, giving us in addition, the arrival on the raft of the Duke of Bilgewater and the rightful King of France, the murder of Boggs, and the attempt to lynch Col. Sherburn. But I shall have time to discuss only a selection from the wealth of description and incident.

The Grangerfords, with their highfalutin manners, their special code of honour, and their interminable feud, are worked out in the broadest caricature. One knows something of Mark Twain's abiding hatred of violence and his unease with romantic pretensions, particularly those of the Southern gentleman.

Yet as *Huck* sees this family, they come to life immediately, the three big men with guns, the two young women with "quilts around them, and their hair down their backs", and "the sweetest old gray-headed lady" that Huck ever saw. We are convinced that Huck means what he says a little later: "I liked all that family, dead ones and all." The two young ladies singing "The Last Link is Broken" or playing "The Battle of Prague" on their little tin-pan piano; the young gentlemen turning from the sideboard, raising their glasses of bitters and bowing to their elders with "Our duty to you, sir, and madam"; the dead Emmeline's crayoned pictures with their lugubrious titles: "Shall I never see thee more alas" and – this time to a dead bird – "I shall never hear thy sweet chirrup more, alas" and, this time with the heroine clasping a black-bordered letter, "And art thou gone yes thou art gone alas" – all these details make the impossible Grangerfords come alive, though they must have been for Mark Twain a kind of horrible object lesson of the baleful influence of Sir Walter Scott upon the antebellum South. It is not that Huck makes allowances for them or sentimentalizes them: his gaze is in its innocence cleansing, but also fortifying. Poor Emmeline's pictures and poetry constitute incidentally the most devastating commentary upon Edgar Allan Poe ever written, for Emmeline is a very precocious young female Poe. Yet even Emmeline, as mediated through Huck's vision of her, manages to be something more than ridiculous. Perhaps Mark Twain here has outwitted himself. The Grangerfords, as Huck sees them, put on flesh and blood, persuade us of their reality, and even seduce us, along with Huck to acknowledge a certain charm in their quixotic mode of living. If their feud is absurd, it is horribly so, not preposterously so. For they are not content with romantic folderol. They shoot to kill. This deadly private war is evoked with immediacy and terror as Huck actually witnesses the death of the Grangerford boy and his cousin: "When I got down out of the tree I crept down along the river bank a piece, and found the two bodies laying in the edge of the water. . . . I cried a little when I was covering up Buck's face, for he was mighty good to me."

The horror and meaningless bloodshed and the sense of waste in the destruction of this household need no moralizing comment. It never occurs to Huck to make such a comment. But the presentation of the state of affairs through Huck's fascinated yet innocent eyes does something more. The Grangerfords have the virtues of their defects. They are ardent in their kindness and sympathy as well as in their feudalistic violence. It is noteworthy that the bourgeois refinements that irk Huck so much at the Widow Douglas's do not seem to trouble him at the Grangerfords. Perhaps the atmosphere of these homespun aristocrats is less constricting to Huck, the born vagabond.

A little later, after the bloody ending of the Grangerford episode, Huck is again on the raft and the two preposterous frauds, to be known as the duke and the king, have now come aboard. These charlatans are soon planning the first of their theatrical ventures. It is to be the balcony scene from *Romeo and Juliet*. Huck tells about it in this way: "So the duke he told him all about who Romeo was and who Juliet was, and said he was used to being Romeo, so the king could be Juliet." To the old man's objection that he can hardly be cast as a young girl, the duke answers airily that "these country jakes won't even think of that. Besides, you know, you'll be in costume and that makes all the difference in the world".

The cream of the jest, it seems to me, is that whether or not the country jakes will know the difference, *Romeo and Juliet* is not in the least remote from this valley of the great river: the situation that Shakespeare treats in his play has just materialized on the other bank. For what are the Grangerfords and the Shepherdsons if not the Capulets and the Montagues? Indeed, Huck himself has been involved in carrying the message from Miss Sophia, the Grangerford Juliet, to young Harney Shepherdson, the Kentucky Romeo. If Huck sees the connection he does not say anything about it. And perhaps the duke in telling "him all about who Romeo was" gave Huck a drastically foreshortened account. But whether Huck realizes that the absurdly remote Shakespearian story to be enacted for the edification of the one-horse Arkansas town bears upon the tragic story which he has just witnessed, the student ought to realize it. For this is simply one of many similar counterpointings. The story-book romance of Thomas Sawyer's boyish fantasies or of Emmeline Grangerford's lugubrious poems or of the duke and king's tatterdemalion theatricals is constantly being put to shame by the actuality that Huck encounters almost daily.

Toward story-book romances, Huck is diligently receptive. Here he trudges dutifully after Tom Sawyer's instruction. Huck tries to instruct Jim in the ways of kings and chivalry, from King Solomon to the "Saxon heptarchies" and after. But it never occurs to Huck to consider as *romantic* the scenes of danger, excitement and death that he actually encounters.

The teasing mixture of good and bad which makes up the world – the confusion of qualities in the concretion of reality – these are things which are rendered for us through Huck's vision in the Grangerford episode. They are rendered perhaps even more vividly in the events which Huck reports in the chapter entitled "An Arkansaw Difficulty". The two charlatans who have now come aboard the raft plan to put on their performance of a Shakespeare revival at a little river town which is, in Huck's words, "pretty well down the state of Arkansaw". Huck goes strolling around the town which is mostly "old, shackly, dried-up frame concerns that hadn't ever been painted" and listens to the village loafers, when to their jubilation old Boggs, the drunkard comes in "for his little old monthly drunk". The villagers assure Huck that Boggs is harmless, though Boggs rides in with the proper vaunt and threat in the best river tradition. We have already heard it from the buckskin-coated raftsmen to whose craft Huck had swum out in an earlier chapter. Boggs declares that he is on the warpath, and promises that the price of coffins is going to rise. He even challenges Huck, riding up to him with the questions "Whar'd you come f'm, boy? You prepared to die?" Huck is scared even though someone assures him that Boggs is really "the best natured old fool in Arkansaw", but Huck is not so scared that he does not take in clearly the events that follow. Boggs in his drunken fury blackguards Col. Sherburn, a proud looking man of about fifty-five, until Sherburn, at the end of his patience, quietly tells Boggs that he will shoot him if he is still in town by one o'clock. There follows, you will remember, Boggs's persistence in his cursing, the decision to call his daughter who can sometimes calm him, Boggs's own dawning fear as one o'clock nears and he begins to sober, and finally the implacable Colonel's stepping out with his pistol, bringing the barrel "down slow and steady to a level" and firing.

At least up until this point one's sympathy has to be with Sherburn. Boggs is a nuisance and worse. He reflects morally the squalor of the town already rendered physically so powerfully in Huck's description of the slovenly houses and muddy streets and rooting pigs. Boggs epitomizes at the least the bad manners of the back country, with its noisy boasting and its cowardly bullying.

But Colonel Sherburn's cool deliberation, his keeping his word so meticulously, his shooting to kill, swing out sympathies the other way. Whether or not they swing Huck's also, Huck does not say. Again, he simply renders to us vividly what happens: ". . . they tore open his shirt first, and I seen where one of the bullets went in. He made about a dozen long gasps, his breast lifting the Bible up" – someone had placed a Bible on his breast – "and letting it down again when he breathed it out – and after that he laid still; he was dead. Then they pulled his daughter away from him, screaming and crying, and took her off. She was about sixteen, and very sweet and gentle looking, but awful pale and scared."

This is superb as reporting; it is so superb as to render commentary superfluous. Dramatically, of course, it is right that it never occurs to Huck to make any commentary here. He is sufficiently caught up in the excitement that he simply goes on telling us what happened next and then next. Somebody remarks that Sherburn ought to be lynched for what he has done and in a moment Huck is part of a yelling mob that snatches down "every clothes-line they come to to do the hanging with". The mob makes its way, with the boy Huck swept along by it, to the fence that surrounds Sherburn's yard.

"Just then Sherburn steps out onto the roof of his little front porch, with a double-barrel gun in his hand, and takes his stand perfectly calm and deliberate, not saying a word. The racket stopped and the wave sucked back." Then Sherburn stares them down, overawing them in a stillness that becomes, as Huck calls it, "awful creepy and uncomfortable". And Sherburn finally proceeds to taunt them with their cowardice, pointing out the absurdity of "*you* lynching anybody". And after a further tongue lashing in which he points out that "the pitifulest thing out is a mob", he actually orders them to leave, and they do. Huck remarks, and presumably here he speaks for the others in the crowd, "I could 'a' stayed if I wanted to but I didn't want to."

Our sympathies surely this time are with Col. Sherburn. He is a brave man, the mob is poor-spirited and contemptible. Yet the Colonel is the same man who a few minutes earlier had shot down a man in cold blood and he is now armed with a double-barrelled shot-gun, rather than with a pistol, presumably because, after shooting Boggs, he had contemptuously "tossed his pistol onto the ground", before he turned on his heel and walked off.

It is a complicated world that Huck sees as he drifts down the river. Huck is the apparently simple observer, but he does not simplify what he sees. He renders it in its full moral complexity. If the student can be brought to see this fact, he will be far on the way to an understanding of Huck's character, of his importance as the focus of narration, and of many other things necessary to an appreciation of the novel.

Huck could have stayed and faced out Col. Sherburn if he had wanted to, but like the others in the crowd about him he didn't want to. Indeed, for a moment, Huck is emotionally a part of the mob – at least to the extent that he shares the fear and abashment that the members of the mob feel as they look into Col. Sherburn's cold glinting eyes. Huck is not in the least self-conscious about this or inhibited by a false pride. He simply puts himself in the mobster's place. But Huck does not let the murder and the collapse of the lynching bee prey upon his spirits. His next sentence indicates that when he decided not to want to stay around Col. Sherburn's, he went off to the circus. He slips under the tent, and since it is a "real bully circus", he soon loses himself in that experience.

This is the scene, you will remember, in which Huck, in his innocence, is completely taken in by the bareback performer who pretends to be a drunken townsman. The obstreperous drunken man insists upon riding the circus horse, cannot be persuaded to go away quietly, is finally allowed to ride, and after precariously hanging on to the horse for a hair-raising first few minutes, suddenly stands upright, throws off his tousled clothes, and reveals himself in all the glory of circus spangles. Huck lives through every moment of this with changing feelings. When the apparently drunken man tries to cling to the rearing horse, Huck says "it warn't funny to me, though; I was all of a tremble to see his danger". And later, when the rider reveals himself in his gaudy professional costume, Huck feels very sheepish to "be took in so" and commiserates with the ring master, now "the sickest ringmaster you ever see". But Huck is not quite so naïve as at first glance may appear. The figure of the drunken man carries for Huck a heavy emotional charge. There is the vivid scene, earlier in the novel, in which Huck's father, when insanely drunk, tries to kill him. A little earlier on this very day, he has seen the fire-eating Boggs, whose fury turns out to be only Dutch courage, reduced suddenly from the heel-clacking half-alligator, half-horse desperado, to the wheezing man dying with a bullet in his chest. And so now this apparently drunken man whose neck is in imminent danger of being broken, finds in Huck a most sympathetic observer.

In the section of the novel about which I have been talking, Huck moves steadily through a world of violence. It is a world in which there are human beings who are either brave men, like Col. Sherburn, or "the best-natured old fool" you ever saw, like Boggs, or perhaps they are what Col. Grangerford might be said to be: both at the same time. These men are killing or being killed and they are doing so because they are drunk with some conception of pride or honour or are indeed quite literally drunk, in addition, with corn whiskey. This world is terrifying because, most of all, these men are not without virtue. Indeed they are most of them in some sense "good" men. Even

Boggs is evidently a weak and foolish man rather than an evil man.

It is a world of violence, then; it is also a world in which things are not what they seem. Everyone has noticed how wary of human beings Huck is. He approaches every stranger cautiously. He rarely tells him the truth about himself. One motive for his caution is the protection of Jim, but the wariness is also part of his character. Our realization of the unpredictable nature of the world in which Huck lives and of its almost casual violence can help account for this. It is a world of boasters and charlatans and liars, and two of the most notable of them are Huck's own companions on the raft.

Through these episodes that I have been discussing, Huck's role has been primarily that of the detached spectator. Even at the Grangerfords, Huck has been guest and stranger. It is a point of honor for the Grangerfords that they should not involve Huck in their blood feud. And though when Huck hears that Buck has left for the fighting, he sets out to find him, it does not occur to him to bring his own gun. Instead, he says: "I clumb up into the forks of a cottonwood . . . and watched." Indeed, one can say that throughout this whole novel. Huckleberry Finn avoids involvement as much as he can. He has a zest for life, but he is perfectly willing to indulge it in merely *observing* life. Even his commitment to Jim is one which he tries more than once to repudiate until the claims of humanity make it impossible for him to betray Jim. If we realize how deep-rooted is Huck's instinct to avoid all such commitments we shall feel an enhanced respect for his moral triumph over himself. It is just because he is uninvolved and uncorrupted that he can be the excellent observer that he is.

But the quality of Huck's vision, I must repeat, is something that cannot be taken for granted. The student must grasp it imaginatively – must participate in it rather than simply be told about it. I see no way to accomplish this except by having him consider the concrete particulars of Huck's experience. Something like an intensive reading is necessary though it need not deal with the episodes from which I have taken my examples. Other passages would do as well. But whatever the passages, the student must come to see what Eliot means in the comment that I have quoted earlier: "[Huck] sees the real world; and he does not judge it – he allows it to judge itself."

Huck's characteristic role of spectator determines the nature and process of his moral growth. Huck begins by holding the Abolitionists in horror, and, a matter that has usually escaped observation, Huck *ends* as he began. Huck, far from feeling a moral shock at Tom's behaviour in reference to the freeing of Jim, seems almost relieved to find that Tom is not an Abolitionist. As Huck puts it: "I couldn't ever understand before, until that minute and that talk, how he *could* help a body set a nigger free with his bringing-up." Huck's own resolve to help the slave Jim escape comes as the result of *concrete* judgements and experiences. His enlarging sympathies are precisely that. It is the concrete experiences that shift Huck's ideas, not the power of an idea which changes his sentiments. This again is what we should expect in a world in which the relationships are all highly personal and concrete, in which the Mr Phelps who is holding Jim in confinement as a run-away slave, comes in to Jim every morning to read the Bible with him and pray with him. Huck's actions and attitudes constitute a mute but penetrating criticism of the ideas and customs of the society about him. But they are the criticism of the detached and un-committed observer. The child was not taken in by the emperor's new clothes. He saw and said that the emperor was naked. This is the quality of Huck's innocent gaze. Huck hangs loose on the fringes of society: he is no reformer.

Huck is then not the doctrinaire Abolitionist. He would scarcely qualify even as a devoted believer in "democracy" if one uses the term in the large and quasi-religious sense in which we tend to use it today. Huck likes individual human beings. He has a powerful dramatic sympathy. He easily pro-jects himself into the plight of others. He can feel pity for even those scoundrels, the duke and the king, as he sees them clad in their tar and feathers, being ridden out of town on a rail. But Huck is tough-minded rather than tender-minded; he has few illusions about man's capacity for depravity. In the chapter appropriately entitled "The Orneriness of Kings", Huck assures the sceptical Jim that the two specimens of royalty on the raft are not too bad: "I don't say that ourn is lambs, because they ain't when you come right down to the cold facts; but they ain't nothing to *that* old ram [Henry VIII], anyway. All I say is, kings is kings, and you got to make allowances. Take them all around, they're a mighty ornery lot." For Huck the spectacle of human history is almost as bleak as it was for his creator, Mark Twain himself.

But I do not mean to suggest that there is bitterness in Huck or despair. That would be to miss the point entirely. The qualities that I would stress in Huck are those of the born artist. Huck's interest in human beings, his dramatic sympathy, his concern for the concrete and the particular – these are the interests and powers of the artist. They accord well with the features of Huck's character that we have already observed: his lack of commitment, his detachment, his willingness to be pure observer, his resistance to the pressures exerted by society – in short, his uncorrupted perceptivity. Small wonder that Huck Finn embodies the finest imaginative qualities of his creator. Indeed, Huck as an artistic intelligence actually surpasses his creator, for some of the traits of Samuel Clemens get in the way of the artist – his bitterness, his rage against man's follies, his verbosity, his preconceptions and prejudices concerning science, religion, and politics.

Is the argument advanced here too fine-spun to present to the student? Perhaps it is. Yet it is almost worth venturing, and with some classes the teacher will be forced to venture it. For a class that is led to reflect upon the artistry of the novel at all soon comes upon this problem: in this book the author is deliberately limiting himself to the perceptions and intelligence and language of an almost illiterate boy. The author, to be sure, gains thereby a certain verisimilitude, a certain flavour of reality; but can these advantages outweigh the apparent losses – particularly in view of the fact that authors do constantly succeed in tales that they tell in their own persons? How then can limitation be a source of positive gain?

I should suggest that we answer by asking the student to think of Huck as a lens – a lens that organizes the picture, giving it a certain depth and focus. And if the student were to protest that this analogy was unfair since a lens is a complex and complicating thing, then I should suggest another analogy, that of the snow glasses made by such primitive men as the Eskimos. These snow glasses – a shield of bone pierced by a tiny slit – are apparently sheer limitation. (The student can test the principle by pushing a pin through a bit of cardboard and see for himself how this primitive lens works.) Through the Eskimo's snow glasses, the eye is forced to peer out at the world through a tiny aperture, but the glare is shut out, and the Eskimo hunter sees as he could not otherwise. Mark Twain, forcing himself to see the world through the sensibility of Huck Finn has apparently seriously limited his view, but the shimmering light of a hundred subjective impressions – abstractions, generalizations, and prejudgings – is cut out, and he sees the world with an almost pristine freshness and with a terrible acuteness. It is that kind of vision that this book accords us.

10

American Literature: Mirror, Lens or Prism?

Literature may tell the truth about a culture, but if so, it tells the truth in varied ways and usually in very special ways. If one thinks that literature necessarily provides a faithful photograph of a culture, he misses the point completely. Realistic photographs there are, to be sure, and one can learn a great deal from its literature about even the detailed daily life of a culture, but anyone so rash as to believe that literature presents a literally faithful account is deluded. Even a writer like James Joyce, who in his *Ulysses* gives us so much of the detail of Dublin in the first years of the twentieth century, and who embedded in that book actual names and incidents that are quite factually correct – the delight of the American graduate student who by checking the Dublin newspapers of the day has proved them to be so – even Joyce in his *Ulysses* has not provided a carefully lighted and proportioned reflection of the details of a typical Dublin day in 1904. If the book is a mirror at all, it is, in its selection, distortion, and overemphasis, much more nearly like one of those mirrors in an American fun-house, and in some respects not like a mirror at all – more like a prism which breaks up the beam of ordinary daylight into a spectrum of rainbow colours.

Literature contains truth, some of it the most profound truth that we know about human beings, but one must know how to read a literary document and how to assess the relation of literal detail to symbolic enlargement and distortion. The magnification achieved through various kinds of lenses, the special focusings and intensifications – properly controlled by a great artist – these may be the appropriate means for showing us what we are. Even when the artist does use a mirror rather than a lens, it is rarely a simple one of the sort that faithfully gives back an undistorted reflection. The writer of comedy, the artist who devises witty caricatures, the social satirist – all make use of mirrors that exaggerate and thereby not only amuse us but often reveal to us what otherwise we should probably not see.

One can learn a great deal about the quality and character of American life through reading American literature. At its very best, it is a great literature, and to say so is to say that it is searchingly profound, it is deeply truthful, and it is certainly not superficially flattering. But one is constantly appalled to be reminded of how people misread and misuse literature by confounding the symbolic with the realistic and by generalizing the exceptional case into a kind of national average. During my two years in Great Britain, reading the reviews of books by Americans and on America, I have been amused and almost as often shocked to see what kind of picture of America emerges from some of these works. (If we reverse the terms, I agree that we get equally ludicrous or appalling results: America will come off no worse than Britain if we read British literature in this fashion.)

What is needed at this point, however, is some illustrative material. How shall I vindicate what I have been saying about the reflection of America in its literature? I shall need concrete examples, and from one fairly narrow segment of the American scene. America covers a lot of ground – specifically the better part of a large continent.

Perhaps I would do well to confine my examples to one region and even to one social class – say, the middle-Western business man or the Eastern suburbanite or the New England villager. I shall in fact talk about the Southern poor white.

I have several reasons for choosing him. A voluminous literature has grown up around him. He has, of late, been much in the headlines, in the British as well as the American newspapers. His is a hard case – that is, this audience may well feel that his image has suffered no real distortion and that he may be fairly dismissed as the bigoted, racist "red-neck" that he is reputed to be. But there is a good deal to be said for deliberately choosing the hard case and framing with it an *a fortiori* argument; for if one can prove the argument for the hard case, then the argument is proved for all the easier ones.

"Southern poor white" can mean rather contradictory things. In the fiction of Erskine Caldwell the Southern poor white tends to be a rather happy-go-lucky creature who carries on his sex life with gusto. For years Mr Caldwell, in increasingly tired prose, has depicted the tireless sexual activities of his characters. James Baldwin's poor whites, on the other hand, lack sexual vitality: their lives are arid. They don't know how to enjoy love or even how to enjoy food. Incidentally, the very speeches that Baldwin, in his play *Blues for Mr Charlie*, puts into the mouths of his white characters betray their bookish unreality. They don't even talk like poor whites.

Baldwin's play is not properly a mirror at all but a lens, a lens set up to focus burning indignation on a particular issue – not to illuminate human beings but to set something on fire. In "Dry September" Faulkner is treating a related issue – and his basic 'moral' is essentially the same as that in Baldwin's play – but Faulkner is also telling us how people can come to do what his characters do. His ability to render their habits of speech accurately, if in itself not very important, is a symptom of something that is very important: his accurate portrayal of their attitudes and values.

But though Faulkner has given us some of the most penetrating indictments of the mind of the Southern racist, Faulkner knows that his poor whites, because he knows them as real human beings, have interests and concerns that have nothing to do with race. So also with his fellow Mississippian, Eudora Welty. Let me illustrate.

One of Miss Welty's stories, "A Piece of News", has to do with a trivial incident in the lives of a poor-white couple. The husband, Clyde Fisher, makes moonshine whisky at his illicit still, and occasionally cuffs his wife Ruby when he discovers – as at least once or twice he has – her adventures with travelling salesmen. The Fishers are plainly a pair no better than they should be: not respectable, not very moral, and – a matter that is of significance for the plot of Miss Welty's story – not completely literate. But theirs is a story worth the telling – at least

Miss Welty has thought it worth the telling – and if the reader decides that she is right, then the essential humanity of this pair and their relevance to other human beings has been established. The stories of monsters and robots, the pointer-readings of non-human machines or the case histories of the clinically insane are another matter. "A Piece of News" is not quite an ordinary mirror, but it is one that will reflect our own human faces when we look into it.

Miss Welty's story is short, and it may appear to be slight. It happens on a rainy day. Ruby Fisher has come into her house, wetted by the rain and therefore a little cross. She has brought back with her a bag of coffee which she had wrapped up in a sheet of newspaper. Now she warms and dries herself before the fireplace in her cabin and awaits her husband's return.

> As she sprawled close to the fire, her hair began to slide out of its damp tangles and hung all displayed down her back like a piece of bargain silk. She closed her eyes . . . at moments when the fire stirred and tumbled in the grate, she would tremble, and her hand would start out as if in impatience or despair.

Presently, roused out of her reverie, Ruby looks at the newspaper and then is suddenly made tense and excited by something in the newsprint that catches her eye:

> 'Ruby Fisher!' she whispered.
> An expression of utter timidity came over her flat blue eyes and her soft mouth. Then a look of fright. She stared about . . . What eye in the world did she feel looking in on her? She pulled her dress down tightly and began to spell through a dozen words in the newspaper.
> The little item said:
> 'Mrs Ruby Fisher had the misfortune to be shot in the leg by her husband this week.'
> As she passed from one word to the next she only whispered; she left the long word, 'misfortune', until the last, and came back to it, then she said it all over out loud, like conversation.
> 'That's me,' she said softly, with deference, very formally.

With primitive people, the printed word carries special potency. For them *grammar* is still *glamour* – I am told that the words are cognate – and to have achieved a place in the newspaper – a hundred million literate Americans, I assure you, yearn to see their names there – has for this primitive woman the urgency of truth. First, she screams out at her absent husband who has done the fell deed:

> "You Clyde!" screamed Ruby Fisher at last, jumping to her feet. "Where are you, Clyde Fisher?"

Then her anger "passed like a remote flare of elation", and her mood changes. Common sense reasserts itself. Her husband had sometimes struck her, but shooting goes beyond anything he has ever done heretofore. 'Clyde had never shot her, even once. There had been a mistake made.' But the suggestion that he might have done so – now given the almost magical authority of the printed word – stirs her imagination. She drifts into reveries about what it would be like.

> Ruby began to cry softly, the way she would be crying from the extremity of pain; tears would run down in a little stream over the quilt. Clyde would be standing there above her, as he once looked, with his wild black hair hanging to his shoulders. He used to be very handsome and strong!
> He would say, "Ruby, I done this to you."
> She would say – only a whisper – 'That is the truth, Clyde – you done this to me.'

The reveries are interrupted by the arrival of Clyde.

> Then Clyde was standing there, with dark streams flowing over the floor where he had walked. He poked at Ruby with the butt of his gun, as if she were asleep.
> "What's keepin' supper?" he growled.

Ruby doesn't at once tell her husband about the newspaper story. She hugs her secret to herself as she prepares his supper and moves about the room.

> Once . . . she saw Clyde looking at her and she smiled and bent her head tenderly. There was some way she began to move her arms that was mysteriously sweet and yet abrupt and tentative, a delicate and vulnerable manner, as though her breasts gave her pain. She made unnecessary trips back and forth across the floor, circling Clyde where he sat in his steamy silence, a knife and fork in his fists.

She is somehow filled with a mysterious happiness. When she spills a drop of hot coffee on Clyde's wrist and he says "Some day I'm going to smack the livin' devil outa you," she dodges mechanically, but her feeling of delight is not affected, and when he has finished with his food,

> she brought him the newspaper. Again she looked at him in delight. It excited her even to touch the paper with her hand, to hear its quiet secret noise when she carried it, the rustle of surprise.

Her anticipation is not disappointed: even Clyde is jarred by what he sees. "It's a lie," he protests. But Ruby does not lack for a rejoinder.

> "That's what's in the newspaper about me," said Ruby, standing up straight. She took his plate and gave him that look of joy.

Common sense is for the moment almost helpless, as Clyde clumsily threshes about with such appeals to reason as "Well, I'd just like to see the place I shot you!"

> But she drew herself in, still holding the empty plate, faced him straightened and hard, and they looked at each other. The moment filled full with their helplessness. Slowly they both flushed, as though with a double shame and a double pleasure. It was as though Clyde might really have killed Ruby, and as though Ruby might really have been dead at his hand. Rare and wavering, some possibility stood timidly like a stranger between them and made them hang their heads.

Then, Clyde finds the effective answer – effective because it is part of the document itself and carries the full authority of the printed word. "Look . . . It's a Tennessee paper." And when his wife cries out passionately that "It was Ruby Fisher! My name is Ruby Fisher," Clyde, his equanimity restored, says:

> 'Oho, it was another Ruby Fisher – in Tennessee . . . Fool me, huh? Where'd you get that paper?' He spanked her good-humoredly across her backside.
> Ruby folded her still trembling hands into her skirt. She stood stooping by the window until everything, outside and in, was quietened before she went to her supper.

And the story closes with a brief reference to the darkness outside and to the last rumblings of the storm that had poured rain on Ruby, now rolling "away to faintness like a wagon crossing a bridge".

The incident, I repeat, is trivial, and if newspapers were as familiar to Ruby Fisher as they are to the inhabitants of New York or London or Leicester, the appearance of her own name in print would doubtless not have made its special impact on this almost illiterate young woman. But that is not quite the point. The point, I take it, is that Ruby's imagination is stirred – and even Clyde's – and that the pair are made to see each other in a new light, and that their whole relationship is renewed by being thrown into fresh perspective. What seems of special importance is that, for all their lack of respectability and the thinness of their book learning, they have imaginations to be quickened and emotions with which to respond, and thus turn out to be people like you and me, the readers of the story, provided, that is, that we as readers possess the imagination required to make out what Miss Welty is doing with the story.

Is this story, then, a mirror? Perhaps, but then it is a rather special mirror. The United States census reports will provide more accurate statistics on the degree of illiteracy, and other government records will doubtless provide better evidence for the number of gallons of whisky made in illicit stills. What "A Piece of News" can reveal is something about the human heart, and that Mississippi poor whites, even those who move their lips when they read the newspaper, may possess such hearts.

If Miss Welty's story does reflect light and thus images things for us, it also has some of the qualities of a prism: it breaks up the light of common day and shows us some of the rich colours of which it is really composed.

Another Mississippi author, in the instance that I now mean to cite, pictures for us a poor white of a very different kind. His name is V. K. Ratliff, and he constitutes one of William Faulkner's most notable creations. He figures prominently in four of Faulkner's novels and in several of his short stories. Ratliff is of yeoman stock. He is a shrewd trader, and enjoys making a good bargain, but he is rigorously honest. Ratliff likes a story; he is himself a redoubtable story-teller, and in his anecdotes and fabliaux he draws fully upon the tall-tale tradition of the old Southwest – the American states between the Appalachian Mountains and the Ohio and Mississippi Rivers.

One of Ratliff's sworn enemies is Flem Snopes, a poor white who preys upon his fellows. Flem is the usurer, the man who squeezes his debtors without mercy, and who, though he is careful to keep within the law, subordinates everything to his cold lust for money.

Ratliff suggests that Flem's impressive financial success comes from his having made a compact with the devil, something like the usual Faustian arrangement, but Ratliff gives the story a special twist. Flem has not sold his soul outright, but has floated a loan from the Prince of Darkness, depositing his soul as collateral. Now he has come down to Hell to settle up, but the collateral has vanished, and the junior officers of the infernal establishment can't find it.

> . . . at last, baffled, they come to the Prince his self.
> "Sire," they says. "He just wont. We cant do nothing with him."
> "What?" the Prince hollers.
> "He says a bargain is a bargain. That he swapped in good faith and honor, and now he has come to redeem it, like the law says. And we cant find it,' they says. 'We done looked everywhere. It wasn't no big one to begin with nohow, and we was specially careful in handling it. We sealed it up in an asbestos matchbox and put the box in a separate compartment to itself. But when we opened the compartment, it was gone. The matchbox was there and the seal wasn't broke. But there wasn't nothing in the matchbox but a little kind of dried-up smear under one edge. And now he has come to redeem it. But how can we redeem him into eternal torment without his soul?"
> "Damn it," the Prince hollers. "Give him one of the extra ones. Aint there souls turning up here everyday, banging at the door and raising all kinds of hell to get in here, even bringing letters from Congressmen, that we never even heard of? Give him one of them."
> "We tried that," they says. "He wont do it. He says he dont want no more and no less than his legal interest according to what

the banking and the civil law states in black and white is hisn. He says he has come prepared to meet his bargain and signature, and he sholy expects you of all folks to meet yourn."

"Tell him he can go then. Tell him he had the wrong address. That there aint nothing on the books here against him. Tell him his note was lost – if there ever was one. Tell him we had a flood, even a freeze."

"He wont go, not without his –"

"Turn him out. Eject him."

"How?" they says. "He's got the law."

Finally, the Prince consents to see Flem.

So they brought him in and went away and closed the door. His clothes was still smoking a little, though soon he had done brushed most of it off. He come up to the Throne, chewing, toting the straw suitcase.

"Well?" the Prince says.

He turned his head and spit, the spit frying off the floor quick in a little blue ball of smoke. "I come about that soul," he says.

"So they tell me," the Prince says. "But you have no soul."

"Is that my fault?" he says.

"Is it mine?" the Prince says. "Do you think I created you?"

"Then who did?" he says. And he had the Prince there and the Prince knowed it.

Time does not allow me to finish the story. In any case, the way in which it will end has already been implied. The Devil himself is no match for Flem's cold legalism. Abstract lust conquers the Devil's own less pure love of the world and of the flesh. The human being who cares only for money is less human than the devil of Christian tradition. Ratliff is too skilful a story-teller to spell this out for his listeners: he simply ends his story with Flem sitting on the throne of Hell and a terrified devil "scrabbling across the floor, clawing and scrabbling at that locked door, screaming . . ."

What does this fantastic episode mirror? Well, in the first place one notes that we have here a double mirror. Ratliff himself is holding the mirror up to Flem – obviously a kind of distortion mirror. For the reflection it presents to us is of something grotesque and fabulous: one that cannot be taken literally. But Ratliff's satiric tall tale about Flem also constitutes a reflection of Ratliff: the character of Ratliff's humour, of his gusto for life, of his basic set of human values. In coming to a judgement on the poor white, the fiction of William Faulkner – provided we know how to read it and what to make of it – can be of a great deal of value.

I am happy, by the way, to exhibit Faulkner in this comic vein. He is a great humourist, and yet this is a side of him that too few readers know. Indeed, the "Gothic" Faulkner, the writer of decadence, of horror for horror's sake, of nameless depravities, has been advertised all too well – to the neglect of his comedy and to the distortion of his tragedies – which are essentially not 'Gothic' at all.

It is amusing to observe that Robert Frost, that stalwart and wholesome New Englander, the smiling Yankee sage, turns out to have his 'Gothic' side too – provided of course that the reader is eager to convict *him* of Gothicism. For example, Frost's "Witch of Coös" tells the story of an old woman, living with her middle-aged son, on a remote mountain farm in one of the New England states. Their house contains more than a skeleton in the cupboard; there is a literal skeleton in the attic, the bones of the woman's lover who was killed by her husband and buried in the cellar. This story of infidelity and murder gradually comes out in their talk with a wayfarer who, overtaken by night, has asked for shelter.

The story, then, has all the accoutrements of the Gothic tale of horror. The old woman is not called a witch for nothing. She can call up spirits. Her son proudly tells the stranger:

> Mother can make a common table rear
> And kick with two legs like an army mule.

And the real excitement of the poem has to do with what might be called a most circumstantial ghost story. Years before, while the husband was still alive, the skeleton buried in the cellar decided to come upstairs. The son tells how

> It left the cellar forty years ago
> And carried itself like a pile of dishes
> Up one flight from the cellar to the kitchen,
> Another from the kitchen to the bedroom,
> Another from the bedroom to the attic . . .

The mother had heard it begin its ascent:

> And then someone
> Began the stairs, two footsteps for each step,
> The way a man with one leg and a crutch,
> Or a little child, comes up.

Then she suddenly realizes that it must be the bones:

> My first impulse was to get to the knob
> And hold the door. But the bones didn't try
> The door; they halted helpless on the landing,
> Waiting for things to happen in their favor.
> The faintest restless rustling ran all through them.
> I never could have done the thing I did
> If the wish hadn't been too strong in me
> To see how they were mounted for this walk.
> I had a vision of them put together
> Not like a man, but like a chandelier.
> So suddenly I flung the door wide on him.
> A moment he stood balancing with emotion,
> And all but lost himself. (A tongue of fire
> Flashed out and licked along his upper teeth.
> Smoke rolled inside the sockets of his eyes.)
> Then he came at me with one hand outstretched,
> The way he did in life once; but this time
> I struck the hand off brittle on the floor,
> And fell back from him on the floor myself.
> The finger-pieces slid in all directions.
> (Where did I see one of the pieces lately?
> Hand me my button box – it must be there.)
> I sat up on the floor and shouted, 'Toffile,
> It's coming up to you.' It had its choice
> Of the door to the cellar or the hall.
> It took the hall door for the novelty. . . .

It took the hall door, and the woman, with the help of her now awakened husband, manoeuvres the skeleton into taking the stairway that leads to the attic, and once he is in, they nail the attic door shut. It's a solution: true, they have lost the use of the attic, but the old woman is philosophical about it:

> The attic was less to us than the cellar.
> If the bones liked the attic, let them have it.

At the end of the story, the old woman, though she has emptied her button-box onto her lap, still "hadn't found the finger-bone she wanted".

The gusto with which the story is told, the folk quality, the use of the ordinary to give conviction to the wildly fantastic, may remind you at points of the passage that I read from Faulkner, and, in any case, it may prompt your retort that this isn't morbid Gothicism at all. To which I would cheerfully agree. Frost is not a Gothic author, but then neither is Faulkner in the sense too commonly urged.

As a matter of fact, Frost's country people, living in the villages or on the small farms of New England, resemble in many ways Faulkner's country people of north Mississippi. Why should they not? Both peoples are basically of Anglo-Saxon stock, are still close to the land, and are conservative in their manners and their beliefs. This matter was brought home to me on a summer afternoon in 1963 when I was strolling through an old Vermont graveyard in the mountains. Here are some of the feminine names I copied from the gravestones: Roxey, Adalineh, Dellie, Achsah, Lucina, Almira, and Tryphena. They are very much like the names that Faulkner bestowed on characters like Dewey Dell, Vynie, Eula, Zilphia, and Drusilla.

My reference to Frost and his rural New England has been a digression – though I hope one that is justified. Let me now return to the Southern poor white with a poem by Robert Penn Warren. The poem bears the rather whimsical title "School Lesson Based on Word of Tragic Death of Entire Gillum Family".

> They weren't so bright, or clean, or clever,
>   And their noses were sometimes imperfectly blown,
> But they always got to school the weather whatever,
>   With old lard pail full of fried pie, smoked ham, and corn pone.
>
> Tow hair was thick as a corn-shuck mat.
>   They had milky blue eyes in matching pairs.
> And barefoot or brogan, when they sat,
>   Their toes were the kind that hook round the legs of chairs.

They had adenoids to make you choke,
    And buttermilk breath, and their flannels asteam,
And sat right mannerly while teacher spoke,
    But when book-time came their eyes were glazed and adream.

There was Dollie-May, Susie-May, Forrest, Sam, Brother –
    Thirteen down to eight the stairsteps ran.
They had popped right natural from their fat mother,
    The clabber kind that can catch just by honing after a man.

In town, Gillum stopped you, he'd say: 'Say, mister,
    I'll name you what's true fer folks, ever-one.
Human-man ain't much more'n a big blood blister,
    All red and proud-swole, but one good squeeze and he's gone'.

Old Slat Gillum admitted that he didn't amount to much –
"Take me, ain't wuth lead and powder to perish" –
but he meant to see that his children got their chance.

So mud to the hub, or dust to the hock,
    God his helper, wet or dry,
Old Gillum swore by God and by cock,
    He'd git 'em larned before his own time came to die.

But one morning he didn't get them to the schoolhouse.

That morning blew up cold and wet,
    All the red-clay road was curled as curd,
And no Gillums there for the first time yet.
    The morning drones on. Stove spits. Recess. Then the word.

Dollie-May was combing Susie-May's head.
    Sam was feeding. Forrest milking, got nigh through.
Little Brother just sat on the edge of his bed.
    Somebody must have said: "Pappy, what now you aimin' to
                                [do?"

An ice pick is a subtle thing.
    The puncture's small, blood only a wisp.
It hurts no more than a bad bee sting.
    When the sheriff got there the school-bread was long burned
                                [to a crisp.

In the afternoon silence the chalk would scrape.
    We sat and watched the windowpanes steam,
Blur the old corn field and accustomed landscape.
    Voices came now faint in our intellectual dream.

Which shoe – yes, which – was Brother putting on?
    That was something, it seemed, you just had to know.
But nobody knew, all afternoon,
    Though we studied and studied, as hard as we could, to know,

Studying the arithmetic of losses,
    To be prepared when the next one,
By fire, flood, foe, cancer, thrombosis,
    Or Time's slow malediction, came to be undone.

We studied all afternoon, till getting on to sun.
There would be another lesson, but we were too young to take up that one.

Whether some such event was actually experienced by Warren in childhood – whether word was one day brought in to the school that a poor-white farmer had gone berserk and killed his five children, his wife, and himself. I do not know. But the shock, to a child, on hearing of sudden, meaningless, violent death encompassing people that he knew at first hand – this experience is rendered very powerfully in the poem.

This account of the Gillums, for all of its tenderness for the simple-minded and deprived human being, refuses to gloss over the uncouth facts of matted hair and illiterate speech. Indeed, it strives to win the reader to the unsentimental compassion that comes only when one has accepted the not very pretty facts. Moreover, the poet refuses to curb his sense of humour as he describes the family – Old Gillum's philosophical pronounce-ments or his wife's preternatural aptitude for conception or the toes of the children that 'were the kind that hook round the legs of chairs".

Indeed, a careless reader who took this poem to be a very simple kind of mirror might miss the tenderness altogether and might conclude that the poet was sneering at the stupid and not-too-well-washed Gillums. It is not easy to make realism and truth, beauty and ugliness, lie down side by side, not quarrelling with, but supporting and sustaining, one another – as I think that they do here.

Let me conclude by summing up in these terms: Literature provides us with a special kind of truth about human beings: it has its own kind of objectivity, and yet its kind of truth is always a kind of truth related to ourselves. The truth that literature gives us about other people is only incidentally historical or sociological or scientific truth. It may involve such truth, but we had better not presume that it necessarily provides any of these kinds of truth. We risk grave distortion if we assume that it does. But authentic literature can give us something precious – something for which there is no substitute. It can cover the statistics of sociology with warm flesh; it can make the dry bones of history live; it can turn the alien with his strange beliefs and customs into a brother whom we can understand. It can even – hardest task of all, I sometimes think – redeem the monsters created by the popular press, by the politician's half-truths, by the advertising-man's snobbery, and by the often superficial and meretricious manipulation of the television and screen writer – it can, I say, redeem into humanity the monsters so created, bringing into focus through the haze of distorting stereotypes and falsifying generalizations their reality as beings whom we can know and understand, even if we disagree with their ideas and condemn some of their actions.

I have used the Southern poor white as an example. For my immediate purpose it is only as an example that I am concerned with him. Let me on some other occasion – or better still, let others – attempt his rehabilitation. What I am concerned with here is not a special but a universal problem. I want to make the case for literature as an indispensable civilizing force. We need it to understand others and to understand ourselves. But I must end with two provisoes. Shoddy and meretricious literature darkens counsel and distorts the truth. Yet even if the literature is genuine, an inadequate and misguided reading will destroy its effectiveness. A particularly damaging misreading of literature is that which demands of it a literalism that denies its true nature – by assuming that it throws back for our gaze the world just as it literally is.

11

The American "Innocence" in James, Fitzgerald and Faulkner

Whether we Americans are really innocent or whether we are not, we have had with us for a long time the notion that Americans *are* innocent and that their innocence is of a peculiar and special sort. In recent years, this notion has come in for increased attention. Americans, in their growing self-consciousness, try to analyze the ways in which their experience differs from that of Europe and the possibly different perspectives in which they are forced to see the claims of the past and the promise of the future.

A number of years ago a friend of mine told me of sitting next to Thomas Mann at a dinner in Princeton, and taking advantage of her proximity to the great man, then a recent emigré from Germany, to say to him: "Dear Dr Mann, please get out of your head that we Americans are a young and innocent people; we are, on the contrary, an old and corrupt people." I mention the incident not in order to insist that my friend was correct or that Thomas Mann stood in special need of her exhortation. I make the allusion simply to indicate that there is no easy consensus on this matter of "innocence" and that the adjective can mean any of several things. But the fervour of my friend's admonition and the fact that she thought that intellectuals from Europe needed to hear it, testifies at least to the fact that the topic was a live one.

The subject is still very much alive. For example, a book review in a recent *Times Literary Supplement* begins with the statement that Americans, of course, "believe that every problem is soluble". And, having just quoted that, if I raise my eyes from my paper at this moment to look into your faces, I think that I can detect a good many that wear an expression which amounts to saying: "Yes, of course– isn't every problem soluble?" And who am I to say that perhaps you are not right? But the Englishman who wrote the review obviously did not see it as one of those self-evident truths that are implied by, if not specifically mentioned in, our Declaration of Independence. If most Americans do feel that every problem is soluble, then this fact too may have some bearing upon this matter of our innocence. So may a great many other things, including aspects of our foreign policy. But, for the purposes of this lecture, I shall respect my own limitations and confine myself to American literature. What I propose to talk about is the way in which three great American novelists have treated the "innocent" American. My texts will be Henry James's *The American* (1877), F. Scott Fitzgerald's *The Great Gatsby* (1925), and William Faulkner's *Absalom, Absalom!* (1936). The novels themselves thus span some sixty years, and the authors may be thought to represent three rather different regional viewpoints, those of the East, the Midwest and the South.

Henry James's story is that of an American millionaire who, at the age of thirty-five, came for the first time to Europe to amuse himself in the Old World, to become acquainted with its culture, and, at the suggestion of an expatriate friend living in Paris, to seek the hand in marriage of a French noblewoman, Claire de Cintré, née Bellegarde. His intended wife is a beautiful and cultured young widow, a descendant of a family proud of its thousand-year-old history. Surprisingly enough, the American's simplicity, directness, sheer audacity – his great wealth, incidentally, is no handicap – almost succeed. But in the end, the engagement is broken. The dowager and her son find that they cannot, after all, accept the upstart American. Claire retires from the world by entering a nunnery, and the businessman prepares to come back to America.

James's hero – his name significantly is Newman – has a great deal of innocence, but it is coupled with a considerable degree of self-awareness. He has his own pride as a self-made man, but he is no vulgarian, and James expects the reader to view him with sympathy. To counterpoise his "innocence", James has made the Bellegardes – at least the mother and the elder son – definitely wicked and, as we learn at the end, they have actually committed a crime.

Fitzgerald's hero, Jay Gatsby, is, like James's Newman, a self-made man. His fortune was built up rapidly during the Prohibition era, and though we are not told in detail just how it was accumulated, his financial manipulations clearly will not bear inspection. But Gatsby, though his great wealth is tainted, is in his own way an idealist – he lives for an idea – and manages to preserve a kind of innocence which, in the total context, is not simply amusing and odd, but magnificent.

Before making his fortune, Gatsby has fallen in love with a young woman named Daisy, but as a soldier preparing to be sent overseas in the First World War, a man moreover without money, he is not able to marry the girl, and Daisy lands in the arms of Tom Buchanan, an eligible suitor who has money and some kind of social position.

The chalice of love that poor deluded Gatsby – born Gatz – bears for four years, safely through the jostling throng, is his idealistic love for Daisy. It is for her that he has accumulated a fortune, and now in the monstrously big house that he has bought across the harbour from the Buchanans, he looks wistfully every night at the little green light on the Buchanan dock. Finally, Gatsby meets Daisy again and tries to reclaim her for true love. The effort fails, of course, as it must; but in contrast to the shoddy, plutocratic society which has swallowed up Daisy, Gatsby's innocence – even though we must put it very carefully within quotation marks – shines with a hard and gem-like flame – or if you prefer Shakespeare to Pater – shines like a good deed in a naughty world. Fitzgerald makes it quite plain that the world inhabited by the Buchanans is a naughty world.

William Faulkner's self-made man is named Thomas Sutpen. He was born in the mountains of western Virginia, but his shiftless family drifts down into the Tidewater country, and there the young boy undergoes an experience that changes his whole life. One day his father has him take a message to one of the planters, and the boy, in his innocence, calls at the front door of the great house, only to be turned away by the liveried Negro servant who tells him to go around to the kitchen door. From this moment onward, Sutpen's life is transformed. It now becomes of the highest importance to him to get the means to build for himself such a plantation house, properly equipped with liveried servants so that he can some day open the door to the wide-eyed, ragged, proud youngster who had been himself.

Sutpen goes to the West Indies and acquires wealth. But there something happens which causes him to abandon his West Indies estate and to start all over again in Faulkner's Yoknapatawpha County. He arrives with a wagonload of wild, French-speaking Negroes and little other than his own courage and zeal and sheer will power. *Absalom, Absalom!* is in part the story of how Thomas Sutpen wrests another great plantation house from the swamps of the frontier country and finds a wife and tries to establish a dynasty. Like Gatsby and like Christopher Newman, he has a qualified success, though he is never able fully to realize his great dream. Like James, Faulkner has his hero partially overcome the resistance which the society sets up against him. Unlike Fitzgerald, Faulkner reveals some sympathies for the values of the society which the intruder would take by storm. Indeed, a close look at Newman, Gatsby, and Sutpen ought to tell us a great deal about the nature of innocence, for in spite of the differences among these three characters, each is obviously to be regarded as in some sense innocent. But since the nature of innocence is the problem at issue – the matter to be defined – let us begin with more objective matters. What is common to the backgrounds of these men?

In the first place, all three, in effect, come out of nowhere: their families can give them nothing and do not share their ambitions. There is no process of nurturing, no family tradition that is handed on. Each of our heroes leaves his family early and strikes out on his own.

In such a situation, there is little place for formal education, and for each of our heroes school attendance is sketchy. Christopher Newman had dropped out of school at the age of ten. When we meet him twenty-five years later, he is so articulate and his grasp of language is that so sound one wonders whether Henry James has not portrayed him as a little too good to be true. But by any standards Newman was a remarkable man, and perhaps the school of experience taught him not only how to make money but how to handle the English language.

Thomas Sutpen "had schooling during a part of one winter". But this boy of thirteen or fourteen found very quickly that the classroom was not for him, and was off to the West Indies to make his fortune. Like James, Faulkner has allowed him a formality of speech that amounts to courtliness. This rhetorical quality in his speech may be hard to account for except that, like Newman, Sutpen evidently took his self-education seriously.

Even Gatsby follows this general pattern. Fitzgerald tells us that his "parents were shiftless and unsuccessful farm people" and that the boy's "imagination had never really accepted them as his parents at all". By the time that he is seventeen Gatsby had managed a few months' attendance at a small Lutheran college in Minnesota, but he is simply a clam digger on the shores of one of the Great Lakes when his patron-to-be discovers him and takes him up.

What is true of all of these men is not that they are all "self-made" merely in the fact that they did not inherit their wealth. In a far more important way, they are self-made – in the sense that they have created their own personalities and disciplined their minds in the service of a dream. Fitzgerald tells us that "the truth was that Jay Gatsby . . . sprang from his Platonic conception of himself". So it is with Thomas Sutpen. Sutpen once told his sole friend in the community that he knew that he possessed courage and as for the cleverness, "if it were to be learned by energy and will in the school of endeavour and experience" he would learn. Sutpen's deepest belief is that a courageous man, if he plans carefully enough, can accomplish anything.

Though Gatsby will seem, when measured against Sutpen's intensity, somewhat relaxed and offhand, his creed is much like Sutpen's. He is possessed by the same kind of devouring idealism. When Gatsby's friend tries to suggest to him that what has happened has happened, and that one simply "can't repeat the past", Gatsby cries out incredulously: "Can't repeat the past? Why, of course you can!"

Much has been made by Faulkner critics of Sutpen's inhuman "design" – his plan to set up a dynasty – a scheme to which he sacrifices everything. Because of the traumatic experience which he had suffered as a boy, he is not only obsessed by the need to achieve his dream of grandeur and success, but he has a fixation upon the specific terms of his dream of success. He must win not just any mansion, but a particular mansion. When he finds that his wife in Haiti possesses a trace of Negro blood, he abandons her and their child – not, if I read his character correctly, because he had any intense racial feeling, but because she did not fit the specific terms of the "design" that had captured his imagination. Much later, in Mississippi, when the son of that first marriage appears at his Mississippi plantation door, he refuses to acknowledge him in any way because a son with even a trace of Negro blood will not fit the details of the design that has become frozen in his imagination. Thus Sutpen sacrifices his colored son to the design, and to it he later sacrifices his two white children just as ruthlessly.

Indeed, Sutpen has not only a "design", as he calls it in his conversation with General Compson, but he has also what he calls his schedule – that is, his time table – in accordance with which the design is to be realized. What he seems most to resent in the family of his Haitian wife is that their deception made him waste time – made him throw his schedule out of kilter.

Jay Gatsby, of South Dakota, lived by a schedule too. One of the most poignant things about this young gangster-idealist is a scrap of paper that turns up late in the story. After Gatsby's death, Nick Carraway comes upon a bit of paper dated September 12, 1906, bearing the word "schedule":

Rise from bed...6 a.m.
Dumbbell exercise and wall-scaling.....,.............6:15-6:30
Study electricity, etc...................................7:15-8:15
Work...8:30-4:30 p.m.
Baseball and sports....................................4:30-5:00
Practice elocution, poise and how
    to attain it...5:00-6:00
Study needed inventions...........................7:00-9:00

GENERAL RESOLVES

No wasting time at Shafters or [a name, indecipherable]
No more smokeing or chewing.
Bath every other day
Read one improving book or magazine per week
Save $5.00 [crossed out] $3.00 per week
Be better to Parents.

It is touching to see how this seventeen-year-old boy sought with a fierce austerity to pull himself up by his own bootstraps. But the discovery has its ominous side, for men who rule their lives in this way are likely to suffer from an elephantiasis of the will. In both Thomas Sutpen and Jay Gatsby that faculty is developed to the point of deformity.

And what of Christopher Newman? Does he too live by a schedule? James has not made of Newman the extreme case that Fitzgerald and Faulkner make of their heroes, but there is enough evidence to show that all three are of the same breed. James has provided plenty of indications of Newman's own self-absorption in his design and the deliberate calculation that went into it. Here is Newman, for example, on the subject of securing a suitable wife. He tells his friend Mrs Tristram: "I want a great woman. I stick to that. That's one thing I can treat myself to. . . . I want to possess, in a word, the best article on the market." When Mrs Tristram reproaches him for being "so cold-blooded and calculating", her comments may, if we like, be put down to friendly banter, and when Newman calls his ideal of a wife "the best article on the market", he is quite possibly speaking tongue-in-cheek. But he is not speaking altogether tongue-in-cheek when he tells Mrs Tristram that to win the most beautiful wife, "a man . . . needs only to use his will, and such wits as he has, and to try".

Madame de Bellegarde, the patrician old lady who is Claire's mother, at one point remarks of her prospective son-in-law that he chooses his future wife "as if he were threading a needle", and we are at liberty to dismiss this, if we like, as the sub-acid remark of a prospective mother-in-law. But to Newman himself the thought occurs that he must seem a "trifle 'pushing'."

At the end, when the engagement has been broken, Newman feels a sense of outrage at Claire's mother and elder brother, and acute sadness for Claire, but he is scarcely heart-broken. His dominant emotion had been "the prospective glory of possession", the possession of a creature so obviously admirable and so much admired by all the world. Romantic love, Newman had from the beginning disclaimed; as for the tenderness of a shared experience, from that, too, he was barred. In a very real sense, and not necessarily through any fault of his own, Newman had had almost no opportunity to know the woman whom he meant to marry.

By contrast, Fitzgerald's Gatsby had had a passionate experience with the girl with whom he was in love. As a young army officer in 1917, he had seemed very attractive to the eighteen-year old girl and there had been for a few weeks a passionate affair which had left him feeling truly married and which had made the girl herself resist for a time what Fitzgerald called "the pressure of the world outside" – pressure that brought about her marriage to another man. Daisy's friend, Jordan Baker, later tells Nick Carraway about finding Daisy just an hour before the bridal dinner "lying on her bed as lovely as the June night in a flowered dress – and as drunk as a monkey. She had a bottle . . . in one hand and a letter in the other." The letter, of course, was from Jay Gatsby.

The marriage arrangements made by Faulkner's hero, Thomas Sutpen, more nearly resemble those of Christopher Newman. In the first place, Sutpen and Newman lived in a more formal age – Newman's courtship occurred in 1869; Sutpen's courtship and marriage in 1833. But it is principally their temperaments which make them differ sharply from Fitzgerald's twentieth-century hero. When Thomas Sutpen, having already made one false start in trying to realize his great design, comes into north Mississippi, this time he chooses with very great care indeed the woman who is to be the mistress of his manor house and mother of his children. Many years later he was to tell General Compson: "You see, I had a design in my mind . . . to accomplish it I should require money, a house, a plantation, slaves, a family – incidentally, of course, a wife." The adverb he employs is eloquent. Sutpen does not make his second marriage driven by some gust of passion or enamoured of a pretty face. His wife is to be adjunctive to the design and her place in the design is calculated to a nicety.

One might have expected Sutpen, the self-made man, who owned nearly one hundred square miles of land, to choose a daughter of one of the plantation owners round about, into whose society he sought to enter. But Sutpen makes his calculation in very different terms. The frontier country was highly suspicious of this strange intruder; his ways were not their ways. There were dark rumours as to how he had accumulated his sudden fortune. Indeed, soon after his entry into Yoknapatawpha County, Sutpen was almost lynched by a group of vigilantes. Sutpen is acutely aware of his lack of respectability. Land and wealth he has in abundance, but respectability is harder to purchase, and Sutpen proposes to acquire a saving measure of it quickly by marriage. He chooses, therefore, for his wife, the daughter of the most respectable man in Jefferson, the austere proprietor of a small store, a man who is a Methodist steward and the principal layman in his little church.

The calculation may strike us as naïve, and as not likely to achieve the desired result. But Sutpen, of course, *is* naïve. After all, he is one of my three exhibits of American innocence, the kind of innocence which General Compson described as involving the belief "that the ingredients of morality were like the ingredients of pie or cake and once you had measured them and balanced them and mixed them and put them into the oven it was all finished and nothing but pie or cake could come out". Sutpen, in short, is not only a man who lives for a design and by a schedule, but a man who makes his dispositions in terms of recipes and formulas: so many ounces of respectability of prime quality will neutralize so many ounces of infamy.

After the collapse of his plans to marry Claire de Bellegarde, Newman's confidante, Mrs Tristram, asks him: "Are you very sure that you would have been happy?" Perhaps she is simply trying to comfort him: the grapes were sour after all; yet, from what has been presented in the novel, we have good reason to believe that her question was pertinent. It is hard to believe that this admirable but ill-assorted pair would have been happy in Europe, nor can I believe that Claire de Bellegarde would really have been happy in St Louis.

Newman sees himself as a kind of St George sallying out of the new world to save a beautiful maiden from the clutches of an old-world dragon, but he fails in his mission. Had Jay Gatsby had better luck and rescued his maiden from her dragon, would he have been happy? Perhaps, but there is nothing in the novel to make one think so, and there are some things in it that seriously call in question any supposal that he and his dream girl – for that is literally what she is – could have lived happily ever after. It is not merely a question of Daisy's superficiality – of her initial weakness or of the corrupting influence of her life with Tom Buchanan. The most ominous portent lies in the character of Gatsby himself – in his "innocence". For Gatsby is a man in the grip of a powerful illusion and his image of Daisy surely could not have survived the flesh-and-blood experience of the actual Daisy. Fitzgerald has hinted that Gatsby himself may have sensed this possibility. Early in his courtship of Daisy, Fitzgerald tells us, Gatsby had a sort of vision: in the evening light the blocks of the sidewalk seemed to form a ladder that "mounted to a secret place above the trees – he could climb it, if he climbed alone, and once there he could suck on the pap of life, gulp down the incomparable milk of wonder". Nevertheless, he seeks Daisy's lips and "forever wed his unutterable visions to her perishable breath".

Here it is appropriate to observe that both Newman and Gatsby dismiss the claims of family, of the past, and of society in general in favor of the intimate communion of two people who feel they need nothing for their happiness but each other. This notion, whether or not it is to be called innocent, is good American doctrine. The American snarls: "I married you, not your family." Or he sings – or sang in the '20's – "We'll build a sweet little nest / Somewhere out in the West / And let the rest of the world go by." The statistics on divorce in America would suggest that this confidence is indeed "innocent". Fitzgerald, who is not innocent in this sense, gives more than a hint that he knows how things would have gone with Daisy and Gatsby, and, as we have remarked, James is willing to have Mrs Tristram suggest that Newman probably would not have been happy.

There is, by the way, something curiously virginal about all three men. General Compson was sure that Sutpen was a virgin until he had won and married his Haitian wife. But in any case, Sutpen never seems to be a man of sensuous indulgence. One senses that he reined in his sexual appetite with all the rigour befitting a Puritan patriarch, and that carnal knowledge for him was merely for the propagation of children. As for Newman, there is also something curiously virginal about him. We are told by the author that Newman likes the company of women, that he was not shy with them, that rather in their company he sat "grave, attentive, submissive, often silent . . . simply swimming in a sort of rapture of respect". Very frankly, I must say that this seems to me to smack of Henry James's own primness and it is not quite what we expect from a go-getting young American of thirty-five, who had lived by his wits from boyhood and had roved about the continent. Be that as it may. Newman does not seem to be a man who knows much about women and his relations with Claire de Bellegarde bear this out. He never acts like a man moved by passion, and it is fitting that his physical relations with Clare amount to no more than a single kiss, his kiss of relinquishment and farewell.

The case of Jay Gatsby is somewhat different. We are told that "He knew women early, and since they spoiled him, he became contemptuous of them, of young virgins because they were ignorant, of the others because they were hysterical about things which in his overwhelming self-absorption, he took for granted." Thus Fitzgerald has made it easier to believe in his hero; yet there is something abstemious about Gatsby after all. In the course of the gay parties given by his older patron, in which "women used to rub champagne into his hair", he "formed the habit of letting liquor alone". At his lavish parties on Long Island, Gatsby moves about with a certain genial detachment and even aloofness. If he lacks the virginal quality of Newman and Sutpen, he resembles them in his Puritanism and in his own special kind of fastidious idealism.

But what of innocence? Can Sutpen really be said to possess the innocence that is characteristic of Newman and Gatsby? Newman and even Gatsby are obviously more sinned against than sinning, and have hurt and injury inflicted upon them which they do not deserve. Sutpen, however, inflicts injury. Yet plainly Sutpen's deficiencies in the matter of sympathy and love are finally an aspect of his defective sense of reality, and his complete self-absorption in his design is possible only to a man who is impervious to the claims of reality. Sutpen's innocence is not mere sinlessness, but an inability to comprehend what sin is.

Thomas Sutpen, as General Compson finds out to his consternation, really believes that the world is a kind of mechanism which can be manipulated if one is shrewd enough and calculates carefully enough, and that the blueprint for an action – or for a life – so calculated, can be realized provided one has the courage to see the plan through. When the child of his first marriage turns up to confront him in Mississippi, he does not feel guilty. He has not committed a sin. He has simply made a mistake – this is his own term for it – and what he wants to do is to recheck his calculations so that he can try once more and this time realize the design. As Quentin Compson tells this part of the story to his room-mate, when Sutpen's son born in Haiti turns up, he is not for "calling it retribution, no sins of the father come home to roost; not even calling it bad luck, but just a mistake ... just an old mistake in fact which a man of courage and shrewdness . . . could still combat if he could only find out what the mistake had been".

Sutpen's innocence, then, amounted to a radical defect in his perception of reality. He has an overweening confidence in his own will and in his power to calculate a course. He tells General Compson how, when he abandoned his first wife, "his conscience had bothered him somewhat at first but that he had argued calmly and logically with his conscience until it was settled. ..." The man who can argue calmly and logically with his conscience until he settles its hash is of course capable of doing anything, but I do not mean to make fun of Sutpen. He makes this statement to General Compson in full seriousness. Perhaps his seriousness is a measure of his capacity for real inhumanity.

I suggest, then, that the monstrous inhumanity of Thomas Sutpen is an extension and specialization of certain American traits which are familiar enough and which in other contexts may even appear admirable. Newman's rather cold-blooded calculation and Jay Gatsby's confidence that one can repeat the past involve similar oversimplifications of reality.

I remarked earlier in this paper that as we compared the attitudes toward innocence of our three authors, certain regional traits might emerge. Perhaps they do. Faulkner's Southern culture, with its stubborn ties with the past, its powerful sense of the claims of family and community, and what might be called its still vital sense of original sin, may be thought to make itself felt in Faulkner's harsher treatment of innocence as compared with the treatment we find accorded by James and Fitzgerald. Thomas Sutpen is, for all of his impressive qualities, a rather obvious villain, whereas Christopher Newman and Jay Gatsby are not. Moreover, Faulkner seems to show more sympathy for the community into which Sutpen comes and with which he collides than James shows for the old-world society against which Newman pits himself, and certainly far more than Fitzgerald shows for the glittering world of money and social prestige that Jay Gatsby plans to take by storm.

This general contrast between Faulkner and the other two novelists would seem to be supported by American literary history. Other Southern writers tend to treat with a certain awe, but also a certain distrust, the new untrammelled man who has cast off the claims of the irrational past and in doing so has tapped a vast new reservoir of energy. I am thinking, for example, of such characters as Bogan Murdoch, in Robert Penn Warren's *At Heaven's Gate,* or George Posey in Allen Tate's novel, *The Fathers.* George Posey is, in personality, very different from Thomas Sutpen, but his basic role is the same: Posey seems to the young Virginian, whose sister he has married, brilliant, resourceful and possessed of a magnetic personal charm. For his young brother-in-law he retains to the very end an attractive boyish innocence, but Tate portrays him as a violently destructive force, wreaking havoc upon the family with which he has become allied.

In this general connection, I ought to cite *The American Adam*, published some years ago, by my colleague, R. W. B. Lewis. Lewis develops in masterly fashion the special view of America that arose in the nineteenth century. The citizen of this new world, it was now proclaimed, had shaken off the evils of the past, had emancipated himself from the burden of time, and, relying upon his natural virtues, was now ready to stride confidently into a beckoning future. In short, Lewis has described, with a special emphasis upon New England, the intellectual climate that produced the self-made men who seem so characteristically "American".

Yet if one is tempted to find in Faulkner's special treatment of innocence something characteristic of his regional culture, one must be careful not to make too much of Faulkner's difference from his fellow novelists. His use of the term "innocence", for example, is not eccentric and perverse. Henry James would have understood what Faulkner meant. The evidence is to be found in James's own novels. Lewis tells us that James's treatment of the theme of innocence involved a "very long series of innocent and metaphorically new-born heroes and heroines", and he points out further that these qualities of innocence are treated by James "with every conceivable variety of ethical weight". Even in *The American* it is plain that James regards the innocence of a man like Newman as not merely, and not wholly, admirable. Lewis remarks that in his fiction James made it quite clear that "innocence could be cruel as well as vulnerable". Indeed, Lewis writes that in James's novel *The Golden Bowl* there "is a startling inversion of the Adamic tradition; it is the world, this time, which is struck down by aggressive innocence". An "aggressive innocence" that destroys the world about it approaches in character the kind of innocence that I find in Faulkner's Thomas Sutpen.

Even Fitzgerald seems to imply such a conception of innocence, for his Jay Gatsby is not the only innocent in his novel. Consider Daisy and Tom Buchanan. The term that Fitzgerald applies to them is, to be sure, not innocent but "careless". He has Nick Carraway observe that "They were careless people, Tom and Daisy – they smashed up things and creatures and

then retreated back into their money or their vast careless-
ness. . . ." This is Nick's bitter final characterization of the pair.
Nick had meant to reproach Tom Buchanan for having in
effect connived at Gatsby's murder. But in his final interview
with Tom, Nick tells us: "I felt suddenly as though I were talking to a child." In saying this, Nick is indeed very close to calling
Tom "innocent" – that is, a man who has not yet found out
what reality is like and who has not yet transcended the child's
self-centred world.

This discussion has seemed to imply that innocence is not a
quality wholly good or desirable; that, on the contrary, it is
something to be sloughed off in process of time – a state to be
grown out of – a negative thing that ought to disappear with the
acquisition of knowledge and moral discipline. I plead guilty
to this emphasis, but it seems also to be the emphasis of two,
and perhaps of all three, of the novelists we have been considering. But I am not one to quarrel over a term as such,
and I am perfectly willing to try to conclude on a positive
note – or at least with a positive value assigned to the term
"innocence".

In order to make a case for innocence as a positive virtue, I
shall appeal to one of the great poems of our century, a poem
about innocence written not by an American but by the
Irishman, William Butler Yeats. Yet I must warn you that
though Yeats celebrates innocence, his view of it will reinforce
rather than contradict the views of it that we have just been
examining. (But then, of course, that is my real reason for wanting to cite the poem.)

Yeats's "A Prayer for My Daughter" was written in 1919.
The occasion is a storm howling in off the Atlantic, sweeping
past the tower home near the west coast of Ireland in which
Yeats was then living. The poet's infant daughter lies asleep in
her cradle, and the father, dreading what the future may have
in store for his child, makes his prayer for gifts and qualities that
shall stay her against the destructive forces that threaten her
future. Yeats proved a true prophet: in this poem, remember
that he is predicting the events of the 'thirties and 'forties and
'fifties when he writes:

> Imagining in excited reverie
> That the future years had come,
> Dancing to a frenzied drum,
> Out of the murderous innocence of the sea.

The storm-tossed Atlantic is murderous in its destructive power, but, ironically, innocent too, for there is no moral implication, no choice, no sense of guilt, merely the play of natural forces.

In contrast to this murderous innocence of nature, the poet invokes for his daughter a different kind of innocence. He hopes that she may live sheltered from the wind like some green laurel "rooted in one dear perpetual place". He hopes that she can keep herself free from intellectual hatred and can, from the depths of her own nature, recover a "radical innocence". The contrast is between two views of the self and two contrasted views of innocence and of nature. The murderous innocence that is amoral and that is associated with the storm winds off the Atlantic is set over against a radical innocence – that is, an innocence *rooted* like the laurel tree. And nature as capricious and cruel, mere brute force, is contrasted with a human nature which is very much like the Platonic view of the soul. One may hope to find in its depths, norms and archetypes of order, indeed a reflection of the divine order.

The last stanza of the poem treats all these matters in their social aspect.

> And may her bridegroom bring her to a house
> Where all's accustomed, ceremonious;
> For arrogance and hatred are the wares
> Peddled in the thoroughfares.
> How but in custom and in ceremony
> Are innocence and beauty born?
> Ceremony's a name for the rich horn,
> And custom for the spreading laurel tree.

Man lives in the society of his fellows. In terms of man's life in human society, what is the cornucopia of Greek legend – the fabled horn of plenty? What is the spreading laurel tree? Ceremony and custom, the poet boldly answers. The true dower of gifts comes from ceremony – it is not blind nature's casual bounty.

Yet we are in the habit of thinking of innocence and beauty as the gift of nature; and we commonly oppose them to custom and ceremony, for we think of custom and ceremony as tending to sophisticate, and even to corrupt. Yeats inverts these relations. Innocence and beauty, he maintains, are not the products of nature but the fruit of a disciplined life. They spring from order. They are not capriciously given. They come from nurture and tradition.

This is a surprisingly "classical" view of man to come from a poet who regarded himself as one of the last Romantics. I would claim something of this view also for Faulkner, so often celebrated as a romantically Gothic novelist, and perhaps I might claim it for our other two novelists as well. The innocence with which we are born – if we *are* born innocent – does not suffice.

Seen in this perspective, the term "self-made" itself takes on new meanings. The self-made man has, to be sure, made his fortune and may have made his "world", but can he be called truly self-made? Or at least *well made* if he is merely *self-made*? Isn't man too much a social and political animal for such self-creation to be other than fantastic? I think that our three American novelists are in agreement on this point. Fitzgerald's remark that Gatsby "sprang from his Platonic conception of himself" hangs somewhere between amused admiration and sardonic awe, and there is a like mixture of patronising tenderness and pointed irony in James's various comments on Christopher Newman. As for Faulkner: there is no question that he sees in Sutpen's innocence what Yeats called the "murderous innocence of the sea".

12

The Southern Temper

At various times during the last several years I have been asked to comment on the place of the South in American literature, and in trying to define some of the characteristics of the literature that has come out of the Southern states during the last forty years, I have tended to stress the presence of a genuine folk culture, white as well as Negro, the importance of the family as a still living force, the powerful sense of community, the peculiar historical consciousness, and – with this feeling for history – a sense of its tragic dimension. These are the aspects of Southern culture that other Southerners stress: Professor Hugh Holman, in a recently published essay,[1] emphasized the Southerner's sense of failure, his sense of guilt, especially as it is connected to the history of slavery, and his sense of frustration encountered when the Southerner's sub-nationalism is snubbed or checkmated by the nation at large.

Professor C. Vann Woodward, in *The Burden of Southern History*,[2] emphasizes the Southerner's sense of history as actually lived, his distrust of abstraction, and his scepticism about the doctrine of human perfectibility. Woodward puts the latter point vividly in a passage that I cannot forbear quoting: "In that most optimistic of centuries in the most optimistic part of the world, the South remained basically pessimistic in its social outlook and its moral philosophy."[3]

But though the cultural traits just mentioned have a bearing upon "the Southern temper", I do not think that I ought to approach my subject in just these terms in this paper.

For one thing, the reader can read for himself Professor

[1] "The Southerner as American Writer", printed in *The Southerner as American*, ed. C. G. Sellers, Jr. (University of North Carolina Press, 1960).

[2] (Louisiana State University Press, 1969.)

[3] *Op. cit.*, p. 21.

Woodward's excellent book and can also read Professor Holman's essay. He can even read me on the subject, if he likes, for I have written about this matter and written in terms not too far different from those of Woodward.[1]

I want, therefore, on this occasion to approach the subject in a rather different way. For one thing, I want to be very concrete. I mean to illustrate my thesis from contemporary Southern writers, and in the interests of economy, I shall confine myself to their treatment of just one kind of fictional character, the middle-aged spinster who has cultural aspirations.

In the interest of economy, I must also forgo setting forth the elaborate set of reservations, qualifications, and cautionary notes that would otherwise be called for. One specific qualification must stand for all the rest. It is this: at the very outset I must concede that not all Southern writers possess the kind of temper that I hope to describe.

Erskine Caldwell, for example, though Georgia-born, participates in the Southern experience largely through his interest in the folk culture. His attitude is either broadly comic or else, when he forgets his own sense of humour, zealously reformist. To take another example, Thomas Wolfe, though in certain respects clearly Southern – Professor Hugh Holman as a fellow North Carolinian has no difficulty in making out his specifically Southern traits – seems to me to partake of the Whitman tradition rather more than do the writers that I regard as typically Southern. Wolfe's mind had in it less of the eighteenth century and more of the nineteenth.

There is no one wholly satisfactory literary example, but the one that I mean to make most use of here is a story by Peter Taylor. If his work is not so widely known as it should be, that is an additional reason, in writing for a journal like *Archiv*, to mention it. The story in question is entitled "Miss Leonora When Last Seen" and is the title story of his latest collection.[2]

The plot is simple. Miss Leonora Logan, now retired after teaching school for many years in the town of Thomasville,

[1] "Southern Literature: the Wellsprings of its Vitality", pp. 215–29 below; first published in *The Georgia Review* Autumn, 1962.

[2] *Miss Leonora When Last Seen and Fifteen Other Stories* (New York: Ivan Obolensky, Inc., 1963).

Tennessee, was last seen – that is, was last seen by a fellow citizen – climbing into the driver's seat of her fourteen-year-old Dodge convertible. As she did so, she was heard to remark that she was going away on a little trip. Two weeks have now elapsed, the narrator of the story tells us, and no one knows where she is. She has, to be sure, sent a half-dozen postcards to friends in Thomasville, and to judge from the towns from which they were posted, Miss Leonora is not very far away. Indeed, she seems to be "orbiting her native state of Tennessee"; but the narrator, who incidentally was the person who helped her into her car when she set off on this last trip, is now worried about her. So is the whole town: as he says, "none of us will rest easy until we know that the old lady is safe at home again".

Miss Leonora is a known eccentric. She has taken such trips for years past: she prefers to drive at night. She usually puts up for the day at some tourist home. If the tourist home is in a town, she likes to dress in an antiquated costume, with lace choker, in the hope that she may be mistaken for the "proprietress's mother or old-maid sister". If however, the tourist home is situated out in the country, she dresses in dungarees and insists on helping out with the chores, either in the house or out in the chicken yard. The narrator is certain, however, that Miss Leonora has really left town in order to avoid being served with papers authorizing the condemnation of her house and land for public use. For some time now, the town has tried to persuade Miss Leonora to sell her property so that a school might be erected on the site. Miss Leonora has kept refusing, and finally the town has had to resort to legal expropriation.[1] Miss Leonora's present trip is, then, more than the foible of a lonesome old maid. It looks like a deliberate act of defiance.

[1] One reason for choosing Miss Logan's property as the site for the new school is that it would eliminate from the town a "colony of Negroes", who, as the narrator indicates, "have always lived up there and who would make a serious problem for us if it became a question of zoning the town . . . as a last barrier against integration". But this is only one of several reasons and the author has not tried to present Miss Leonora as a civil-rights liberal. If her attitude towards the Negroes irritates some of the townspeople, we may be sure that it would fall far short of satisfying Mr Stokely Carmichael. I mention the matter here only because I ought to make it plain that Peter Taylor is not dodging the issue in this story of the present-day South.

It is natural that an author writing about what is happening to the older culture of the South should choose a woman to typify the anti-commercial, traditional spirit, with its indifference to, if not actual antipathy toward, progressive measures, and its fixation on the concrete and the personal. A woman fits this role more plausibly than a man – though I confess that it may be simply my own Southern temper that makes it seem so to me. But in any case, the isolation so often imposed upon a person who clings thus to the past is easier to account for when the person is a woman and may prompt from the reader a more sympathetic response. Miss Leonora, though she is no mere allegorical figure, in a very special way does embody the spirit of a place and the culture of a period. I think she herself exhibits some aspects of the Southern temper, but I don't mean to present her as my primary example of it. She is a special case, not typical, though her eccentric traits, as we shall see, exhibit aspects of the Southern temper.

The man who tells the story is a former pupil of Miss Leonora's, and all that we learn about Miss Leonora we learn through him. He too is a special case. He still resents Miss Leonora's attempts to "improve" him and his schoolmates. He connects it with what he regards as the Logan family's persistent attitude toward the town. As the owner of the Thomasville hotel, he wants to see the town grow, and he bitterly observes that "It was a Logan . . . who kept the railroad from coming through town; it was another Logan who prevented the cotton mill and the snuff factory from locating here . . . [The Logans'] one idea was always to keep the town unspoilt, unspoilt by railroads or factories . . ." Yet as a boy he had thought Miss Leonora to be a beautiful woman. He knows from personal experience that she was a good teacher. He still stands in a kind of awe of her inherent dignity and of her force of character.

This inn-keeper, then, in spite of the fact that he is one of the top men in the Thomasville Exchange Club, is no ordinary small-town booster. Something about the Southern temper, then, might be gleaned from his somewhat contradictory responses to Miss Leonora and the problems she raises. Contrast him with, for example, one of the townspeople of Gopher

Prairie in Sinclair Lewis's *Main Street*. Or compare him with the nameless citizen of Jefferson, Mississippi, who tells the story of Miss Emily Grierson in Faulkner's "A Rose for Emily". Miss Emily, like Miss Leonora, is an eccentric old maid, whose arrogance and aristocratic ways are resented by the people of the community in a special and rather complex way. As the narrator of "A Rose for Emily" puts it: "Thus she passed from generation to generation – dear, inescapable, impervious, tranquil, and perverse."[1] Faulkner's Miss Emily, of course, turns out to be clinically mad; whereas Miss Leonora is only mad north-northwest, but the relation of the two women to the community is not unlike and the men who tell the stories are not wholly unlike either.

Yet, though one might learn something of the Southern temper from the way in which the Thomasville hotel-keeper talks about Miss Leonora, no more than Miss Leonora will he provide an index of it. For something like adequacy in this matter, we shall have to look to the author of the story, for it is in his selection and disposition of events, in his conception of his characters, and in his interpretations of their attitudes and actions that we shall find revealed the quality of mind with which we are presently concerned. Later on in this essay, I shall venture a few comments by way of summary, but at this time we have not gone far enough with our examination of the story.

Miss Leonora's salient quality is her dedication to culture. She has a mission to civilize the town. This trait has come up for much attention throughout American literature: Carol Kennicott's attempt to civilize Gopher Prairie is an obvious and rather crudely handled instance; the formidable Olive Chancellor in Henry James's *The Bostonians* is a more complex case, and is, of course, handled with a great deal of subtlety. The theme is American, then, and the expression of it – through the character of a genteel and high-minded spinster, somewhat warped by her isolation – is sufficiently familiar. But Peter Taylor's treatment of the theme seems to me characteristically Southern.

As Miss Leonora's pupil remembers her: "She was eternally

[1] *The Collected Stories of William Faulkner* (New York: Random House, 1950).

instructing us. If only once she had let up on the instruction, we might have learned something – or I might have. I used to watch her for a sign – any sign – of her caring about what we thought of her, or of her *not* caring about her mission among us, if that's what it was." He goes on to say that he knows now "that all along she was watching me and others like me for some kind of sign from us – any sign – that would make us seem worthy of knowing what we wanted to know about her".

And what was it that he and his schoolmates wanted to know? In the next sentence he tells us: they wanted to know, beyond any doubt, that "the old lady had suffered for being just what she was – for being born with her cold, rigid, intellectual nature, and for being born to represent something that had never taken root in Thomasville and that would surely die with her".

How rigid and how intellectual was Miss Leonora's nature? Not very intellectual, really, if we compare her to Henry James's blue-stocking, Olive Chancellor. Miss Leonora's mental world is limited and provincial: moreover, Miss Leonora's nature is not really very cold and rigid – according to the narrator's own evidence. Just before setting off on the last of her little trips, Miss Leonora told him: "When I think of the old days . . . I realize I was too hard on you. I asked too much of my pupils. I know that now . . . I was unrealistic. I tried to be to you children what I thought you needed to have somebody be. That's a mistake, always. One has to try to be with people what they want one to be."

Is this a recantation on Miss Leonora's part – a hauling down of the flag? Well, not exactly, if one interprets, as I do, Miss Leonora's last trip as a gesture of defiance to the new order. But the admission of mistaken policy, however we are to take it – with whatever mixture of ironic qualification – is at least knowing and sensitive. It points to a nature that is aware of the feelings of others and it points – there is other evidence of this sort in the story – to a yearning for sympathy and understanding. Miss Leonora's social sense is highly developed. She is fully aware of why her former pupil has called on her on this particular morning: she knows that he has been delegated to break the

news to her that her property has at last been legally condemned. But let us listen to the way in which he tells it: "What
[Miss Leonora] actually said was much kinder and was what
anyone might have said under the circumstances. 'I've felt so
bad about your having to come here like this. I knew they
would put it off on you. Even you must have dreaded coming,
and you must hate me for putting you in such a position.'"
Miss Leonora's aspiration for the "higher things in life" are
quite genuine, but her love of culture does not take precedence
over her love of Thomasville. As the narrator remarks, not without a tinge of sarcasm, "No matter how far up in the world a
Logan may advance, he seems to go on having sweet dreams
about Thomasville." Indeed, Miss Leonora's love of culture is
a function of her love for her community.

It is rather otherwise with Sinclair Lewis's heroine in *Main
Street*. Carol's reaction to the hideousness of Gopher Prairie
allows Lewis a long innings of satire, after which he huddles
together a reconciliation and a happy ending. (Incidentally, I
do not apologize for including Carol Kennicott in my present
collection of spinsters. For even though she is married and has
borne a child, it is not until she and Dr Kennicott set out on
their second honeymoon that she ceases to be, spiritually at
least, the genteel spinster, unhappy in her isolation.)

If Carol Kennicott is a rather ordinary culture-vulture,
Henry James's heroine Olive Chancellor, of course, is a bird of
a rather different feather. She *is* an intellectual and she *does*
have the rigidity of nature rather resentfully attributed to Miss
Leonora by her former pupil. It is worth noting that, when he
calls Miss Leonora an "intellectual woman", he adds that she
was "at the same time . . . an extremely practical and simple
kind of person". Simplicity and practicality are not traits that
one would attribute to Miss Chancellor. Olive Chancellor, with
her complicated psyche and only half-understood yearnings,
Olive Chancellor with her latent lesbianism, is not at all simple.

Is it fair, then, to compare Miss Chancellor with Miss
Leonora? Is the contrast between these women relevant to this
discussion of the Southern temper? I should have to concede
that it is probably not relevant, except that James himself

evidently thought that it was. It is no accident that Henry James – there are no accidents in the work of Henry James – chooses a Southerner as the character who is to be the antithesis of all that Olive Chancellor believes and is. But I do not mean to produce Basil Ransom triumphantly as a positive instance of Southern attitudes and values. In the interest of space and the general symmetry of this essay, I prefer to stick to my basic illustration: the genteel spinster. Moreover, I am quite aware that James had his reservations about Ransom as certainly he had about culture south of the Potomac River.

It will be well enough for my present purposes here simply to point out that when James needed a convenient stick with which to beat what he regarded as a significant, if extreme, example of Boston culture, he knew where to go to get it. What James's novel implies about the Southern temper may at points confirm, and at least will not contradict, the general line that I am taking here.

Basil Ransom dislikes what he calls Olive Chancellor's cant about progress, equality, and the emancipation of women. To one feminist sage, he expostulates: "My dear madam, does woman consist of nothing but her opinions?"[1] In answer to the plea that we should end the suffering of women, his retort is that their suffering "is the suffering of all humanity . . . Do you think any movement is going to stop that . . .? We are born to suffer – and to bear it, like decent people."[2]

James evidently thought Olive Chancellor, special case that she is, relevant to her culture just as I would argue that Leonora Logan, though eccentric to the point of caricature, is relevant to hers. Miss Leonora Logan is as unthinkable in Massachusetts as is Olive Chancellor in Tennessee. But is Miss Leonora really typically Southern? I believe so. I have already mentioned Faulkner's Miss Emily of Mississippi. A nomination from Texas might be Cousin Eva, one of the characters in Katherine Anne Porter's "Old Mortality".[3]

We meet Cousin Eva as her young kinswoman Miranda meets her, quite by accident, in the Pullman car of a train. She is a

---

[1] *The Bostonians* (Modern Library Edition, 1956), p. 225.   [2] Ibid., p. 288.
[3] In *Pale Horse, Pale Rider, Three Short Novels* (New York: Harcourt, Brace, 1939).

"thin old lady" with "choleric black eyes . . ." She has "two immense front teeth and a receding chin, but she [does] not lack character". When Miranda first sees her, the old lady has "piled her luggage around her like a barricade . . ." She possesses "a certain brisk, rustling energy. Her taffeta petticoats creaked like hinges every time she stirred". But when Cousin Eva discovers that Miranda is her kinswoman and that they are both *en route* to the same destination, to attend the same family funeral, she unbends. She tells Miranda about her own life and is lavish in bestowing wholesome advice.

Among other things, Cousin Eva debunks the romantic legend about Amy, the family beauty, who died young; and she has some blistering remarks to make about the plight of women.

"It was just sex," she said in despair; "their minds dwelt on nothing else. They didn't call it that, it was all smothered under pretty names, but that's all it was, sex," She looked out of the window into the darkness, her sunken cheek near Miranda flushed deeply. She turned back. "I took to the soap box and the platform when I was called upon," she said proudly, "and I went to jail when it was necessary, and my condition didn't make any difference. I was booed and jeered and shoved around just as if I had been in perfect health. But it was part of our philosophy not to let our physical handicaps make any difference to our work. You know what I mean", she said, as if until now it was all mystery. "Well, Amy carried herself with more spirit than the others, and she didn't seem to be making any sort of fight, but she was simply sex-ridden, like the rest. She behaved as if she hadn't a rival on earth, and she pretended not to know what marriage was about, but I know better. None of them had, and they didn't want to have, anything else to think about, and they didn't really know anything about that, so they simply festered inside – they festered –"

Miranda found herself deliberately watching a long pro-cession of living corpses, festering women stepping gaily towards the charnel house, their corruption concealed under laces and flowers, their dead faces lifted smiling, and thought quite coldly, "Of course it was not like that. This is no more true than what I was told before, it's every bit as romantic," and she realized that she was tired of her intense Cousin Eva, she wanted to go to sleep, she wanted to be at home, she wished it were tomorrow and she

could see her father and her sister, who were so alive and solid;
who would mention her freckles and ask her if she wanted something to eat.

But Cousin Eva has her grievance and it is a real one.

"'Hold your chin up, Eva', Amy used to tell me," [Cousin Eva]
began, doubling up both her fists and shaking them a little. "All
my life the whole family bedeviled me about my chin. My entire
girlhood was spoiled by it. Can you imagine," she asked, with a
ferocity that seemed much too deep for this one cause, "people
who call themselves civilized spoiling life for a young girl because
she had one unlucky feature? Of course, you understand perfectly
it was all in the very best humour, everybody was very amusing
about it, no harm meant – oh, no, no harm at all. That is the
hellish thing about it. It is that I can't forgive," she cried out, and
she twisted her hands together as if they were rags. "Ah, the
family," she said, releasing her breath and sitting back quietly,
"the whole hideous institution should be wiped from the face of
the earth. It is the root of all human wrongs," she ended, and
relaxed, and her face became calm. She was trembling. Miranda
reached out and took Cousin Eva's hand and held it. The hand
fluttered and lay still, and Cousin Eva said, "You've not the
faintest idea what some of us went through, but I wanted you to
hear the other side of the story. And I'm keeping you up when you
need your beauty sleep," she said grimly, stirring herself with an
immense rustle of petticoats.

Yet it is the younger woman, not the older, who feels cut off
from her tradition. Miranda is surprised to find that when her
father meets them at the station next morning, Cousin Eva,
the embattled feminist, enters easily into rapport with him.
Once in the automobile,

[Cousin Eva and her father] were precisely themselves; their eyes
cleared, their voices relaxed into perfect naturalness, they need
not weigh their words or calculate the effect of their manner.
"It is I who have no place," thought Miranda. "Where are my
own people and my own time?" She resented, slowly and deeply
and in profound silence, the presence of these aliens who
lectured and admonished her, who loved her with bitterness and
denied her the right to look at the world with her own eyes, who
demanded that she accept their version of life and yet could not
tell her the truth, not in the smallest thing. "I hate them both,"

her most inner and secret mind said plainly, *"I will be free of them, I shall not even remember them . . ."*

"Come back with us, Miranda," said Cousin Eva, with the sharp little note of elderly command, "there is plenty of room."

"No, thank you," said Miranda, in a firm cold voice. "I'm quite comfortable. Don't disturb yourself."

Neither of them noticed her voice or her manner. They sat back and went on talking steadily in their friendly family voices, talking about their dead, their living, their affairs, their prospects, their common memories, interrupting each other, catching each other up on small points of dispute, laughing with a gaiety and freshness Miranda had not known they were capable of, going over old stories and finding new points of interest in them.

Miss Porter, as her stories and essays reveal, has in her own nature a wide streak of the feminist, and she has presented Miranda's sense of frustration and her spirit of rebelliousness with dramatic sympathy, but the closing sentences of her story are significant. Miranda continues talking to herself:

"Let them go on explaining how things happened. I don't care. At least I can know the truth about what happens to me," she assured herself silently making a promise to herself, in her hopefulness, her ignorance.

The final phrases – "in her hopefulness, her ignorance" – represent an instance of what I mean by the Southern temper.

Miss Leonora is a more complicated and more interesting woman than is Cousin Eva (whose primary function in the story is, after all, to serve as a foil for Miranda). Part of the complication is the mixture of traits that are admirable along with others that are hardly endearing. Miss Leonora's pupil remembers, for example, her strange conduct at the death of one of her pupils years before. That was when Miss Leonora taught at the Institute, a private school for girls, before it burned and Miss Leonora became a teacher in the Thomasville high school. One of the boarding students, a distant kinswoman of Miss Leonora, had been stealing from the other girls. It was Miss Leonora who obtained unmistakable evidence of her guilt and pronounced sentence on her. She was to be expelled and sent back home to Omaha. A few hours later the girl disappeared, and when they dragged the sluggish water near the school, they found her body. The narrator, then a boy of nine, remembers how Miss Leonora suddenly turned on the crowd, calling out "Go away! Go away! What business have you coming here with your wailing and moaning? A lot you care about that dead girl!" And then: "Go away! Take your curious eyes away! What right have you to be curious about *our* dead?"

He also remembers how, a few years later, on the night that the Institute building burned, Miss Leonora dashed about, "screaming orders to everyone, even to the fire brigade when it arrived. She would not believe it when the firemen told her that the water pressure could not be increased. She threw a bucket of water in one man's face when he refused to take that bucket and climb up a second-story porch with it."

But a little later on, with the fire obviously devouring the building, Miss Leonora subsided and simply watched the spectacle like everyone else, and what the boy saw written on her face was not "self-pity or despair". You saw "an awareness of what was going on around her, and a kind of curiosity about it all that seemed almost inhuman . . . She looked dead herself, but at the same time very much alive to what was going on around her."

To sum up, Peter Taylor has not been easy on Miss Leonora, and he allows his hotel-keeper narrator adequate grounds for adverse criticism. (In "A Rose for Emily" Faulkner, of course, has gone much further: Miss Emily's pride and arrogance, her insistence on living her life on her own terms, ends in madness and murder. But even Faulkner's narrator finds something in Miss Emily that stirs his admiration, and his way of telling her story will suggest to the sensitive reader why he says that for the community she was "dear" as well as "perverse", a "treasure" as well as a "burden".)

Miss Leonora seems such to the hotel-keeper in Peter Taylor's story. The hotel-keeper tries very hard to justify the town's treatment of Miss Leonora. He insists that "Wherever Miss Leonora Logan is today, she knows in her heart that in the legal action recently taken against her . . . there was no malice directed against her personally." In fact, people have gone out of their way to be kind: "Two of us," he points out, "even preferred to resign from the school board" to avoid voting for the condemnation proceedings. Besides, Miss Leonora's action is really foolish: "she knows that her going away can only delay matters for a few weeks at most." And yet he has clearly connived at her running away.

It happened in this way: In spite of their quarrel with Miss Leonora, common courtesy forbids the town's officials to serve the condemnation papers on Miss Leonora without some prior notice: the occasion must be a kind of social call. The narrator is chosen as one of a small delegation to make this call. But when he learns at the filling station, from Buck Wallace, the only other man in town with whom Miss Leonora is still on speaking terms, that she is evidently dressed for a journey, he dismisses the rest of the delegation and takes care to go to her house alone. He tells Miss Leonora the news about the condemnation, they chat for a while, and then he hands her into her car and she escapes.

The way in which Miss Leonora was dressed had surprised Buck Wallace and it shocks our narrator. That experience may have a bearing on his final attitude toward her. This is what he saw when he entered her house.

> Her splendid white mane, with its faded yellow streaks and its look of being kept up on her head only by the two tortoise-shell combs at the back, was no more. She had cut it off, thinned it, and set it in little waves close to her head, and, worse still, she must have washed it in a solution of indigo bluing. She had powdered the shine off her nose, seemed almost to have powdered its sharpness and longness away. She may have applied a little rouge and lipstick, though hardly enough to be noticeable, only enough to make you realize it wasn't the natural coloring of an old lady and enough to make you *think* how old she was. And the dress she had on was exactly right with the hair and the face, though at first I couldn't tell why.
>
> As I walked beside her from the center hall into her "office" her skirt made an unpleasant swishing sound that seemed out of place in Miss Leonora's house and that made me observe more closely what the dress was really like. It was of a dark silk stuff, very stiff, with a sort of middy-blouse collar, and sleeves that stopped a couple of inches above the wrists, and a little piece of belt in back, fastened on with two big buttons, – very stylish, I

think. For a minute I couldn't remember where it was I had seen this woman before. Then it came to me. All that was lacking was a pair of pixie glasses with rhinestone rims, and a half-dozen bracelets on her wrists. She was one of those old women who come out here from Memphis looking for antiques and country hams and who tell you how delighted they are to find a southern town that is truly unchanged.

Has Miss Leonora indeed hauled down the flag – given up the fight, agreeing that if you can't beat them, you join them? Or in putting on the uniform of the enemy, has she simply adopted a protective disguise? Whatever her motive, the narrator wonders how she can ever be identified now and brought home if out on the highway she now looks like "a thousand others". It is possible too that she may have completed her disguise by altering her driving habits to conform to those of the world about her, such as "letting other people pass her, [and] dimming her lights for everyone."

But, "I like to think," he tells us, "that in her traveling bag she [has] the lace-choker outfit that she could change into along the way, and the dungarees, too; and that she is stopping at her usual kind of place today and is talking to the proprietors about Thomasville."

By the end of this story, it should be plain to the reader what the narrator values in Miss Leonora, though I am not sure that the narrator is fully clear about it in his own mind. In any case, he would certainly not state it in the way that I am going to have to state it now; but I am forced to summarize.

I should say that he admires Miss Leonora's non-conformity, her insistence on doing things her own way, and her courage to be herself. I doubt that he has ever read David Riesman's *The Lonely Crowd*, but he knows an "inner-directed person" when he sees one. Though he tells himself that he believes in progress, he finds something refreshing in knowing a person who honestly doesn't give a hoot for it. Miss Leonora's attempt to find grace and meaning in life and to live her own life with a certain style has impressed him far more than she, or he, had guessed.

There had been a time when the narrator had supposed that Miss Leonora's careering around the country on her little trips was a kind of madness, but now he tells us that he has come to realize that "For years her only satisfaction in life [had] been her periodic escape into a reality that is scattered in bits and pieces along the highways and back roads of the country she travels". Hers is not an attempt to escape from reality but *into* it, and if Miss Leonora's reality is enmeshed in a past way of life, doomed to extinction, this does not mean that she does not stand in judgement over the "citified place" that Thomasville now aspires to be. The narrator, with at least one side of his mind, concedes that Thomasville is judged and found wanting – wanting in flavor, in vitality, and in essential humanity.

Whatever Miss Leonora's motive in transforming herself into one of those old harpies, blued and burnished in the city beauty-shops, seeking out antiques and country hams, her present appearance evidently served to bring into focus for her former pupil – perhaps into sharp definition for the first time – the values that he had, over the years, come to associate with her. He realizes that he doesn't want her brought up to date. With at least a part of his mind, he dislikes having her surrender to the town and its shallow modernity.

Many writers of the twentieth-century South have found the Miss Leonoras of their region fascinating creatures and have found it absorbing to explore their relation to the communities in which they live. I do not mean to imply that Southern writers have become fixated on this kind of character: Faulkner's alienated Joe Christmas and his Lena Grove with her almost mindless instinctive rapport with nature; the vacuum-centered tycoons like R. P. Warren's Bogan Murdock; the hearty folk heroes like Faulkner's V. K. Ratliff; the confused young men of the 1930's trying to find themselves, men like Jack Burden in Warren's *All the King's Men;* the old hunters or fishermen who keep their sanity and integrity in an unpropitious age, men like Caroline Gordon's Aleck Maury or Warren's Willy Proudfoot; and many other kinds of characters are to be found in the Southern fiction of the last forty years.

But there are good reasons why old maids like Miss Leonora have in this literature a place of some prominence, and what the Miss Leonoras mean to those who write about them can tell us a good deal about the writer's minds and indeed about the Southern temper.

Let us begin with the attitude towards the past: as Taylor's treatment of Miss Leonora, or Faulkner's treatment of Miss Emily reveals, the past is scarcely romanticized. The old woman who is so much attached to the past is not without fault, and may even be guilty of crime. The past is in some ways worse than the present, but it is also better than the present. The attitude toward the past, in short, is discriminating. There is no enthusiastic faith in progress, but neither is there any blind worship of the past. William Butler Yeats would have understood this point of view.

Next, the attitude toward the Establishment. (I dislike the term, but to use it here may by its very anomaly in this context sharpen my point.) The artist and the writer are traditionally "agin" the government. The artist's instinctive position is that of the anarchist, and in a great deal of recent American writing this feeling has been carried to a new pitch of intensity. But the Southern writer's natural tendencies toward anarchy as artist are tempered by his Southern sense of community. An almost instinctive acceptance of the community is still strong, and the community, in the region he knows best, has not yet withered into something so rigidly dead as an Establishment. All of this is not to say that the Southerner is unsympathetic with rebels or that he is willing to accept any community as an act of piety. But the fight that his rebellious characters wage is of a special kind – a sort of civil war – a fight within the family. Faulkner's novels will provide plenty of illustrations.

Next, the issue of conformity. Few things are so interesting as a genuine eccentric; few things so boring as a manufactured eccentricity, got up for purposes of exhibition. The interesting eccentric wants to be himself, not to impress his fellows as being shockingly different from them. Moreover, one can be himself to the point of eccentricity if he can take his values for granted – can assume that they are part of the truth of the universe and that others in their secret hearts accept them too. Lacking this confidence, he may, in his anxiety not to be different, be frightened into falling into step with the man just ahead of him.

Miss Leonora is herself, and can be as eccentric as she pleases as long as she feels that she has some real relation to a true community; when that relation lapses, she adopts the disguise of creatures whom she evidently regards as fakes and therefore as truly grotesque. I think that it is conceivable that she may some day actually put on that pair of "pixie glasses with rhinestone rims" and thus adopt a literal false face in further defiance or for the sake of a deeper disguise; but in either case she will know what she is putting on.

Finally, to mention an issue that is not explicitly noticed but surely implied in Peter Taylor's story: for the Southern writer, nature, including human nature, still has something of the numinous about it. The writer may have ceased to go to church. He may acknowledge no formal religious belief, but he still responds to nature with a kind of religious awe. He respects a mystery lying at the heart of things, a mystery that at some level always evades the rational explanation, a reality that can be counted on to unpredict prediction. He takes a great delight in contemplating the variety of the human scene. He finds human beings wonderful in their courage and generosity, but also wonderful in their "orneriness" and folly. He is continually fascinated by the teasing mixture of elements that is man. He is willing to concede that Miss Leonora is a woman no better than she should be, but he also rejoices that she exists.

13

Southern Literature:
The Wellsprings of its Vitality

Many years ago a very bright young New York woman who dabbled in the arts asked me why it was that the South produced so much significant literature. With some confidence I began to tell her why, but found to my surprise that it was not easy to do. Since that time I have heard the question put often and in various forms. A typical recent posing of the question occurs in one of the essays of John Aldridge's book entitled *In Search of Heresy*. He properly discerns the importance of the Southern background to writers like William Faulkner and Robert Penn Warren. He writes that only in the South and in "certain ailing portions of the moral universe of New England" is there "still a living tradition and a usable myth". But Mr Aldridge accepts a thoroughly stereotyped view of the South. It is his little joke that "nearly every Southerner who preserves his sanity into adulthood emigrates to New York and becomes a novelist". Or is it a joke? For Mr Aldridge seems honestly convinced that life in the South is so grim that the sensitive child is forced to develop his imagination by turning away from the horrors around him. But the Southern novelist who emigrates to the North would seem, if we continue to listen to Mr Aldridge, to be jumping out of the frying pan into the fire, for "Opposed to [the Southerner's] world" Aldridge goes on to say, "is the world of the urban North", a world of grey conformity, but which, for this very reason is also a "world of discontinuity, loneliness, psychoanalysis, nervous breakdown, the world you are exiled to and give your sanity to. . . ." In this last statement Mr Aldridge is clearly not joking, for throughout his book, he insists that this deplorable "grey" world does indeed exist.

So we are free to work out, if we like, a neat set of antitheses: a decadent Southern world that somehow produces art under the very compulsion of its decadence versus a grey world of all too stodgy sanity and conformity; Yoknapatawpha County, Mississippi, versus Fairfield County, Connecticut; what Aldridge calls "the timeless Southern gentlewoman madness" versus the vapidity of the female exurbanite.

Mr Aldridge's account is attractive in a rather fantastic way, and one could perhaps qualify the terms sufficiently to make them yield a modicum of truth. But the sins of the South are not quite so vividly scarlet, the virtues of the North so depressingly grey; and in any case, Mr Aldridge's theory throws the writer too violently back into himself. No literature – and certainly not our present Southern literature – is *that* subjective.

Yet in rejecting an account like the foregoing, I am not prepared to come forward with some confident explanation of my own. I have said that I would talk about the springs of literary vitality, but I cannot trace all the subterranean veins of water that feed those springs. I cannot claim to be able to map the special configurations of the cultural landscape that force those springs to gush out at certain places. Least of all do I understand the process of literary creation, for we are here dealing with more than the contours of the cultural landscape; we are dealing with the inner processes of the mind.

I shall therefore make no pretense to be exhaustive. I shall be content to point to a few special features in the Southern cultural situation that seem to be obviously important. But first, in order to place our problem within a larger perspective, we might note what has been going on all over the English-speaking world during the past half century. Our most authentic literature has been coming from the province and not from the great metropolitan centers. Whether it be Thomas Hardy's Wessex, or W. B. Yeats's Ireland, or Dylan Thomas's Wales or Robert Frost's New Hampshire, a literature rooted in a regional culture stands out in sharp contrast to the rootless urban civilization. What has been going on in the South during the last fifty years, therefore, is analogous to what has been going on in other parts of the English-speaking world.

The Southern writer, therefore, need not be nettled at the reproach that he is a provincial. What else can he be – granted the general international situation – without forfeiting his spiritual integrity and committing a kind of cultural suicide? I do not recommend a parochial blindness, or complacent ignorance, but the South, in the present scheme of things, is committed to provincialism; and the best and truest of the Southern writers accept that fact. South Carolina, for example, cannot become Connecticut. With all due respect to the neat and tidy and quite admirable little state of Connecticut, where I now live, South Carolina ought not to try to be Connecticut. The South must be itself and not merely a synthetic replica of the East, or perhaps a watered-down version of the Midwest.

Only if the South realizes as richly as possible its potentialities as a region will it have a great contribution to make. The literature that it is producing is in itself a great contribution. If the South should foolishly surrender its own personality through some futile effort to keep up with the Joneses, we can confidently say that it will cease to produce literature, and its loss of fruitfulness in this era would be symptomatic of its own spiritual death.

But it is time to be much more concrete and specific. What are some of the elements in the life of the South which have an important bearing on its literature and which clearly reflect themselves in that literature? Let me mention only a few: (1) the concreteness of human relationships including the concreteness of moral problems; (2) the conflict and tension which everywhere confront one in the Southern scene and which, because they are conflict and tension, make for drama; (3) the pervading sense of community; (4) the sense of religious wholeness – I dare say that the South is the last part of the country which still believes instinctively in the supernatural; (5) the belief that human nature is mysterious and relatively intractable, and that it is not a kind of social putty which can be shaped as the politician or the social scientist may be tempted to shape it; and (6) a sense of the tragic dimension of life. If the South still believes in the "American dream", it is at least chastened in its belief, not naïve and uncritical. I remember my

old professor from Oxford University visited me many years ago
in Baton Rouge. I drove him up past the great Standard Oil
plant, on into West Feliciana Parish to look at some of the
plantation houses there. He was very much moved by what
he saw and remarked that on this and other trips to America,
people had shown him only the machinery of success, the great
new buildings, the thriving cities, the powerful means of
production. What I had shown him was not merely the confident future but also the past with its sense of loss and defeat.
Nowhere else in America, he told me, had he seen any such
thing, and the very fact of its existence had reassured him. The
South in this regard was closer to the older European tradition,
for it had some access to a more profound vision of human life.

My list of elements might be extended far beyond the six that
I have named. The six actually represent a selection from a
much longer list that I once jotted down, but even six are too
many for my purposes here. I shall not have time to talk about
more than two or three.

To recur to the first: the concreteness of Southern experience
rests primarily upon the fact that life in the South is still a life
on farms or in small towns. Even in the larger cities, the
Southerner has been able, up to this point, to escape the anonymous life of the great metropolis. I do not want to get too deep
into sociology at this time and I certainly want to avoid
statistics as I would the plague. Let's admit the exceptions.
Some may feel that their lives are not concrete but all too abstract. On the other hand, in Connecticut, life in the village in
which I now live – with its town meetings, its two churches, and
its one village store – though this one has a frozen food counter
rather than a cracker-barrel – can be very concrete. But I
think that my generalizations will hold; namely, that a certain
concreteness is accessible to the modern Southern writer as it is
not to the non-Southerner.

Katherine Anne Porter's story "Pale Horse, Pale Rider"
provides a fine illustration of this quality of concreteness. It is a
story of youthful idealism and the searing frustration that such
an idealism inevitably suffers. This of course is a perennial
theme of literature. It is a story that has been told over and over

again – at no time more often than during the last fifty years. But in Miss Porter's telling, how concrete it all is! – so much that every nuance of Miranda's revolt against the stuffy and the hypocritical seems to find its objective embodiment effortlessly. The story, indeed, is no mere lyrical effusion, but a drama in which, for every action, there is an opposite and comparable reaction. Miranda's idealism that is being lacerated is not a kind of emotional ectoplasm that hovers vaguely around her frustrating situation. We can believe in Miranda's action because we can sense so clearly that against which it is a *reaction*. Joyce's *Portrait of the Artist as a Young Man* manages to incarnate in a kind of objective drama the same order of lyrical idealism, though of course in so different a key, and as the exploitation of so different a theme. But if I mention Joyce here I am simply re-invoking the analogy between Ireland and the South. In both the Joyce and the Porter stories, the family is a force that is almost palpable, though in "Pale Horse, Pale Rider" Miranda is already away from her family, and we know her family only through its effects upon her.

The concrete quality of experience, and again as it involves the sense of family relationships, is to be found in Tennessee Williams's *Cat on a Hot Tin Roof*. To my mind, this is a bad play, a play which is ultimately to be judged incoherent. And yet even this play exhibits powerfully the concrete quality of which I am speaking. I have called the play ultimately incoherent, for I cannot really believe in the characters. I cannot believe that Big Daddy would say some of the things that Mr Williams has forced him to say. I am sure that Williams has badly muddled Brick's motivation. Still, many of the scenes are very powerful. They are so because in this play, as in "Pale Horse, Pale Rider", the family is a real force and not a kind of scheme of abstract relationships.

The South, of course, has no monopoly on the family, and, as I said a few moments ago, it would be silly to claim that life in America outside the Southern states is all of it brittle and abstract. Yet certain relationships among human beings can apparently be presented by the Southern writer without the sense of strain or shrillness or even conscious manipulation.

Surely the Southern writer has his native region to thank for this.

I said a few moments ago that the concreteness of life in the South included the concreteness of moral problems. In modern civilization it is this moral component that tends to disappear or at least to lose any sharpness of outline. The American citizen of the present day finds much of his life merged into great corporate bodies whose policies he can determine only slowly and indirectly if at all, but whose powerful drift relentlessly forces him toward certain actions and decisions. Consider the suburbanite who is moderately well off and owns some shares of *AT & T* or *IBM*. He obviously has no real means for determining the management policies of these giant corporations, and his own particular job in a bank or sales organization hardly gives him more autonomy. He is still merely a cell in a greater organism, whose destinies he can do little to direct though much of his own destiny is bound up with its fate. Indeed, he may find that the area of his own personal life in which he can choose and make decisions is often very narrowly circumscribed. What I have said of the white-collar worker and junior executive will fully apply to the labourer, skilled or unskilled. He is often simply one integer in a great labour union. Unless he makes a career out of leadership – and he would have to be rather exceptional to do this – he must on the whole accept the decisions of the group. Hence so much of the talk that we hear today about the evils of conformity. In modern society the dominant virtues of necessity become those of the well-adjusted extrovert, of the nice guy who is easy to get along with, and of the decent colleague who is all too often merely the man who cheerfully complies with the powers that be.

W. H. Auden has described this kind of man in a poem entitled "The Unknown Citizen". I quote the concluding lines:

The Press are convinced that he bought a paper every day
And that his reactions to advertisements were normal in every
way.
Policies taken out in his name prove that he was fully insured,
And his Health-card shows he was once in hospital and left it
cured.

Both Producers Research and High-Grade Living declare
He was fully sensible to the advantages of the Installment Plan
And had everything necessary to the Modern Man,
A gramophone, a radio, a car, and a frigidaire.
Our researchers into Public Opinion are content
That he held the proper opinions for the time of year;
When there was peace, he was for peace; when there was war,
    he went.
He was married and added five children to the population,
Which our Eugenist says was the right number for a parent of his
    generation,
And our teachers report that he never interfered with their
    education.
Was he free? Was he happy? The question is absurd:
Had anything been wrong, we should certainly have heard.

With the world that Auden thus describes we return to the world described by Mr Aldridge in his book *In Search of Heresy*, to which I referred at the beginning of this paper. It is the world of the urban North, the world in Aldridge's phrase "of discontinuity, loneliness, psychoanalysis, nervous breakdown". These are peculiarly the ills of modern man, and the South, you need not be told, is not exempt from them. Still I think that it is fair to say that up to this time, the South has better resisted the grey anonymity and the complacent conformity that Aldridge associates with the dominant civilization. And the South has been able to resist such dehumanization largely because it has retained a notion of reality still informed by religion, and because it has clung to old-fashioned and now sometimes despised virtues. In this older view of reality, man is constantly being put to the test. He is confronted with moral choices and he has to assume responsibility for his actions. An older world-view persisting in a simpler and less urbanized context: this is the situation that still obtains in much of the South. I am convinced that it is a situation that has helped determine the characteristic stance of the Southern writer. For him, evil is a fact that cannot be explained away. Moreover, it is something involved with the innermost being of the self. It is not the result of a defective social organization or merely the consequence of an unfortunate childhood. Therefore one cannot hope to eradicate evil by making the right decision at the polls or by relaxing on the couch of the right psychoanalyst. (This is not to say that it is useless to vote or that one may not need to consult a psychiatrist: it is to say that man is a moral being and not merely a mechanism.)

Perhaps I can best make my point by dealing with the apparent exception, the work of William Faulkner. Faulkner is frequently described as a writer who deals with will-less compulsive, driven men. Indeed, no less an authority than André Gide has asserted that Faulkner's characters lack human souls because they lack will. But Faulkner's characters are not soulless automata. Even those of his characters who seem most compulsive in their actions, characters like Joe Christmas in *Light in August*, or like Quentin Compson in *The Sound and the Fury*, actually live in an old-fashioned moral universe. Indeed the terror of their predicament could be fully manifested only against such a background. Furthermore, a novel like *Absalom, Absalom!*, unless I completely misunderstand it, is a massive parable about the necessity for moral action.

There is some reason, however, for misunderstandings of Faulkner on this score of compulsion and free will, for Faulkner rarely elects to present a passionate debate in which the choice is fought out. Instead, he usually gives us the already committed character, "devoted, concentrated in purpose". His fine story, "An Odor of Verbena", will furnish a good example of what I mean. An attentive reader soon comes to realize that Bayard's decision not to avenge his father's death is a deliberate decision, one made after a good deal of soul-searching, and adhered to in spite of the most powerful counter-pressures. But since the story proper begins only after Bayard has made his decision, and since Faulkner chooses to focus attention upon Bayard's resistance to the counter pressures, the inattentive reader, or the reader who knows little of the Southern scene, might easily conclude that Bayard has not freely chosen a course of action at all – that he is simply in the grip of an obsession.

With this matter of the hard choice – the choice between two evils or the choice between two goods – we touch upon two of the points that I made earlier about the Southern experience:

first, the presence of conflict and tension, which make for drama, and second, the sense of the tragic dimension of experience. I think that it is with this sense of the tragic that Robert Penn Warren is concerned in his poem entitled "Dragon Country". In its vividness of detail and its air of complete conviction, the poem is one of the most brilliant that Warren has ever written. But its meaning has puzzled many readers, and some have confessed that they end up in bewilderment. According to the poem, a dragon has appeared in the state of Kentucky. Everybody knows, of course, that dragons don't really exist and yet how account for some of the things that have happened? What possibly could have done the damage to Jack Simms's hogpen, for example? And what creature could have torn the mules from the trace chains of the wagon, leaving burst harness and splintered, blood-stained wood? And how account for the fact that when men hunted the marauder, the bloody trail always ended suddenly as if the beast had simply flown up and away?

> So what, in God's name, could men think, when they couldn't bring to bay
> That belly-dragging earth-evil, but found that it took to air?
> Thirty-thirty or buckshot might fail but then at least you could say
> You had faced it – assuming, of course, that you had survived the affair.
>
> We were promised troops, the Guard, but the Governor's skin got thin
> When up in New York the papers called him Saint George of Kentucky.
> Yes, even the Louisville reporters who came to Todd County would grin.
> Reporters, though rarely, still come. No one talks. They think it unlucky. . . .

Turned tongue-tied by the metropolitan press, which laughs at the dragon-story, and thus not able to admit that the evil has reality, even the friends and relatives of the victims explain the facts away. When a man disappears, his family report that he has gone to work in Akron, "or up to Ford, in Detroit". When Jebb

Johnson's boot was found with a piece of his leg inside it, his
mother refused to identify it as her son's.

Now land values are falling; lovers do not walk together by
moonlight. Certain fields are going back to bush and undergrowth. The coon "dips his little black paw" undisturbed each
night in the stream.

> Yes, other sections have problems somewhat different from ours.
> Their crops may fail, bank rates rise, loans at rumor of war be
>   called,
> But we feel removed from maneuvers of Russia, or other great
>   powers,
> And from much ordinary hope we are now disenthralled.
>
> The Catholics have sent in a mission, Baptists report new attend-
>   ance.
> All that's off the point! We are human, and the human heart
> Demands language for reality that has not the slightest dependence
> On desire, or need – and in church fools pray only that the Beast
>   depart.
>
> But if the Beast were withdrawn now, life might dwindle again
> To the ennui, the pleasure, and night sweat, known in the time
>   before
> Necessity of truth had trodden the land, and our hearts, to pain,
> And left, in darkness, the fearful glimmer of joy, like a spoor.

Thus the poem ends. The bewildered reader may be tempted
to try to find in it a kind of justification of evil – even a Mani-
chaean celebration of evil as the necessary and inevitable
counterpart of good – that is, the reader may interpret the poem
to mean that the Kentuckians who inhabit the dragon's country
are really better off than others are, since the inhabitants of the
dragon's country have to live so dangerously and are kept so
constantly on the moral *qui vive*. But this is not quite what Warren
is saying. The "joy" of which a "a fearful glimmer" glows in the
last line comes not from evil as such but from an acceptance of
the "necessity of truth". If one admits the element of horror in
life, if he concedes the necessary mystery, if he faces the terrifying
truth about it, if he admits the existence of the dragon of evil,
that very facing of the truth constitutes the promise – and the
only promise – of ultimate joy.

The third aspect of Southern culture that I mentioned earlier is the sense of community. Communities are obviously to be found *in partibus infidelium* as well as in our blessed South. Yet I think that I am justified here in emphasizing the sense of community, for there is a cohesiveness in the South which is distinctive. The cohesion is sometimes so strict that it is regarded as a smothering rather than a nurturing force. The social scientist frequently deplores it. The young literary rebel lashes out against it. The neurotic finds it peculiarly oppressive. And, goodness knows, all of us at one time or another have voiced our exasperation with it. But as a living force it has its virtues, and insofar as literature is concerned, it constitutes a necessary and tremendously valuable milieu. Deprived of this circumambient medium in which he lives and moves and has his being, the artist may soon find himself like a fish out of water, gasping frantically for air. Even the artist in exile, the artist in the guise of the cursed wanderer, needs something to be exiled *from*. How else can he realize his role?

The sense of community is the very stuff out of which most of the literature of the South is made. Yet it is something that easily goes unnoticed, and indeed the Southerner himself, since it is as familiar as the air that he breathes, may take it, like the air, for granted. Conversely, the outlander who does not take it for granted may find a novel like Faulkner's *Light in August* quite baffling, simply because he is unaware of the force of community which pervades that novel, and being unaware of it, misses the central structure of the novel.

Yet a little reflection will show that nearly all the characters in *Light in August* are outside the community – they are pariahs, defiant exiles, withdrawn quietists, or simply strangers. Miss Burden, the daughter of carpet-bagger intruders, has lived within a kind of cultural cyst. As for the Rev. Mr Hightower, the community has tried its best to expel him, though having failed in the attempt, it has finally accorded him a sort of grudging acceptance. The curious little man, Byron Bunch, is considered by the community to be a harmless eccentric. Joe Christmas is, of course, a true Ishmael, who defies both white and black communities. But the community itself, the great counterforce to which these characters are attracted, or against which they are reacting, has no specific representatives in *Light in August* and need have none. For the sensitive reader, the community is everywhere in the novel, represented here by the sheriff, there by the woman who runs the boarding house, and again there by Byron's fellow workers at the sawmill. Yet many modern critics, even when they are struck with the brilliance of individual characters, make heavy weather of the novel, simply because they cannot "see" the community any more than they can "see" the air that pervades the scene, and consequently cannot understand what really is happening. Yet the importance of the community for the meaning of the novel is easy to demonstrate. If you try to imagine *Light in August* transferred to the east side of Manhattan Island, where the community, at least in Faulkner's sense, does not exist, you can quickly see how much the novel does depend upon this powerful though invisible element. Plotwise, everything in the novel could still be accounted for. The frustration and rage of Joe Christmas, the murder of the lonely old maid, Miss Burden, and the impotence and moral defeat of the Rev. Mr Hightower, are familiar enough happenings in the setting of our great modern world cities. But they are given a very special focus by being put, as Faulkner has put them, in a pastoral setting, where the flock still exists as an entity, with its shepherds and bellwethers and often cruel sheepdogs. In such a context, with a visible flock, the plight of the lost sheep and the black sheep can be given special meaning.

The importance of the community could be illustrated from almost any work that Faulkner has written. "A Rose for Emily", for example, is told by a nameless spokesman for the community. Characteristically, he says "We thought this," "Then it seemed to us," "Then we said that," etc. But more is involved than a mere trick of narration: the meaning of the story is lost – it indeed becomes nothing but a Gothic horror story – unless we take into account Miss Emily's relationship to the community.

Again, the meaning of *Absalom, Absalom!* has been badly distorted by readers who think that Sutpen is the embodiment of the community instead of an outsider who has tried to seize upon the values of the community by abstraction and violence.

The sense of the community in modern Southern literature could be illustrated from almost any Southern writer. If I have chosen in this paper to confine my illustrations to Faulkner and one or two others, that has simply been because, in speaking before a general audience, I have wanted to confine myself to two or three of our most widely known authors. But there are dozens of Southern writers, who would have furnished instances of the aspects of experience about which I have been speaking. Apparently the richness and immediacy and complexity of his cultural community has fascinated the typical Southern author. If he has had to rebel against it, as Thomas Wolfe did, still his very rebellion is a tribute to it. It has challenged one author after another to discover its meaning. It has refused, however, in its density, to yield neat abstract propositions except to the most brutal sociological handling, such as that which Erskine Caldwell has given it from time to time.

As long as this experience exerts its urgent demand to be redeemed in knowledge and yet at the same time resists all the simplifications that undercut *true* knowledge, presumably it will call out from the perceptive Southern writer novels, dramas, and poems, which strive to articulate its meaning. Poem after poem in Robert Penn Warren's fine volume, *Promises*, might be used to illustrate. In his "Walk by Moonlight in a Small Town", the speaker returns to his boyhood home and finds the little town, in spite of all its tawdry "matter of fact", filled to the brim with mystery.

And pitiful was the moon-bare ground.
Dead grass, the gravel, earth ruined and raw –
It had not changed. And then I saw
That children were playing, with no sound.
They ceased their play, then quiet as moonlight, drew, slow, around.

Their eyes were fixed on me, and I
Now tried, face by pale face, to find
The names that haunted in my mind.
Each small, upgazing face would lie
Sweet as a puddle, and silver-calm, to the night sky.

> But something grew in their pale stare:
> No reprobation or surprise,
> Nor even forgiveness in their eyes,
> But a humble question dawning there,
> From face to face, like beseechment dawning on empty air.

Here the children remembered from his boyhood put the question to him, not he to them. It is a question that he would answer, but obviously one that no man can answer.

> Might a man but know his Truth, and might
> He live so that life, by moon or sun,
> In dusk or dawn, would be all one—
> Then never on a summer night
> Need he stand and shake in that cold blaze of Platonic light.

But what the poet yearns for here is humanly impossible. Man can never know his truth so thoroughly that he will not need to shake in the cold blaze of the light of the ideal.

In another poem Warren encounters the way in which a remembered experience cries out for utterance into meaning, and deals with the problem more quietly but I think even more brilliantly. The poem is entitled "Hands are Paid". It has to do with a commonplace event. The scene, presumably out of childhood, is one in which a farmhand has worked all day in the threshing field for his silver dollar, gone home to eat sowbelly and cornbread by the light of the coal-oil lamp, kicked off his shoes, and finally fallen into bed.

> The bullbat has come, long back, and gone.
> White now, the evening star hangs to preside
> Over woods and dark water and far countryside.
> The little blood that smeared the stone
> Dropped in the stubble, has long since dried.
>
> The springs of the bed creak now, and settle.
> The overalls hang on the back of a chair
> To stiffen, slow, as the sweat gets drier.
> Far, under a cedar, the tractor's metal
> Surrenders last heat to the night air.
>
> In the cedar dark a white moth drifts.
> The mule's head, at the barn-lot bar,

> Droops sad and saurian under night's splendor.
> In the star-pale field, the propped pitchfork lifts
> Its burden, hung black, to the white star,

Someone in the threshingfield uncovered a black snake and snagged him on the pitchfork where he continues to make "Slow arabesques till the bullbats wake".

> And the years go by like a breath, or eye-blink,
> And all history lives in the head again,
> And I shut my eyes and I see that scene,
> And name each item, but cannot think
> What, in their urgency, they must mean,

> But know, even now, on this foreign shore,
> In blaze of sun and the sea's stare,
> A heart-stab blessed past joy or despair,
> As I see, in the mind's dark, once more,
> That field, pale, under starlit air.

Many a Southern author, surely, shuts his eyes and sees some such scene, turns over each item lovingly with the hands of the mind, but "cannot think / What, in their urgency, they must mean". Or perhaps he does try to indicate what these imagined events mean, even as Warren in other poems and in his novels has tried to indicate what some of them mean. But it is significant that the urgency with which they strive toward meaning is felt, and that whether one can formulate their meaning or not, the contemplation of the scene holds for such writers "a heart-stab blessed past joy or despair". As long as the stuff of the Southern experience continues to exert this claim upon the imagination of its sons, the South will continue to give us a powerful literature.

14

Faulkner's Treatment of the Racial Problem: Typical Examples

The racial problem is, in the first place, only one of the many problems that America faces at the present time. Indeed, we share in the problems that seem endemic to the twentieth-century societies of the West, particularly those societies that have been industrialized for a considerable time. In the second place, the racial problem has its own relation to the whole complex of such larger problems and, in my opinion, cannot be fully understood in isolation from them. But race has been much in the headlines of late. The problems of race are certainly urgent, and it is these problems that have attracted the special attention of some of our finest literary minds.

Moreover, in this matter of the racial problem a "close" reading of texts may be particularly useful, if we are really concerned with what the writer in question is saying in his fiction, and especially if that writer is William Faulkner. Because of its very urgency, of its topicality, and of the emotional charge that it carries for a great many Americans of the present time, the reader may very well attribute to Faulkner's texts meanings that are not actually there. Such a reader, if challenged, can of course reply that what he finds is surely what Faulkner ought to be saying since a sensitive and imaginative writer like Faulkner must surely be as enlightened a man as the reader himself is.

Such reasoning is very human, and who am I to say that this or that particular reader has not seen the truth and that whenever we have doubts as to what Faulkner meant we should read the passage in question by the clear light of that privileged reader's perceptions. That, however, is not the way that literary criticism works – or perhaps I should say that I am so old-fashioned that I think that is not the way it ought to work. For every reason, it seems to me important to try to see what Faulkner's text actually says. If we value Faulkner as an artist, we must do this. In so far as we really believe that the insights provided by a sensitive artist may tell us something about the state of society in a particular historical period, it is all the more important to determine as precisely as we can what the import of the work actually is.

Before taking up the concrete examples, however, I think I ought to make one brief preliminary comment on "close reading". Some actors and actresses strenuously object to being "typed" – as the ingenue or the witless and zany comic or the wise and fatherly counsellor or whatever, for the actor who is so typed may be condemned to play that same role forever after. I sometimes feel that I too have been typed in something like this fashion – as the rather myopic "close reader", the indefatigable exegete. In fact I am interested in a great many other things besides close reading. But I do believe that if we are not to talk nonsense about literary texts, we must have accomplished an adequate reading of them. What is an adequate reading? How "closely" must one read a Hemingway story? Or a Shakespearian tragedy? Or the childhood lyric, "Twinkle, twinkle, little star"? The degree of closeness will depend upon a number of things. I have no dogmatic prescription to offer. But – to cite a specific example – I am convinced that a closer reading of Faulkner's novels would have saved certain critics from egregious mistakes. It would, for instance, have prevented Leslie Fiedler's writing that the mother of Joe Christmas tried to convince the doctor who delivered her child that the child's father was a Mexican and not a Negro. But there was no attending physician at the birth of this child. The girl's grimly fanatical father was nicknamed "Doc". But Old Doc Hines is not Dr Hines, and it is Mr Fiedler's own imagination that has supplied him with his medical degree.

Again, a more careful reading of Faulkner's page would have

prevented a reader as astute as Mrs Olga Vickery from attributing to Temple Drake, the daughter of a judge, an episode involving Ruby Goodwin, the wife of a moonshiner. This confusion of persons necessarily distorts Mrs Vickery's conception of Temple's character. (One ought to add, however, that this error is corrected in the revised edition of her study of Faulkner, a work that contains much excellent commentary on Faulkner's novels.)

Where shall we begin? It is tempting to choose a problem from Faulkner's masterpiece, *Absalom, Absalom!* What is Thomas Sutpen's real attitude towards the Negro? In what sense is he a racist? He refuses to acknowledge his own son because the son has a trace of Negro blood and yet in effect he acknowledges a daughter whom he has begotten on one of his slaves and he brings her up in the household along with his legitimate son and daughter. Again, he invites his neighbours to watch him fight with one of his slaves. He fights with the slave not at all to punish him, but as a kind of test of his own manhood. Such actions, by the way, scandalize the Mississippi community in which he lives.

What is the attitude of Sutpen's son by the quadroon wife, Charles Bon, the son whom Sutpen will not acknowledge? What is Bon's own attitude toward race and specifically toward his quadroon mistress and their little son? How much is his attitude towards them, and towards his white brother and sister, affected by race? I've heard Chales Bon referred to as the first "freedom rider", and his quiet but stubborn pressure upon his father to acknowledge him might make the epithet seem apt. But is it? Could one not argue that, in abandoning his own little son, he is simply repeating his own father's behaviour towards himself? There are problems here, and whatever the final answer some of the confident assertions made about Charles Bon and Sutpen are called in question by the richness and the complexity of the novel.

On the other hand, it is also tempting to look into the character of Lucas Beauchamp, the man with Negro blood who is a descendant of old Carothers McCaslin. Lucas plays a prominent part in *Go Down, Moses* and he is the acknowledged hero of *Intruder in the Dust*. Thus, though the character of Lucas is very different from that of Charles Bon, he too has been praised as a champion of Negro rights. Lucas insists upon his own dignity. He refuses to be pushed around by some of his rough white neighbours.

Yet Lucas seems to be actually proud of his white ancestry and regards as weak and perhaps pusillanimous Issac McCaslin's repudiation of his heritage because of his sense of guilt at what the white man has done to the Negro and specifically because of the ruthless cruelty of his grandfather, old Carothers McCaslin. What is Lucas Beauchamp's attitude towards the white man? What is his attitude toward the other Negroes? What is his attitude toward race?

These are matters that I am tempted to discuss; yet I think that I shall begin with a simpler problem. In "That Evening Sun", Nancy, a Negro woman who has served as a temporary cook for the Compson family, lives in mortal fear of her husband Jesus. Nancy has prostituted herself to a white man and is now carrying his child. Though Jesus has left town some months before, Nancy has become convinced that he has returned and means to cut her throat.

Apparently many readers of this story have not known how to deal with Mr Compson. Why doesn't he do more to help Nancy? Why doesn't he offer a more effective response to her plight? A note published in *The Explicator* by Mr William Toole will provide a typical expression of this point of view. Mr Toole remarks that in this story none of the white characters comes off very well. Even Mr. Compson, whom Toole describes as the "finest [of the] white character[s]", fails Nancy and through that failure becomes "strangely diminished in moral stature". By contrast, Nancy grows in moral stature. As Mr Toole puts it, "the debauched and ignorant Negro woman is elevated all the more as she awaits a grim and primitive punishment of her sins".

On one level I suppose that his judgement makes a kind of sense. Mr Compson cannot allay Nancy's fears and Faulkner does indeed succeed in evoking in his reader a very sensitive awareness of Nancy's plight – of her helpless desperation. It is

Nancy's story and not Mr Compson's, and it is proper that our sympathies should be focussed on her and that the other characters in the story should serve finally as mere foils to her. But a somewhat more careful reading of the text will indicate that it would be difficult – if not impossible – for anyone to free Nancy from her terror and that most men would have acted pretty much as Mr Compson did. Whether or not we think well of Mr Compson, doesn't, I suppose, matter very much, but if we are to comprehend the story, it is important that we understand Nancy. That is the issue of consequence.

One of Mr Compson's real difficulties is that there is no proof that Jesus has returned. Nancy produces no specific evidence. She does say that she has been sent a sign, but is the sign, this "hogbone, with blood on it", as Nancy describes it, the product of Nancy's perfervid imagination? Or if it did exist, is it meant to be a portent of death? And was it left in Nancy's cabin by her estranged husband? Nobody has yet had a glimpse of him, not even Nancy, and when she is asked for proof that he is now in Jefferson, all that she can offer is her irrational sense of his vengeful presence. (I say "irrational", for it is interesting that before he left town Jesus already knew that Nancy was carrying Mr Stovall's child and yet at that time had made no move against her.) Mr Compson, therefore, in expressing his scepticism that Jesus really means to return and kill Nancy, is not being fatuously reassuring. In fact I see no reason to doubt Mr Compson's sincerity when he tells Nancy that Jesus is "probably in St Louis now. Probably got another wife by now and forgot all about you". But even if he thinks her terror irrational and her fears imaginary, he does recognize that for her they are real and so he tries to help her.

The reader also ought to notice that it is not merely the white people who are sceptical about Jesus's return. So are the Negroes. Dilsey asks Nancy: "How do you know he's back? You ain't seen him" and Nancy can only reply "I can feel him. I can feel him laying yonder in the ditch."

Dilsey then comes at the matter from a somewhat different angle, by asking Nancy how she knows that Jesus is "out there tonight? How come you know it's tonight?" Nancy has no evidence apart from the profound intuition that has gripped her whole being. She tells Dilsey: "He's there, waiting. I know. I done lived with him too long. I know what he is fixing to do fore he know it himself."

Later, Dilsey asks Nancy why she won't let Mr Jason – this is her way of referring to Mr Compson – telephone the marshal. Then Dilsey tries to persuade Nancy to go on down to her own cabin. Frony, Dilsey's daughter "will fix you a pallet and I'll be there soon". But Nancy replies that no mere Negro can stop Jesus. She can be safe only in the house of a white man, though as we shall see by the end of the story Nancy believes that a white man's house would provide no protection either. When Mr Compson offers to take her to stay with Aunt Rachel, another Negro, Nancy tells him that "it wont do no good. When even your own kitchen wouldn't do no good. When even if I was sleeping on the floor in the room with your chillen, and the next morning there I am, and blood—"

Preoccupation with Mr Compson's adequacy or inadequacy in the situation has tended to obscure another complication of the story, one that I believe has never been mentioned by any of the numerous commentators. It is this: Nancy's own sense of guilt and the strong emotional ties that still bind her to Jesus make her feel that she deserves to suffer at his hands.

I don't believe that we should press this issue very hard, but the ambivalence of Nancy's feelings toward Jesus and the fact that she still feels strongly possessive toward him is put very emphatically in the story. When Mr Compson tries to quiet her fears by telling her that Jesus is now in St Louis and has probably got himself another wife, what does Nancy say? "If he has, I better not find out about it. I'd stand there right over them, and every time he wropped her, I'd cut that arm off. I'd cut his head off and I'd slit her belly and I'd shove . . ." Mr Compson conscious that the children are present, tries to make her hush, but not in time to prevent the little girl's asking: "Slit whose belly, Nancy?" Nancy is indeed afraid of Jesus, but she is still fiercely possessive and her feeling that he still belongs to her whether or not she belongs to him, obviously has something to do with her obsession with the notion of his return.

So too does her sense of guilt. When the five-year-old Jason, fascinated with the conversation going on between Dilsey and Nancy, asks: "Are you a nigger, Nancy?" Nancy answers: "I hellborn, child. I wont be nothing soon. I going back where I come from soon."

As the story ends, Mr Compson arrives at Nancy's cabin. He is looking for the children who are here because Nancy has enticed them to come home with her. Whether or not she thinks that the presence of the children – the eldest is only nine years old – would be a protection against Jesus, in her misery she craves some kind – indeed any kind – of company. Mr Compson is still sympathetic but now he is at his wit's end. Nancy won't go with him to Aunt Rachel's to spend the night. She won't lock up her house; and he asks her: "Then what do you want to do?" Nancy tells him: "I don't know. I cant do nothing. Just put it off. And that don't do no good. I reckon it belong to me. I reckon what I going to get ain't no more than mine."

In a sense one feels that Nancy may even be anxious to get it over with, but she doesn't want it to happen in the dark. As she tells Mr Compson: "I scaired of the dark. I scaired for it to happen in the dark." The story ends with the children and Mr Compson departing, the younger children not comprehending the situation, prattling to each other as they go. But the eldest of the children, Quentin looks back to see Nancy sitting by the fire with her kerosene lamp turned as high as she can turn it, and the door of the cabin left wide open, waiting for Jesus to enter, but hoping that it won't happen in the dark.

It is a beautifully told story, a brilliantly told story, and it must be judged so even if Jesus did not come that night or on any subsequent night. For this story is concerned to render the terror and the helplessness of a human being who feels that she is to die. This feeling is transmitted with utter conviction.

Well, what did happen? Did Jesus come that night and cut Nancy's throat? We simply don't know. Malcolm Cowley, in his important introduction to the *Portable Faulkner*, a work that did so much to revive Faulkner's reputation in the United States after most of Faulkner's books were out of print, remarks that we do learn in another story, the novel *The Sound and the Fury*, that Nancy had her throat cut and that her husband left her body in a ditch for the turkey vultures to eat. But Cowley, as several people have since pointed out, had confused the bones of Nancy, the mare once owned by the Compsons, with Nancy, the heroine of this story. As far as Faulkner is concerned, there is no way to tell whether we are to regard Nancy's fears as a delusion or as well founded.

It is true that in Faulkner's novel *Requiem for a Nun*, Nancy reapppears as Nancy Manigoe. The same incident about Nancy's having her teeth kicked in by the white man to whom she has prostituted herself is also told of Nancy Manigoe, and the author has acknowledged (in *Faulkner in the University*) that the two women are the same. But this in itself does not prove very much. It would not be the first time that Faulkner had changed his mind about a character, Faulkner is not at all above summoning a character like some Lazarus from the tomb to serve his turn in another story or novel. Therefore I shall not claim that the fact that Nancy occurs in a later novel proves that Jesus did not kill her, and that therefore her fears were merely a delusion, though the author of a well regarded book on Faulkner, Mrs Olga Vickery, has been willing to do so. She writes that "in view of Nancy's disconcerting resurrection in *Requiem for a Nun*, a careful rereading [of "That Evening Sun"] discovers how much emphasis is placed upon the foolishness of her fears."

Perhaps so, though I think that we are on safer ground as far as literary criticism is concerned if we say that the worth of "That Evening Sun" is independent of later events about which we can only speculate and which are no part of the story itself. If a painting is properly composed and has its own unity, it can convey its meaning within the section of canvas to which the painter has confined his brush. We are not required to try to trace a portion of a picture on out beyond the picture frame. Yet I dare say that readers like Mr Toole might have been inclined to be less hard on Mr Compson if they had borne in mind that Nancy lives beyond the time of "That Evening Sun", if not like Falstaff to live and fight another day, at any rate, to suffer and die on another occasion.

Now I should like to turn to a more complicated problem, one that arises with reference to that massive novel, *Light in August*, surely one of Faulkner's masterpieces. The problem can be put briefly in this fashion. What is Joe Christmas's attitude toward the Negro? What is his attitude toward the white man? What is his attitude toward himself? Many critics have insisted that in the end Joe dies as a Negro and as a conscious representative of the Negro race. In what sense, if any, can one say that he does?

I had first planned to discuss in some detail a related question: is Joe Christmas really a Negro? What evidence – in spite of the fact that commentators occasionally refer to him as a *mulatto* – what evidence is there for believing that he possesses any Negro blood at all? But I must confine this paper, if I can, to the amount of pages prescribed and besides I have already dealt with this matter of Joe's racial inheritance in a book on Faulkner. At this time, I shall do no more than offer a brief summary of the argument that I offered there.

A careful reading of *Light in August* suggests the unlikelihood of Joe's possessing any Negro genes. The evidence that he has even a trace of Negro blood rests on the assertion of Joe's crazed old grandfather, Eupheus Hines. Joe's grandmother, Mrs Hines, is thoroughly aware that her husband is an obsessed man and she herself doubts that Joe has any Negro blood. But in any case, it is plain that Joe becomes what he becomes, not by any biological inheritance but by the way in which society regards him and the way in which he is constrained to regard himself.

Two terrifying passages in the novel make this point with great power. They are both short and I shall read them here. The first (on p. 105 of the Penguin edition) describes Joe as a child in the orphanage, conscious of the way in which the janitor, old Hines, keeps him under observation.

"He knew that he was never on the playground for an instant that the man was not watching him . . . with a profound and un-flagging attention. If the child had been older he would perhaps have thought *He hates me and fears me. So much so that he cannot let me out of his sight*[.] With more vocabulary but no more age he might have thought *That is why I am different from the others: because he is watching me all the time*[.]"

The second passage (p. 288) describes the child's own intent observation of a Negro workman in the orphanage yard. Old Doc Hines tells of how Joe "was watching the nigger working in the yard, following him around the yard while he worked, until at last the nigger said, 'What you watching me for, boy?' and he said, 'How come you are a nigger?' And the nigger said, 'Who told you I am a nigger, you little white trash bastard?' and he says, 'I aint a nigger,' and the nigger says, 'You are worse than that. You dont know what you are. And more than that, you wont never know. You'll live and you'll die and wont never know.'"

What does Joe Christmas himself think of his Negro blood? Obviously he hopes to shock the woman in the brothel by telling her that he is part-Negro. Later, perhaps as a test of her love, he confides to the waitress-prostitute Bobbie Allen, the first girl with whom he was ever in love, that he thinks he has some Negro blood. But when Joanna Burden asks him one evening whether he has any idea who his parents are, he tells her that he doesn't know "Except that one of them was part nigger. Like I told you before."

> "She was still looking at him: her voice told him that. It was quiet, impersonal, interested without being curious. 'How do you know that?'
> "He didn't answer for some time. Then he said: 'I don't know it.' Again his voice ceased; by its sound she knew that he was looking away, toward the door. His face was sullen, quite still. Then he spoke again, moving; his voice now had an overtone, unmirthful yet quizzical, at once humorless and sardonic: 'If I'm not, damned if I haven't wasted a lot of time.'"

The occasion of this conversation is a rather special one. It occurs in a period in which Joe seems moderately happy in his relationship with Joanna. Faulkner has gone to some pains to suggest an atmosphere of confidence between two people talking about themselves and his mention of the overtone in Joe's voice, "unmirthful yet quizzical", suggests that here Joe is speaking sincerely. He doesn't really know whether or not he has Negro blood. Incidentally, had old Doc Hines ever told him that his father was part Negro, Joe probably would have said, "my father was part nigger," not what he does say: "One of them was part nigger." Joe does not know but has been simply acting out his alienation, carrying on his shoulder, like a chip of defiance, the imagined stigma of black blood (see p. 191).

Did Joe persist in his defiance to the end? Or did he, just before his death, finally accept the Negro as his brother? In a recent book, Mr Melvin Backman interprets Joe's final fateful actions as a Negro – that is, Backman argues that Joe voluntarily returns to Jefferson and puts himself in the hands of the law because he has resolved to die at its hands as a Negro murderer.

Backman's interpretation acquires a certain plausibility in the light of certain passages that occur in Chapter 14. For example, Joe, dazed and lightheaded from hunger, goes into a Negro house where he smells food (p. 252). But the Negroes immediately recognize Joe as the wanted murderer and flee in panic. There Joe seats himself at the table,

"waiting, thinking of nothing in an emptiness, a silence filled with flight. Then there was food before him, appearing suddenly between long, limber black hands fleeing too in the act of setting down the dishes. It seemed to him that he could hear without hearing them wails of terror and distress quieter than sighs all about him, with the sound of the chewing and the swallowing. 'It was a cabin that time,' he thought. 'And they were afraid. Of their brother afraid.'"

The last phrase may be thought to count powerfully in favour of Backman's case, particularly if we put beside it Joe's reflection (three pages earlier on p. 249), as he pulls on a pair of black shoes that had belonged to a Negro man. As he does so, Joe "could see himself being hunted by white men at last into the black abyss which had been waiting, trying, for thirty years to drown him and into which now and at last he had actually entered, bearing now upon his ankles the definite and ineradicable gauge of its upward moving".

It is in this passage in particular that Mr Backman finds justification for his belief that Joe's actions do testify to his acceptance of himself as a Negro. Backman writes that "paradoxically, it is only after the murder that [Joe] felt ready to become one with his black brother. He put on the 'black shoes' even though he 'could see himself being hunted by white men at last into the black abyss . . .'"

The suggestion that Joe's putting on the shoes signifies that he is ready to become one with his black brother may, however, seem much less plausible if one will recall his motive for putting on these shoes "smelling of Negro". Joe was being tracked by the sheriff's bloodhounds and he wishes to confuse the dogs. In fact, as we are told on p. 248, he persuades a Negro woman to accept his own shoes in exchange for her husband's.

The stratagem works. The bloodhounds rush to the Negro cabin and have to be pulled by main strength away from the Negro woman who is now wearing Joe's shoes. Now it is perfectly true that when Joe puts on the Negro's brogans, there does arise in his mind a vision of himself "being hunted by white men at last into the black abyss which had been waiting". Joe is so poised between the white world and the black world that he is hypersensitive to the implications of any action as tending toward, or away from, the one or the other of those worlds. Joe is thus alive to all the ironies implied in enveloping himself if only momentarily in the Negro odour. One takes a step down into the black abyss in order to escape being swallowed up in it. But having taken the first step downward, will one be able to escape?

Some days later, Joe, still wearing the Negro's shoes, does start back of his own accord to Jefferson. But why? Mr Backman, as we have already remarked, associates Joe's return with an acceptance of himself as a Negro. Mr Lawrance Thompson has his own variation on this theme; Joe's return is "his masochistic bid for torture". Thus, Joe wants to be killed and since Thompson uses the word "torture", apparently Joe foresees and yearns for Percy Grimm's butcher knife. Thompson writes: "After the murder and after the escape [Christmas] chooses to circle back, within the larger of his runnings, to avail himself of that ultimate and masochistic luxury of death at the hands of his enemies – the death he expects and wants." But this is a clumsy and foreshortened account of Joe's action. Joe's

motivation is more than this. Moreover, Joe at this moment is
not any more or less masochistic than he has been for years past.
But in any case, Joe has not laid aside his defiance. What I hope
will constitute the proof of this last statement will be forth-
coming in what I shall say a little later.

After invading the Negro cabin and eating some cooked food
– we are told that it is the first decent food that Joe had eaten
for a long time – Joe feels a compulsive need to ascertain the
day of the week as though "at last he had an actual urgent need
to strike off the accomplished days toward some purpose, some
definite day or act, without either falling short or overshooting".
From this time onwards he becomes irritated when the people
whom he accosts run away from him in terror. He says to himself

> "Any of them could have captured me, if that's what they want.
> Since that's what they all want: for me to be captured. But they
> all run first. They all want me to be captured, and then when I
> come up ready to say here I am *Yes I would say Here I am I am
> tired of running of having to carry my life like it was a basket of eggs* they
> all run away".

Joe is evidently now fully resolved: he knows precisely what
he is going to do. When he elicits from a terrified Negro the
information that it is Friday, he immediately sets off toward
Jefferson. We are told that Joe's "direction is straight as a surveyor's line, disregarding hill and valley and bog". Yet we are
also told, he is not hurrying. "He is like a man who knows where
he is and where he wants to go and how much time to the exact
minute he has to get there in. It is as though he desires to see his
native earth in all its phases for the first or the last time."

Does this last sentence imply that Joe is finally accepting his
homeland and nature itself? The next sentence might seem to
indicate as much:

> "He had grown to manhood in the country, where like the un-
> swimming sailor his physical shape and this thought had been
> molded by its compulsions without his learning anything about
> its actual shape and feel. For a week now he has lurked and crept
> among its secret places, yet he remained a foreigner to the very
> immutable laws which earth must obey. For some time as he

walks steadily on, he thinks that this is what it is – the looking and seeing – which gives him peace and unhaste and quiet . . .''

But it is not an acceptance of his homeland as home or his reconciliation with nature that accounts for his present sense of "unhaste and quiet", for the passage goes on to say: "suddenly the true answer comes to him. He feels dry and light. 'I dont have to bother about having to eat anymore,' he thinks, 'That's what it is.'"

If the account of Joe's state of mind had not taken this last turn, one would be tempted to say that something like the instinct that directs the homing bee has put Joe on his "bee-line" course back toward Jefferson or that Joe's compulsion as he moves back toward Jefferson is like that of the salmon fighting its way up the falls, back to the pool in which it had been spawned. No more than the salmon, does Joe feel any need to bother about eating: his body has enough stored energy to reach the destination sought and that destination is sensed as final.

Yet what urges Joe to return to Jefferson is something more than the blind compulsion that determines the movements of a natural creature. What is this "true answer" that suddenly comes to Joe, this answer that makes him feel suddenly "dry and light". It has not been spelled out for us by Faulkner, but surely it has been implied by what Joe is to say to himself a little later, as he sits in the wagon headed toward Mottstown and Jefferson: he tells himself that he has been "farther in these seven days than in all the thirty years [before]. . . . 'But [he says to himself] I have never broken out of the ring of what I have already done and cannot ever undo . . .'" The course on which Joe instinctively sets off on towards Jefferson, a course as "straight as a surveyor's line, disregarding hill and valley and bog," denies the circle in which he has been running for thirty years. His "unhaste and quiet" – the fact that he is not hurrying – denies the running to which he has condemned himself through those thirty years. He is tired of running and if this going back to Jefferson to face the consequences means, as Joe knows it must mean, death, well, Joe is tired of having to handle life as if it were a basket of eggs. His life will have to take its chances though Joe as a realist can make an informed estimate of what those chances are.

The bee's return to the hive, "straight as a surveyor's line", is a powerful assertion of Joe's desire to break out of the circle, but Joe's motive for returning deserves an analogy more nearly adequate to himself as a conscious being. I find the analogy that seems to me best in a speech that Milton in his *Paradise Regained* assigns to Lucifer. Christ has just chided Lucifer for offering him his aid in assuming the throne of David, for, as Christ points out to Lucifer, "my promotion will be thy destruction". But the great Adversary has his answer. He will welcome his destruction when it comes.

> Let that come when it comes; all hope is lost
> Of my reception into grace; what worse?
> For where no hope is left, is left no fear;
> If there be worse, the expectation more
> Of worse torments me than the feeling can.
> I would be at the worst; worst is my Port,
> My harbour and my ultimate repose.
> The end I would attain, my final good.

Yet if Joe does decide to return to Jefferson where, as he must know, he will meet his death, does this final decision indeed signify his acceptance of himself as a Negro? Does he feel ready, as Mr Backman has put it, "to become one with his black brothers"? Or as Mrs Olga Vickery states it, "to assume the role of Negro which Jefferson has prepared for him"? We may be tempted to think so because of the last sentence in Chapter 14 (p. 255) where Joe is described as sitting on the seat of the wagon, with, "planted on the dashboard before him the shoes, the black shoes smelling of Negro: that mark on his ankles the gauge definite and ineradicable of the black tide creeping up his legs, moving from his feet upward as death moves."

Yet if we turn to the next chapter and read (on p. 263) the account of how Joe was captured, we will find that Joe does not really "give" himself up at all. He does not go up to the sheriff and say I am the Negro murderer whom you are seeking. Far from it. There is a brilliant passage in which we are allowed to overhear the account of the capture of Joe as reported by a countryman who had come into Jefferson to market on Saturday. He tells us that when Christmas arrived in Jefferson, he "went into a white barbershop like a white man, and because he looked like a white man they never suspected him. Even when the bootblack saw how he had on a pair of second-hand brogans that were too big for him, they never suspected. They shaved him and cut his hair and he paid them and walked out and then went right into a store and bought a new shirt and a tie and a straw hat, with some of the very money he stole from the woman he murdered." Finally someone did recognize him and asked him "Aint your name Christmas?" and Christmas made no ado about admitting that he was. As the countryman puts it, "He never denied it. He never did anything. He never acted like either a nigger or a white man. That was it. That was what made the folks so mad. For him to be a murderer and all dressed up and walking the town like he dared them to touch him, when he ought to have been skulking and hiding in the woods, muddy and dirty and running. It was, like he never even knew he was a murderer, let alone a nigger too."

The important matter here is that even though Joe has decided to stop running away, he has not made his peace with either the white or the black community. He is still the defiant rebel. His alienation is the most important thing just as his search to find himself is perhaps the most admirable thing about him. He refuses to be distracted from that search or to accept any compromise with his real identity. Because his formative years were spent in the American South, and because of the special circumstances of his childhood, his alienation is intimately involved with the Southern caste system and crucially so. But we shall miss the terrifying poignance of Joe's situation and the richness of the whole novel if we treat *Light in August* as simply a footnote on the racial situation in the United States. Because Joe evidently cannot honestly say, he does not say: the Negro is my brother and I accept brotherhood with him. This modern Ishmael recognizes no brothers and he is no nearer to the Negro consciousness than he is to the white.

Indeed, Joe's problem is a more complicated affair. It is connected with his latent homosexuality – his fear of women and his fear of Nature. But I have no more space to pursue these connections.

To pursue these matters might also seem to lead us away from any positive moral judgement and away from any specific incitement to social and political action. But these objections, before they are to be accepted as valid, call for further scrutiny. I concede that the reader of a novel is a moral being and that as such he must be ultimately willing to make a moral commitment. But surely his actions and the actions of all of us ought to be taken in the light of the fullest moral calculus to which we can attain and, again, surely the prime virtue of a good novel is not that it should prove to be effective "*agit-prop*" but that it should provide us with a profound revelation of reality.

T. S. Eliot somewhere makes a helpful distinction between prose and verse. He observes that though it is legitimate that a writer should in his prose reflect upon his ideals, in his verse he must deal with reality. In his discursive prose – that is to say, in his speeches and essays, which have been collected into one volume by Mr James Meriwether – Faulkner speaks out positively and emphatically in favour of racial justice and according to the Negro his full civil rights. But in his fiction – which at his best attains the subtlety and the massive concreteness of poetry – Faulkner is concerned with reality – in its richness, its manifold complications, and even in its ambiguities. In his *Light in August*, the plight of Joe Christmas is revealed in all its poignance but it is made to transcend the topicalities of our day. Faulkner relates Joe's tragic alienation to universal issues and to predicaments of the human spirit that transcend the agonies and frustrations of the American South and the special problems of our troubled twentieth century.

15

Faulkner as a Poet

Like James Joyce, Faulkner began by thinking of himself as a poet, but went on to discover that his richest and most sensitive and fully formed writing – his "poetry" in short – could be realized in his prose. Faulkner refers more than once to himself as a "failed poet".[1] The remark is, of course, too emphatically disparaging to be taken literally. In Faulkner's early work there are certainly the stirrings of poetry and who is to say that had he not become intensely interested in fiction he might not have developed into a very considerable poet. William Butler Yeats, like Faulkner, began as a rather dreamy and ineffectual poet and did not acquire muscle and power until he was a man in his forties. But speculation about what kind of poet Faulkner might have turned out to be had he not given his full attention to fiction is arid. Far more to the point is to trace the development from the poet of *The Marble Faun* to the author of *The Hamlet* and *Go Down, Moses,* and to show why the more ample forms of fiction allowed his "poetry" to come to full fruition there.

One can hardly overstate the fact that Faulkner's verse is late romantic verse. Indeed, one might fairly call his verse decadent. The poets who had caught his imagination and whom he was consciously and unconsciously imitating were the poets of the 'nineties. Like theirs, this young poet's world has grown tired and old. He harks back to a brighter and ampler day in which the presence of the gods of the fields and forests could still be felt. Nature, to be sure, still moves through its beautiful rituals and modern man is still able, in imagination at least, to sense what nature must have meant to an ancient Greek. But a sensitive

---

[1] "Interview with Cynthia Grenier", *Lion in the Garden*, eds. J. B. Meriwether and Michael Millgate (New York: Random House, 1963), p. 217.

observer cannot conceal from himself the fact that the antique world lingers today only in an occasional nook of sequestered beauty and in the memory of poets and other dreamers.

Faulkner spells out for us part of the story of his early verse in telling us that "at the age of sixteen I discovered Swinburne. Or rather, Swinburne discovered me, springing from some tortured undergrowth of my adolescence, like a highwayman, making me his slave. . . . It was years later that I found in him much more than bright and bitter sound, more than a satisfying tinsel of blood and death and gold and the inevitable sea."[1]

The influence of Swinburne would seem to be general and pervasive rather than a matter of specific borrowings.[2] It is true that Faulkner published in *The Mississippian* (26 November, 1919) a poem entitled "Sapphics",[3] which represents itself as a definite response to, and a further commentary upon, Swinburne's poem of that title. Faulkner's opening phrase "So it is", implies that the speaker here has just put down Swinburne's poem and is stating his general agreement with it. Faulkner has imitated the metre (as the title implies) but nowhere else, as far as I can see, does he try to follow Swinburne's intricate metrical patterns. Swinburne's flickering anapests and complicated rhyme schemes were not for this young poet. He does not venture into them.

There are other readily discernible influences to be seen in Faulkner's poetry: Verlaine (some of whose poems Faulkner translated), Keats, T. S. Eliot, perhaps Edna Millay, and I should think the early verse of W. B. Yeats. But with the exception of Eliot, Faulkner is not much interested in the experimental verse of 1914–20. He shows small patience with Carl Sandburg or Amy Lowell, and though he wrote[4] that he had read "Robinson and Frost with pleasure, and Aldington", and though he tells us that "Conrad Aiken's minor music still

---

[1] "Verse Old and Nascent: a Pilgrimage", first published in *The Double Dealer*, April, 1925; reprinted in *William Faulkner: Early Prose and Poetry*, ed. Carvel Collins (Boston: Little, Brown, 1962), p. 114.

[2] R. P. Adams collects a number of borrowings and adaptations, chiefly from the early fiction: *Tulane Studies in English*, XII (1962), p. 120.

[3] *Early Prose and Poetry*, pp. 51–2.

[4] "Verse Old and Nascent", *Early Prose and Poetry*, pp. 116–17.

echoes in my heart", it is plain that these poets have left few visible traces on Faulkner's own poetry. (It is curious that nowhere in this essay or in his other early reviews does he mention Eliot.)

The poet whose influence Faulkner *is* willing to acknowledge in 1925 as tonic and exhilarating is A. E. Housman. Faulkner writes:

> "I found a paper-bound copy [of *A Shropshire Lad*] in a bookshop and when I opened it I discovered there the secret after which the moderns course howling like curs on a cold trail in a dark wood, giving off, it is true, an occasional note clear with beauty, but curs just the same. Here was reason for being born into a fantastic world: discovering the splendor of fortitude, the beauty of being of the soil like a tree about which fools might howl and which winds of disillusion and death and despair might strip, leaving it bleak, without bitterness, beautiful in sadness,."[1]

If *A Shropshire Lad* did influence the poetry of *The Marble Faun*, it is a vague and diffused influence: there are few echoes, if any, that I can hear. With the poems collected in *A Green Bough*, the matter is entirely different. Poem after poem, especially the poems written in quatrains, acknowledge Faulkner's debt to Housman. In addition to the three examples cited by Harry Runyan[2] a number of years ago, I call attention to such parallels as these:

The opening couplet of Poem VII

> Trumpets of sun to silence fall
> On house and barn and stack and wall

clearly echoes the first line of Poem VIII of *A Shropshire Lad*,

> Farewell to barn and stack and tree.

The last stanza of Poem IX of *A Green Bough* reads:

> . . . and found this peace as he
> Who across the sunset moves to rest
> Finds but simple scents and sounds;
> And this is all, and this is best.

[1] "Verse Old and Nascent", *Early Prose and Poetry*, p. 117.
[2] "Faulkner's Poetry", *Faulkner Studies*, II (Summer–Autumn, 1954), 26.

Compare the last quatrain of Poem VII of *A Shropshire Lad*:

> Lie down, lie down, young yeoman;
>   The sun moves always west;
> The road one treads to labour
>   Will lead one home to rest,
>   And that will be the best.

Faulkner has the mother in Poem XIV say of her son

> He'll be strong and merry
> And he'll be clean and brave. . . .

The last phrase answers to these lines in Poem XVIII of *A Shropshire Lad*:

> Oh, when I was in love with you,
> Then I was clean and brave. . . .

Poem XXI brings together phrases from several Housman poems. Line 10 begins "Woman bore you"; compare the last line of Poem XXXV of *A Shropshire Lad*, "Woman bore me, I will rise." Line 11 of Faulkner's poem begins "Life's gale may blow". Here Faulkner is undoubtedly remembering line 14 of Poem XXXI of *A Shropshire Lad*: "Through him the gale of life blew high."

Faulkner begins Poem XXXIV of *A Green Bough* with an elaborate metaphor:

> The ship of night, with twilightcolored sails,
> Dreamed down the golden river of the west. . . .

Compare the first stanza of Poem IV of *A Shropshire Lad*:

> Wake: the silver dusk returning
>   Up the beach of darkness brims,
> And the ship of sunrise burning
>   Strands upon the eastern rims.

This little sheaf of echoes and reminiscences does not pretend to be exhaustive, but one need not cite further instances to show that Faulkner did not exaggerate when he stressed the impact of *A Shropshire Lad* on his mind and art.

A Green Bough is not, of course, simply woven out of Housman.

The first three poems seem to me to have a good deal of Eliot in them and there is a clear echo in Poem XXVII. Undoubtedly there were other influences: Keats obviously in Poem XL, and possibly Edna St Vincent Millay in Poem XLIV. Moreover, it ought to be said, there is also a great deal in *A Green Bough* – and in *The Marble Faun* – that is Faulkner himself, instances of accomplished art even though usually fragmentary – interesting phrases, fresh images, significant metaphors.

A rabbit bursts into view, "its flashing scut / Muscled in erratic lines of fright"; "A pewter bowl of lilies in the room / Seems . . . to weigh and change the gloom / Into a palpable substance [one] can feel"; the Marble Faun looks around him at a snow-covered garden "soundless in the falling light"; a man walks his life "As through a corridor rushing with harsh rain" and "reaching the end / He turns it as one turns a wall." The world in autumn turns "to cold and death / When swallows empty the blue and drowsy days / And lean rain scatters the ghost of summer's breath."

Yet the really important things to be found in Faulkner's verse are the anticipations of the great metaphors and analogies which would achieve their full development only when they reappeared in his fiction. As Faulkner told a student audience in 1947: "My prose is really poetry."[1]

Miss Rosa Coldfield, of Faulkner's *Absalom, Absalom!*, might claim as much for her prose. Faulkner, to be sure, tells his reader that she is a poet: Miss Rosa is the self-appointed Poet Laureate of Yoknapatawpha County and the principal theme of her verse is the gallantry and heroism of the Confederate soldier. But Faulkner evidently felt that it was pointless to provide his reader with samples of her verse, for it is easy to imagine its banal and hackneyed quality. But Miss Rosa's prose – her long tirade against Thomas Sutpen which comprises nearly all of Chapter V – is a very different matter. It rises at times to the intensity of poetry. It is a very special and contorted poetry, to be sure, a dithyramb of hate, – obsessed, bardic, self-intoxicated – but it is poetry, nevertheless. Miss Rosa's "poetry" can throw light on Faulkner's own, for

[1] *Lion in the Garden*, p. 56.

Faulkner quite clearly put a good deal of himself into Miss Rosa, and though as author he always stands outside and above her Norn-like frenzy, undoubtedly she provided him with an outlet for an elevated, involved, highly mannered strain of rhetoric which was very dear to his own heart.

Miss Rosa, who, some forty-three years before had been shocked by Thomas Sutpen's bald proposal that they should breed a child with the promise that if the child should prove to be a male, he would marry her, has lived ever since, as Mr Compson puts it, in a state of permanent outrage. Now in Chapter V, as she sits in her parlor with Quentin Compson through the long September afternoon, she pours out her indignation against Sutpen, the "demon". Thrice she exclaims: "I, self-mesmered fool!" "Self-mesmered" is obviously a clipped form of "self-mesmerized". Perhaps Faulkner himself saw nothing odd in the phrase or perhaps he consciously tailored it to fit Miss Rosa's rather eccentric use of the language. But in any case, the epithet fits her like a glove: we know that this is the way in which she would have put it, and though what we hear is the furious, exuberant rhetoric of a "self-mesmered fool", nevertheless the more passionate parts of it are telling and effective.

Like all passionate speech, Miss Rosa's is highly rhythmic and some of it comes very close to a formalized accentual structure. One can clearly hear the beat and cadences in the following passage in which Miss Rosa tells how as a young girl she observed the garden paths through which the lovers, Judith and Bon, walked:

> I was not spying, who would walk those raked and sanded garden paths and think 'This print was his save for this obliterating rake, that even despite the rake it is still there and hers beside it in that slow and mutual rhythm wherein the heart, the mind, does not need to watch the docile (ay, the willing) feet'; would think 'What suspiration of the twinning souls have the murmurous myriad ears of this secluded vine or shrub listened to? what vow, what promise, what rapt biding fire had the lilac rain of this wisteria, this heavy rose's dissolution, crowned?'

Much of Miss Rosa's speech is taken up with trying to suggest to Quentin how she, as a fourteen-year-old girl, lonely, shy, yearning for love, participated vicariously in the courtship of Bon for Judith. The motive was not envy, she assures him, nor was she spying on the young couple. She was certainly not in love with Bon. She tells Quentin:

> "(I did not love him; how could I? I had never even heard his voice, had only Ellen's word for it that there was such a person) and quick not for the spying which you will doubtless call it, which during the past six months between that New Year's and that June gave substance to that shadow with a name emerging from Ellen's vain and garrulous folly, that shape without even a face yet because I had not even seen the photograph then, reflected in the secret and bemused gaze of a young girl: because I who had learned nothing of love, not even parents' love – that fond dear constant violation of privacy, that stultification of the burgeoning and incorrigible I which is the need and due of all mammalian meat, became not mistress, not beloved, but more than even love; I became all polymath love's androgynous advocate."

"All polymath love's androgynous advocate" is of course absurd; but on reflection, one realizes that it is a perfectly accurate description of Miss Rosa's state of mind in that long-ago summer. Moreover, by this time we have been convinced that Miss Rosa is quite capable of this phraseology: this is just what she would have said. Since the speech is in character and since it describes (though with a prim pedantry) the state of mind in question, one hardly need defend calling it "poetry". If the adjective "androgynous" sticks in the reader's craw, he might turn back to an earlier page in which Miss Rosa confesses that during this "miscast summer of my barren youth which (for that short time, that short brief unreturning springtime of the female heart) I lived out not as a woman, a girl, but rather as the *man* which I perhaps should have been [*italics mine*]". Indeed the special pathos of her situation, as Miss Rosa now sees it, was that she was trying to be born into some kind of womanhood, and Judith's love affair summoned her own stunted womanhood to birth.

Miss Rosa describes her childhood as having been "not living but rather some projection of the lightless womb itself;

I [,] gestate and complete, not aged, just overdue because of some caesarian lack, some cold head-nuzzling forceps of the savage time which should have torn me free. . . ."

"Caesarian lack" represents a fierce compression which would earn the blue pencil on any freshman's essay. But again, it is a phrase that one would rather expect Miss Rosa to invent, and perhaps it makes the notion more compact by its violent ungrammatical compression: her womanhood's being brought to birth required a caesarian section or at least a "cold head-nuzzling forceps" to pull her into the light.

On the next page she continues with birth imagery:

"instead of accomplishing the processional and measured milestones of the childhood's time I lurked, unapprehended as though, shod with the very damp and velvet silence of the womb, I displaced no air, gave off no betraying sound, from one closed forbidden door to the next and so acquired all I knew of that light and space in which people moved and breathed as I (that same child) might have gained conception of the sun from seeing it through a piece of smoky glass – fourteen, four years younger than Judith, four years later than Judith's moment which only virgins know: when the entire delicate spirit's bent is one anonymous climaxless epicene and unravished nuptial . . ."

Absurd or no, Miss Rosa can rise to the occasion with the proper metaphor. She does so when she describes her coming into the house in response to the news that Henry has killed Charles Bon. As she faces the house she sees in it

"some desolation more profound than ruin, as if it had stood in iron juxtaposition to iron flame, to a holocaust which had found itself less fierce and less implacable, not hurled but rather fallen back before the impervious and indomitable skeleton which the flames durst not, at the instant's final crisis, assail; there was even one step, one plank rotted free and tilting beneath the foot (or would have if I had not touched it light and fast) as I ran up and into the hallway whose carpet had long since gone with the bed- and table-linen for lint, and saw the Sutpen face. . . ."

This Sutpen face is the face of Clytie, the mulatto woman who is Sutpen's natural daughter and Judith's half-sister. Miss Rosa had always despised and feared Clytie and now Clytie is "there

in the dim light, barring the stairs: and I running out of the
bright afternoon, into the thunderous silence of that brooding
house where I could see nothing at first: then gradually the face,
the Sutpen face not approaching, not swimming up out of the
gloom, but already there, rocklike and firm and antedating
time and house and doom and all, waiting there (oh yes, he chose
well; he bettered choosing, he created in his own image the cold
Cerberus of his private hell) – the face without sex or age
because it had never possessed either: the same sphinx face
which she had been born with. . . ."

One assumes that Miss Rosa had, as a matter of course, read
Byron and Scott; but evidently she knows her Shakespeare too.
When she bursts into the house, aghast at what she had heard,
eager to find out just what had happened, she is met by more
than Clytie's sphinx face; she is arrested by Judith's quiet and
apparently unperturbed voice. Rosa is like Hamlet standing
before the arras behind which is concealed some dread or
terror. But she is afraid to slash through it to reveal the truth.
She tells Quentin that "even at nineteen [I] must have
known that living is one constant and perpetual instant when
the arras-veil before what-is-to-be hangs docile and even glad
to the lightest naked thrust if we had dared, were brave enough
(not wise enough: no wisdom needed here) to make the
rending gash".

Miss Rosa's mind, like Faulkner's, was evidently also
saturated with Macbeth's great final soliloquy: "Life's but a
walking shadow, a poor player", etc. The shadow image comes
into her speech as she tries to convey to Quentin the demonic
quality of Thomas Sutpen. She insists to Quentin that

"he was not articulated in this world. He was a walking shadow.
He was the light-blinded bat-like image of his own torment cast
by the fierce demonic lantern up from beneath the earth's crust
and hence in retrograde, reverse; from abysmal and chaotic
dark to eternal and absymal dark completing his descending (do
you mark the gradation?) ellipsis, clinging, trying to cling with
vain unsubstantial hands to what he hoped would hold him,
save him. . . ."

I don't contend that all of Faulkner's rhetoric can be defended

– not even in this novel and certainly not in some of the others. But Faulkner is much more the master of it than his early critics have given him credit for being, and by making Miss Rosa responsible for the most overblown rhetoric of *Absalom, Absalom!*, Faulkner has gone far toward giving it dramatic justification.

Since Miss Rosa does not know the truth about the fall of the house of Sutpen or why Henry killed Charles Bon, she is bound to make her own misjudgments and, under the circumstances, is quite powerless to make any sense of the events that have destroyed her family. She is forced into a "devil theory" in order to account for them. But Miss Rosa is no fool – nor, in spite of her overblown rhetoric, does she lack a certain literary flair. She has a good sense of the histrionic. She is conscious that she is acting a part: for several pages she actually refers to herself in the third person as if she were a character in a play.

To listen to her, as Quentin is compelled to listen to her that September afternoon, is to witness the eruption of a small volcano, pouring forth its long pent-up subterranean fires. The perfervid emotion is there, and her torrent of words is impelled by an inner necessity.

Miss Rosa, by the way, is largely responsible for the often-remarked "Gothic" quality of this novel. Mr Compson's stoical perspective and his cynical weariness hardly points in this direction. It is Miss Rosa who invests Sutpen's Hundred with nameless horrors and demonic presences. Again and again, in her long tirade, she speaks of hearing, through Clytie's or Judith's voice, an inhuman voice, that of the house itself speaking, and she creates for the reader, if he will attend to her, what that house means to her. The house called Sutpen's Hundred is the physical shell of the master who has fashioned it for his own purposes. Thus she describes her life in that house with Clytie and Judith while Sutpen was away at the War:

> "Something ate with us; we talked to it and it answered questions;
> it sat with us before the fire at night and, rousing without any
> warning from some profound and bemused complete inertia,
> talked, not to us, the six ears, the three minds capable of listening,
> but to the air, the waiting grim decaying presence, spirit, of the

house itself, talking that which sounded like the bombast of a madman who creates within his very coffin walls his fabulous immeasurable Camelots and Carcassonnes."

For Miss Rosa, Sutpen speaks "the bombast of a madman", and she takes her cue from him, replying with a "bombast" of her own, that of a woman warped by loneliness and outrage. But even bombast, in the hands of a master rhetorician, can on occasion touch poetry, can become the inevitable means of revealing something about Miss Rosa and even perhaps, in its own perverse way, something about Sutpen himself.

Miss Rosa's "poetry" is a very special kind of Faulkner's prose-that-is-really-poetry. As has been remarked earlier, much of this passionate prose has to be seen as the development of images and metaphors which first appeared in the early verse. In fact, one has sometimes to examine passages in the novels in order to see what some of the more obscure poems are "about". In *A Green Bough*, for example, Poem III is filled with complicated imagery, much of it brilliant and powerfully evocative; but the references are obscure and the articulation of the image clusters is very shaky. One conjectures that the poem is about the passing of night and the coming of dawn. (The sixth section of the poem is clearly a dawn scene.) This conjecture is strengthened when one notices the several links that connect the poem with the great dawn scene in *The Hamlet*. In *The Hamlet* and in Poem III, light is likened to sound: "The cave is ribbed with music; threads of sound / Gleam on the whirring wings of bats of gold, / Loop from the grassroots to the roots of trees, / Thrust into sunlight, where the song of birds / Spins silver threads to gleam from bough to bough." With this passage, compare: "[light] upward-seeking, creeps the knitted bark of trunk and limb [of trees] where, suddenly leaf by leaf and dispersive in diffusive sudden speed, melodious with the winged and jeweled throats, it upward bursts and fills night's globed negation with jonquil thunder."

There is one quite specific link between the poem and the dawn passage in *The Hamlet*: in the novel the dark from which the light wakes and rises, the "dark of time's silt and rich refuse", holds within itself "Troy's Helen and the nymphs and the snoring mitred bishops, the saviors and the victims and the kings". But the bishops and the kings had appeared long before in Poem III:

> . . . snored
> Kings and mitred bishops tired of sin
> Who dreamed themselves of heaven wearied
> And now may sleep, hear rain, and snore again.

Later in the poem, we find "Kings in hell, robed in icy flame" and "Glutted bishops . . . / Couched in heaven, mewed [?up] for paradise," and still farther on, "duke and king / And scarlet cardinal. . . ." This medieval pageant with Dantesque echoes ("robed in icy flame") – "A priest on thin gray feet" and "Whispering nuns" are alluded to in the closing lines – continued to hold Faulkner's imagination. (Nineteen years after the publication of *The Hamlet*, the same configuration occurs in *The Mansion*. The earth which is drawing Mink Snopes down into itself is "already full of the folks that had the trouble but were free now . . . all mixed and jumbled up comfortable and easy now . . . Helen and the bishops and the kings and the unhomed angels. . . .")

To return to Poem III: if the matter of this poem *is* the beginning of day, then the dawn passage in *The Hamlet* shows how the novice poet, at a later date and in a different medium, was able to clarify and develop his first clogged and murky expression without losing any of the boldness and energy of the original conception.

In his fiction, then, Faulkner was eventually to move toward a tougher and more realistic poetry. Did his discovery of the *Shropshire Lad* bring about such poetry? The honest answer has to be no. Housman's emphasis on Stoic endurance appealed to something very deep and abiding in Faulkner's own nature and Housman's insistence that his young soldiers and athletes and shepherd lads face the facts of a hard and finally meaningless world is the quality which evidently called forth Faulkner's early tribute to Housman. Housman had provided, Faulkner wrote, a "reason for being born into a fantastic world" and for displaying "the splendor of fortitude". But Housman's poetry

is itself essentially a poetry of the nineties. Its theme is of a lost
Arcadia:

> We'll to the woods no more,
> The laurels all are cut,
> The bowers are bare of bay
> That once the Muses wore. . . .

It is full of desolate shepherds; it emphasizes the fragility and
pathos of young love; and at its weakest it verges on prettiness
and sentimentality.

In any case, Housman's influence did not send Faulkner back
to his native land. In fact, nearly all of Faulkner's early verse –
perhaps all of his verse – finds its setting in a faraway country.
The landscape is a literary landscape in the most damaging
senses of that term.

In the introduction that he contributed to *The Marble Faun*,
Faulkner's Oxford friend, Phil Stone, wrote that "the sunlight
and mocking-birds and blue hills of North Mississippi are a part
of this young man's very being". Certainly this statement is true,
profoundly so, but it is misleading if it is taken with any
reference to the poetry of *The Marble Faun* or indeed to most of
the rest of Faulkner's verse. For example, *The Marble Faun* is
filled with copses and glades and brakes. Instead of the blue
hills of North Mississippi, there are wolds, leas, and downs. On
these downs grow heath and gorse and may. The cottages have
thatched roofs. The birds that fly about these cottages and out
of these brakes are rooks, nightingales, and blackbirds.

To an American ear, these words are disconcertingly literary.
They sound even more outlandish to a Southern ear. Though it
is true that Faulkner uses the word *glade* in one of his novels, this
word is unknown to the common folk. Glades and brakes occur
in Swinburne. One remembers Swinburne's celebrated line
"The breasts of the nymphs in the brake." But in Mississippi
a brake would be inevitably a canebrake and certainly would
not contain white-breasted nymphs. Furthermore, in
Swinburne's poem there are downs as a matter of course but
they are not to be found in Yoknapatawpha County any more
than heather or gorse or thatched cottages.

Consider the birds in Faulkner's poetry which are, with the

exception of an occasional mockingbird, simply not the birds of this continent. Hence the anomaly of his English rooks, European nightingales "Whose cries like scattered silver sails / Spread across the azure sea," and his singing blackbirds.

These blackbirds (I have counted at least eight instances of them in Faulkner's poetry) make the point most strikingly. For the blackbirds that sing so sweetly in Faulkner's verse just as they do in the verse of Housman, belong to the thrush family and so come legitimately by their music. The blackbirds that Faulkner could have known in the Southern states – or elsewhere in America for that matter – can hardly be said to sing at all. They don't belong to the thrush family, and in his *Field Guide to the Birds*, Roger Peterson deposes as follows: "The 'song' [of the rusty blackbird] is a split creak like a rusty hinge . . . rather penetrating." The purple grackle's "'song' [is] a split rasping note that is both husky and squeaky". The cowbird's "Courtship song [is] bubbly and creaky, (*glug-glug-gleeee*, last note thin, on high pitch)." Even if, to be exhaustive, one includes the redwing blackbird among the possibilities, the case is not helped. Peterson describes the song of the redwing as "a gurgling *konk-la-reeee* or *o-ka-leeee*, the last note high and quavering". Anyone who has heard redwings challenging each other or singing their courtship song near a swamp or pond may find the chorus of powerful *konkarees* very pleasant to the ear, but no one who has ever heard them will associate them with Faulkner's blackbirds with "gold wired throats" or think their songs "Piercing cool and mellowly long".

If Faulkner as a young poet was indeed finding in the Marble Faun the mouthpiece for his own youthful yearnings and poetic imaginings, the bonds that rendered the faun relatively "mute and impotent" were not marble but literary. Until Faulkner was able to break these bonds, his writing, in spite of an occasional felicitous expression or nicely turned passage, remained empty and sterile.

Yet, though the discovery of *A Shropshire Lad* did not free the young poet for vigorous and graceful poetic activity, *A Shropshire Lad* did represent, as Faulkner saw, the placing of the poem within a known landscape, a device that allowed the poet to use particular and even local materials in which to clothe the universal things that he was moved to say. (One remembers Faulkner's praise of *A Shropshire Lad* that in it the poet had shown "the beauty of being of the soil like a tree". One remembers too that he had, in his essay "American Drama", asked the American writer to use the "language as it is spoken in America", complaining that in comparison with it, "British is a Sunday night affair of bread and milk – melodious but slightly tiresome nightingales in a formal clipped hedge.")[1]

In this general connection it is also worth looking at Faulkner's short review of William Alexander Percy's *In April Once*, which he contributed to *The Mississippian* on 10 November 1920.[2] Faulkner writes that "Mr Percy – like alas! how many of us – suffered the misfortune of having been born out of his time. He should have lived in Victorian England and gone to Italy with Swinburne, for like Swinburne, he is a mixture of passionate adoration of beauty and as passionate despair and disgust with its manifestations and accessories in the human race. His muse is Latin in type – poignant ecstasies of lyrical extravagance and a short lived artificial strength achieved at the cost of true strength in beauty." One is tempted to say that writing about his fellow Mississippian, Faulkner is writing more or less consciously about his own situation. One does not mean to claim that Faulkner is here, with cool detachment, discovering in his own poetry the deficiencies that he found in Percy's. But surely the passage quoted indicates that this highly intelligent if still somewhat confused young man, was aware of the inherent weakness in his own poetry. And surely there is evidence that Faulkner felt that he too had been born out of proper time, since his poetic heroes are the late Victorians, and that – at least for his own happiness – he ought to have gone to Italy with Swinburne.

Yet a full realization of the necessity to call his own muse home apparently came to Faulkner somewhat later. Sherwood Anderson had told Faulkner, during their acquaintance in New Orleans: "You have to have somewhere to start from: then

[1] *Early Prose and Poetry*, p. 95.
[2] *Early Prose and Poetry*, pp. 71–3.

you begin to learn. It don't matter where it was, just so you remember it and aint ashamed of it. Because one place to start from is just as important as any other. You're a country boy; all you know is that little patch up there in Mississippi where you started from. But that's all right. . . ."[1]

But Faulkner in his verse never really took this advice and, as a fiction writer, he did not act on it until his third novel, *Sartoris* (1929) – unless one admits that the small town in his first novel, *Soldier's Pay* (1927), though formally set in Georgia, reflects at points Faulkner's home town of Oxford, Mississippi.

Faulkner needed to call his muse home. But he needed something more. His poetry, like Joyce's, required an ample context for its proper development. Again like Joyce, most of all he needed in that context elements of realism sufficient to purge it of any sense of effete prettiness and faded romanticism. This is not to argue that had he continued to write verse he might not have achieved the requisite muscular force and power through a process of condensation and compression. Perhaps he might have. The best of his poems suggest the possibility. Yet, on the other hand, the kind of thing which he did so magnificently in the best of his fiction might have been wasted had he persisted in trying to fine down and tighten rather than to expand and complicate and enrich the effects of work conceived on a larger scale.

One can illustrate by asking the reader to compare Poem XLIV of *A Green Bough* with the great prose hymn to nature that is sung in the closing pages of "The Bear". The eight-line poem beginning "If there be grief" is, in fact, one of Faulkner's most successfully and completely formed poems. The last stanza has a special effectiveness. No grief is to be expended on him: he will not die,

> . . . for where is any death
> While in these blue hills slumbrous overhead
> I'm rooted like a tree! Though I be dead,
> This earth that holds me fast will find me breath.

As Ike McCaslin walked through the big woods on a June

[1] "A Note on Sherwood Anderson," *Essays, Speeches, and Public Letters by William Faulkner,* ed. by James B. Meriwether (New York: Random House, 1965), p. 8.

morning to visit the graves of Lion and Sam Fathers and Old Ben, he was caught up in an experience of nature's immortality. It came to him that "there was no death" and that neither Lion nor Sam were "held fast in earth but [were] free in earth and not in earth but of earth, myriad yet undiffused of every myriad part", merged now into the unwearied processes of nature. The statement that Sam Fathers is "not held fast in earth but free in earth" is bolder than what is said in Poem XLIV: "This earth that holds me fast will find me breath." Though the prose passage denies the literal fact that a buried corpse is indeed held fast in earth, it is nevertheless more realistic than the poem: the earth will not find the dead man breath, but it will, having taken the man back to itself, turning him into earth again, allow him to merge into the 'immutable progression" of the seasons and the unquenched vitality of nature.

One does not want to claim too much: neither variation on the theme "there is no death" can be taken literally: both of them require a kind of ecstatic leap of faith. But one feels that Faulkner, in writing the conclusion to his great story, has got his priorities right and has based Ike's exalted vision not on a fancy but on a fact that one can cling to.

Something further should be said of the prose version. The man who has the vision in "The Bear" is a person with whose mind and heart the reader has become acquainted, and whose growing up he has witnessed. Ike's vision of the immortality of nature is plausible – in its time and place and motivation. But the young man who speaks Poem XLIV is not quite real. His ancestry is essentially literary. He is a kind of displaced Shropshire lad, whereas Ike McCaslin – faults, virtues, and all – is a Yoknapatawpha boy who demands and gets the reader's belief.

The Hamlet contains some of Faulkner's finest "poetry". In this novel, the idiot Ike becomes a kind of faun, not a wistful marble statue, not a being who is Arcadian in any literary sense, but the human animal presented in his full animality and so deeply sunk into nature that he is all but without speech, shorn of all the ordinary complexities of intellect and emotion.

The marble faun yearns to follow Pan over the hills, to feel the pressure of sun and rain on his body, and to move in rhythm to the dance of the seasons. Ike, the flesh-and-blood faun, does indeed move, with his companion and goddess, the cow, through the round of the day, and it is interesting to match some of the "nature" passages in Faulkner's first book of verse with comparable passages in *The Hamlet*. For example, the marble faun imagines Pan, pausing and brooding

> Beside [a] hushèd pool where lean
> His own face and the bending sky
> In shivering soundless amity.

These lines constitute no mean achievement, but how much more brilliant is Faulkner's account of how the idiot found "a brown creep of moisture in a clump of alder and beech", and scooped out a basin for it, "which now at each return of light stood full and clear and leaf by leaf repeating until [the cow and the idiot] lean and interrupt the green reflections and with their own drinking faces break each's mirroring, each face to its own shattered image wedded and annealed".

The Marble Faun recalls a day in which the "air is gray with rain". He tells us that he sits

> . . . beneath the weeping sky
> Crouched about the mountain's rim
> Drawing her loose hair over them.
>
> My eyes, peace-filled by falling rain,
> Brood upon the steamy plain. . . .

With these verses compare the account in *The Hamlet* of the rainstorm that descends on Ike. Gone are the clichés of "weeping sky" and "peace-filled" eyes. Instead we are told that the rain came down "without warning" and that Ike watched it "for some time and without alarm". The gathering rainstorm was at first

"wanton and random and indecisive before it finally developed, concentrated, drooping in narrow unperpendicular bands in two or three different places at once, about the horizon, like gauzy umbilical loops from the bellied cumulae, the sun-belled ewes of summer grazing up at the wind from the south-west. It was as if the rain were actually seeking the two of them [cow and boy], hunting them out where they stood amid the shade, finding them finally in a bright intransigent fury. . . . striking in thin brittle strokes through [Ike's] hair and shirt and against his lifted face, each brief lance already filled with the glittering promise of its imminent cessation like the brief bright saltless tears of a young girl over a lost flower. . . ."

This is vigorous – even exuberant writing. The writer has let himself go. He is not even pretending in his description to be following the movement of the idiot's mind, but how vividly he makes us participate in the scene!

The Marble Faun contains several passages suggesting the approach of night. Thus,

> Sunset stains the western sky;
> Night comes soon, and now I
> Follow toward the evening star.
> A sheep bell tinkles faint and far,
> Then drips in silence as the sheep
> Move like clouds across the deep
> Still dusky meadows wet with dew.

In *The Hamlet*, a "rapid twilight effaces [boy and animal] from the day's tedious recording". Faulkner describes the reversal of light, the absorption of light into the earth, and writes:

Then ebbs afternoon, until at last the morning, noon, and afternoon flow back, drain the sky and creep leaf by voiceless leaf and twig and branch and trunk, descending, gathering frond by frond among the grass, still creeping downward in drowsy insect murmurs, until at last the complete all of light gathers about that still and tender mouth [of the spring] in one last expiring inhalation. [Ike] rises. The swale is constant with random and erratic fireflies. There is the one fierce evening star, though almost at once the marching constellations mesh and gear and wheel strongly on.

One need not stress the difference between the vaguely "literary" poeticizing of the verse ("Follow toward the evening star," "sheep / Move like clouds") and a prose rhetoric so magnificent that one cannot fail to accord it the name of poetry.

If such parallels as these between bits of description in *The Marble Faun* and lengthy descriptive passages in *The Hamlet* seem too vaguely general to indicate any specific development of Faulkner's earlier imagery, it will not be difficult to show how certain images in the verse are, in the later fiction, amplified and developed to their immense advantage. For example, in Poem III of *A Green Bough* the poet describes an underwater scene in which "Hissing seas rage overhead," and someone "Staring up through icy twilight, sees / The stars within the water melt and sweep / In silver spears of streaming burning hair." Such an image of bright hair streaming up through water closes an elaborate description in *The Hamlet*.

> The pear tree across the road opposite was now in full and frosty bloom, the twigs and branches springing not outward from the limbs but standing motionless and perpendicular above the horizontal boughs like the separate and upstreaming hair of a drowned woman sleeping upon the uttermost floor of the windless and tideless sea.

In the prose passage Faulkner has accounted for the up-streaming hair: it floats from the head of a woman lying on the seafloor. This passage in *The Hamlet* also absorbs into itself another image from his poetry. In the tenth section of *The Marble Faun*, Faulkner had described a different tree, a dogwood, shining in the moonlight:

> Dogwood shines so cool and still,
> Like hands that, palm up, rigid lie
> In invocation to the sky
> As they spread there, frozen white,
> Upon the velvet of the night.

Here the analogy is more obvious: the boughs of the tree are likened to human hands lifted in prayer – almost as in one of the couplets in Joyce Kilmer's masterpiece of sentimentality, "Trees".

The developed image in *The Hamlet* is not only more elaborate than the early image in the verse: it is much bolder. It is exotically romantic and unearthly. But, it may be asked, isn't the analogy ("drowned woman", "uttermost floor") *too* romantic? Doesn't it give off a whiff of Swinburnian decadence? If the reader met with the elaborated figure in *The Marble Faun* he would probably have to agree that it did. The comparison occurs, however, in another context, and in these matters, context is all. What is the context? The spotted horses have just arrived from Texas. V. K. Ratliff is sitting with Quick and Freeman and other neighbours on the porch of Varner's store, talking about the horses and making conjectures as to their true owner. Ratliff opines that Flem Snopes is up to some skulduggery. As usual, he is sharp in his observations on Flem and the Snopes tribe: "A fellow can dodge a Snopes if he just starts lively enough." He rallies his listeners for their interest in the ponies and asks with mock incredulity: "You folks aint going to buy them things sho enough, are you?"

Nobody answers him and, in the ensuing silence, Faulkner introduces his elaborate figure of the pear tree. Thus it forms a background for the conversation – the natural scene weirdly beautiful under the moonlight, in sharp contrast to men's petty schemes and picayune rascalities. Ratliff's dry wit and earthy wisdom make the appropriate comment upon them. Indeed, the salt in Ratliff's comments is necessary to keep the "poetic" element wholesome and sweet.

One of the men sitting on the porch does take note of the tree – but not until a bird curves "across the moonlight, upward" into it and begins to sing. Does the tree call up to him an image of the floating hair of a drowned woman? No; his comment is that it's the first mockingbird he's noticed this year. To which a companion replies that he's heard one earlier, singing in a gum tree. And the talk goes on from gum trees to willow trees and on to the observation that a willow is not a tree but a weed.

The next night, after the auction of the wild Texas ponies, much the same group of men are again sitting on the same moonlit porch and looking across to the pear tree. "It rose in mazed and silver immobility like exploding snow; the mockingbird still sang in it." This second description of the pear tree incorporates, by the way, another image from *The Marble Faun*. The Faun sees

> Slow exploding oak and beech
> Blaze up. . . .

The foliage of the burgeoning trees seems to surge upward as if there were a blast of green ascending from the ground - a "slow" explosion, the shape of the tree's bursting energy, seen in slow motion, hovering in the air.[1] What the Faun sees is lighted by the sun; here the illumination is from the moon ("exploding *snow*") and the image is brought to sharper focus (a particular tree, not the collective "oak and beech").

The image is again ethereally beautiful, but it is once more in tension with an earthy context. One of the countrymen, Varner, this time does comment on the tree. But what does he say? "Look at that tree. It ought to make this year, [that is, it ought to bear fruit], sho." To which one of his companions replies: "Corn'll make this year too."

Yet the contrast, as Faulkner uses it here, is not simply that between beautiful nature and callous man. We are not necessarily to conclude that because the Yoknapatawpha farmers lack capacity for Faulknerian metaphors they are totally insensitive to the poetry of life. Ike Snopes, as idiot-faun, participates in the poetry of nature. Hard-bitten Will Varner, in his own way, worships the moon-goddess and acknowledges her power over all female kind. For Varner, having remarked about the pear tree's "making" this year, goes on to say that "A moon like this is good for every growing thing outen earth." And he tells a story. He and his wife wanted one more child, a girl child. He remembered what an old woman had once told his mother, "that if a woman showed her belly to the full moon after she had done caught, it would be a gal. So Mrs Varner taken and laid every night with the moon on her nekid belly, until it fulled and after. I could lay my ear to her belly and hear Eula kicking and scrounging like all get-out, feeling the moon."

Superstitious nonsense? Coarse folk humour? Poetry? The

---

[1] The reader may find it interesting to compare with the two tree images quoted from *The Hamlet* the following series of tree images that occur in the early novel, *Soldier's Pay* (1926): (p. 99) "The oaks on the lawn became still with dusk, and the branches of trees were as motionless as coral fathoms deep under seas." (158) "At the foot of the hill a dogwood tree spread flat palm-like branches in invocation among dense green, like a white nun." (247) ". . . a tree near the corner of the veranda, turning upward its ceaseless white-bellied leaves, was a swirling silver veil stood on end, a fountain arrested forever: carven water." (272)". . . the silver tree at the corner of the house hushed its never-still never-escaping ecstasy." (289–90) "The sky was bowled with a still disseminated light that cast no shadow and branches of trees were rigid as coral in a mellow tideless sea."

reader will make up his own mind, but if Faulkner is indeed aiming at poetry here, it is poetry of a special kind. Not that of moonlight and magnolias, but a poetry which will everywhere acknowledge the unpoetic, the realistic, and even the ugly and digest and absorb these into itself. There is a great deal of such poetry in *The Hamlet*. The atmosphere is that of an Arcadian landscape but not of the Arcadia painted in luminous colours by a Claude Lorrain. In spite of a "mythic" and pastoral quality – many observers have remarked on it – this Arcadia is evidently located within Yoknapatawpha County.

For his poetry, Faulkner needed a medium which was at once more and less demanding than that of conventional verse. He needed room to turn around, room for repetition, and room for expansion generally. Most of all he needed the kind of context which would allow him to set up a real tension between his more purely "literary" tendencies and his sense of a solid and believable world.

One can make what is essentially the same point in another way: when Faulkner gave up his Swinburnian model and came to see that even Housman's was a dangerous one (William Butler Yeats had high praise for *A Shropshire Lad* but went on to say that one more foot in that direction and all would have been marsh) – when, in short, Faulkner did call his muse home, she had to become homebred, in her rhythms, her language patterns, and everything else that went with a Yoknapatawpha girl. I do not mean to say that Faulkner ever gave up completely a certain hankering for extravagantly literary words and high-falutin allusions. To the end of his life he flirted from time to time with the exotically "literary". (As we have seen, he allowed Miss Rosa Coldfield to express herself in this fashion.) But Faulkner possessed a high literary intelligence and his basic literary instincts were dead right. In his great work he writes like the born poet that indeed he was.

16

The Doric Delicacy

Modernist poetry is characterized by a complete revulsion against poetic diction. It has banished the *e'ens*, and *thou's*, the *pleasant leas*, and *soft gales*, and with them archaic diction in general. But the poetry of John Crowe Ransom, though its modernity is patent, makes constant use of archaic diction, some of it as quaintly antique as that of Spenser, whom Ben Jonson chided for having "writ no language". For example, in Ransom's verse the enemy "up clomb . . . in the airy towers"; "the rooster" is seen "footing the mould"; a warrior slain in battle is a "lugubrious wight"; the poet can even frame such a salutation as "Sweet ladies, long may ye bloom, and toughly I hope ye may thole."

Ransom's use of the archaic, it scarcely need be said, is not Spenserian, either in method or effect: the ancient words are not chosen to poetize the matter; they are not amiably decorative; as Ransom employs them, they are absorbed into a special idiom of distinct character whose very principle is a kind of tough-minded modernity. Yet it is startling that the archaic occurs at all; and among the modern poets, the fact is almost unique. It is worth pondering, for it may indicate a way in which to engage the special quality of Ransom's work. And though this use of the archaic does not point back to the poetry of Spenser, there is one elder poet to whom it does point unmistakably: John Milton.

For Milton too devised an idiom which was at once highly personal and yet for his time distinctively modern; and in it he too incorporated elements of archaic diction such as one hardly finds in contemporaries like Donne or Denham or Marvell. We can, to be sure, isolate out of Milton's verse, Chaucerian forms arrived at perhaps *via* Spenser, but the total impact of the verse is not Spenserian. It is sharply contemporary. Most of all, it is distinctively Miltonic.

But I should hesitate to suggest this parallelism between Milton and Ransom if I did not feel that it was simply one item in a larger parallelism; and, in any case, I hesitate to raise the question of parallels without some rather precise qualifications.

The use of literary parallels is nowadays a somewhat discredited critical device, and justly so; for the matching of "parallels", like source hunting, has too often been pursued as a mechanical exercise. The statistics which it yields are usually quite barren. Yet, a comparison of the work of one poet with another can, on occasion, be illuminating – most of all perhaps when we have put away any preoccupation with borrowings and influences, and are content to use the one case merely to provide a perspective from which to view the other.

The minor poems of Milton seem to me to stand in some such relation to Ransom's poetry. Ransom's poetry enables one better to discern the Miltonic strategy, and the poems which Milton published in the 1645 volume can throw a good deal of light on *Chills and Fever* and *Two Gentlemen in Bonds*.

But having claimed so much for this relationship, I want to make doubly clear what I do *not* maintain: that there is any conscious imitation on Ransom's part. I have collected no specific "borrowings". So far as I know they do not exist. In any case, they are not to my purpose here.

Even the more general parallels between the two men are scarcely to my purpose, though I think that it may be interesting to mention a few of the more striking ones: their common "Protestantism", their learning, their sense of tradition and their insistence on maintaining the continuity of the tradition. The poetry of both men shows the deep impress of classical letters. (Ransom read "Greats" at Oxford.) Yet there is in both men something which at a first glance seems at variance with the suavity which we associate with a predominant training in humane letters: there is a kind of logical rigour, something of a penchant for positivism. It is not quite fair to say with Saurat that Milton is unhappy with all mysteries including the great Christian mysteries, and demands that everything be plain as a pikestaff. But there is in Milton what amounts to an inveterate rationalism; and there is a comparable quality in Ransom, as his interest in positivism, particularly as displayed in his critical volumes, indicates.

One is tempted to go on and name an even more curious parallel: Milton wrote, and Ransom has written, on theology. Ransom has wryly called his *God Without Thunder* "home-brew theology", but it is a descriptive term which somewhat scandalously applies to *De Doctrina Christiana*. For Milton's book is a brilliant personal recording of his own position rather than an ecumenical document, and, whatever Milton's intention, was scarcely calculated to win any more converts, had it been published, than the publication of *God Without Thunder* actually did win.

But this parallel is probably too special and accidental to be significant. Better to return to the common trait of a highly personal idiom, a striking trait which has already been mentioned. In this quality Ransom certainly matches Milton. Someone has remarked that, if he found any three consecutive lines of Ransom scribbled on a scrap of paper on a desert island, he would have no difficulty in pronouncing them to be Ransom's. Milton's individual quality is almost as indelible; yet, as we know, it is won from a mélange of borrowings. Any one of Milton's poems is a tissue of allusions, semi-quotations, and echoes from the classic writers and the Elizabethans; but the borrowed matter is always digested and absorbed. The Miltonic poem is not a mosaic; it is an articulated whole; the tone is unified, individual, almost unique.

I have already forsworn source hunting in this examination of Ransom's poetry. But the nature of his characteristic fusion of the archaic and the contemporary, of the Latinized diction and the native idiom – the terms on which the fusion is made, the tensions involved, the tone thereby established – an examination of such matters as these can tell us a good deal about the essential poetry of both Milton and Ransom.

In the case of Ransom, of course, the prevailing tone is ironic, and Ransom's consistent role as an ironist was brilliantly treated some years ago by Robert Penn Warren. With Ransom, one of

the obvious functions of the Latinity and the hint of the archaic
is to parody the grand manner and to establish the ironic tone
which is the consistent tone of Ransom's verse. There is no need
here to repeat Warren's discussion. In what follows I have
something a little more special in mind: the examination of
further qualities which are related to irony, but which transcend
irony, being indeed common to Milton's minor poetry as well as
to Ransom's.

It scarcely needs to be observed that Milton too is a witty
poet, and nowhere more so than in his diction. Milton early
gave up the metaphysical conceit, at least in the form in which
we associate it with Donne. But, even in his latest poetry, he
continued to make use of what I should call a submerged wit,
and his more verbal wit (corresponding to the puns in Donne)
is characteristically achieved by playing the Latin meaning of a
word off against its developed English meaning. The earth, for
example, becomes "this punctual spot" (Latin *punctum*, a dot);
or "Hell saw / Heav'n ruining from Heav'n," i.e. Heaven
sloughing off from Heaven as a ruin and Heaven falling (Latin
ruina, a falling down). The witty quality is easily obscured by
the academic habit of regarding these instances as merely the
result of Milton's scholarship or pedantry. But when Milton
has Heav'n ruin from Heav'n, or writes, of the fallen angels'
rebellion, that God "tempted [their] attempt", there can be no
question of the wit.

Much of Ransom's more verbal wit takes precisely this form;
one can find half a dozen examples in a single poem. Consider,
for example, his "Vaunting Oak". The anecdote around which
the poem is built is slight. The girl walking with her lover, in
her happiness, points to a great oak tree as a proper symbol of
the endurance of their love. But her lover, with sorrowful irony,
is forced to point out that the aged tree is hollow, already
prepared to fall.

It is the Latinized diction (along with archaic diction and a
rather formal patterning of sentence structure) which the poet
uses to invest the anecdote with its special quality. The great
tree, imagined as fallen, is described as "concumbent". Its
massive bole (symbol of the eternal) rears up against the sky:

"Only his *temporal* twigs are unsure of seat. . . ." The leaves flutter in the wind "in panic round the stem on which they are captive" – literally *held* (*captivus*) though the poet is glad to retain the English sense of *captive* also. That is, the leaves would flee in their panic if they were not held prisoners.

Thus far in the poem, the Latinisms have been used primarily for a kind of conscious grandiloquence, a kind of parody of the grand manner. But the instances that follow play meaning against meaning for witty ironical effects. The heart of the young girl has been "too young and mortally / Linked with an unbeliever of bitter blood." *Mortally* is darkly, ominously, but the word is presumably used also because the two are linked by marriage, irrevocably, "till death do them part". The girl finds in the great tree an "eminent witness of life"; *eminent*, of course, in the general sense of "signal" or "remarkable", but the specific Latin sense of *eminent* becomes a normal extension of the metaphor of the tree – Latin *eminens*, projecting, lofty. The great tree projects above the humbler "populace / Of daisies and yellow kinds," which are too ephemeral to serve as symbols for the perdurability of love.

Suddenly the poem shifts into the colloquial (though the Latinized diction and formalized phrasing intermittently occur for ironic effect):

> And what but she fetch me up to the steep place
> Where the oak vaunted?

As they run up the steep hill the girl knows better than to make her boast among the ephemeral flowers of a season. But once arrived beneath the great tree, she murmurs

> "Established, you see him there! forever."

But the "unbeliever of bitter blood" cannot allow her to remain in her "pitiful error". He tests the tree:

> I knocked on his house loudly, a sorrowing lover . . .

At the hollow reverberation.

> "The old gentleman," I grieved, "holds gallantly,
> But before our joy shall have lapsed, even, will be gone."

Up to this point the poem is half playful, half wistful commentary on the frailty of human love. But the opening measures of the poem, even if we regard them at a first reading as an almost wicked parody on the grand style, have done something to universalize the experience. The little anecdote has been told against a background. The lover's original mockery of himself as an "unbeliever of bitter blood" now becomes more than playful. His challenging the oak is not trivial and special: it is typical. The highly personal little anecdote has thus been taken out of a merely personal context. When, therefore, he proceeds to knock more sternly, the tone of the poem modulates into a deeper and more serious note in which the grand manner, earlier parodied, is reasserted this time with full seriousness, so that the answering reverberation from the hollow tree can be justly called a "dolorous cry".

> I knocked more sternly, and his dolorous cry
> Boomed till its loud reverberance outsounded
> The singing of bees; or the coward birds that fly
>
> Otherwhere with their song when summer is sped,
> And if they stayed would perish miserably;
> Or the tears of a girl remembering her dread.

The poem achieves a proper climax and a powerful one as the boom from the hollow oak is made to swell into a great cry of lament which smothers every sound in the spring scene – the singing of bees, the calls of the birds and the sobbing of the girl. But if we are to express the poet's strategy in terms of diction, we have to say that the ironic use of the formal and pompous diction of the earlier lines of the poem has guaranteed and made possible the powerful and utterly serious use of "dolorous" and "reverberance" in the closing lines of the poem.

But the most important special characteristic which Ransom shares with Milton is what must be called, for want of a better term, aesthetic distance. Indeed, the poem just discussed provides an instance: it employs a considerable measure of aesthetic distance. The scene is given an almost formal quality; the reader is kept well back from the scene; characteristically, the "unbeliever" is not revealed as the "me" of the poem – the speaker – until the poem is half over.

With Milton, the measure of aesthetic distance is nearly always great. This aesthetic distance is not aloofness: the prim young puritan keeping his distance from the common world that lies about him. It is not to be characterized as a sense of form: Donne's "Canonization" is as firmly and as exquisitely "formed" as anything in Milton. (Both Donne and Milton at their best give us poetry in which form and content cannot be separated.) The quality to which I refer is not even to be defined as a high degree of formality, for whereas Milton is rarely casual, he can be surely "informal" enough. He does not stand on his dignity in "L'Allegro" and "Il Penseroso".

Yet there is in all of Milton's work a large measure of aesthetic distance. The scene is framed, the stance of the observer is carefully implied, a sense of perspective is definitely, if quietly, indicated. Even in "L'Allegro" and "Il Penseroso" a certain detachment is always indicated, and it is this detachment as much as anything else that gives these poems their special flavour of coolness. Indeed, an inspection of Milton's earliest show piece, the "Nativity Hymn" will reveal that Milton's sense of aesthetic distance is already fully developed. The scene is panoramic – the whole world, quieted and stilled, is laid out beneath our gaze. We see the dove of peace descending through the successive spheres; and later, from a comparable vantage point, we are allowed to view the slinking away of pagan gods in Greece, in Syria, in Lybia, as the divine influence flows over the whole known world. Even at the end of the poem, we are not brought up to the manger to kneel with the poet. It is evidently from a distance that we see the whole scene, for it is a tableau conceived amply enough to include "Heaven's youngest teemed star" shining above the stable, "and all about the Courtly Stable, bright harnessed angels . . . in order serviceable."

I would not make too much of what may be thought an accidental quality of Milton's poetry, but I am convinced that it is not accidental. As a device it is closely related to the characteristic tone which is set and sustained in one after another of the minor poems. It is closely related to Milton's particular vision of reality – his characteristic way of "seeing" his world.

The measure of aesthetic distance in Ransom's poetry is thoroughly comparable to Milton's. It is controlled by the poet for his own effects, to be sure. But it is quite as pervasive as in Milton and as fundamental to Ransom's variations of tone.

"Necrological" will furnish a nice and apposite example. The youthful friar who views the battlefield is quite removed from the issues. The battle is over, "the living all were gone", and the young friar himself as observer is withdrawn, at the end of the poem, lost in a "vast surmise", as still as the dead men themselves.

But this last example is rather special. The very theme of the poem is the remove at which the young friar stands from the issues of a torn and violent world. "Spectral Lovers" will provide a less specially weighted and therefore more cogent illustration of Ransom's characteristic use of aesthetic distance.

> By night they haunted a thicket of April mist,
> Out of that black ground suddenly come to birth,
> Else angels lost in each other and fallen on earth.
> Lovers they knew they were, but why unclasped, unkissed?
> Why should two lovers go frozen apart in fear?
> And yet they were, they were.

The lovers are spectral indeed: they are, as it were, made to materialize out of the mist. They "haunt" a thicket of April mist; it is as if they had suddenly come to birth out of that black ground; or else they are angels "fallen on earth", and perhaps fallen in that they are lost in each other. But they are spectral also in the sense that is to provide the torment described in the poem: their lack of grossness, the restrictions which they impose upon the flesh, their ideal quality.

A less tough-minded poet, a less ambitious and brilliant poet, would scarcely have dared to humanize and agonize these creatures of the mist. He would have left them a shade too ethereal, glimmering "white in the season's moon-gold and amethyst". It is typical of Ransom that he should be able to present them realistically.

Ransom presents the man even wittily:

> And gesturing largely to the moon of Easter,
> Mincing his steps and swishing the jubilant grass,
> Beheading some field-flowers that had come to pass,
> He had reduced his tributaries faster
> Had not considerations pinched his heart
> Unfitly for his art.

But if the realistic and witty description jars with the spectral quality of the lovers, it would seem to jar also with the uncolloquial and "literary" language that the lovers are made to speak.

This for the woman:

> Should the walls of her prison undefended yield
> And open her treasure to the first clamorous knight?
> "This is the mad moon, and shall I surrender all?
> If he but ask it I shall."

This for the man:

> "Blessed is he that taketh this richest of cities:
> But it is so stainless the sack were a thousand pities.
> This is that marble fortress not to be conquered,
> Lest its white peace in the black flame turn to tinder
> And an unutterable cinder."

The power of the contrasts and of the tensions which are thus set up is obvious. The interesting question will be how, in view of the violence of these tensions, the poem holds together at all. The answer surely lies in the last stanza and the perspective which it establishes.

The first line of this last stanza, "They passed me once in April in the mist," pushes the whole scene back into a past time. It does something more. This is the first time that the "me" of the poem, the observer who speaks the poem, has been mentioned. The speaker, then, is not one of the lovers. The lovers have been described actually from the outside. The calculated language which the lovers have spoken has been imagined for them, since their words are not audible even to each other. The formalized, almost ritual-like quality of their action is thus accounted for. For the spectral lovers prove to be, now that the vantage point of the speaker is established for us, a construction evoked with pity, with understanding, with irony, by the "me" of the last stanza, out of himself and out of the two forms which have silently passed him in the mist.

It is much the same kind of effect that one gets at the end of Milton's "Lycidas" when the "I" of the poem, he who has spoken the passionate though formalized lament, suddenly is reduced to a figure mentioned in the third person, the uncouth swain whose thought is "eager", but who, in spite of his confident declaration that Lycidas, like the day star, has risen and now "flames in the forehead of the morning sky", himself inhabits a workaday world in which suns rise and set and in which now, at the end of his song, the actual sun has dropped again "into the western bay".

I have said that the effect is much the same. Perhaps I should say rather that the effect is comparable, for the device as Milton uses it just reverses Ransom's: we conclude with a figure in the third person rather than, as with Ransom, with a first person, a "me" whom the spectral lovers have passed. But the effect gained by the sudden establishment of a controlling perspective is much the same.

I should like, however, to conclude these notes with a later poem and a finer poem than those I have discussed. For the large measure of aesthetic distance is a constant in Ransom's poetry and can be illustrated from his latest work as easily as from his earliest. The poem I have in mind is the beautiful "Prelude to an Evening". On the surface it is an intensely personal poem with a husband speaking to a troubled wife and addressing her directly as "you". The directness suggested by the "you" is further enforced by his imagining her in the domestic scene "dainty at [her] orange-cup", her "heels detonating the stair's cavern", "freshening the water in the blue bowls", "smoothing the heads of the hungry children", etc.

But the poem must not be allowed to work itself out as an intensely personal poem, for managed so it would violate its theme. If there were real closeness between the speaker and the "you" to whom ostensibly he speaks the poem, the "drift of fog on your mornings" would be dispelled. She would not hear in the pines a "warning sibilance".

The speaker of the "Prelude" apologizes wryly for himself as the "tired wolf / Dragging his infected wound homeward". But he has succeeded in infecting his mate, and for her the "images of the invaded mind", because only hinted at, become more monstrous than for him. This he knows, and the poem is a delicate and tender account of her day as he imagines it from his vantage point of guilt and tender concern. He can see the "too banded Eumenides"; she cannot see them, but can only sense them through their troubling effect upon him.

But the tenderness must not be permitted to cloud the picture. Each detail must be registered with clean detachment and with full realism if the experience presented is not to be robbed of its significance. The details in their realism and in their domesticity are faithfully rendered: her "mouth unbeautied against the pillow" as she cries out in her sleep from some nightmare: the "needles clicking" as she knits; her abstracted air as she makes her "Noes but wanderingly" to the questioning children.

All of this means, however, that the imagined scene must be patterned, ordered in a particular perspective, "seen" by the tired husband from his stance outside the room and outside the context of a special day. He has said that it is by "our perverse supposal" that the drift of fog has come upon her mornings; but the re-created scene too is a "supposal", his supposal, his imagined recreation of the scene, and it gains its intimacy and its tenderness because it is "supposed" with clarity and detachment.

> You in your peignoir, dainty at your orange-cup,
> Feel poising round the sunny room
>
> Invisible evil, deprived and bold.
> All day the clock will metronome
> Your gallant fear; the needles clicking,
> The heels detonating the stair's cavern.
>
> Freshening the water in the blue bowls
> For the buckberries with not all your love,
> You shall be listening for the low wind,
> The warning sibilance of pines.

You like a waning moon, and I accusing
Our too banded Eumenides,
You shall make Noes but wanderingly,
Smoothing the heads of the hungry children.

Like so many of Ransom's finest poems, this poem is a triumph of tone; and aesthetic distance is, of course, an aspect of tone, a special ordering of the poet's attitude toward his material, a liberation of the elected poem from the particular and accidental emotions of the poet as man rather than as artist.

Ransom's poems, I have suggested, are always ordered very carefully in this fashion, just as Milton's are so ordered, and it is this control of perspective that institutes Ransom's special claim to a kind of classical decorum. It is a claim well worth pressing. It is a quality which is rare enough in modern poetry and for the want of which the modern poets have suffered and, one predicts, are likely to suffer more.

Be that as it may, there is in modern poetry nothing else quite like this quality of Ransom's. Wallace Stevens, our other special master of perspective and of tone, is perhaps a comparable figure, but his general method is quite other than Ransom's and perhaps much more special and limited than Ransom's. In any case, our age has produced nowhere else a poetry so fine grained, so agate hard, so tough minded as that contained in *Chills and Fever* and *Two Gentlemen in Bonds*. It wears well. After some twenty-odd years, it has worn very well indeed, outlasting verse that once appeared a great deal more exciting or profound. It belongs to that small body of verse which, one predicts, will increasingly come to be regarded as the truly distinguished poetry of the twentieth century.

17

Edgar Allan Poe as an Interior Decorator

Poe is notorious for the "Gothic" quality of his stories. His haunted castles, often ruinous, are darker, more ominous and more spiritually depressing than even those in the novels of Horace Walpole and Mrs Radcliffe. The melancholy house of Roderick Usher, with its "bleak walls.' and "vacant eye-like windows", broods over a "black and lurid tarn". The house of Ligeia, though not itself specified as gloomy or ruinous, is situated in a "dim and decayed city by the Rhine". When Ligeia dies, her widowed husband moves to England and characteristically chooses to set up his new household in a ruined abbey. Evidently he values its "gloomy and dreary grandeur" and does not so much as clear away the grasses that grow upon its ancient stones.

The relevance of such edifices to the dramas that are enacted within their Gothic walls is plain enough and has come in for proper attention; yet not much has been made of the way in which Poe has furnished his nightmare houses. The furnishings, incidentally, are not usually in themselves Gothic at all; that is, they are not medieval. But they have been chosen with care. Poe was very much interested in the decoration of a room and the relationship of the carpet, the wall and curtain hangings, the furniture, and even the *objets d'art* to each other and to the total effect of the room. (One remembers that Poe wrote an essay rather grandly entitled "The Philosophy of Furniture".)

As soon as Ligeia's bereaved husband has removed to the ruined English abbey, he makes great alterations in the interior, filling it with rich furniture, tapestries, and hangings. In such stories as "Berenice", "Morella", "The Fall of the House of

Usher", and "The Oval Portrait", one finds these same elaborate furnishings. Usually a lamp burning scented oil hangs like a censer from the ceiling. Ottomans are disposed about the room. There are elaborate tapestries and heavy draperies which, in their rustling, give "a hideous and uneasy intonation to the whole".

Poe may have genuinely admired such overstuffed and grandiloquent elegance. But in any case, splendidly gloomy interiors provide the appropriate habitat for Poe's heroes, so often morbidly melancholy or actually mad, and the proper setting for the return from the tomb of his Ligeias and Morellas and Berenices.

Siegfried Giedion, the Swiss architect and historian of culture, has some very interesting comments to make on nineteenth-century taste in furniture and furnishings.[1] Though Giedion nowhere mentions Poe, the period rooms that he describes might very well be those to be found in Poe's characteristic tales. In the first place, there was in the nineteenth century, as Giedion observes, the increasing influence of the upholsterer. The upholsterer tended to control the situation. "Picturesque disorder fascinated people, for it was the reflection of the chaotic state of feeling. The upholsterer, by embellishment of furniture and artistic hangings, sets up a fairy land to enchant the drabness of the industrial day."

Giedion connects the ponderous armchairs and sofas and ottomans with what he calls an "orientalizing romanticism". He observes that "the Oriental influence must be counted as one of the many strivings for escape that darkened the emotional life of the last century and gave it a tragic note. Man was not content to live in his own skin. This could lead to nothing but the grotesque." (One remembers that Poe entitled his 1840 volumes *Tales of the Grotesque and Arabesque*.)

It may be significant that some of Giedion's most interesting examples of nineteenth-century style come from France, the country that from the beginning saw in Poe the great pioneer

[1] *Mechanization Takes Command*, New York: Oxford, 1948. See especially the section entitled "The Nineteenth Century: Mechanization and Ruling Taste", pp. 329–89.

artist. In particular Giedion mentions Alfred de Musset's comments made in 1836 that "We have left no imprint of our age either on our dwellings, on our gardens, or on anything else. We have culled something from every century but our own. . . . We live off fragments."

Did Poe think that the men of his own day were living off fragments? It would be hard to say. But the issue here is not what Poe consciously intended but has to do rather with the characteristic instinct that made him provide such settings for the particular examples of breakdown, frustration, and horror which he chose to depict. In any case, in at least one of his tales of the grotesque Poe has provided an instance of a character who is clearly aware of what his furniture means and how it is related to his own state of mind.

The hero of "The Assignation" tells his guests that

> "to dream has been the business of my life. I have therefore framed for myself, as you see, a bower of dreams. . . . You behold around you, it is true, a medley of architectural embellishments. The chastity of Ionia is offended by antediluvian devices, and the sphynxes of Egypt are outstretched upon carpets of gold. Yet the effect is incongruous to the timid alone. Proprieties of place, and especially of time, are the bugbears which terrify mankind from contemplation of the magnificent. Once I was myself a decorist [that is, a person who venerates decorum]; but that sublimation of folly has palled upon my soul. All this is now the fitter for my purpose. Like these arabesque censers, my spirit is writhing in fire, and the delirium of this scene is fashioning me for the wild visions of that land of real dreams whither I am now rapidly departing."

His is the speech of a dying man, for he has poisoned himself in order to keep an assignation in the kingdom of death with his beautiful mistress.

Giedion finds in the nineteenth century a horror of empty space: every room has to be filled up as fully as possible with sumptuous furniture. Second, there is a devaluation of symbols: all the miscellaneous lumber of the past is dumped together for merely decorative or spectacular effects. Lastly, there is a basic confusion of feeling, a fact which accounts for the reign of the upholsterer, for he was the man "to gather superficially loose ends".

But for the best account of what the time-style of this period really meant, Giedion appeals to the Surrealists of our own century. His reference to the Surrealists, by the way, is thoroughly relevant to a consideration of Poe, for Poe was a kind of fore-runner here also and one need only intensify the characteristic Poe-esque atmosphere in order to find oneself in a Surrealistic world.

Giedion chooses for his principal illustration a "ghoulish *collage*" fabricated by Max Ernst. He describes it thus: "Of the billowing drapes, of the murky atmosphere, Ernst's scissors make a submarine cave. Are these living creatures, plaster statues or models of the academic brush found reclining here, or rotting? To this question no answer can or should be given. The room, as nearly always, is oppressive with assassination and non-escape. . . .

"Such is the demonic side of [the] nineteenth century, ever scented behind the banal forms. [In Ernst's representations, the demonic aspect] has been overcome and, at a safe distance, may be evoked through the Dadaistic *collage*. The pathos of a decadent society that has made its house an operatic setting is not to be taken in earnest." Yet Giedion asks us to observe that "what the Surrealists mockingly portray is at bottom the phenomenon that Henrik Ibsen, living within the period, attacked in deadly earnest and incarnated in his personages – the ceaseless roaming in search of one's soul: Nora's longing to escape from her domestic prison [in *A Doll's House*] the mill-stream débâcle in *Rosmersholm*, Oswald's madness in *Ghosts*."

Poe does indeed dramatize for us what Giedion calls "the demonic side of the nineteenth century" and his tales are "oppressive with assassination and non-escape", or, as Giedion puts it in another passage, with "violence and death". Many of Poe's characters are obsessed with a fear of death. Some of them strive to come back from the tomb; others are terrified of being buried alive or indeed are buried alive like Madeline in "The Fall of the House of Usher". The two obsessions are, of course, actually the same: the horror of

retaining consciousness in a world that is dead – of living in
thought while still tied to one's own rotting body.

Poe was fascinated with the deviousness of the human spirit
(as, for example, he reveals in "The Imp of the Perverse)" and
its inner conflicts (as, for example, in "William Wilson").
Indeed, he is interested in the whole phenomenon of consciousness and the deeper realm of hidden motivations – what we
should today call the unconscious. These were the interests of
the romantic poets generally, but Poe forces the central issue
further than most of his fellows in romanticism, either American
or British. He endeavours to explore even more deeply than they
the depths of the psyche.

A poet like Wordsworth, by writing about peasants and
children and idiots, attempts to get down to layers deeper than
those of the rational mind. But Poe writes about madness,
spiritual incest, and vampirism. Byron hints darkly at incest and
nameless crimes, but Poe will take this sense of horror one stage
further. As I have indicated earlier, it is perhaps just here that
we are to look for the most significant expression of Poe's
"American" quality. For Poe's mind reveals the cultural lag
that one would expect of a man born on this side of the Atlantic
in the early nineteenth century, a lag accentuated in his case by
his emotional allegiances to the social order of Virginia – an
order more conservative than that of America as a whole – a
society based on the land and knit closely together by ties of
family and tradition.[1] In such a situation, the very cultural lag –
the inertia of society – can accentuate the avant-garde position
of the individual.

As several writers of our own time have remarked, Poe

---

[1] It ought to be conceded, however, that Poe was not actually an integral part of
the social order of Virginia. His ties with Virginia society through his foster-parents
left him merely hanging on the fringes of the planter society to which he aspired to
belong. Poe's own father was a Marylander, but *his* father, Edgar, for whom the
poet was named, had begun life as an immigrant Irish wheelwright, though he had
later attained wealth and, by the end of the Revolutionary War, the rank of
Assistant Quartermaster General. Had Poe been more fully a part of the society
that he claimed as his own, he might have been less attracted to the Gothic world of
dream and romance. Some more cynical modern critics would even argue that had
Poe been fully integrated into the planter society he would not have written at all.
His talents might have found their fulfillment in politics or in a military career.

combined both primitivism and decadence; that is to say that Poe applies a freshness and energy (that go with provincial rawness) to the problems of an over-refined and hyper-civilized consciousness. Poe's typical hero is consciously living (but with an abnormal energy) on the "fragments" of the past. The hero of "The Assignation" will serve as an example. Because he is no longer committed to any particular tradition, he gathers around himself *objets d'art*, not because any of them has any symbolic meaning for him, but because of their immediate decorative value or because their very random meaninglessness piques and amuses him.

Allen Tate, in an essay entitled "Our Cousin, Mr Poe",[1] sees Poe's preoccupation with the disintegration of culture in not very different terms. Poe, he says, more than any other writer "in England or the United States or, so far as I know, in France", gives us a vision of "dehumanized man". Tate goes on to specify what he means by the term "dehumanized"; Poe's characters are "'dead to the world'; they are machines of sensation and will. . . ." This is Tate's own way of coming at Giedion's point that men of the nineteenth century were not willing "to live in their own skins". (I do not mean to imply, however, that Tate writes with conscious reference to Giedion's book: he has told me that he has never read it.) For Poe's characters, the body is a mere machine: it is effectively cut off from the consciousness which lives within, but which aspires to live beyond, the body. The sensibility tries to cut itself loose from the flesh: it refuses to be reconciled to it.

Certainly Poe's characters do aspire to live with an intensity that has no relation to physical law. They seem never to eat or drink; they have no sensuous appetites of any kind. They inhabit, as we have remarked, fantastically gloomy though gorgeous settings. They do no work. Occasionally they read or play on musical instruments. They meditate a great deal. They speak to each other intensely and with passion. They seethe with all sorts of emotions, but their "living" is all in their heads – is all a matter of intellect and imagination. Even so, Poe's characters walk in fear of death, for though their consciousness

[1] *The Forlorn Demon* (Chicago, Regnery, 1953).

manages rather successfully to float above the life of the body and of the senses, it cannot entirely cut its connection with the body; and this means that with the end of the body, consciousness itself will cease to be. (It also means that Poe's characters sometimes fear that consciousness will *not* cease to be and that one will suffer the recurrent nightmare of being buried alive.)

Consider Poe's typical heroines. They are usually afflicted with mysterious diseases. They visibly waste away before their lovers' eyes. A closer inspection reveals that they are not dying of spiritual anaemia but rather of an intensity that drains the body of its energy. Their lovers or husbands can see that they are perishing and the heroines themselves are thoroughly aware of it, but the process cannot be halted. Yet Poe's heroines are not content to die; they are not willing to let go of their lovers, even though their relationships seem scarcely those of physical love: the lovers simply share an intense contemplation of each other. These women, "of monstrous will and intellect," as Tate describes them, in the end turn into vampires. They return from the tomb, literally as the Lady Madeline does, or by taking over the body of her husband's second wife, as Ligeia does, or by appropriating the body of her child, as Morella does.

Poe's characters do fear the final annihilation, the dread nothingness which always threatens them even while they are alive since they have no real contact with the world of nature or with the world of religion, being purely intense sensibilities, sheer intelligences, operating in a vacuum. As Tate implies these revenants who like Ligeia return from the tomb are now the "undead" precisely because they were never truly alive. In fact, Tate remarks that Poe "is not interested in anything that is alive. Everything in Poe is dead: the houses, the rooms, the furniture. . . ." To say this is to overstate matters, and yet there is a very real sense in which the world depicted by Poe is a dead world. Typical examples are those somber mansions furnished – to use Giedion's phrase – like "operatic settings". No one could conceivably spill tobacco ashes on the oriental carpets or upset a teacup or open a window. The very fact that Poe's characters occupy such stage sets hints that they are themselves dead, zombies, of preternatural intuition and ravenous imagination, who are shut up in bodies which they do not really control and in environments with which they have no meaningful relationship. One thinks of Roderick Usher spinning his morbid fancies as he sits within his melancholy house with its bleak walls and its vacant eye-like windows and – not to forget the furnishings – in a room whose "general furniture [is] profuse, comfortless, antique, and tattered", a room littered with "books and musical instruments" that fail "to give any vitality to the scene".

Poe's typical hero, cut off from the world of nature, surrounded by "dead" furniture, living only in terms of an intense imagination, is unable to find in any human relationship an outlet for his feelings or any human activity an occasion for his actions. Such a setting reflects a situation increasingly familiar to men of our time. One could even argue that Poe is one of our first writers to have intimations of "the world of the absurd", that anti-universe which has come in for so much attention during the last quarter century.

Such an argument would not, of course, require the assertion that Poe was fully conscious of all the implications of his stories or that he foresaw in the next century the appearance of books like Henry Miller's *The Air-Conditioned Nightmare*. A writer who could not possibly conceptualize the future might well have been preternaturally alive to currents in the contemporary culture that pointed toward the culture to come. Poe's literary work considered as a portent and a prophecy of things to come may amount to nothing more than an uncommonly sensitive response to his own spiritual environment.

Yet those who believe that Poe was always quite conscious of what he was doing might be tempted to make a bolder claim. James Southall Wilson, for example, argued[1] that many of Poe's most celebrated stories were written tongue-in-cheek. In the course of his argument he cited Poe's own statement to his friend Kennedy that Kennedy was "nearly, but not quite right" in denying the allegation that Poe's stories were intentionally satiric. Poe writes to Kennedy: "Most of them were *intended*

[1] "The Devil Was in It", *The American Mercury*, XXIV (1931).

for half-banter, half-satire – although I might not have fully acknowledged this to be their aim even to myself."

Banter and satire – especially if the satire is at the expense of fashions, social modes, and attitudes – imply intellectual judgement, no mere emotional response. Poe's discriminations ("half-banter, half-satire"; not "fully acknowledged" even to himself) are in themselves highly significant. Perhaps they are meant to temper his disagreement with his friend's conception; in any case, however, they point to a sophisticated and highly self-conscious artist who realized that he was at once inside and outside of his "bizarreries" – at once caught up in these fantastic imaginings *and* judging them in detachment. Perhaps Poe not only was infected with but diagnosed rather accurately the cultural malaise of his day and even had intimations as to the ultimate outcome of the disease. Poe, one might suppose, could have viewed with an indulgent eye Max Ernst's Surrealistic high jinks with the furnishings of the House of Usher.

18

A. E. Housman

It is tempting to regard A. E. Housman's poetry as classical –
in its lucidity, its symmetry, its formal patterning, its laconic
bite and edged intensity. Our disposition to do so is encouraged
by the fact that Housman was a professor of Latin at Cambridge
University and an eminent scholar of the classics. But, as has
been frequently observed, Housman is actually the most
romantic of poets, and he himself pointed to thoroughly
"romantic" sources for his own poetry in naming "Shakespeare's
songs, the Scottish border ballads, and Heine". The essentially
romantic nature of his conception of poetry was confirmed in
Housman's famous lecture, *The Name and Nature of Poetry*. To a
Cambridge that had largely shifted its allegiance and worshipped new gods, Housman proclaimed the old gospel: his
summary of the history of English poetry still saw the Romantic
revolt as the one far-off divine event to which, from its first
beginnings, the whole creation of English poetry had moved.
But Housman's poetry is not only generally and fundamentally
romantic: it reflects its particular era, the romanticism of the
late nineteenth century. As the late John Peale Bishop once put
it: "He is the poet of the end of an age. . . ."

But, of course, this again is not the whole story. Here, on the
centenary of the poet's birth, we are concerned with what in his
poetry transcends his own time and speaks to us now in the
mid-twentieth century. Beyond even that, of course, we are
interested in what is truly timeless in Housman's poetry.
Perhaps a useful means for realizing this timeless quality is to
see what he has in common with some of the writers of our own
day.

Two of Housman's constant themes are courage and stoic
endurance, and these are themes which are almost obsessive for

several of our best contemporary writers. To name only two, there are William Faulkner and Ernest Hemingway. The gap between Housman's Shropshire lads and Hemingway's bull-fighters or boxers or big-game hunters may seem shockingly wide, but it is actually less wide than we think. The gap narrows when we place beside Housman's doomed young soldiers the typical Hemingway hero as man-at-arms during the First World War. The idioms used, I grant you, are sharply dissimilar. Hemingway's brilliantly realistic, acrid Midwestern American speech is a whole world away from the faintly archaic, wholly British idiom which is the staple of Housman's lyrics.

> The street sounds to the soldiers' tread,
>   And out we troop to see:
> A single redcoat turns his head,
>   He turns and looks at me . . .
>
> What thoughts at heart have you and I
>   We cannot stop to tell;
> But dead or living, drunk or dry,
>   Soldier, I wish you well.[1]

But, I repeat: beneath these surface differences, the situation, the stance taken, the attitude assumed, may not be different at all. Indeed, Hemingway, it seems to me, can throw a great deal of light upon Housman and, though I venture this more hesitantly, Housman may throw a good deal of light on Hemingway.

A good place to start is with one of Housman's finest short poems, but a poem too little known, his "Epitaph on an Army of Mercenaries":

> These, in the day when heaven was falling,
>   The hour when earth's foundations fled,
> Followed their mercenary calling
>   And took their wages and are dead.

---

[1] Quoted poems from *Complete Poems* by A. E. Housman, copyright © 1922, 1940, © 1959, by Henry Holt & Co., Inc. Copyright 1950 by Barclays Bank, Ltd. By permission of the publishers.

> Their shoulders held the sky suspended;
> They stood, and earth's foundations stay;
> What God abandoned, these defended,
> And saved the sum of things for pay.

It has been said that this brilliant little poem commemorates the small British professional army which heroically took its beating in the early days of the First World War, and which, in spite of terrible losses, managed to slow down and finally to stop the German advance, and so held the Channel ports. I dare say this may be true, so far as concerns the specific occasion. But the poem has a universal application. It does not celebrate merely the tough professional soldier who fights for his country, not because of some high-sounding ideal but because fighting is his profession – because that is the way he makes his living. The poem also celebrates all of those hardbitten realists who are often regarded as mere materialists and yet who frequently outdo the perfervid idealists and self-conscious defenders of the good.

If this is what the poem celebrates, then we are not so far from Hemingway's characteristic stance after all. One remembers, in *A Farewell to Arms*, Lt. Henry's disgust for the great value terms which, for him and his comrades, had become pretentious and empty and therefore lying.

> There were many words that you could not stand to hear and finally only the names of places had dignity. . . . Abstract words such as glory, honor, courage . . . were obscene beside the concrete names of villages, the numbers of roads, the names of rivers, the numbers of regiments and the dates.

But can one really be hired to die? Do Housman's "mercenaries" save the sum of things, as the poet asserts that they do, "for pay"? Isn't there a concealed idealism after all, despite the poet's refusal to allow anything more than the materialistic reason? Of course there is, and this, I suppose, is the point that the poem is making: that the courage to stand and die rather than to run away usually comes from something like *esprit de corps* or professional pride or even from a kind of instinctive manliness rather than from adherence to the conventional rubrics of patriotism and duty. But if this is what Housman's poem implies, then we are indeed in the general realm of Hemingway's fiction, for the mercenaries' gesture is completely consonant with the Hemingway ethos. The Hemingway hero, like Housman's, faces the insoluble "troubles of our proud and angry dust", and in his own way subscribes to the sentiment that

> Bear them we can, and if we can we must.
> Shoulder the sky, my lad, and drink your ale.

Of course, it must be added that the drink of the Hemingway hero is more likely to be *grappa* or brandy or seven-to-one martinis.

But Hemingway can show what is *wrong* with a Housman poem just as effectively as he can show what is right. Consider a well-known poem by Housman which I think has to be set down as a failure:

> Could man be drunk for ever
> With liquor, love, or fights,
> Lief should I rouse at morning
> And lief lie down of nights.
>
> But men at whiles are sober
> And think by fits and starts,
> And if they think, they fasten
> Their hands upon their hearts.

These tough lads who avoid a contemplation of the essential horror of life by keeping the senses occupied with liquor and lechery and fighting are obviously in the same plight as those that we find in *The Sun Also Rises*. Jake, the hero of that fine and sober book, is in spite of himself sober at times, and thinks by fits and starts. But in this case, Hemingway has all the advantage. We can believe in the toughness of his hero and also in his pathos, for both are presented realistically and convincingly. Jake Barnes is never made to fasten his hand upon his heart, and it is this theatrical gesture, so out of keeping with these lusty, brawling, hard-drinking young men, that lets Housman's little poem collapse. The failure does not stem from the fact that the poem falsifies the typical Hemingway situation; it fails because it is inconsistent with its own premises. It is not that the gesture is foreign to Hemingway's Nick Adams: it is a gesture which could not occur in the Shropshire pub of the 1890's. But of course in justice to Housman, Hemingway has his failures too. *Across the River and into the Trees* sentimentalizes the heroic gesture into its own kind of theatricality.

I do not mean to press unduly the Hemingway-Housman analogy. I shall be principally concerned with those qualities that make the finest of Housman's poetry perdurable. But I think that the comparison with Hemingway's can be extremely useful in opening up to a contemporary audience the problems which Housman faced and the characteristic failures and characteristic successes which he achieves. In both authors, so dissimilar in so many ways, there is a fairly narrow ambit of interests. The same theme and the same kind of character occur over and over. There is the danger of monotony, the danger of repetition. It seems sometimes to a reader that Housman has only one poem to write, which he writes and rewrites tirelessly, though oftentimes with very brilliant and beautiful variations. With the general narrowness of the ambit there is, as we have seen, the possibility of sentimentality. In general there is a serious problem of tone. The poem must not seem arch or cute. It must achieve its intensity while making use of understatement or laconicism. The close-lipped courage and the stoic endurance must elicit an intense sympathetic response and yet the hero, from the very terms of the situation, is forbidden to cry out or make any direct appeal for our sympathy.

This is the general problem that besets the presentation of the Hemingway hero: he is the tough guy who because of his very toughmindedness sees into the nature of reality and indeed is more sensitive to the tears of things than are those soft and blurred sensibilities whose very fuzziness of response insulates them against the tragic aspects of reality. Yet Housman is a poet who elects to work within a tiny lyric form, barred from the factuality and massively detailed sense of the world which a writer of fiction like Hemingway rightfully has at his disposal.

Let us see how Housman manages the matter in a tiny lyric,

which after years of reading remains one of my favourites, a
poem entitled "Eight O'Clock".

> He stood, and heard the steeple
>   Sprinkle the quarters on the morning town.
> One, two, three, four, to market-place and people
>   It tossed them down.
>
> Strapped, noosed, nighing his hour,
>   He stood and counted them and cursed his luck;
> And then the clock collected in the tower
>   Its strength, and struck.

We learn in the poem almost nothing about the condemned
man. We are never told what his crime was. The poem does no
more than give us the last half minute of his life. But how
brilliantly that half minute is evoked, and with it some sense of
his incorrigible spirit as he waits for the clock's stroke which
announces the hour of his execution. Everything in the poem
co-operates to dramatize the experience. In the last moments of
this man's life, time takes on a monstrously heightened quality.
The clock, I take it, is one which sounds a musical phrase for
each of the quarter hours and finally, at the hour, after the little
tune has been completed, the number of the hour is hammered
out with separate strokes. The musical phrases, then, are the
"quarters" which he hears the steeple "Sprinkle . . . on the
morning town". By the way, an earlier draft of the poem is
preserved in one of the notebooks possessed by the Library of
Congress – notebooks which the Library owns through the
generous gift of Mrs Gertrude Clarke Whittall. The notebook
draft reads:

> One, two, three, four, on jail and square and people
>   They dingled down.

Housman's second thoughts make an immense improvement.
One does not need the mention of the jail. Suspense requires
that the reason for the man's intent listening should not be
divulged until we come to the second stanza. Contrast requires
too that the "morning town", as it is called in the first stanza, be
simply presented as a crowded market-place town to which the
steeple clock almost gaily "tosses" its chiming quarters.

But with the second stanza, now that we know that the listener is strapped and noosed, the clock, though it continues to dominate the scene, changes character and collects itself to strike the prisoner himself. True, the eighth stroke will not be launched vindictively at the prisoner. It will only signal to the hangman the moment to pull the trap. But by a brilliant telescoping, the clock, the recorder and instrument of time, becomes itself the destroyer:

> And then the clock collected in the tower
> Its strength, and struck.

Time is, with Housman, always the enemy. Housman's Shropshire lad characteristically views the window pane, "blind with showers" and grudgingly checks off one day of his brief springtime that is ruined. Or he speaks to a loved one urgently

> Now – for a breath I tarry
> Nor yet disperse apart.

One of Housman's finest poems turns not upon reference to a clock but to a calendar. The speaker faces the advent of the first winter month and faces it with a heavy heart.

> The night is freezing fast,
>   To-morrow comes December;
>   And winterfalls of old
> Are with me from the past;
>   And chiefly I remember
>   How Dick would hate the cold.

Dick, the friend who is mentioned almost casually in the last line, is of course the occasion for the poem, and as we shall see in the next stanza, it is the first fall of snow upon Dick's grave that becomes the matter of the poem. But Dick, his friend observes with a kind of wry humour, has outwitted winter.

> Fall, winter, fall; for he,
>   Prompt hand and headpiece clever,
>   Has woven a winter robe,
> And made of earth and sea
>   His overcoat for ever,
>   And wears the turning globe.

Housman has been very daring here. The metaphor with which the poem ends is as bizarre and witty as one of John Donne's. For the speaker insists that the earth has not swallowed up Dick but that the dead man has wrapped the earth about himself "And wears the turning globe". For a poet so Victorian in his tastes as Housman was, and a poet generally so inimical to witty conceits – in his famous lecture on poetry Housman will hardly allow the seventeenth-century metaphysicals the name of poets – his conceit of Dick's wearing the globe is very curious indeed. But the bold figure works. The suggestion of schoolboy slang, "prompt hand and headpiece clever," helps to prepare for it, and something of extravagance is needed if the poem is not to dissolve into a kind of too pure and direct pathos. But what makes the last lines work is Housman's audacity in using the commonplace and matter-of-fact word "overcoat". He has already called it a "winter robe", and now if he were to name it a "cloak" or a "toga" or even a "garment", the poem would close on a kind of strained embarrassment. But *overcoat* here is triumphantly right. It represents the brilliant handling of tone which is to be found in nearly all of Housman's successful poems. Dick, with his "headpiece clever", the man never at a loss, has finally outwitted the cold, which he always used to hate. This at least is the way in which one might imagine Dick's accounting for the situation: it is a gay piece of schoolboy extravagance and the jest, because it is characteristic of the dead youth, actually renders the sense of grief not less but more intense. There is not a trace of sentimentality.

Sentimentality is a failure of tone. The emotion becomes mawkish and self-regarding. We feel that the poet himself has been taken in by his own sentiment, responds excessively, and expects us to respond with him in excess of what the situation calls for. And so the writer who, like Housman, insists so uniformly upon the pathos of loss, upon the imminence of death, and upon the grim and loveless blackness to come, must be adept at handling the matter of tone.

Housman's great successes (as well as his disastrous failures) are to be accounted for in terms of tone. It does not matter that Housman never himself employs the term. *We* need it, nevertheless, in order to deal with Housman's poetry: for control of tone is the difference between the shrill and falsetto and the quiet but resonant utterance; it is the difference between the merely arch and self-consciously cute and the full-timbred irony; it is the difference between the sentimental and the responsibly mature utterance. Housman's characteristic fault is a slipping off into sentimentality. (One may observe in passing that this is also Hemingway's characteristic fault.) Conversely, Housman's triumphs nearly always involve a brilliant handling of tone – often a startling shift in tone – in which the matter of the poem is suddenly seen in a new perspective.

"The night is freezing fast" exhibits the kind of tonal shift of which I am speaking. "The Immortal Part" will furnish an even clearer example. In this poem, the speaker perversely insists that the immortal part of man is his skeleton – not the spirit, not the soul – but the most earthy, the most nearly mineral part of his body. The bones will endure long after the "dust of thoughts" has at last been laid and the flesh itself has become dust.

The device on which the poem is built is the grumbling complaint of the bones. The speaker begins by telling us that he can hear his bones counting the days of their servitude and predicting the day of their deliverance in which the flesh will fall away from them and leave them free and unfettered. Housman allows to the bones a certain lugubrious eloquence.

> "Wanderers eastward, wanderers west,
> Know you why you cannot rest?
> 'Tis that every mother's son
> Travails with a skeleton.

The reference to "wanderers" makes one suppose that "travails" is spelled "travels," but in fact the word is "travails"; and this suggestion of the travail of childbirth is developed fully in the next two stanzas:

> "Lie down in the bed of dust;
> Bear the fruit that bear you must;
> Bring the eternal seed to light,
> And morn is all the same as night.

"Rest you so from trouble sore,
Fear the heat o' the sun no more,
Nor the snowing winter wild,
Now you labour not with child.

"Empty vessel, garment cast,
We that wore you long shall last.
– Another night, another day."
So my bones within me say.

The colloquy of the bones is brilliant. But can the brilliance be indefinitely sustained? After nine stanzas, there is every danger of monotony. What climactic threat is there left for the bones to utter? And if there is none, how end the poem?

What Housman does is to introduce a shift in tone. The man answers back:

Therefore they shall do my will
To-day while I am master still,
And flesh and soul, now both are strong,
Shall hale the sullen slaves along,

Before this fire of sense decay,
This smoke of thought blow clean away,
And leave with ancient night alone
The steadfast and enduring bone.

But this defiance of the bones implies in fact a conviction of the truth of their ultimate triumph. Indeed, the "I" who speaks concedes the bones' eventual victory, and furthermore the last four lines of his speech of defiance simply turn into an echo of the chant of the bones. But the tone of the poem has shifted: the conscious sentient being has refused to collapse before the certain onslaught of time. The human spirit is given its due. The worst has been faced and faced down, though not denied.

Housman's use of a shift in tone is so important in his poetry generally that I should like to exhibit still another instance – one of Housman's finest, that which he employed in "Bredon Hill".

The lovers on many a Sunday morning on Bredon Hill have listened to the church bells ringing out through the valleys.

In summertime on Bredon
The bells they sound so clear;
Round both the shires they ring them
In steeples far and near,
A happy noise to hear.

Here of a Sunday morning
My love and I would lie,
And see the coloured counties,
And hear the larks so high
About us in the sky.

In their own happiness the lovers would put words to the sound
of the bells:

The bells would ring to call her
In valleys miles away:
"Come all to church, good people;
Good people, come and pray,"
But here my love would stay.

And I would turn and answer
Among the springing thyme,
"Oh, peal upon our wedding,
And we will hear the chime,
And come to church in time."

But his sweetheart comes to church before their time.

But when the snows at Christmas
On Bredon top were strown,
My love rose up so early
And stole out unbeknown
And went to church alone.

They tolled the one bell only,
Groom there was none to see,
The mourners followed after,
And so to church went she,
And would not wait for me.

This last stanza, as the notebooks preserved in this Library
reveal, gave Housman great trouble. He made at least five
attempts to get the phrasing right. I hope that it is not too
irreverent of me to suggest that he never did get it precisely

right. I cannot help resenting the line "The mourners followed after" – not because it is not true – presumably there were mourners – but because it is unnecessary – we do not need to be *told* in so many words that the girl died. Moreover, the direct reference to her death works against the indirect presentation of it through the poem's basic metaphor – which treats the funeral as if it were a marriage, in which the lover is betrayed by his sweetheart who jilts him and steals away to church to be wed to another.

> And so to church went she
> And would not wait for me –

not *could* not wait, but *would* not wait, as if her failure to wait for him were a matter of her own volition.

But whether or not I am right in thinking that Housman's "explaining his metaphor" is a slight blemish in the sixth stanza, how brilliantly the poem recovers in the seventh, and is brought to an ending that is beautifully right! I think that you can "hear" the shift in tone as I read this last stanza:

> The bells they sound on Bredon,
>   And still the steeples hum.
> "Come all to church, good people," –
>   Oh, noisy bells, be dumb;
>   I hear you, I will come.

The note of exasperation – the irritated outburst against the noise of the bells – is a powerful, if indirect way, of voicing the speaker's sense of loss. All come to death; he will come to the churchyard too; but now that his sweetheart has been stolen from him, what does it matter *when* he comes. The bells whose sound was once a happy noise to hear have become a needless and distracting noisiness. The lover shuts them up as he might the disturbing prattle of a child:

> Oh, noisy bells, be dumb;
>   I hear you, I will come.

One of Housman's surest triumphs of tone is the first poem of *A Shropshire Lad,* the poem simply entitled "1887". The year 1887 was that of Queen Victoria's Jubilee. The village is celebrating the fiftieth year of her accession to the throne. The beacons have been lighted and in the village pub they are singing "God Save the Queen".

> From Clee to heaven the beacon burns,
>   The shires have seen it plain,
> From north and south the sign returns
>   And beacons burn again.

> Look left, look right, the hills are bright,
>   The dales are light between,
> Because 'tis fifty years to-night
>   That God has saved the Queen.

But after the light dancing measures and the flickering alliteration of the opening lines, line eight brings us down with a solid bump. "God save the Queen" is a ritualized phrase. One invokes God's favour. One recommends the sovereign to His mercy. But one does not bring the prayerful imperative down into the dust and sweat of ordinary syntax by turning it into the present perfect of an ordinary work-a-day English verb:

> Because 'tis fifty years to-night
>   That God has saved the Queen

It is as if a piece of ritual furniture were suddenly put to some common use: we get a comparable shock.

I shall have more to say of this device in a moment: suffice it to observe at this point that notice has been served that this will be no ordinary Jubilee tribute. And it is not. For the speaker goes on in the stanzas that follow to talk about the absentees on this occasion, the lads who had been abroad on the Queen's business, who did not come home.

> Now, when the flame they watch not towers
>   About the soil they trod,
> Lads, we'll remember friends of ours
>   Who shared the work with God.

Again, with the last line there is a shock: God has saved the Queen, but He has required the services – or at least has chosen to make use of the services – of human helpers. And some of these have proved to be expendable. The irony is as edged as a knife –

and yet it is a quiet and unforced irony; for the statement "Who shared the work with God" is perfectly consonant with the stated premises. For if the defeat of the Queen's enemies is to be attributed ultimately to God, the humbler means, the British infantryman who have stood off her enemies, have had a share, even if only a humble share, in God's work. But many of the Shropshire lads who went into the armies of the Queen have not returned.

> To skies that knit their heartstrings right,
>   To fields that bred them brave,
> The saviours come not home to-night:
>   Themselves they could not save.

Here the irony achieves a sort of climax, for the last lines echo the passage in the Gospels in which Christ, hanging on the cross, is taunted with the words: "Others he saved; himself he cannot save." To apply the words associated with the Crucified to the dead soldiers is audacious, but again the words are perfectly applicable, quite simply and literally fitting the case of the absent soldiers. Indeed, a reader who failed to catch the Biblical allusion would not feel that the lines were forced or strained. For soldiers, who must necessarily risk losing their own lives in order to save others, are often to be found in such a plight: Others they saved, "Themselves they could not save."

With the fifth stanza, the poem moves away from the local scene. The speaker lets his imagination wander over the far places of the earth where the dead soldiers now lie.

> It dawns in Asia, tombstones show
>   And Shropshire names are read;
> And the Nile spills his overflow
>   Beside the Severn's dead.
>
> We pledge in peace by farm and town
>   The Queen they served in war,
> And fire the beacons up and down
>   The land they perished for.

We need this expansion of view and we need a momentary rest from the irony that has closed so powerfully stanzas two, three, and four. But after this shift of perspective and alteration of tone, we are returned once more to the Jubilee occasion. The lads of the Fifty-third Regiment – those who did come back, that is – join in the celebration.

> "God save the Queen" we living sing,
> From height to height 'tis heard;
> And with the rest your voices ring,
> Lads of the Fifty-third.

> Oh, God will save her, fear you not:
> Be you the men you've been,
> Get you the sons your fathers got,
> And God will save the Queen.

It is a powerful ending of a brilliant poem. Anyone can feel that. But it may be worth examining a little further the speaker's final attitude. Is the poem anti-royalist? Anti-religious? More specifically, is the man who speaks the poem contemptuous of the lads of the Fifty-third because they naïvely sing "God save the Queen" and do not realize that it is they who have had to do the dirty work themselves?

As a matter of fact, Housman's own views on the ending of his poem are on record. Frank Harris, in his *Latest Contemporary Portraits,* tells of a talk with Housman about this poem. He writes:

> I recited the last verse as if it had been bitter sarcasm which in all sincerity I had taken it for and I went on: "It stirs my blood to find an Englishman so free of the insensate snobbishness that corrupts all true values here. I remember telling Kipling once that when he mixed his patriotism with snobbery it became disgusting to me; and here you have poked fun at the whole thing and made splendid mockery of it."
> To my astonishment, Housman replied sharply: "I never intended to poke fun, as you call it, at patriotism, and I can find nothing in the sentiment to make mockery of: I meant it sincerely; if Englishmen breed as good men as their fathers, then God will save their Queen." His own words seemed to have excited him for he added precisely but with anger: "I can only reject and resent your – your truculent praise."

Housman's angry outburst might seem to settle the matter. But does it? It may dispose of Harris's attempt to read a "bitter

sarcasm" into the last stanza. But even Housman's own word
for it will hardly smooth the irony out of this poem.

> Lads, we'll remember friends of ours,
> Who shared the work with God.

> The saviours come not home to-night:
> Themselves they could not save.

These passages simply defy an innocently literal reading: and in
view of Housman's frequently expressed scepticism about the
existence of God, the last lines of the poem likewise defy a literal
reading.

In angrily rejecting Frank Harris's bitter sarcasm, Housman
over-corrected the error. If one reads the entire account printed
by Harris, it is easy enough to see what happened. Harris and a
pair of his friends had got to talking about Housman's poetry,
and one of them proposed that they look the poet up at King's
College, London, where he was teaching and take him to lunch.
They called, introduced themselves, and fairly swept him along
with them. This was not the sort of thing that Housman, a shy
and fastidious man, would take to, and Frank Harris, with his
breezy confidence and his trace of vulgarity, was exactly the sort
of man that Housman would abominate. Harris makes it quite
plain that no rapport had been established; the conversation
had been forced and difficult throughout the luncheon.
Resentments of a more pervasive kind and a general antagonism
burst forth in Housman's explosion over the meaning of his
poem.

We are back, then, once more with the problem of tone. Is it
possible to describe the tone of this poem without misrepre-
senting it on the one hand as a heavy sarcasm and without, on
the other hand, falsifying its evident irony? I think that it is
possible.

The key to the poet's attitude is to be found in a line of the
poem upon which we have already commented:

> Because 'tis fifty years tonight
> That God has saved the Queen.

There, as we remarked, a ritualistic phrase, a pious sentiment, a patriotic cliché is suddenly taken seriously and is made to work in a normal English sentence. It is as shocking as if a bishop suddenly used his crozier like a shepherd's crook to lay hold upon a live sheep.

But to consider soberly the implications of the phrase that is bandied about so thoughtlessly on this jubilant occasion – to reflect upon what is involved in the prayer "God save the Queen" – does not necessarily involve mockery of the Queen or of the young men who have helped to save her. Housman's protest here is well taken. His consideration of the cliché, however, does involve a realistic appraisal of the issues and a penetration beneath patriotic shows and appearances. The speaker clearly admires the lads of the Fifty-third but his angle of vision is different from theirs. What they accept naïvely and uncritically, he sees in its full complexity and ambiguity. But his attitude is not cynical and it is consonant with genuine patriotism. The irony that it contains is a mature and responsible irony whose focus is never blurred. The closing stanza, with its quiet insistence that God will save the Queen but with its conjoined insistence on the all important proviso that they shall get them the sons their fathers got dramatizes the speaker's attitude to a nicety.

A little while ago, I called Housman a romantic poet, a late romantic. If I have emphasized Housman the ironist, it is because I think his irony is important and that its presence does not make him the less a romanticist. But a more obvious aspect of his romanticism may be his treatment of nature.

Many of the poems – and not only those of *A Shropshire Lad* – are given a pastoral setting. The English countryside is everywhere in Housman's poetry. A typical appearance is revealed in the charming lyric which is printed on the back of your programs. To see the cherry in blossom is one of the delights of the year, and how few years there are vouchsafed us in which to see it. Time is the enemy of delight and yet the cherry tree is the product of time. The very description of the springtime beauty is ominous: if "hung with snow" is a way of stressing the unbelievable whiteness of the blossoms, the phrase also hints of winter and the death to come.

But Housman's view of nature looks forward to our time rather than back to that of Wordsworth. If nature is lovely and offers man delight, she does not offer him solace or sustain him as Wordsworth was solaced and sustained. For between Wordsworth and Housman there interpose themselves Darwin and Huxley and Tyndall – the whole achievement of Victorian science. The effect of this impact of science is not, of course, to make Housman love nature less: one could argue that it has rendered nature for him more poignantly beautiful. But his attitude toward nature is not that of the early Romantics and we must take into account this altered attitude if we are to understand his poems.

In this general connection allow me to remark, by the way, that we have had in our day the revival – though it has gone largely unnoticed – of a very fine nature poetry. This nature poetry reveals the somewhat altered perspective of the twentieth century – as is natural and inevitable. But the delight in the rich qualities of the natural scene is extraordinary. Let me extend the term *poetry* to include some of our finest prose fiction. Look at the rendering of nature – to be found, say, in Hemingway and Faulkner. There is a loving attention to detail and faithful evocation of the quality of a scene. The natural world is reflected with beautiful delicacy and even radiance in the fishing episode in Hemingway's *The Sun Also Rises*, or in the hunting scenes of Faulkner's "The Bear". This latter story concludes with what can only be described as a great hymn to nature. If keeping in mind such nature poetry as this, we remember also the characteristic depiction of nature by poets like Thomas Hardy or Robert Frost, we may begin to realize that the twentieth century, in spite of industrialization and the growth of world cities, has indeed produced a rich nature poetry.

Our immensely increased knowledge of nature has not destroyed her charm. Even the so-called scientific neutralization of nature has not done that – not at least for many of our poets. But it has altered their attitudes toward her and it has tended to stress man's sense of his alienation from nature. (Of course, even this sense of alienation is not strictly "modern" – I find it, for example, in Keats' "Ode to a Nightingale".) But the fact of alienation tends to be determinative for the modern nature poet. The poems of Robert Frost testify again and again to the elemental attraction of nature of which man is a part, but Frost never yields to the delusion that man can slip through the invisible barrier to merge himself into nature. The speaker of the poem in every case remembers his manhood and ruefully or with a half-serious jest or with a stoic brusqueness puts down the temptation. When the falling leaves of autumn beckon to Frost's "leaf-treader" to come with them in their descent to death, the man acknowledges the "fugitive in his heart" that wants to respond to the leaves' "invitation to grief", but finally, with a small's boy's impudence, he shrugs off the impulse:

> But it was no reason I had to go because they had to go.
> Now up, my knee, to keep on top of another year of snow.

Again, the traveller in "Stopping by Woods on a Snowy Evening" pauses and as he enjoys the beauty of the lovely scene, feels the attraction of nature:

> The woods are lovely, dark and deep . . .

But he has promises to keep and it is significant that he drives on. Or again, the man who comes upon the site of the burned farmhouse and abandoned barn is struck by the melancholy of the scene. The very birds who haunt the scene seem to be mourning. But the observer knows better, though

> One had to be versed in country things
> Not to believe the phoebes wept.

But he *is* versed in country things, and in spite of the temptation to feel that nature sympathizes with man, he knows that she does not. However melancholy the birds may sound to him, they are simply singing out of the fullness of their own activity; they know nothing and care nothing for man's sorrow.

Frost's treatment of nature can help us to understand Housman's, particularly that revealed in what is in some respects Housman's finest poem, with a comment on which I mean to close this lecture. But I am not, of course, so absurd as to suggest that the attitudes of Frost and Housman are identical; and in any case, the poetic strategies of these two fine poets differ in a

dozen ways. They speak in different idioms, different intonations. But the resemblance is worthing pointing out in order to
stress an element of the modern in Housman that we may easily
overlook.

Housman expressed his characteristic attitude toward nature
in the beautiful poem numbered XL in *Last Poems* his farewell
to nature. The matter of the poem is the speaker's resignation of
his mistress Nature to another. The resignation is forced; he
does not willingly relinquish her. He has possessed her too
completely to feel that she is less than a part of himself and his
appetite for her is not cloyed. At this moment of conscious
relinquishment, nature has never been more compellingly the
enchantress.

> Tell me not here, it needs not saying,
>   What tune the enchantress plays
> In aftermaths of soft September
>   Or under blanching mays,
> For she and I were long acquainted
>   And I knew all her ways.

How thorough is his knowledge of her ways is quietly but
convincingly made good in the second and third stanzas.

> On russet floors, by waters idle,
>   The pine lets fall its cone;
> The cuckoo shouts all day at nothing
>   In leafy dells alone;
> And traveller's joy beguiles in autumn
>   Hearts that have lost their own.

> On acres of the seeded grasses
>   The changing burnish heaves;
> Or marshalled under moons of harvest
>   Stand still all night the sheaves;
> Or beeches strip in storms for winter
>   And stain the wind with leaves.

These beautiful stanzas do more than create a series of scenes
from nature. They insinuate the speaker's claim to his possession
of nature through an intimate knowledge of her ways. Each of
the vignettes suggests the secret life of nature revealed to a rapt

and solitary observer: the tap of the falling pine cone, audible only because the scene is hushed and breathless; the shouts of the solitary cuckoo, who seems to be calling to no other bird and not even to a human listener but with cheerful idiocy shouting "at nothing"; the flower called "traveller's joy" in the autumn sunshine silently extending to the joyless wayfarer its grace of self, the namesake of joy.

The "changing burnish" on the "acres of seeded grasses", I take to be the shimmer of light that one sees play upon a hayfield in late summer when the wind heaves and ripples the long grass stems to catch the light. You who have seen it will know that "burnish" is not too extravagant a term, for the grass sometimes shimmers as if it were metallic. The wind that heaves the grass is a fitful wind of late summer. That which strips the beech trees of their leaves is a late autumn gale. But the third scene portrayed in this stanza –

> Or marshalled under moons of harvest
> Stand still all night the sheaves –

is windless: that is the point, I take it, of the statement that under the harvest moon the sheaves "Stand *still* all night". The secret life of nature is thus depicted through all weathers and throughout the round of the seasons. All of it has been observed by the speaker, all of it has been made his own possession through knowledge and is held now in memory. But the various scenes of the changing year are but the magic spells woven by the one enchantress.

The fourth stanza stresses his claim to possession. The first line rings the changes upon the word "possess" and the very last word of the stanza, the emphatic closing rhyme word, is "mine". But the action of the stanza is a relinquishment of his claims. The speaker conjures the companion to whom he speaks the poem to

> Possess, as I possessed a season,
>   The countries I resign,
> Where over elmy plains the highway
>   Would mount the hills and shine,
> And full of shade the pillared forest
>   Would murmur and be mine.

His claim to possession is based upon a shared experience, a secret knowledge, the kind of bond that unites two lovers who feel that they belong to each other. But in this instance, the beloved is nature; and nature is not one to recognize any lover's claim to possession.

> For nature, heartless, witless nature –

Nature is not only the fickle mistress, she is the idiot mistress, having no more mind than heart.

> For nature, heartless, witless nature
>   Will neither care nor know
> What stranger's feet may find the meadow
>   And trespass there and go,
> Nor ask amid the dews of morning
>   If they are mine or no.

Nature, for all her attractiveness to man, is supremely indifferent to him. This is the bedrock fact upon which the poem comes to rest, but if the fact constitutes a primal irony, it is accepted in this poem without rancor or any fierce bitterness. The very charm of nature is the way in which she can give herself freely to all of us who will strenuously try to claim her. And moreover, if nature, in this last stanza, is heartless and witless, she is still as freshly beautiful as the morning. Notice how concretely Housman says this in the closing lines. Nature spreads her dewy meadow as virginally fresh for the imprint of the feet of the trespasser as for those of the old lover who would like to believe that he alone possessed her.

The attitude toward nature here is not Wordsworth's confident trust that "Nature never did betray / The heart that loved her." Yet the poem may be said to illustrate the Wordsworthian formula

> How exquisitely the individual Mind . . .
> . . . to the external World
> Is fitted: – and how exquisitely, too – . . .
> The external World is fitted to the Mind.

True, it is Housman's mind, not Wordsworth's, that is fitted to the landscape here described; but the exquisite fitting is there just the same – so much so that the nature that Housman depicts seems to answer at every point the sensitive and melancholy mind that perceives it, and in its turn implies in its aloof and beautifully closed order the loneliness and austerity of the mind of its observer.

Housman's feet no longer print the dew of his favourite English meadow. The enchantress nature spreads her blandishments now for other men – for us, if we care to respond. But it ought to be noted that Housman has himself responded with an enchantment of his own: I mean the poem itself. The poem matches the immortality of nature with its own kind of immortality – the immortality of art. For, if nature, changeless through all the vicissitudes of change, is unweariedly the same, so also the experience that Housman has dramatized for us here may be endlessly repeated and is eternally recapturable. *Ars longa, vita brevis. We* may trespass into the poet's ancient dominion, see and possess as the poet himself "possessed a season" the woods and fields of Shropshire or of Cambridgeshire. But in participating in his *poem* we will possess more: we will possess his hard-won knowledge of the meaning of possession. Through the poem we shall come to know more deeply what our relation to nature is and what we as men are. Our feet, then, that "trespass" on the poet's ancient dominion, in the magical world of his poem, commit no trespass. His footprints become our own; we stand in his shoes; we share in his experience, which has been treasured up and given a life beyond life. That is what art can do. That is why we must always feel a deep gratitude to the poet. That is why we celebrate Alfred Edward Housman's one hundredth birthday this evening.

19

Wordsworth and Human Suffering: Notes on Two Early Poems

In the Fenwick note on "The Old Cumberland Beggar", Wordsworth tells us that the poem was written in his twenty-eighth year at a time when the "political economists were . . . beginning their war upon mendicity in all its forms, and by implication if not directly, on Almsgiving also". This war upon mendicity Wordsworth calls a "heartless process" and there is, of course, no reason to doubt Wordsworth's fervour in terming it such. Yet to modern ears Wordsworth's own attitude toward the beggar may seem somewhat heartless: he does not want the old beggar shut up within doors; he wants him to be unconfined, able to pursue his usual rounds. He wants him to have the advantages of solitude and, as the last two lines of the poem indicate, to be able to die in the eye of nature "as in the eye of nature he has lived".

These are not modern sentiments. That the old man should be allowed to wander on the roads and in various weathers is something that the modern humanitarian feels to be cruel treatment. And indeed, a superficial reading of this poem might very well convey the impression that Wordsworth primarily wanted the beggar to remain, even though to his own discomfort, a kind of picturesque adornment to the countryside or a means for prompting in the people of the countryside moral feelings which otherwise they might not experience.

Wordsworth thus may seem to contemplate the beggar as he might a noble stag or any other fine wild animal that ought not be penned up but allowed to live out its own life at large in nature. Wordsworth, to be sure, regards man as nobler than any mere animal, but the argument does take something of this form: like an old stag, the beggar deserves to live out his days unconfined, and to be allowed to die in his native habitat.

Later in the poem, Wordsworth is to admonish his reader: "deem not this man useless." Yet throughout the first part Wordsworth has presented him as completely useless. The beggar has placed his staff upon the pile of stones and we see him looking over his profits for the day, "the dole of village dames". He is examining one scrap and fragment after another,

> with a fixed and serious look
> Of idle computation.

As described here, the beggar becomes a kind of parody of the business man, casting up his accounts, or of the miser fingering his treasures. One notices that Wordsworth passes over an opportunity to have the beggar consciously share his meal with the little birds, he, having received charity, passing on his own bit of charity to lesser creatures. He only *seems* to be dispensing his largess to the birds as the crumbs shower from his hands, for Wordsworth makes it plain that his palsied hands cannot hold the crumbs, and that the feast for the birds is being spread quite involuntarily. The stress on the birds' caution points up this fact: they are attracted, but they dare not approach closer than half the length of his staff.

After this picture, so very vividly done, and honestly done, the speaker, telling us that since his childhood he has known the beggar, describes the beggar's relation to other people on the road – the sauntering horseman, the woman who minds the toll gate, the postboy. All know the beggar and all in some sense show that they pity him. With line 44 we return to the beggar as solitary, and to the world that he experiences as he moves along the high road. In terms of the thesis that Wordsworth is to present a little later in the poem, one would expect him to make much of the old man's friendly intercourse with nature and the compensations which, in spite of his age and infirmities, his life with nature gives him. Instead, Wordsworth honestly

records the fact that the stooped old man sees very little of the
world except that which lies just before his feet:

> One little span of earth
> Is all his prospect.

As he goes along, he sees no more than some scattered leaf or
wheel marks on the road, and even here "seldom knowing that
he sees. . . ." Such is his little constricted world, and he creeps
through it so quietly and so slowly that everybody passes him
by, even the "slow-paced waggon".

The songs of the birds are there for him to hear, but Wordsworth concedes that the beggar does not necessarily attend to
them. Wordsworth will maintain that the beggar is better off
because these influences of nature can play about him even if no
longer upon him. But the concessions he makes to realism are
important, for it behoved Wordsworth to avoid the trap of
turning the old beggar into a person as sensitive as himself,
simply another Wordsworth. (We have already mentioned
another trap into which the poet risked falling: that of making
the old beggar a picturesque object affording the well-fed and
well-housed poet aesthetic delight. We shall consider later
whether the poet succeeded in avoiding this trap.)

It is only after his detailed and realistic presentation of the
beggar's "useless life" that Wordsworth utters his challenge:
deem not this man useless. The poet's argument will be: they
also serve who only creep and beg. But before he comes to a
specific justification of the usefulness of the beggar, Wordsworth
makes a bold generalization:

> 'Tis Nature's law
> That none, the meanest of created things,
> Of forms created the most vile and brute,
> The dullest or most noxious, should exist
> Divorced from good. . . .

This proposition is stated absolutely: presumably it will have to
include the viper, the flea, and the mosquito. Life is one, and
the pulse of good is "inseparably linked" to "every mode of
being".

If this is true of the meanest of creatures, then it has to be true of someone who once

> owned
> The heaven-regarding eye and front sublime
> Which man is born to.

Even this comment has its precision. Wordsworth is careful to put the verb in the past tense, for he has made it perfectly plain that the beggar's eye is not now heaven-regarding, for, as we have seen, the beggar keeps his look fixed on the ground. Still, the beggar is more than a "dry remnant of a garden-flower" or an "implement / Worn out and worthless". He affects the world and exercises a function that is important and unique:

> The villagers in him
> Behold a record which together binds
> Past deeds and offices of charity
> Else unremembered, and so keeps alive
> The kindly mood in hearts which lapse of years,
> And that half-wisdom half-experience gives,
> Make slow to feel, and by sure steps resign
> To selfishness and cold oblivious cares.

The beggar is like a kind of inverse scapegoat: instead of bearing away the sins of the community into the wilderness, he bears back and forth *through* the community a memory of its good offices and charities.

Here again Wordsworth is very honest. He tells us that

> Where'er the aged Beggar takes his rounds,
> The mild necessity of use compels
> To acts of love; and habit does the work
> Of reason. . . .

This is indeed to put it bluntly and even paradoxically. Can acts of love be compelled? Can habit really do the work of reason? Strictly speaking no, though perhaps the influence of Hartley made the notion seem more plausible to the young Wordsworth than it now seems to some of us. Yet as presented in the poem, Wordsworth's account of the matter has a fine common sense. What Wordsworth is really talking about is education, and it is true that men can be coaxed and even compelled into uses which are tinged with goodness. The villager who falls into the habit of giving charity may finally become disposed to "true goodness".

One remembers in what high repute sympathy was held by men of the eighteenth century. Sympathy worked its miracles and in some late eighteenth-century thought becomes the effectual mother of all the virtues. So the beggar, by prompting that "first mild touch of sympathy", may indeed engender what will later flower into genuine philanthropy. The beggar reminds the prosperous and unthinking of the existence of another world, a world of want and sorrow. Thus, he prompts such people to remember their blessings, and he makes – what Wordsworth calls "no vulgar service" – these blessings "felt". So much for the prosperous. But for the very poor the beggar performs a service that is unique. He confers upon the poorest of the poor the opportunity to be a benefactor. They too

> Long for some moments in a weary life
> When they can know and feel that they have been,
> Themselves, the fathers and the dealers-out
> Of some small blessings. . . .

The beggar, as the lowest rung on the social ladder, provides a footing for the happiness of the very poor: they at least are better off than he.

The cynic may make such remarks as these bitterly. Wordsworth apparently feels that he can make them simply with cheerful honesty. At any rate, this is his case for the usefulness of the old beggar. Yet carrying out this function costs the old man something. The beggar serves, but he suffers in the process. How justify, for example, letting an old man walk the roads in all weathers? Here Wordsworth has been shockingly candid. In the very act of breathing a blessing on the beggar's head, the poet rather goes out of his way to express a wish that the beggar's blood should "Struggle with frosty air and winter snows", and adds:

> let the chartered wind that sweeps the heath
> Beat his grey locks against his withered face.

Does Wordsworth succeed with his rather audacious procedure? And if he does, can one suggest why? Well, for one thing, the implication is that the beggar has been brought to his present state by natural processes. It is the "tide of things" that "has borne him" to "that vast solitude" in which he now finds himself. But the tide of things has not merely drifted a bit of random flotsam to shore. The "vast solitude" is referred to as if it were a goal that one would long to reach, and in bearing the beggar to it the tide has evidently carried out "the law of Heaven". Though the beggar appears "to breathe and live for himself alone" in this solitude, he does not in fact bear only himself on his journeys but carries with him

> The good which the benignant law of Heaven
> Has hung around him. . . .

Moreover, the beggar does not merely remind people of the uses of charity. He makes them think – "pensive thoughts" – and deepens their knowledge of themselves and of reality.

The argument that is advanced here is really very cunningly put. It is as if the poet were forbidding officious men to disorder what nature itself has ordered by daring to disannul services so important as those of the Cumberland beggar.

It is only after having made this point that Wordsworth boldly insists upon the hardships to which the beggar will be exposed as he makes his rounds, the "Struggle with frosty air and winter snows". Even in this recital, hardships are mingled with joys: for example,

> let him breathe
> The freshness of the valleys. . . .

Finally, Wordsworth plays his trump card. After the reference to the chartered wind beating the old man's grey locks, Wordsworth goes on to exhort us to

> Reverence the hope whose vital anxiousness
> Gives the last human interest to his heart.
> May never HOUSE, misnamed of INDUSTRY,
> Make him a captive!

The essence of the beggar's hope is a vital anxiousness, and it is this anxiousness that provides for his heart a human interest. I am not sure that the grammar here can be confidently unravelled, but even so – and perhaps because the phrasing is ambiguous – the passage constitutes a very brilliant and effective piece of special pleading. For these cloudy lines suggest that one's interest in living depends upon a hope whose other face is necessarily anxiety, and that the beggar, in losing his vocation with its attendant incitements and apprehensions, would lose his very reason for being. His freedom depends upon a "vital anxiousness". Remove the anxiousness, and the beggar, though certain of food in the workhouse, is merely a captive.

Moreover, the workhouse will deprive the beggar of "that vast solitude" which the phrasing of the poem has suggested is the crown of a lifetime. The workhouse is noisy, a place of "pent-up din", no place for the old man who has won his right to "the natural silence of old age!" Silence and solitude are cunningly associated with freedom; for the beggar, freedom means freedom from all "life-consuming sounds". The poet thus argues: "Let him be free of mountain solitudes" and a little later the poet will pray that the light too may find a "free entrance" to his "languid orbs".

The general tone of the argument, I repeat, is that of a plea that some noble animal may enjoy its right to continue its natural freedom and to live out its life in its own accustomed way. The beggar ought, for example, to have around him the pleasant song of the birds, whether he can hear it or whether he cares to hear it. He ought to be allowed to behold "The countenance of the horizontal sun", even if his eyes have now "Been doomed so long to settle upon earth". Finally, he has earned his right to die "in the eye of Nature" even as he has always lived in the eye of Nature. The beggar has not been shut out from nature. He has always been able to view it. But, more importantly, nature has been able to view *him* so that he has lived out his life in "the eye of Nature" – whatever this may mean – and whatever it may mean, it certainly possesses powerful emotive force. A lesser poet would have emphasized the need for the old beggar to look upon nature in death as he has in life, and thus would have contradicted the fact that the old man now keeps his eyes on the ground. By reversing the pattern, Wordsworth has strengthened his case, and has at last implied that nature takes a special cognizance of the old man.

The poem, even if considered as a piece of special pleading, is very clever indeed. It may well be judged too clever to represent actually a matter of Wordsworth's *conscious* manipulation of language. Yet I would not want Wordsworth to act as attorney against me in a law suit. In this poem, all the tricks of rhetoric are skillfully employed to enforce very successfully a point which a modern reader is disposed to resist and resent. (F. R. Leavis, writing in another connection, in *Revaluation*, makes something like this point about Wordsworth's "innocently insidious tricks".)

Lest it be thought that I have overemphasized the risks that Wordsworth has taken and the complications of tone that he has dared to develop, one might compare "The Old Cumberland Beggar" with his poem beginning "I know an aged Man constrained to dwell". In this late poem – composed in 1846 – Wordsworth tells the story of an aged man who had been forced to leave his cottage and remove to "a large house of public charity" where he lives "as in a Prisoner's cell". Before this time, when he could "creep about, at will" like the Cumberland beggar, he had fed a red-breast at his cottage door. The bird had learned to peck crumbs "upon his knee". Between the bird and the man there sprang up a "dear intercourse":

> Months passed in love that failed not to fulfil,
> In spite of season's change, its own demand,
> By fluttering pinions here and busy bill;
> There by caresses from a tremulous hand.

But now the aged man, as captive, is separated from his one friend and, though surrounded by many men, has "alas! no company", unfriended, truly alone, and with only the memory of the bird to comfort him.

In this poem everything is spelled out. The man shares his food with his fellow creatures, here reduced to one companionable robin, and the memory of this friendship is apparently all that warms the old man's life while he pines within the house of "charity". But the later poem is much too explicit, and comes perilously close to descending into sentimental bathos in the last stanza. "The Old Cumberland Beggar" is, in its honesty and realism, more ambitious and, perhaps not in spite of, but because of, the risks that the poet takes, much more successful.

In this general connection, one ought to notice the little poem entitled "Animal Tranquillity and Decay". Wordsworth's note, as delivered to Miss Fenwick, indicates that these verses were an overflowing from "The Old Cumberland Beggar". "Animal Tranquillity" shows this relation unmistakably in the way in which it too transposes natural infirmity into awesome strength and defeat into virtue. For example, every limb of the old man, his look and his bending figure, the poet says, bespeak

> A man who does not move with pain, but moves
> With thought.

Is the old man in fact simply painfully arthritic? Are his deliberate movements really deliberate in that they are instinct with thought? Or is the poet saying that the old man's motions, slowed though they may be by the pain in his limbs, do not appear painful but impress an observer as those made by a man of thought?

The poet goes on to observe that the old man has been "insensibly subdued" to "subtle quiet". He has been so habituated to long patience that

> patience now doth seem a thing of which
> He hath no need.

Finally, the poet describes him as a person led by nature

> To peace so perfect that the young behold
> With envy, what the Old Man hardly feels.

(This is again an instance of brilliant double-talk – though the reader may prefer to say, as I do, that in this instance duplicity has been transmuted into the richness and subtlety of great poetry.) The old man hardly feels the perfect peace to which he has been led by nature and which the young behold with envy. This is indeed to put the best possible face on decay and the slowing down of age. There is, of course, a peace that is deeper still: the peace of death, and the recipient of that peace is so thoroughly pacified that he is not aware of it at all: he is simply not aware. I do not, by the way, mean to imply that Wordsworth had excluded the possibility of this last interpretation. The child of the "Intimations" Ode does not know it is going to die, and the little maid of "We Are Seven" cannot comprehend what death is. The old man of "Animal Tranquillity" has almost re-entered the peace that the child abandons on growing up.

Rather early in his career, Wordsworth touched upon the problem of man's self-consciousness and his alienation from nature. Consciousness becomes the very barrier which separates man from nature. The theme is to become explicit in Keats's "Ode to a Nightingale", where the bird's immortality derives from the fact that the bird, completely submerged in nature, having no memory of the past and no prevision of the future, lives in an eternal present with no sense that it can ever die; whereas man, knowing what the bird "amongst the leaves" has never known, is indeed, as the bird is not, "born for death". Man's consciousness, through which he is able to savour so fully the bird's special kind of happiness, is the very barrier which keeps him from slipping into nature and joining the bird in its state of timeless being.

Some of the problems that pertain to "The Old Cumberland Beggar" are at least implicit in other Wordsworth poems. The young poet who appears in "Resolution and Independence" presumably hopes that the old leech-gatherer will never have to be shut away from nature, and that, *faute de mieux*, he will be allowed to die in his boots beside one of the lonely pools on the moor. But the poem is focused upon something else: what haunts the "mind's eye" (of the young man and of the reader of the poem) as the poem ends is a vision of the leech-gatherer, now become almost a natural presence endowed with nature's immortality, pacing

> About the weary moors continually,
> Wandering about alone and silently.

The story of Margaret in "The Ruined Cottage" raises much more specifically the problem of loneliness, loss, and death – more sharply indeed than does "The Old Cumberland Beggar".

Why is the younger man calmed and strengthened by the
Wanderer's recital of Margaret's sufferings? Why does the
Wanderer feel that the "purposes of wisdom" are served by
attendance on her story? What consolation was there for
Margaret herself?

The answer to these questions is not easy, and the difficulties
are not merely those raised by a modern reader. Wordsworth's
contemporaries registered some uneasiness in this area. De
Quincey thought that the Wanderer would have done better to
give Margaret some cash rather than mere sympathy. John
Wilson ("Christopher North") admired the poem but he
remarks that the poet has "described, or rather dissected, with
an almost cruel anatomy – not one quivering fibre being left
unexposed – all the fluctuating, and finally all the constant
agitations laid bare and naked that carried [Margaret] at last
lingeringly to the grave". Wilson is not convinced of the truth
of Margaret's psychology as depicted, and he rejects the
Wanderer's conclusion that

> sorrow and despair
> From ruin and from change, and all the grief

that we "can suffer here below, appear an idle dream among
plumes, and weeds, and speargrass, and mists, and rain-drops".
It is interesting to observe that David Perkins, in *Wordsworth
and the Poetry of Sincerity*, makes a related point: ". . . even poor
Margaret," he notes, "seems a mere shade when compared to
the final, vivid images of 'spear-grass . . . By mist and Silent
rain-drops silvered o'er.'" Perkins's general point is that Wordsworth loved nature "as a reality, man as an idea".

The story of Margaret is beautifully and movingly told. To
the younger man, the ruined cottage seems a "cheerless spot".
But for the Wanderer, the spot is suffused with the sense of
human pathos and loss. To him the hills, streams, and senseless
rocks can speak

> with a voice
> Obedient to the strong creative power
> Of human passion. Sympathies there are
> More tranquil, yet perhaps of kindred birth,

> That steal upon the meditative mind,
> And grow with thought. Beside yon spring I stood,
> And eyed its waters till we seemed to feel
> One sadness, they and I.

Thus, for the Wanderer, the spring shares his own sadness for the woman who once lived near here. The Wanderer goes on to tell the younger man about Margaret, but after some talk about her the Wanderer is willing to let the subject drop. Why, he asks, should one

> feeding on disquiet, thus disturb
> The calm of nature with our restless thoughts?

This last remark is curious. It may even seem subversive of the Wanderer's real feelings about nature. For a little later on the Wanderer is going to extract nourishment from these same sad and restless thoughts and, by feeding on disquiet, promises to achieve a deeper quiet. The Wanderer is more subtle than he seems. Perhaps he has meant to plant a disquieting thought to which the younger man will be forced to return. At any rate, after some talk on more trivial things, the younger man begs the Wanderer to resume the story of Margaret, and this time the Wanderer speaks something that is apparently nearer to his own notion in saying

> But we have known that there is often found
> In mournful thoughts, and always might be found,
> A power to virtue friendly; . . .

The Wanderer tells Margaret's story very effectively indeed. His is an art that conceals art. He uses restraint and is careful not to make any overt bid for sympathy. He also has an eye for the exact detail. And it is interesting to see how much he makes the details tell the story of Margaret's grief. For example, the untrimmed honeysuckle beginning to hang down in heavier tufts, the garden of the cottage, losing its pride of neatness, bits of sheep's wool hanging to the corner stones on either side of the porch of the cottage

> as if the sheep,
> That fed upon the Common, thither came
> Familiarly, and found a couching-place
> Even at her threshold.

Margaret knows what is happening to her. She parts with her elder child in order to apprentice him to a "kind master on a distant farm" – presumably for the child's own good. Presumably too she would do so with her other child if this were not impossible, for she tells the Wanderer that she knows that she has done much wrong to the helpless infant. She is so careworn and abstracted that she cannot give it a proper rearing. Her effect upon the child comes out poignantly in the Wanderer's statement that

> Her infant Babe
> Had from its mother caught the trick of grief,
> And sighed among its playthings.

Margaret's grief is like that of Wordsworth's character Michael in that it does not break her heart and quickly end her life. For nine tedious years she lives on – long after the death of her baby. Her own sad decay is reflected in the gradual decay of her poor hut. Margaret is identified very cunningly with her cottage, and what is happening to the building reflects what is happening to its occupant.

When the Wanderer's tale has been completed, the younger man is overcome with the sense of pathos, and his outpouring of grief has to be checked finally by the Wanderer himself who tells him that

> enough to sorrow you have given,
> The purposes of wisdom ask no more: . . .

Margaret herself found her own consolation, so the Wanderer tells his younger friend. But what precisely is the meaning of Margaret's story? How does it promote wisdom? And why does this story of helpless suffering console us about the human predicament? I have already said that I am not at all sure of the answer here.

In the long speech of the Wanderer, which begins with line 932 and goes through line 956, the references to Christianity provide something like an orthodox answer. The way of the Cross is suffering; the problem of evil and suffering has always been finally a mystery; yet it is clear that human beings may be asked to express their deepest love and loyalty by being willing to suffer. Through suffering, they come to a deeper sense of themselves and of God, and in discovering the divine, they may find the way to a transcendent joy which makes present earthly suffering finally irrelevant. But the earlier Wordsworth's view of this matter was surely not quite so orthodox as this, and even in the text as revised in 1845, the earlier, more pantheistic notions are still present. For example, the Wanderer tells us that Margaret "sleeps in the calm earth, and peace is here". The ruined cottage and the ruined garden have conveyed to the heart of the Wanderer an image of tranquillity that is so calm and still and beautiful that the sorrow and despair that one feels in experiencing a world of mortal change simply becomes an idle dream, a dream that can

> maintain
> Nowhere, dominion o'er the enlightened spirit . . .

Is Wordsworth saying here that, seen in the full perspective of nature, seen as a portion of nature's beautiful and unwearied immortality, Margaret with her sorrows is simply one detail of an all-encompassing and harmonious pattern? One can, for example, look at the rabbit torn by the owl in something like this fashion, and the rabbit's agony, no longer isolated and dwelt upon in itself, may cease to trouble us when understood as a necessary part of a total pattern, rich and various and finally harmonious, in which even the rabbit's pain becomes not a meaningless horror since it partakes of the beauty of the whole.

One shrinks from concluding that such an interpretation as this is Wordsworth's own; and I do not mean to so conclude. But it is useful to state it as a limiting term of Wordsworth's position. Behind Wordsworth there lies the eighteenth-century view of human suffering which was not wholly different from that just described. The universe was an orderly universe, and a poet like Alexander Pope had been able to argue plausibly that much that appeared to be evil was simply partial good, or good only partially understood. A great many eighteenth-century modes of thought linger in Wordsworth's poetry, but it is obvious that "The Ruined Cottage" has a different quality of feeling and a different tone from that of the quasi-deistic poetry of the Age of Reason. So much for a backward look.

If we look forward to the poetry that comes after Wordsworth, for example, to the later poetry of Yeats, we find what might be called the reconciliation of suffering in the aesthetic vision. I should describe this latter in something like this fashion: man is so various, so wonderful, capable of so much triumph and agony, suffering and joy, malice and goodness, that if one can take his stance far enough away from the individual case to allow him to see life in its wholeness, with all its rich variety – if one can do that, he can accept not only suffering but active wickedness as an inevitable and necessary part of the human drama, and can even rejoice in it as a testimony to the depths of man's feeling and his power to experience and endure.

I gave this summary not necessarily to cast scorn upon it. There is a sense in which we do enjoy the suffering of a Lear or of an Oedipus. Their power to suffer and to endure is a testimony to their own greatness, and a testimony to the dimensions of the human spirit. The deepest knowledge of ourselves, that given by the greatest art, always seems to require the experience of tragic suffering. But an aesthetic attitude toward the human spectacle, so valuable and necessary and indeed even so clearly enjoined upon us if we intend to get all that we can from *literature*, is not necessarily the same thing as an ethics or a metaphysics by which one can live. Literature has its own function, a very important one, though I question whether it can become an altogether satisfactory substitute for a philosophy or a religion. There is a good deal of evidence to indicate that Wordsworth himself found in later life that there could no be substitute for a religion. Did he ever feel, even at the beginning of his career, that an imaginative vision was enough? I am not sure that he did, though the notion has been recently urged.

In any case, the view of human suffering taken by the Wanderer is much more than what I have called the aesthetic vision. It is deeply tinged with religion: the point is that it is not the Christian religion. On this matter, John Wilson's remarks can be helpful. As he put it, more than a century ago: "the religion of this great Poet – in all his poetry published previous to the 'Excursion' – is but the 'Religion of the Woods'. In the 'Excursion', his religion is brought forward – prominently and conspicuously. . . . And a very high religion it often is; but is it Christianity? No – it is not. There are glimpses given of some of the Christian doctrines," but Wilson's point is that the various interlocutors in *The Excursion* may, "for anything that appears to the contrary, be deists."

I dare say that Wilson is probably right in remarking that the Wanderer's attitude is not Christian, and certainly right in calling it religious. Yet it would not be easy to give a systematic account of the "theology" that underlies the Wanderer's religious experience. I am not sure that Wordsworth could have done so himself. But what is important is that Wordsworth has been able to dramatize this religion for us and to do it so winningly that we are convinced of the integrity of the Wanderer's emotions and share in the catharsis that he and his young friend experience.

In short, the poet has enabled us to know what it "feels like" to hold the Wanderer's faith. This he has done through his art – through what reveals itself as a most skilful and delicate management of the resources of language. The accomplishment is of the highest importance and it must not be misunderstood: the art is not cosmetic but structural – not a rhetorical presentation of plausible arguments but a poetic creation. But to try to show this in detail would involve a commentary that would far exceed the limits of this paper.

20

Milton and the New Criticism

The most celebrated metaphor of our time is probably John
Donne's comparison of the souls of the lovers to the legs of a
pair of compasses.

> Such wilt thou be to me who must
>   Like th' other foot, obliquely run;
> Thy firmness makes my circle just,
>   And makes me end, where I begun.

It has become a touchstone of metaphysical poetry, perhaps *the*
touchstone – though we ought to remember that Donne uses far
more frequently condensed metaphors rather than elaborated
comparisons. Nevertheless, upon it has been erected a whole
aesthetic.

John Milton employs the compass in a very different fashion.
Listen to this:

> He took the golden Compasses, prepar'd
> In Gods Eternal store, to circumscribe
> This Universe, and all created things:
> One foot he center'd, and the other turn'd
> Round through the vast profunditie obscure,
> And said, thus farr extend, thus farr thy bounds,
> This be thy just Circumference, O World.
>
> (Paradise Lost, VII, 225–31)

We are likely to say: how like Milton! his compasses *would* be
golden, and he would be intent upon, and contented with, the
grandiose pictorial effect. Donne's poetry is founded on
functional metaphor; Milton's, on large and eloquent statement. Furthermore, even when Milton gives us a comparison,
and even when he employs a technical instrument, the effect
for which he strives is still pictorial and grand. The telescope,

most of us would concede, is a sufficiently technical instrument quite as much so as the geometer's compass. But how does Milton use it? Here is Milton's description of Lucifer's shield and spear:

> his ponderous shield
> Ethereal temper, massy, large, and round,
> Behind him cast; the broad circumference
> Hung on his shoulders like the Moon, whose Orb
> Through Optic Glass the Tuscan Artist views
> At Ev'ning from the top of Fesole,
> Or in Valdarno, to descry new Lands,
> Rivers or Mountains in her spotty Globe.
> His Spear, to equal which the tallest pine
> Hewn on Norwegian hills, to be the Mast
> Of some great Ammiral, were but a wand . . .
>
> (*P. L.*, I, 284–94)

So much for a contrast between Donne's abstruse, muscular metaphors and Milton's grand measured similes. This is the orthodox account of the matter, and to some readers, it will seem merely perverse not to leave it at that.

I should like to suggest, however, that Donne and Milton in their use of metaphor are not radically different – even though the suggestion is likely to prove irritating to the literary historian. One can image such a historian exclaiming: "Aha! Trying to turn Milton into Donne! Why can't you let matters be? These two poets are fundamentally different. You are blurring the very distinctions which we historians labour to make." And then, as he frowns, and somewhat loudly sweeps the string, this: "Your generation has gone so mad over Donne that you are actually unable to admit that Milton is a poet unless you can translate his effects into Donne's effects."

Now I sympathize with the historian's exasperation. I am not intent on turning Milton into Donne, but I think it worth while to explain why I am forced into a manœuvre which is susceptible of such interpretation.

Our age rejoices in having recovered Donne; but in doing so we have recovered not just Donne's poetry, but poetry. This is so generally true that for many of us the quality of poetry –

as distinguished from that of the more empty rhetorics – is bound up with functional metaphor, with dramatic tension, and with the fusion of thought and emotion – qualities which we associate with the poetry of Donne. Small wonder then if we try to find these qualities, or comparable qualities, in the work of anyone to whom we give the name of poet. For, if the scholar can afford to occupy himself with differences, the critic must finally assume resemblances. That is, the critic is never interested solely in Milton: he is interested in poetry – Milton's poetry, to be sure, but the term becomes meaningless unless it has some relation to an underlying concept. If one is interested only in Milton's *expression*, he will find that quite as characteristically given in Milton's prose.

The scholar's abiding danger is that he will abandon poetry altogether in his preoccupation with individual peculiarities and the accidents of history, finally ending up with a sort of biographical and historical total recall. That the critic, on the other hand, has his typical way of failing I hasten to concede. His danger, I suppose, is to narrow poetry too strictly toward some norm, and to exclude from the commonwealth of poetry those poets who do not measure up.

Obviously, humility and tact are required here. We want to see how poets are related to some common concept of poetry, though we shall want also to take due account of their differences. We want to have it both ways; and with a little tact and a real sensitiveness to the issues, I think that it is possible for us to have it both ways. But in the present muddled state of scholarship-criticism, the charge that the critic is engaged in turning one poet into another – Milton into Donne – is to be expected. I suspect that Professor Douglas Bush, for example, might see it in that way.

The new poetry and the new criticism, for Professor Bush, involve a disparagement of Milton, they tend to exalt Donne over Milton. And Milton's own fervent angel Abdiel could not resent this inversion of just hierarchy more indignantly than Professor Bush resents it. I am thinking not only of his Messenger Lectures, but of his volume on the seventeenth century in the *Oxford History of English Literature.*

Naturally, Professor Bush fixes upon T. S. Eliot as the Satan who has drawn off the third part of the host of Heaven (or at least a third part of the graduate students) from their proper allegiance. Eliot's recent paper on Milton is an interesting and curious performance. I am sure that Eliot has been somewhat embarrassed, and probably quite surprised, to find how much weight has been attached to his various animadversions on Milton. His recent essay impresses me as an entirely honest attempt to undo some of the unintended damage. Unfortunately, Eliot's admiration for Milton is special and partial and whereas he is able to find matters to praise – Milton's great music and his consummate skill in verse paragraphing – he does in fact find little to say about the imagery.

Eliot says that Milton is a great poet because he is the "greatest master of free verse in our language". Bush says, in effect, that Milton is a great poet because he is a great moralist. I agree on the judgement of greatness, but I am not entirely satisfied with the reasons. Eliot's account seems partial; Bush's, finally, irrelevant. I think that better – at least more nearly adequate – reasons can be adduced.

But in seeking those reasons I think that we might well take leave of the embattled moderns (though I have tried to indicate that they are battling over a real issue) in order to go back to a notable seventeenth-century critic, who read Donne and Milton, and apparently read them both with pleasure. I refer to Sir Henry Wotton, who was the author of at least one fine lyric, and whom we reckon as one of John Donne's good friends. Donne addressed several of his verse letters to Wotton. The young Milton, launching his career as a poet, was proud to print in his 1645 edition a letter from Wotton on the subject of *Comus*. It is a handsome letter. Wotton writes: "I should much commend the Tragical part, if the lyrical did not ravish me with a certain Dorique delicacy in your Songs and Odes. . . ." But Wotton does not rest in compliment: he fills his letter with the names and addresses of his friends on the Continent whom he wishes his young friend to meet.

I propose that we use Wotton as a kind of link between Donne and Milton. Wotton could discriminate between them – of that we need have no fear. (If Milton's songs have a "Dorique delicacy", how would Wotton have characterized Donne's? As possessing a Corinthian opulence? A Baroque vigour?) Would he have found resemblances between Donne's poetry and Milton's? I think so. Take, for example, a passage from the "tragical part" of *Comus*, Comus's speech on Temperance.

> Wherefore did Nature powre her bounties forth,
> With such a full and unwithdrawing hand,
> Covering the earth with odours, fruits, and flocks,
> Thronging the Seas with spawn innumerable,
> But all to please and sate the curious taste?
> And set to work millions of spinning Worms
> That in their green shops weave the smooth-hair'd silk
> To deck her Sons, and that no corner might
> Be vacant of her plenty, in her own loyns
> She hutch't th' all-worship ore, and precious gems
> To store her children with; if all the world
> Should in a pet of temperance feed on Pulse,
> Drink the clear stream, and nothing wear but Freize,
> Th' all-giver would be unthank't, would be unprais'd,
> Not half his riches known, and yet despis'd,
> And we should serve him as a grudging master,
> As a penurious niggard of his wealth,
> And live like Natures bastards, not her sons,
> Who would be quite surcharg'd with her own weight,
> And strangl'd with her waste fertility;
> Th' earth cumber'd, and the wing'd air dark't with plumes,
> The herds would over-multitude their Lords,
> The Sea o'refraught would swell, & th' unsought diamonds
> Would so emblaze the forhead of the Deep,
> And so bestudd with Stars, that they below
> Would grow inur'd to light, and com at last
> To gaze upon the Sun with shameless brows.
> List Lady be not coy, and be not cosen'd
> With that same vaunted name Virginity,
> Beauty is natures coyn, must not be hoorded,
> But must be currant, and the good thereof
> Consists in mutual and partak'n bliss,
> Unsavoury in th' injoyment of it self
> If you let slip time, like a neglected rose
> It withers on the stalk with languish't head.
> Beauty is natures brag, and must be shown

> In courts, at feasts, and high solemnities
> Where most may wonder at the workmanship;
> It is for homely features to keep home,
> They had their name thence; course complexions
> And cheeks of sorry grain will serve to ply
> The sampler, and to teize the huswifes wooll.
> What need a vermeil-tinctured lip for that . . .

It is good Elizabethan dramatic verse; and like such verse, it has sufficient and important kinship with the poetry of Donne. To enumerate a few particulars: the pleasant conceit of the silkworms.

> That in their green shops weave the smooth-hair'd silk;

the witty treatment of beauty as a coin that shines by being kept current, with its implication that chastity is mere miserliness; the paradox of earth "strangl'd with her *waste* fertility"; the extended metaphor in which the "forhead of the Deep", bestudded with "unsought diamonds" becomes assimilated to the "shameless brows" beneath which the monsters of the deep come to gaze upon the sun; the ironic pun

> It is for homely features to keep home,
> They had their name thence. . . .

Most interesting of all, in this connection, are the lines

> course complexions
> And cheeks of sorry grain will serve to ply
> The sampler, and to teize the huswifes wooll.
> What need a vermeil-tinctured lip for that. . . .

You certainly don't need a vermeil-tinctured lip to ply the sampler. You need fingers; and the "course complexions" and "cheeks of sorry grain" are thus strictly no more relevant than are the lady's beautiful lips. But by his condensation, Milton has forced the "coarse complexions" and "cheeks of sorry grain" into a kind of relevance. If they are not actually needed to ply the sampler, they do furnish a kind of model for it. For the sampler is of coarse cloth, and its crude colours may be said to be of "sorry grain". The sampler (with its pious motto) is homely workmanship that reflects perfectly the homely features that belong to the needlewoman who makes it.

But these examples are from an early work. We had better turn to the major poetry even though that entails parting company with Sir Henry Wotton, who died, of course, long before the major poetry was written.

Let us begin with a relatively easy simile from the first book of *Paradise Lost.* The fallen angels have just been called back into battle order, and have formed ranks on the "burning marl" of Hell. Satan inspects them:

> Millions of Spirits for his fault amerc't
> Of Heav'n, and from Eternal Splendors flung
> For his revolt, yet faithful how they stood,
> Thir Glory witherd. As when Heavens Fire
> Hath scath'd the Forrest Oaks, or Mountain Pines,
> With singed top thir stately growth though bare
> Stands on the blasted Heath.
>
> (*P. L.,* I, 609–15)

The pictorial effect is pre-eminent, of course. We are presented with nothing less than the wreck of a mighty forest, rising out of – since this is the burning soil of Hell – the still glowing ashes. But the comparison will bear a great deal of weight: it is not general but particular, not vague but rich. For one thing, the files of blackened boles suggested a ranked army as the still-green forest mass could not. We should, then, see the forest, rather than the trees; a great mass of boughs rather than the military files. For another, the forest is now in a sense nobler than before: the great trees, in their ruin, stand out for what they are. But though the stateliness of the growth is more nakedly evident now than before, the *growth* has ended. The trees are as dead as the fallen angels whom they represent, for the fallen angels are now in a real sense dead, great monstrous hulks who have lost their real life. "Heath" is really anticipatory: a heath is a tract of waste land which the former forest will now become. With "blasted" we are back to the tenor once more. The fallen angels have literally been blasted, and we are reminded that the lightning ("Heavens Fire"), God's thunderbolts, which has wasted the metaphorical forest, is the actual artillery that has wreaked havoc on the angelic army.

Consider another simile from the same general context. Here Milton describes the fallen Satan, who does not appear

> Less then Arch Angel ruind, and th' excess
> Of Glory obscur'd: As when the Sun new ris'n
> Looks through the Horizontal misty Air
> Shorn of his Beams, or from behind the Moon
> In dim Eclips disastrous twilight sheds
> On half the Nations . . .
>
> (*P. L.,* I, 593–8)

Again, I pass over the associations of grandeur and majestic scope, for those qualities are not in question. The picture is grandiose: that is conceded. Is it also rich?

The poet wants, first of all, of course, a figure of diminished light – and one which will stress the disparity between the normal sun and an altered sun. Here Satan is not a sun high in the heavens, but a sun that seems on a level with earth, a dawning sun, whose light must struggle through the thicker air near the horizon, and through misty air, at that. In that struggle his beams are shorn away. The beams are "th' excess of Glory", the overflowings from the fountain of light. The sun in Herrick's "Corinna's Going A-Maying", for example, wears his beams – is the "god unshorn", for he is the preponent masculine force of spring. Milton has been very cunning here. He is carefully just to Satan: he specifies that he appears no less than "Arch Angel ruind, and th'excess / Of Glory obscur'd," but the specification itself ironically comments upon Satan's aspirations and his contest with the Almighty. For the sun, the fountain of light of the universe, *must* spill over, *must* have his excess, if he is the true sun. The winter sun, shorn of his beams, cannot fructify, or create anything. Satan is a merely negative and destructive power.

The alternative picture which Milton offers – the sun eclipsed – is more than a simple option: It constitutes an extension of significance; for it is a foreshadowing of what will come out of Satan's defeat. Satan's eclipse bodes ill for men. For Milton knew (and his fit audience knew also) that a "disaster" is literally "the baleful aspect of a planet or star". The obscuration of the sun's brightness is literally the sun's *disaster*; and "disastrous twilight" properly flows from it. In later times monarchs will be perplexed by such disasters of the sun, and will fear that they presage great changes. But Satan's disaster is, for all men, the prime eclipse which presages mortal change for everyone, king and commoner alike.

I have dealt with the way in which this simile looks forward to human history and the results of Satan's fall; but it is tempting to extend it the other direction, to the *cause* of Satan's fall. For it is all here. The simile is a microcosm of the whole poem.

In Satan, as we have seen, "th'excess / Of Glory [is] obscur'd." A glory (Latin *gloria*) is a halo or crown of light. Before his fall, Satan possessed such glory, but the phrase "th' excess of Glory" suggests Satan's motive for revolt – excessive desire for glory. If we as *readers* are not reminded of this, we may be very sure that Satan himself found little difficulty in making the association. Here is his greeting to the Sun when in Book IV he first gazes upon it:

> O thou that with surpassing Glory crownd,
> Look'st from thy sole Dominion like the God
> Of this new World; at whose sight all the Starrs
> Hide their diminisht heads; to thee I call,
> But with no friendly voice, and add thy name,
> O Sun, to tell thee how I hate thy beams
> That bring to my remembrance from what state
> I fell, how glorious once above thy Spheare;
> Till Pride and worse Ambition threw me down
> Warring in Heav'n against Heav'ns matchless King . . .
>
> (32–41)

To sum up: Milton's sun simile is tightly integrated with the theme of the poem. It is not loosely decorative; and in it Milton is using language to something like its maximum power.

I have argued in each of these cases for the interconnections between the metaphor and the total context. I have argued that the so-called epic-similes are not loosely attached decorations, which may be peeled away from the epic structure with little or no loss. But if the similes are so related to their context, one variation which one would expect to find would be metaphors which interpenetrate a whole passage – and which indeed become fully developed only as one followed them through the whole passage. Consider the following: Eve is alone, working in her rose-garden. Satan, having concealed himself in the body of the serpent, catches sight of her:

> As one who long in populous City pent
> Where Houses thick and Sewers annoy the Aire,
> Forth issuing on a Summers Morn to breathe
> Among the pleasant Villages and Farmes
> Adjoynd, from each thing met conceaves delight,
> The smell of Grain, or tedded Grass, or Kine,
> Or Dairie, each rural sight, each rural sound;
> If chance with Nymphlike step fair Virgin pass
> What pleasing seemd, for her now pleases more,
> She most, and in her look summs all Delight.
> Such Pleasure took the Serpent to behold
> This Flourie Plat, the sweet recess of *Eve*
> Thus earlie, thus alone; her Heav'nly forme
> Angelic, but more soft, and Feminine,
> Her graceful Innocence, her every Aire
> Of gesture or lest action overawd
> His Malice, and with rapine sweet bereav'd
> His fierceness of the fierce intent it brought:
> That space the Evil one abstracted stood
> From his own evil, and for the time remaind
> Stupidly good, of enmitie disarm'd,
> Of guile, of hate, of envie, of revenge;
> But the hot Hell that alwayes in him burnes,
> Though in mid Heav'n, soon ended his delight,
> And tortures him now more . . .
>
> (IX, 445–69)

Ostensibly the declared comparison simply records Satan's brief feeling of delight in the fresh pastoral scene. There seems to be so little difference between Eve in her rose-garden and the milkmaid with "Nymphlike step" – particularly when we remember that Eve has, only a few lines earlier, been called a nymph – that we may well feel that the simile fails to pass D1

Samuel Johnson's test; namely, that the things compared should be sufficiently unlike.

The comparison, however, is richer and more complex than that, and Milton is using it, not only to control our attitude toward Satan, but to define precisely Satan's state of mind. Earlier metaphors have compared Eve to a goddess, to Diana or to Ceres. She is now being humanized for the temptation: the scene is a pleasant rural one, and Eve becomes a rustic maid. She is naïvely simple.

But one may well ask: what then does the comparison do for Satan? Surely, he isn't a young Keats, oppressed with the noisome city, now delightedly breathing in the country air and charmed with the country grace of the pretty milkmaid? He is not, to be sure, and I suppose that it would be foolish to put much weight on the vague terms in which the spectator is described, as one who has been "long in populous City pent". It certainly does not seem very promising to make Hell the populous city, though it is sufficiently noisome with the smell of brimstone. But Satan has been out of Hell for eight days at least, and has for some time breathed the sweet air of the Earthly Paradise.

Yet the sense of release and escape suggested by the simile is relevant after all. For Satan is a "pent" spirit – now literally pent up in the serpent but most of all pent up in himself and in the "Hell that alwayes in him burnes". What the sight of Eve does is to draw him for a moment out of himself:

> That space the Evil one abstracted stood
> From his own evil. . . .

And for Satan to be transported out of himself, even for a moment, is a relief. For that moment, he can actually enjoy Paradise. He is, after all, a "Spirit of Heav'n" as he has proudly insisted to Death, and this Garden, as he remarks more than once, is heavenly. To breathe the air of Paradise for a moment gives the sense of enlargement and release. His malice dies away in a kind of grateful homesickness.

Our earlier glance at the young Keats, then, is not completely amiss after all, though we should probably do even better if we substituted for Keats the young Byron. For what is suggested by the metaphor is the relation of the roué and the pretty milkmaid. Does that vulgarize the relationship that Milton has in mind? It does, I fear. Granted. Then let us see how Milton develops and refines it; for he does not ignore, or avoid, the issue.

Eve's virginal innocence is in itself an incitement to the Prince of Evil: if it enchants him for a moment out of his bitterness, and thus releases him into Paradise, its final effect will be to inflame him the more – to thrust him back into "the hot Hell that always in him burnes". He will repay her bereavement of his fierceness with a bereavement of her innocence.

But I am here primarily concerned with the phrase with which Milton sums up the impact upon Satan of the whole natural scene:

> That space the Evil one abstracted stood
> From his own evil, and for the time remaind
> Stupidly good. . . .

"Stupidly good" constitutes the pivot for the whole passage. What does it mean? "To stupify" originally is to astound, to stun. Satan is momentarily "good" from bewilderment. But "stupify" suggests too a kind of torpor, a numbness or stupor. Satan is like a torpid snake – like the snake in which he has encased himself, if numbed, and torpidly harmless. But when the Evil one is abstracted from his own evil, he is not only good (as separated from evil), but stupidly so, for he has so thoroughly given himself up to evil that he is now abstracted from part of himself, and can be "good" only in a dazed and stupid manner, having lost his wits, his directing purpose. If, on the other hand, we remember the pleasant rural scene, with its smell of grain and tedded hay, "stupidly good" acknowledges the rural setting, and accommodates Satan to the rustic scene – like one of Thomas Gray's villagers whose thoughts have never *learned* to stray into the sophistications of evil. It has never occurred to the villager to be evil – he doesn't know how. But to be stupidly good, of course, is not to be good at all: "stupidly" twists goodness away from any moral meaning. Such goodness is not an active virtue at all. And this again fits the situation.

For Satan's goodness cannot last, and Satan cannot be stupidly anything. As soon as the shock wears off, his negative goodness will collapse. Even the sharp revulsion to intense evil is already contained in the phrase "stupidly good". We can in fact read the line thus: for the time Satan stupidly remained good. That will be the way in which Satan, in a moment, will see himself: as being stupid, forgetting his purpose, being foolishly good when his long-sought prey is miraculously alone and at hand.

I do not believe that I have exhausted the meanings of the phrase – certainly not all the shadings of meaning. But all that I have been able to think of are relevant. The phrase in its richness can accept and absorb into it every strand of meaning in the preceding twenty lines.

Sometimes Milton's decisive metaphor is embedded even more deeply in the context, and is even more dependent upon a large context for its full power. Some of Milton's finest passages accordingly seem flat when taken in isolation. The power is that of momentum, not mere swiftness. The dense style has little surface excitement – little apparent speed, but like the slowly rolling cannonball, it can break a man's leg if he puts out his foot to stop it. Mass has been integrated with movement. Unless a poet can make this integration, he has little business in writing a long poem. But by the same token, the dense style may seem devoid of metaphor. For this reason, it would doubtless be the best strategy to avoid altogether *Paradise Regained*, that high Bolivian plateau of Milton's austere style. But *Paradise Regained* is so much underrated that I prefer not to miss an opportunity to mention it.

Paradise Regained is a debate, a debate, I take it, over ends and means. But it is anything but a dry exercise in dialectics. It is dramatic; intensely so, and I suppose that wherever one feels intense drama, he properly suspects that metaphor is present and active, even if there are no showy images to be seen.

In his debate with Christ, Lucifer's constant method is to take the Scriptural prophecies of a Messiah for granted, to assume the validity of Christ's purpose, and to raise each time only the question of means. Christ's kingdom is to be brought to pass. On that point the debaters will agree – the question is how: ends suppose means. Lucifer, as lord of this world, can provide – and will be happy to provide – the means. And he interprets Christ's unwillingness to accept the proffered aid as lack of zeal – a tardy unwillingness to serve the God whose Son he has been proclaimed to be. Christ asks: Why are you so concerned to bring in my Kingdom? Do you not know that its coming involves the destruction of your kingdom? Satan answers as follows:

> Let that come when it comes; all hope is lost
> Of my reception into grace; what worse?
> For where no hope is left, is left no fear;
> If there be worse, the expectation more
> Of worse torments me then the feeling can.
> I would be at the worst; worst is my Port,
> My harbour and my ultimate repose,
> The end I would attain, my final good.
> My error was my error, and my crime
> My crime; whatever for it self condemn'd,
> And will alike be punish'd; whether thou
> Raign or raign not; though to that gentle brow
> Willingly I could flye, and hope thy raign,
> From that placid aspect and meek regard,
> Rather then aggravate my evil state,
> Would stand between me and thy Fathers ire,
> (Whose ire I dread more then the fire of Hell)
> A shelter and a kind of shading cool
> Interposition, as a summers cloud.
> If I then to the worst that can be hast,
> Why move thy feet so slow to what is best . . .
>
> (III, 204–24)

At the least, this is brilliant rationalization. Satan makes plausible his interest in bringing about Christ's reign. Is he lying, or is he sincere? I suppose that the obvious answer is that he is lying. (He is the father of lies.) But the matter is more complex than that: for me, a real weariness breathes through the speech; and in this instance to admit a genuine weariness does not force us to question the genuineness of his present purpose – his attempt to entrap Christ. Satan is weary but he is dogged. We can accept both elements, for they work together –

not only in the sense that real weariness makes his speech plausible and therefore seductive, but in a deeper sense. Satan yearns for the *end*, the end as cessation of activity and the end as goal, purpose. *Worst* is his ultimate port, toward which he journeys, his goal as the realization of himself and as the safe harbour in which he can rest. For Satan has said "Evil be thou my good": the worst is, then, his best. It is his total fulfillment, and because so, only in it can he attain his final peace. Satan is in deadly earnest: he wants victory or death, conquest or annihilation. In any case, he wants the end.

I am not trying to make Satan "noble", and I am sure that Milton was not trying to make him noble. Milton is doing something much more important: he is making the full dramatic commitment to his character, allowing Satan to realize himself in his speeches, doing justice to the tensions that exist in the yearning for rest on the part of a spirit whose essence is restlessness. If there is a contradiction in Satan, Milton is not content to expose it logically; he presents it dramatically.

I have tried to show how much emotional pressure in this context "harbour", "port", and "end" can bear. Let us take the matter a step further. All three attach to a large concealed metaphor, that of a journey, whether by land or by sea. Even the word "error" fits the metaphor: an "error" is literally a wandering. But even if Satan has wandered away, so he argues, his path and Christ's now coincide, for he can accept Christ's goal as his own. They are in the same boat, he argues; or if you like, both are lost in the same desert. It is a weary journey in a weary land. Satan would be grateful for

> A shelter and a kind of shading cool
> Interposition, as a summers cloud. . . .

But Christ seems to hold back, to hestitate, and his would-be companion taunts him as if he lingered:

> If I then to the worst that can be hast,
> Why move thy feet so slow to what is best . . .?

The lines are the brilliant climax to an underlying metaphor which, though I have pointed it up, I have not forced upon the passage: it is implicit in Satan's speech. The smooth, marmoreal surface of Milton's verse is not to be accounted for as the imposition of a classic decorum upon unresisting material. The decorum is there, but it is not stamped down upon inert dead-ness. At Milton's best, it is a dynamic thing, in which the pressures of living language are absorbed, accepted, and brought into equilibrium.

In concluding, I should like to return to the Tuscan-artist simile, for I do not want to seem to evade problems raised by perhaps the most famous simile of them all.

Mr Eliot has written: "Here I think that the two sudden transitions, to the Tuscan astronomer and thence to the Norwegian pine, followed by the concentrated astonishing image of sea-power, are most felicitous. If I may put it in this way without being misunderstood. I find in such passages a kind of inspired *frivolity*, an enjoyment by the author in the exercise of his own virtuosity, which is a mark of the first rank of genius."[1]

But this comment, even when taken as Mr Eliot insists it be taken, with proper reverence, still leaves the simile very close to a mere *tour de force*. No poet has earned the right to display his virtuosity until he has mortised his simile into the larger structure of the poem. We still have to ask: can the simile be justified? Here follows one scholar's attempted justification:

> We are invited to see the moon through the eyes of the most quick-witted and intelligent astronomer of modern times, under ideal atmospheric conditions, under the clear dry sky of Italy. See it thus "with the daring imagination and furtively proud mind of a scientist" in the days of the Inquisition and you are prepared to imagine more vividly and with more emotion the shield of Satan. The fact that the moon is not smooth but ridged and channeled intimates the same of Satan's shield, and "faintly suggests the most superb shield in Homer and in literature, that of Achilles".

Thus far Professor Hanford, and he has indeed here gathered together for us God's own plenty, but scarcely in a form that we can use.

---

[1] *The Sewanee Review*, Vol. LVI, No. 2.

Let us try sorting and shaping it. Satan's shield is of "ethereal temper", of "sphear-metal", to use the phrase of one of Milton's youthful poems, "sphear-metal, never to decay". It is large, round, and like the moon (which also is properly of ethereal temper), but it appears larger than the moon as seen by human eyes – it is like the moon as seen through the telescope. I do not know that the "clear dry sky of Italy" really has anything to do with the case, but I am sure that the mention of Galileo's telescope does. It effects something of the first importance. Ostensibly the comparison merely describes the moon, but actually it establishes the necessary perspective. A few lines earlier, we have listened to Satan and Beëlzebub conferring. But we must now be moved back and made to see them from sufficient distance to take in the whole tremendous scene. I grant that the effect is achieved by an illogical transfer. *We* are not looking at Satan through the telescope as if he were some distant object. But the transfer works. The spectator of the shining shield-orb is located very firmly in this world and very far off from what he sees. Our perspective is sympathetically lengthened: we view Satan from afar.

Yet how defend the last details of the simile as it tails off into apparent digression? Milton specifies not only the time of the observation ("At Ev'ning") and the place ("from the top of Fesole, / Or in Valdarno") but the purpose

> to descry new Lands,
> Rivers or Mountains in her spotty Globe.

Yet this farthest elaboration of the vehicle turns us back to the tenor. The great simile curves back on itself. I have quoted Professor Hanford's reference to the shield of Achilles. It is very much to the point; Milton's "fit audience" would get more than a "faint reminiscence" of Achilles' shield on which were wrought pictures of war and peace, city and country, meadow, field, and stream. Like that of Achilles, Satan's shield contains, and is, a whole world. But the last phrase, "spotty Globe", suggests something further still: namely, that Satan's shield, for all its "ethereal temper" does not properly pertain to the Aristotelian heavens, which were perfect, changeless, not subject to decay.

Satan's shield is rather Galileo's moon, a celestial body, but which, on better inspection, shows as suspiciously earthy. The shield is thus appropriate to its owner. If Milton makes it grand and awesome, not merely like the moon, but like a brighter, magnified moon, he can afford to accept all the other consequences of the magnification. They make for a just picture of the fallen Archangel, now majestic though in ruin.

If the reader is inclined to protest a little at the last point, I would remind him that it was the spots found by Galileo in the sun and moon which helped to get him into trouble. Milton was certainly alive to their significance, and was clearly fascinated by them. In all three telescope metaphors in *Paradise Lost*, the spots duly appear. But, to speak more generally, I certainly do not mean to imply that all the aspects of the simile ought to be, or have to be, in the reader's consciousness. Many people have felt the rightness of the simile without any such conscious exploration. Allow me, however, to reiterate my original point: the complexities are here in Milton's poetry. They probably affect us unconsciously. If we care to explore, we can find them.

With a poet like Donne, we usually *have* to explore them – have to be conscious of them – to get into the poem at all. The complexities involve even the superficial structure of the poem. We get from point to point in the poem only by taking them into account, and though this quality of the structure is not an end in itself (as if Donne preened himself upon being perverse or difficult), still it has a very important practical consequence: it effectively locks us out of the poem until we have actually mastered the poem. The metaphorical complexities stand guard over the inner meanings.

That this is not true of Milton's poetry, surely does not make Milton a less profound poet than Donne, but it does make him a poet easier to *misread*. The way into a Milton poem seems so deceptively easy, and the splendid surface of the poetry may beguile us into glib talk about Milton's grand "simplicity". It may also suggest to us that Milton's use of metaphor is radically different from that of Shakespeare's or Donne's. Worse still, a cocksure confidence in Milton's "simplicity" may deprive us of any real basis for discriminating between Milton's style and that of his eighteenth-century imitators like James Thomson of *The Seasons*.

Eliot is surely quite right in seeing Milton's style as highly personal and special. It is a style which invited imitation. I think that our generation still tends to see Milton in terms of the qualities of style which could be isolated and were isolated, and rather mechanically imitated, in the following century.

This is no occasion for vituperation against Thomson, who like many of the eighteenth-century Miltonists was an amiable and pleasant gentleman, and whose rather tepid and diffuse poem, *The Seasons*, has its own merits. But I am talking now about great poetry and a great poet, John Milton. If we want to get back to Milton and into his poetry, James Thomson or Thomas Warton or even Thomas Gray is not, for us at least, the best guide. I think we have to approach Milton from his own century, and if we need mediation, through the judgement of his seventeenth-century contemporaries. There is, for instance, Sir Henry Wotton, to whom I alluded earlier in this essay. There is, to mention a greater name, Andrew Marvell, for whom Milton was the "mighty poet", yet whose own admirable poetry is metaphysical enough to suit even the "newest" critic.

21

Eve's Awakening

Perhaps more than any other poet Milton has suffered from misapplied biographical interest and misapplied interest in his ideas. A great deal of the distaste for Milton's poetry in the last seventy-five years has sprung from a dislike of Milton the man – as I once heard Professor Douglas Bush ruefully remark. And though Milton's ideas are important – *Paradise Lost* is not just a superb organ music throbbing in an intellectual void – still, our concern for his theological and philosophical consistency can push us into ruinous distortions of his poetry.

There is, of course, no patented way to read Milton, indeed, and if there were such a way, I, least of all, would lay any claim to possessing it. But I do think that a consideration of the structure of the poem, of the interplay of part with part, of image with image, and an emphasis upon the way in which ideas are bodied forth and thus qualified as well as defined by the images might furnish a partial corrective to overweening biographical and ideological emphases. I shall lean very hard upon the Milton scholarship of the last twenty years, and I do not promise that I shall write anything that is fresh and new about Milton's ideas as such. The point that I should like to make in this essay is a highly important point: that Milton's great poem shows the thinking through images which must characterize any genuine poem.

For example, the passages with which I am concerned in this paper bear heavily upon the relationship of man to woman, and thus we run at once into a problem that sets the modern reader's teeth on edge. Does Milton really think that man is superior to woman – that a wife should be subject to her husband? So many of us are made angry by what we are told was Milton's treatment of his first wife, Mary Powell, and by what we take to be

his stiffnecked Puritan opinions, that we are quite unable to
read his great poem. We stop reading the poem to quarrel with
Milton the defective sociologist. I could wish that Professor W.
R. Parker would be able to prove that the sonnet beginning "Me-
thought I saw my late espoused saint" was actually written to
commemorate Mary Powell rather than Katherine Woodcock,
his second wife. Perhaps this cannot be proved. And surely truth
and rigidly honest scholarship have first place. But if it could be
proved convincingly, that proof would do more, I am satisfied,
to commend Milton to the modern reader than anything else
that I can think of. Be that as it may, Milton is on record in one
of his divorce pamphlets to the effect that a woman may have
more intelligence than her husband, and that wisdom, not the
mere fact of maleness, should govern the family decisions. But
whatever may be said in extenuation of Milton's ideas on the
subject, in his poetry Milton, as a matter of course, makes use
of the traditional concept of woman. And if that in itself be
irritating, then we must be prepared to be irritated with such
moderns as William Butler Yeats, D. H. Lawrence, and William
Faulkner, where, unless I utterly mistake myself, the traditional
view of woman is also dominant.

One of the most charming passages in the poem occurs in
Book IV when Eve gives her account of her first moments of
consciousness and of her first meeting with Adam. It is worth
pondering for its own sake, but we shall find it is also a nice
example of the careful articulation of Milton's poem.

Eve tells how she waked, and immediately began to wonder,
as she says, "where / And what I was, whence thither brought,
and how." Eve is no infant for whom the world is a confused
blooming buzz. She has been created mature, and moreover she
represents unfallen humanity with its keen perceptions and its
vigorous and powerful intellect. These she proceeds to apply at
once to the situation in which she finds herself. René Descartes
could do no better: she says not *Cogito, ergo sum*, but *Admiror,
ergo sum* – I wonder, therefore I am. She is a conscious being:
she immediately speculates on what kind of being, and she
infers at once that some power has brought her here from some
place and by some means. But she is charmingly feminine

withal. She is quickly attracted by the murmur of running water to the banks of a little lake, a lake that mirrors the sky and that seems to be another sky. Peering into it she sees an image with "answering looks / Of sympathie and love":

> I started back,
> It started back, but pleasd I soon returnd,
> Pleas'd it returnd as soon . . .

From this Narcissistic indulgence, Eve is called away by the voice of God. He is invisible but by addressing her as "Fair creature", He takes cognizance of her love of beauty, and by telling her that what she sees is an image of herself, he takes account of her bewilderment and her need for companionship. He promises her

> I will bring thee where no shadow staies
> Thy coming, and thy soft imbraces, hee
> Whose image thou art, him thou shalt enjoy
> Inseparablie thine . . .

Adam has been made in God's image; Eve has been made of Adam's substance, and as the invisible Voice here tells her, she has been made in Adam's image as well, and she is to bear to him, "Multitudes like thy self" – that is, beings made in his image and hers.

Milton's scheme of hierarchy is thus set forth concretely and succinctly. The sense in which Man is made in God's image – and the sense in which Eve is made in Adam's image – will come in for more attention in Book VIII: it is that quality which distinguishes man from the brute creation, the possession of reason, already exemplified in Eve's first conscious response to the world in which she finds herself. More of that anon.

For the moment I want to point out that Milton has also in this brief passage touched on what will be Eve's difficulty and what will constitute later the devil's prime means for tempting her. She is sensitive to beauty, and she finds it easier to love the image of herself as mirrored in the forest pool than the image of herself as mirrored less obviously in Adam. For when she is led into Adam's presence, as she confesses to him later,

> yet [thee] methought less faire,
> Less winning soft, less amiablie milde,
> Then that smooth watry image . . .

and so she retreats from him. Later at the climax of the poem, Adam too will have to choose between images: his image mirrored in Eve and God whose image he himself mirrors. He will choose the more obviously enchanting image, that reflected in Eve. The act will be a kind of Narcissism, a kind of self-love. It will cut him off from the primal source of life and power, and throw him back upon himself, though of course he is not capable of sustaining himself.

I must apologize for being drawn away from our chosen passage again and again to follow up implications. But the passage is rich, and this very process of deserting it to point its ties with other sections of the book may become a virtue if it shows us how tightly Milton has articulated his great poem.

But to recur to the narrative. For Eve it is not a matter of love at first sight; but for Adam, it is, and his plea to Eve constitutes one of the most moving passages in the poem;

> Return fair Eve,
> Whom fli'st thou? whom thou fli'st, of him thou art,
> His flesh, his bone; to give thee being I lent
> Out of my side to thee, neerest my heart
> Substantial Life, to have thee by my side
> Henceforth an individual solace dear;
> Part of my Soul I seek thee, and thee claim
> My other half . . .

Adam, who seems to the modern reader so often priggish and pedantic, will not seem so here. It is a love speech, and it moves Eve. She speedily comes to see Adam as more amiable than "that smooth watry image" – sees, as she later puts it,

> How beauty is excelld by manly grace
> And wisdom, which alone is truly fair.

Milton's doctrine that wisdom is superior to sensuous beauty is present here, but for once Milton almost gets by with his presentation of it. By dramatizing the doctrine, and by putting it – not into Adam's mouth but into the mouth of Eve – Milton renders the doctrine inoffensive to any but the most belligerent modern reader.

The psychology of Eve is sound and convincing. To the student of Freud it may seem even preternaturally so; for Milton has made Eve recapitulate the whole process of the child's growing up and transferring the affections to the other sex. According to Freud, the child must transcend the mother image with which it has first associated warmth, nourishment, and affection, and center its affections elsewhere. In the case of the female child the task is more difficult, for it must transcend an image of its *own* sex. But neatly as the symbolism fits into the Freudian system, it is not part of my purpose to place any stress on this.

What I want to emphasize is the power of the passage as an integral part of the poem. We need not fear that we are over-reading it. Milton has been careful to give not only the first conscious thoughts of Eve, but also the first conscious thoughts of Adam, of Lucifer, and of Sin and Death. He has built to, and away from, our passage most cunningly. For instance, Sin is born from Lucifer as Eve is born of Adam. Like Athena, Sin bursts fully armed from Lucifer's head. But with Lucifer it is not love at first sight. *He* recoils from her, and only later she comes to please him – only later that he finds himself as Sin says, "full oft / Thyself in me thy perfect image viewing. . . ." But the Narcissism of Lucifer soon leads to incest, and of this union Death is born.

Milton then doubles the theme once more; for Sin tells that when she had borne Death, she fled from him, but that Death immediately pursued her and raped her, begetting the horde of yelling monsters that now surround her and feed upon her. These passages prepare for, and insist upon, a parallelism between Eve's relation to Adam and Sin's to Lucifer. If we still have any doubt of this, listen to Sin's speech to Lucifer:

> Thou art my Father, thou my Author, thou
> My being gav'st me; whom should I obey
> But thee, whom follow?

And compare it with Eve's speech to Adam in Book IV:

> My Author and Disposer, what thou bidst
> Unargu'd I obey; . . .

So much for the relation of the female characters to the male. But I want to return to the larger theme – in this case, to Adam's first thoughts as a conscious being. Like Eve, Adam first contemplates the sky, but not the sky reflected in a pool. He looks up "Strait toward Heav'n," he says. Next he observes the created world, and infers at once that the creation including himself as creature implies a creator. He addresses the "fair Creatures", which he sees about him, entreating them to

> Tell me, how may I know him, how adore,
> From whom I have that thus I move and live,
> And feel that I am happier then I know.

But the creation – though its very presence testifies to a great Maker – is dumb; it cannot name Him, and it is necessary that the Divine Being himself appear to tell Adam that He is the Author of "all this thou seest" and to offer him life in the Garden with the sole prohibition of the fruit of one tree. Adam then gives names to the fish, birds, and beasts, over whom he has been given dominion. But whereas Eve soon discovers her own image and longs for union with it, Adam from the first looks about to find his own image and cannot find it. He does not find it in the beasts about him and he asks of his Maker

> In solitude
> What happiness, who can enjoy alone,
> Or all enjoying, what contentment find?

In the colloquy that follows between Adam and God, Milton has been daring enough to imply in God a sense of humour – the merest trace of good-humoured teasing. I think that Milton's manœuvre is successful, or almost so. But that is not my point here: I call attention to the fact because most of us are so convinced that Milton is unbendingly solemn, that we ourselves become rigidly solemn readers – to the detriment of the poem.

To summarize the argument briefly: God asks why Adam, in

view of the plenitude of the creatures, should worry about
solitude. And He forestalls Adam's easiest reply by pointing out
that reason is not the sole and absolute prerogative of man, for
God is made to say that the beasts have "Thir language and
thir wayes, they also know / And reason not contemptibly".
To this Adam replies by urging the fact that there can be no true
fellowship among unequals: and it is fellowship that he seeks,
fellowship "fit to participate / All rational delight". I would
emphasize the word *delight* quite as much as the word *rational*.
Adam's point is evidently that reason as a mere instrument of
the will – for example, reason as exemplified by the white rat
that has learned to run a maze for food or by the ape that has
been taught to put one box on another to reach a banana –
reason as pure means is not enough. There must be the ability
to share in rational pleasures.

This view of reason is out of fashion in our times. Milton
reborn today might easily come to feel that our ideal was to
produce highly skilled technicians who should relax from their
technical labours by amusing themselves with the trash of
Hollywood and television. But the meaning of "rational delight"
is crucial if we are to understand this poem.

When God, still apparently refusing to concede Adam's point,
calls attention to His own solitude, Adam correctly puts the
distinction between God and His creatures: God is perfect;
man is not; man's only recourse to remedy his defect is to "beget /
Like of his like, his Image multipli'd". Man, that is to say, can
solace himself only in a human community. With "his Image
multipli'd" we are back to our word Image once more. Man
needs to see himself in the creation and he cannot find himself
mirrored in the creation of fish, birds, and beasts.

This is the answer that God is waiting for. And he picks up
this term *image* in his next speech to Adam, congratulating him
on "Expressing well the spirit within thee free, / My Image, not
imparted to the Brute". His questions to Adam have been but a
test. He has known all along that it was "not good for Man to be
alone", and he promises to create forthwith

Thy likeness, thy fit help, thy other self . . .

It is now time to turn to Lucifer's account of what he felt at his creation. The relevant passage is that in which Lucifer is replying to Abdiel's charge that Lucifer is the creature of God, made by God, and now rebelling against his Maker. Lucifer haughtily replies as follows:

> That we were formd then saist thou? . . .
> . . . . . strange point and new!
> Doctrin which we would know whence learnt: who saw
> When this creation was? rememberst thou
> Thy making, while the Maker gave thee being?
> We know no time when we were not as now;
> Know none before us, self-begot, self-rais'd
> By our own quick'ning power, when fatal course
> Had circl'd his full Orbe, the birth mature
> Of this our native Heav'n, Ethereal Sons.
> Our puissance is our own, . . .

Now Satan is very clever here, and I am not sure that C. S. Lewis's admirable commentary quite does him full justice. Lucifer, like a good scientist, demands evidence of the senses: "We know no time when we were not as now." Of course not; one cannot as a conscious being have experience of a period in which one was not a conscious being. (How quickly Eve can master this devil's logic we shall see in Book IX.) Lucifer rejects all hypotheses of creation. The mirror is here demanding equality with the source of light which it reflects: that is, the mirror is saying: "I am no mere reflector of light; I am a source of light."

It is true that Lucifer, in his debate with Abdiel, does not use the word *image* nor does he make use of the light-mirror configuration. But that basic symbolism runs through the poem. One remembers that Lucifer in Book I is compared to the sun, the wintry sun peering through the mists, or a sun in dim eclipse, shedding disastrous twilight. And one remembers his address to the sun in Book IV in which he expresses his hatred of its beams. And one remembers most of all the great parable of just hierarchy as represented in the starry heavens:

> Of Light by farr the greater part [God] took,
>   . . . and plac'd
> In the Suns Orb, made porous to receive

And drink the liquid Light, firme to retaine
Her gather'd beams, great Palace now of Light,
Hither as to thir Fountain other Starrs
Repairing, in thir gold'n Urns draw Light,
And hence the Morning Planet guilds her horns. . . . .

Even those stars which have a modicum of their own light, "Thir small peculiar," draw upon the great fountain of the sun "By tincture or reflection." The Morning Planet is of course the morning star, Lucifer, and Milton could count upon his reader's – though not apparently upon modern editors' – remembering Isaiah, 14:12–13: "How art thou fallen from heaven, O Lucifer, son of the morning! how art thou cut down to the ground . . . For thou hast said in thine heart. I will ascend into heaven, I will exalt my throne above the stars of God . . ."

Lucifer has been unwilling to augment his own light – *his* "small peculiar" – by reflecting light from the great source of light. He has set himself up as a source. He puts himself in competition with God. Small wonder that the fervent angel Abdiel addresses Lucifer as one "alienate from God, . . . Spirit accurst . . ."

This is the sin into which Adam and Eve are to fall: that of alienation from God. The mirror will turn away from the light in the vanity of thinking itself as light-giving. God's image will no longer be reflected in it because it has tilted itself away from God. When in Book XI, Adam wonders that God will allow Man made in His image to become deformed with plague and pestilence, the angel Michael answers him by saying

Thir Makers Image . . . then
Forsook them, when themselves they villifi'd. . . .

The motivation for this act of secession will be pride – both in Lucifer and in Adam and Eve. God will be regarded no longer as father but as tyrant; not as loving overlord but as rival; and man, seceding from God, will attempt to set himself up as a god. When Eve tastes the forbidden fruit, the poet grimly comments "nor was God-head from her thought".

Now in summarizing thus, I am of course saying little that is new. The general point is a familiar one, though not an

unchallenged one. My justification in proceeding through the
account once more is to indicate how carefully Milton has
worked it out in certain dominant images and how he has
implied the nature of the fall in his account of the creation of
Adam and Eve. Eve must not forget what she was once able to
infer so clearly: that she is a creature and therefore cannot
assume the prerogatives of the Creator; and Eve must not
become obsessed with her own lovely image; the superficial
reflection of herself in a lower element. As for Adam, he must
not become obsessed with that lovely image either – to the point
of preferring that image to the image of God.

But I mean to go beyond this summary to some speculations
about the kind of knowledge to which Adam and Eve attain
by eating the fruit. Here there is no widespread agreement
among Milton authorities. Conjectures range from the acquisition of scientific knowledge to no knowledge at all. I have
already written on this topic recently, and perhaps my best
expedient here is to cite a portion of that paper as published in
PMLA (December, 1951).

"What knowledge, then, does the Forbidden Fruit confer? I
think that an earlier section of Eve's speech can set us on the
right track. She has exclaimed:

> For good unknown, sure is not had, or had
> And yet unknown, is as not had at all.

This seems plausible to her, and since we are fallen men, it
probably seems plausible to us. How can you have something
that you don't know you have? Or if you have it, how does an
ignorant possession of it do you any good? For most of us this is
not devil's logic; it is just logic. If Milton is to maintain the
opposite – and I think that he does – then he will have to present
his case through extralogical devices including paradox.

"The Forbidden Fruit gives Adam knowledge of good and
evil as *we* know them. But it gives him such knowledge only at
the price of extirpating another kind of knowledge. Milton
maintains that the other kind of knowledge was possible –
though none of his readers, being mortal men, could have
experienced it. God is made to say that Adam would have been

happier 'to have known / Good by itself.' That state is properly mythical. Has Milton been able to intimate it – to suggest to us what it was like? We must expect to see him play upon the various senses of the word *know* – not as an idle rhetorical gesture but in order to refashion from our various dictionary uses a sense of *know* which will be relevant to the myth that he is presenting.

"The good that Adam possesses, he does not 'know' he possesses. He will know that he had it only after he has lost it. Adam states this in so many words after the Fall:

> we know
> Both Good and Evil, Good lost, and Evil got,
> Bad Fruit of Knowledge, if this be to know. . . .

But this state of affairs has been implicit in all the earlier action. Earlier, Adam could say: '[I] feel that I am happier then I know.' One cannot substitute for this: '[I] know that I am happier than I know.' Grammatically this is literal nonsense; theologically it is also nonsense. One can only say: '[I] know that I *was* happier than I *knew*.' Earlier the angels have sung:

> thrice happie if they know
> Thir happiness . . .

Later God pronounces:

> Happier, had it suffic'd him to have known
> Good by it self, and Evil not at all.

Milton, speaking as chorus in Book IV, and with all the stops of verbal wit pulled out, stresses the paradox:

> Blest pair; and O yet happiest if ye seek
> No happier state, and know to know no more.

"The unfallen Adam is really very much like the child described in Wordsworth's Immortality Ode: Wordsworth might indeed be describing Adam in the epithets he bestows upon the child: 'Nature's Priest,' 'best Philosopher', 'Seer blest,' 'Thou, over whom thy Immortality / Broods like the Day, a Master o'er a Slave.' Yet the Child cannot impart his philosophy and does not 'know' that he possesses it. If he is an 'Eye among the blind', he is also 'deaf and silent'. One cannot even acquaint him with the knowledge that he possesses without destroying his knowledge by making self-conscious and abstract what is concrete and joyful and unself-conscious. The poet was himself once such a child, and having lost the child's knowledge, knows at last what it was that he once possessed. But he cannot 'know' it *and* possess it. I am tempted to complete the parallel by saying that Wordsworth at the end of the Ode speaks very much like the fallen but repentant Adam at the end of *Paradise Lost*: both have attained a wisdom out of suffering and 'the faith that looks through death'.

"One is tempted to go still further and say that for Adam and Eve, their immortality does indeed brood over them like 'a Master o'er a Slave'; that Eve responding to Lucifer's words, throws off her immortality because she is persuaded that she is enslaved; that her assertion of individuality and separateness challenges the complete harmony in which she moves, and finds in death its necessary consequence."[1]

In the paper from which I have just been quoting. I was concerned primarily with the use of the word *fruit* in *Paradise Lost*, and with the necessity for making use of myth – a necessity which the very nature of his problem had enjoined upon Milton. But I should like to go on to connect this account with the whole matter of God's image as reflected in Adam and Eve. As I have remarked in commenting on the child of Wordsworth's poem: one cannot even "acquaint him with the knowledge that he possesses without destroying his knowledge by making self-conscious and abstract what is concrete and joyful and unself-conscious". It is this kind of self-consciousness that constitutes the knowledge that Adam and Eve gain from eating the forbidden fruit.

Dorothy Sayers remarks that St Augustine suggests that the Fall is a lapse into self-consciousness, and though I am not certain that I have located in Augustine the passage or passages to which she refers, it is very true that there are passages in his *City of God* that do point toward self-consciousness as the knowledge conferred by the act of plucking and eating the fatal

[1] *PMLA, LXVI* (1951), 1051–3.

apple. For example, in Book XIV, Ch. XIII, St Augustine writes:

> This then is the mischief: man liking himself as if he were his own light turned away from the true light, which if he had pleased himself with, he might have been like . . . it is good that the proud should fall into some broad and disgraceful sin, thereby to take a dislike of themselves, who fell by liking themselves too much. . . . Therefore says the Psalmist: "Fill their faces with shame, that they may seek Thy name, O Lord": that is, that they may delight in Thee and seek Thy name, who before delighted in themselves, and sought their own.

For anyone who knows how heavily Milton draws on this fourteenth book of *The City of God* and how closely he follows St Augustine even in the nuances of interpretation of the Garden story, Augustine's emphasis on the human pair's preoccupation with self suggests that such will be Milton's emphasis. But the evidence is in *Paradise Lost* itself.

The theme of self-consciousness comes out clearly in Satan's opening words to Eve in the great temptation scene. He begins by flattering Eve, for to succeed he must draw her attention back to the image of herself which she first saw in the forest pool. He calls her "Fairest resemblance of thy Maker faire, . . ." She it is who most beautifully represents God's image. All things in the universe that are fair and good are united in her "Divine/ Semblance". I shall not detail the Serpent's argument. It is brilliantly plausible. Suffice it to say that it ends as it begins; in an appeal to Eve, to Eve's own pride in herself – a pride that will blot out any sense of inferiority to God and hence of any obligation to him.

Adam's decision to taste the forbidden fruit seems very differently motivated. He knows at once that Eve is lost and says so at once. But he means to die with her:

> som cursed fraud
> Of Enemie hath beguil'd thee, yet unknown,
> And mee with thee hath ruind, for with thee
> Certain my resolution is to Die; . . .

Milton furnishes Adam with the noblest motivation to sin, and properly so. The poem gains thereby. But Adam's sin is ultimately of the same kind as Eve's: the first words that he addresses to her tell the story:

> O fairest of Creation, last and best
> Of all Gods Works

he calls her in his agony. And if the words are primarily a testimony to his genuine love for her, and so have their pathos, they also imply the choice that he is to state a few lines later. For him, the Creation is summed up in her, not in the Creator. It is a hard choice, but there is no hesitancy in his mind if he is to be forced to choose. Adam's choice, to be sure, seems to be a detached and unselfish choice, but only apparently so. It is a choice between his community and the divine community – between his little empire and the whole realm of God.

This far I have, I am sure, seemed to stress not the human pair's self-consciousness – as we usually employ that word – but their consciousness of self. But the consciousness of self with its pride is nearly related to self-consciousness with its sense of shame, and if the motivation to sin springs from too much regard for self, with the Fall comes self-consciousness in the senses that associate it with shame, with isolation and alienation, and with the loss of the innocent rapport with the world about one. This is the only knowledge that the act of eating the apple brings the human pair.

The fact comes out nowhere more plainly than in their changed relation in the sex act. The life of the senses had existed before the Fall, and Milton is as fervent as D. H. Lawrence in emphasizing the parity and holiness of their sexual desires and just as emphatic as Lawrence in recognizing the physical implications. But the sex act now after their rebellion against God's order has a different focus. Adam begins to regard Eve with the eye of a sensual connoisseur; he makes comparisons between the emotion aroused in him now as compared with that on other occasions; he has never known "true relish" until now that he has tasted the fruit and he anticipates a special relish now in the act of love. Adam and Eve are each preparing to use the other for his own enjoyment. They are "knowing" and self-conscious about the sexual relations in a way in which they have not been before this.

It is usual to take this passage as a symbolization of the conquest of reason by passion – of the conquest of the lower faculties over the higher faculties. And surely this is a proper and important interpretation. Milton himself has underlined it. Bu the over-emphasis on the sensual aspect of the relation which now occurs puts an end to the old harmonious relationship in which body, mind, and spirit all had due part. The sleep into which Adam and Eve fall is restless and full of troubled dreams, and when they wake, their eyes, as Adam complains, are opened; but opened only to see that they have been deceived. The Serpent has cheated them with his promises

> since our Eyes
> Op'nd we find indeed, and find we know
> Both Good and Evil, Good lost, and Evil got,
> Bad Fruit of Knowledge, if this be to know.

Adam's reproaches to Eve bring on a bitter wrangling between the human pair. The breakup in the universal community implies a further breakup in the human community itself. Adam cannot maintain his loyalty to Eve stated so generously when he elected to die with her. And Eve, reproached by Adam, retorts by making a stinging defense of herself as self.

> Love was not in thir looks, either to God
> Or to each other. . . .

The Cavalier poet Lovelace has dealt with the essence of the situation in his little poem "To Lucasta, on Going to the Wars": "I could not love thee dear so much, / Loved I not honour more." Adam cannot love Eve as much as he ought unless he loves God more: unless he loves God more, ultimately he cannot love Eve at all. Doubtless Milton had read the Lovelace poem, though I am not arguing that he remembers it here. But Milton would have understood the Cavalier poet's paradox, and he was prepared to take it seriously.

There remains one curious further passage to deal with in which man's likeness to God – the sense in which he reflects

God's image – is the matter at issue. It is the speech which God makes to the angels in Book XI:

> O Sons, like one of us Man is become
> To know both Good and Evil, since his taste
> Of that defended Fruit; but let him boast
> His knowledge of Good lost, and Evil got,
> Happier, had it suffic'd him to have known
> Good by it self, and Evil not at all.

The temptation has been to say that Milton here is bound to his source in Genesis and makes the best of an embarrassing business by turning Genesis 3:22 into a sneer upon God's part. But I think that we can do more with it than this. Man is like God in that he has been made in the image of God. God has said so earlier in congratulating Adam upon "Expressing well the spirit within thee free / My image not imparted to the brute." The brutes cannot sin, for their actions are not free – they are instinctive. The great gift imparted to man lies in Adam's capacity to choose – and this implies the capacity to choose wrongly as well as the capacity to obey God's behests not instinctively but freely and consciously.

Yet if the "knowledge" that Adam gains is only self-consciousness, how can Milton have God say that Adam has now become like "us" in coming to know both good and evil? Is God, then, self-conscious and not innocent? I am prepared to answer yes, that God is self-conscious, but that self-consciousness as applied to God does not carry the implications that self-consciousness must carry for a limited being. As perfect omniscience – as creator and not creature – as a limitless being endlessly contemplating his own virtues, God is self-conscious indeed. The whole Western tradition from Aristotle onward is behind Milton here; Milton could assume acquaintance with this tradition and assume it not merely for his fit audience though few. And in *Paradise Lost* itself God is constantly referring to the Son as "My image" and contemplating himself as perfectly reflected in this "radiant image of his Glory". But Adam is not prepared to assume this burden of consciousness. God as creator has, in the fall of the angels, experienced loss and yet he has not been lessened thereby. He is capable of dealing with rebellion and even of bringing good out of that rebellion. But Adam cannot assume the obligations and responsibilities that go with the Creator's self-knowledge. He is a part, not the whole; a creature, not the Creator. If he ventures to know evil, not as a possibility but as an experience, the process is irreversible – irreversible that is in so far as his own efforts avail him. The arm that has cut itself loose from the body cannot rejoin it at will: indeed Adam knows Good lost, and Evil got. Happier indeed it would have been for Adam to know good alone – that is, happier would it have been for him to have remained loyal subject and happy child of God rather than to have tried to set up as a god for himself.

Of course had Adam persisted in his innocence he would have invited the same satiric jeer that Satan darts at the loyal angel Gabriel: "To thee no reason; who knowst only good, / But evil has not tri'd." And this will almost certainly be a modern reader's attitude toward the unfallen Adam; for the modern reader believes in experience as the only guide, and innocence for him connotes callowness and immaturity. He forgets that Milton's Garden state is not static and not ultimate; that Milton has provided for Adam's growth in grace and knowledge, until at last Adam's body shall turn "all to spirit". (See Book V, 497.) Moreover for many readers the issue has been further complicated by the fact that Milton has stressed so powerfully God's plan for making of Adam's very sin the ground and occasion for Christ's redemption of man. But we leap to conclusions if we assume that because the divine plan foresaw Adam's fall and was prepared to turn it to account, Adam's sin was not really sin but "good" after all. Too many modern critics of Milton have erred in just this fashion. They have argued that Milton as a renaissance humanist couldn't really have believed that Adam could have been happy to continue in paradise, that Adam's moral development required his sowing his wild oats, and that Milton was really on Lucifer's side unconsciously if not consciously. The real remedy for these misconceptions is to read the poem itself. A careful reading is rewarding. It reveals that Milton is not absent-mindedly repeating theological ideas in which he had really ceased to believe. Quite the contrary. Milton's insight into the perennial problem of man is profound. It is our modern inability to deal with myth that is at fault. If it is, Milton can aid us. For his great poem is not only an enlightened critique of the mythical method. It is a brilliant example of that method.

22

The Unity of Marlowe's Doctor Faustus

In his *Poetics*, Aristotle observed that a tragedy should have a beginning, a middle, and an end. The statement makes a point that seems obvious, and many a reader of our time must have dismissed it as one of more tedious remarks of the Stagirite, or indeed put it down to one of the duller notes taken by the student whom some suppose to have heard Aristotle's lectures and preserved the substance of them for us. Yet the play without a middle does occur, and in at least three signal instances that I can think of in English literature, we have a play that lacks a proper middle or at least a play that *seems* to lack a middle. Milton's *Samson Agonistes* is one of them; Eliot's *Murder in the Cathedral*, another; and Marlowe's *Doctor Faustus*, the third. Milton presents us with Samson, in the hands of his enemies, blind, grinding at the mill with other slaves, yet in only a little while he has Samson pull down the temple roof upon his enemies. There is a beginning and there is an end, but in the interval between them has anything of real consequence happened? *Murder in the Cathedral* may seem an even more flagrant instance of an end jammed on to a beginning quite directly and without any intervening dramatic substance. Thomas has come back out of exile to assume his proper place in his cathedral and act as shepherd to his people. He is already aware of the consequences of his return, and that in all probability the decisive act has been taken that will quickly lead to his martyrdom and death.

Marlowe's *Doctor Faustus* may seem to show the same defect, for very early in the play the learned doctor makes his decision to sell his soul to the devil, and after that there seems little to do except to fill in the time before the mortgage falls due and the devil comes to collect the forfeited soul. If the consequence of Faustus's bargain is inevitable, and if nothing can be done to alter it, then it doesn't much matter what one puts in as filler. Hence one can stuff in comedy and farce more or less *ad libitum*, the taste of the audience and its patience in sitting through the play being the only limiting factors.

In what I shall say here, I do not propose to do more than touch upon the vexed problem of the authorship of *Doctor Fastus* in either the A or B version. But I think that it is significant that the principal scenes that are confidently assigned to Marlowe turn out to be the scenes that open and close the play. To other hands is assigned the basic reponsibility for supplying the comedy or sheer wonder-working or farce that makes up much of the play and is the very staple of Acts III and IV.

For their effectiveness, *Doctor Faustus, Samson Agonistes* and *Murder in the Cathedral*, all three, depend heavily upon their poetry. One could go further: the poetry tends to be intensely lyrical and in the play with which we are concerned arises from the depths of the character of Faustus himself; it expresses his aspirations, his dreams, his fears, his agonies, and his intense awareness of the conflicting feelings within himself. The poetry, it ought to be observed, is not a kind of superficial gilding, but an expression – and perhaps the inevitable expression – of the emotions of the central character. If there is indeed a "middle" in this play – that is, a part of the play concerned with complication and development in which the character of Faustus becomes something quite different from the man whom we first meet – then the "middle" of the play has to be sought in this area of personal self-examination and inner conflict, and the poetry will prove its most dramatic expression. One observes that something of this sort is true of *Samson Agonistes*. The Samson whom we meet at the beginning of the play is obviously incapable of undertaking the action that he performs so gloriously at the end. Something very important, I should argue, does happen to Samson in the course of the play, and his awareness of some "rousing motions" after Harapha has left him is no accident – that is, the rousing motions did not simply happen to occur at the propitious moment. I should argue that the encounter between Samson and his father, his wife, and the giant, all have had their part in transforming the quality of his response to the world about him, and that the sensitive auditor or reader will, if he attends to the poetry with which Milton has invested the play, come to see that this is true.

I think that a similar case can be made for Eliot's *Murder in the Cathedral*, though I must concede that Eliot has cut it very fine. An attentive reading or a good production of the play will make the reader aware that the Thomas who is presented early in the play is not yet ready for martyrdom. True, Thomas thinks he has prepared himself. He has foreseen the three tempters. But the Fourth Tempter is indeed, as he tells us, unexpected, and Thomas himself is clearly shaken by the encounter and does not experience *his* rousing motions until after a further conflict.

But before attempting to get deeper into the problem of whether *Doctor Faustus* has a proper middle, it will be useful to make one or two general observations about the play. *Doctor Faustus* is a play about knowledge, about the relation of one's knowledge of the world to his knowledge of himself – about knowledge of means and its relation to knowledge of ends. It is a play, thus, that reflects the interests of the Renaissance and indeed that looks forward to the issues of the modern day. There is even an anticipation in the play, I should suppose, of the problem of the 'two cultures'. Faustus is dissatisfied and even bored with the study of ethics and divinity and metaphysics. What has captured his imagination is magic, but we must not be misled by the associations that that term now carries for most of us. The knowledge that Faustus wants to attain is knowledge that can be put to use – what Bertrand Russell long ago called power knowledge – the knowledge that allows one to effect changes in the world around him. When Faustus rejects philosophy and divinity for magic, he chooses magic because, as he says, the pursuit of magic promises "a world of profit and delight, / Of power, of honour, of omnipotence." He sums it up in saying: "A sound Magician is a mighty god." But if one does manage to acquire the technical knowledge that will allow one to "Wall all Germany with brass" or to beat a modern jet plane's time in flying in fresh grapes from the tropics, for what purpose is that technical knowledge to be used? How does this knowledge of means relate to one's knowledge of ends? Marlowe is too honest a dramatist to allow Faustus to escape such questions.

This last comment must not, however, be taken to imply that Marlowe has written a moral tract rather than a drama, or that he has been less than skilful in making Faustus's experiments with power-knowledge bring him, again and again, up against knowledge of a more ultimate kind. Marlowe makes the process seem natural and inevitable. For example, as soon as Faustus has signed the contract with the devil and has, by giving himself to hell, gained his new knowledge, his first question to Mephistopheles, rather naturally, has to do with the nature of the place to which he has consigned himself. He says: "First will I question with thee about hell, / Tell me, where is the place that men call hell?" In his reply, Mephistopheles explodes any notion of a local hell, and defines hell as a state of mind; but Faustus cannot believe his ears, and though getting his information from an impeccable source, indeed from the very horse's mouth, he refuses to accept the first fruits of his new knowledge. He had already come to the decision that stories of hell were merely "old wives' tales" – one supposes that this decision was a factor in his resolution to sell his soul. Yet when Mephistopheles says that he is an instance to prove the contrary since he is damned, and is even now in hell, Faustus cannot take in the notion. "How? Now in hell? / Nay and this be hell, I'll willingly be damned here. . . ."

The new knowledge that Faustus has acquired proves curiously unsatisfactory in other ways. For instance, Faustus demands a book in which the motions and characters of the planets are so truly set forth that, knowing these motions, he can raise up spirits directly and without the intervention of Mephistopheles. Mephistopheles at once produces the book, only to have Faustus say: "When I behold the heavens, then I repent / . . . Because thou has deprived me of those joys." Mephistopheles manages to distract Faustus from notions of repentance, but soon Faustus is once more making inquiries that touch upon the heavens, this time about astrology; and again, almost before he knows it, Faustus has been moved by his contemplation of the revolution of the spheres to a more ultimate question. "Tell me who made the world," he suddenly asks Mephistopheles, and this thought of the Creator once more wracks Faustus with a reminder of his damnation. Marlowe has throughout the play used the words *heaven* and *heavenly* in a tantalizingly double sense. *Heavenly* refers to the structure of the cosmos as seen from the earth, but it also has associations with the divine – the sphere from which Faustus has cut himself off.

Thus, technical questions about how nature works have a tendency to raise the larger questions of the Creator and the purposes of the creation. Faustus cannot be content – such is the education of a lifetime – or such was Marlowe's education, if you prefer – cannot be content with the mere workings of the machinery of the universe: he must push on to ask about ultimate purposes. Knowledge of means cannot be sealed off from knowledge of ends, and here Faustus's newly acquired knowledge cannot give him answers different from those he already knew before he forfeited his soul. The new knowledge can only forbid Faustus to dwell upon the answers to troubling questions that persist, the answers to which he knows all too well.

To come at matters in a different way, Faustus is the man who is all dressed up with no place to go. His plight is that he cannot find anything to do really worthy of the supernatural powers that he has come to possess. Faustus never carries out in practice his dreams of great accomplishments. He evidently doesn't want to wall all Germany with brass, or make the swift Rhine circle fair Wittenberg. Nor does he chase the Prince of Parma from Germany. Instead, he plays tricks on the Pope, or courts favour with the Emperor by staging magical shows for him. When he summons up at the Emperor's request Alexander the Great and his paramour, Faustus is careful to explain – Faustus in some sense remains to the end an honest man – that the Emperor will not be seeing "the true substantial bodies of those two deceased princes which long since are consumed to dust." The illusion is certainly life-like. Faustus has gone beyond a mere cinematic presentation to the feelings of Aldous Huxley – the Emperor is invited to go up and touch the wart on the Grecian paramour's neck – but even so, Alexander and his paramour are no more than apparitions. This magical world lacks substance.

With reference to the quality of Faustus's exploitations of his magical power, one may point out that Marlowe is scarcely answerable for some of the stuff that was worked into the middle of the play. Yet to judge only from the scenes acknowledged to be Marlowe's and from the ending that Marlowe devised for the play, it is inconceivable that Faustus should ever have carried out the grandiose plans which he mentions in Scene iii – such matters as making a bridge through the moving air so that bands of men can pass over the ocean, or joining the hills that bind the African shore to those of Spain. Faustus's basic motivation – his yearning for self-aggrandisement – ensures that the power he has gained will be used for what are finally frivolous purposes.

I have been stressing the author's distinction between the different kinds of knowledge that Faustus craves, and his careful pointing up of the inner contradictions that exist among these kinds of knowledge. I think that these matters are important for the meaning of the play, but some of you may feel that in themselves they scarcely serve to establish the requisite middle for the play. To note the confusions and contradictions in Faustus's quest for knowledge may make Faustus appear a more human figure and even a more modern figure. (I am entirely aware that my own perspective may be such as to make the play more "modern" than it is.) Yet, if Faustus is indeed doomed, the moment he signs, with his own blood, his contract with the devil, then there is no further significant action that he can take, and the rest of the play will be not so much dramatic as elegiac, as Faustus comes to lament the course that he has taken, or simply clinical, as we watch the writhings and inner torment of a character whose case is hopeless. Whether the case of Faustus becomes hopeless early in the play is, then, a matter of real consequence.

On a purely legalistic basis, of course, Faustus's case *is* hopeless. He has made a contract and he has to abide by it. This is the point that the devils insist on relentlessly. Yet there are plenty of indications that Faustus was not the prisoner of one fatal act. Before Faustus signs the bond, the good angel twice appears to him, first to beg him to lay his "Damned book aside" and later to implore him to beware of the 'execrable art' of magic. But even after Faustus has signed the bond, the good angel appears. In Scene vi he adjures Faustus to repent, saying: "Repent, yet God will pity thee." The bad angel, it is true, appears along with him to insist that "God cannot pity thee". But then the bad angel had appeared along with the good in all the early appearances too.

There are other indications that Faustus is not yet beyond the possibility of redemption. The devils, in spite of the contract, are evidently not at all sure of the soul of Faustus. They find it again and again necessary to argue with him, to bully him, and to threaten him. Mephistopheles evidently believes that it is very important to try to distract Faustus from his doleful thoughts. The assumption of the play is surely that the devils are anxious, and Mephistopheles in particular goes to a great deal of trouble to keep Faustus under control. There is never any assumption that the bond itself, signed with Faustus's blood, is quite sufficient to preserve him safe for hell. At least once, Lucifer himself has to be called in to ensure that Faustus will not escape. Lucifer appeals to Faustus's sense of logic by telling him that "Christ cannot save thy soul, for he is just, / There's none but I have interest in the same." But Lucifer employs an even more potent weapon: he terrifies Faustus, and as we shall see in Scene xiii, a crucial scene that occurs late in the play, Faustus has little defence against terror.

In Scene xiii, a new character appears, one simply called "an Old Man". He comes just in the nick of time, for Faustus, in his despair, is on the point of committing suicide, and Mephistopheles, apparently happy to make sure of Faustus's damnation, hands him a dagger. But the Old Man persuades Faustus to desist, telling him: "I see an angel hovers o'er thy head, / And with a vial full of precious grace, / Offers to pour the same into thy soul: / Then call for mercy, and avoid despair".

The Old Man has faith that Faustus can still be saved, and testifies to the presence of his good angel, waiting to pour out the necessary grace. But Faustus has indeed despaired. It may be significant that Faustus apparently does not see the angel now. At this crisis when, as Faustus says, "hell strives with grace for conquest in my breast", Mephistopheles accuses him of disobedience, and threatens to tear his flesh piecemeal. The threat is sufficient. A moment before, Faustus had addressed the Old Man as "my sweet friend". Now, in a sudden reversal, he calls Mephistopheles sweet – "Sweet Mephistopheles, intreat thy lord / To pardon my unjust presumption, / And with my blood again I will confirm / My former vow I made to Lucifer." The answer of Mephistopheles is interesting and even shocking. He tells Faustus: "Do it then quickly, with unfeigned heart, / Lest greater danger do attend thy drift." There is honour among thieves, among devils the appeal to loyalty and sincerity. "Unfeigned heart" carries ironically the very accent of Christian piety.

Faustus, for his part, shows himself, now perhaps for the first time, to be truly a lost soul. For he suddenly rounds upon the Old Man and beseeches Mephistopheles to inflict on him the "greatest torments that our hell affords". The pronoun is significant. Faustus now thinks of hell as "our hell", and the acceptance of it as part of himself and his desire to see the Old Man suffer mark surely a new stage in his development or deterioration. The shift-over may seem abrupt, but I find it credible in the total context, and I am reminded of what William Butler Yeats said about *his* Faustian play, *The Countess Cathleen*. The Countess, as you will remember, redeemed the souls of her people from the demons to whom they had sold their souls by selling her own. Many years after he had written the play, Yeats remarked that he had made a mistake, he felt, in his treatment of the Countess. As he put it in his *Autobiography*: "The Countess sells her soul, but [in the play] she is not transformed. If I were to think out that scene to-day, she would, the moment her hand has signed, burst into loud laughter, mock at all she has held holy, horrify the peasants in the midst of their temptations." Thus Yeats would have dramatized the commitments she had made. The comment is a valid one, and I think is relevant here. Yeats, in making the signing of the bond the decisive and effective act, is of course being more legalistic than is Marlowe, but he vindicates the psychology of the *volte face*. When Faustus does indeed become irrecoverably damned, he shows it in his conduct, and the change in conduct is startling. Faustus has now become a member of the devil's party in a sense in which he has not been before.

I think too that it is a sound psychology that makes Faustus demand at this point greater distractions and more powerful narcotics than he had earlier required. In the scene before this, it was enough for Faustus to call up the vision of Helen. Now he needs to possess her. And if this final abandonment to sensual delight calls forth the most celebrated poetry in the play, the poetry is ominously fitting. Indeed, the poetry here, for all of its passion, is instinct with the desperation of Faustus's plight. Helen's was the face "that launched a thousand ships and burnt the topless towers of Ilium". If the wonderful lines insist upon the transcendent power of a beauty that could command the allegiance of thousands, they also refer to the destructive fire that she set alight, and perhaps hint at the hell-fire that now burns for Faustus. After this magnificent invocation, Faustus implores Helen to make his soul immortal with a kiss, but his soul is already immortal, with an immortality that he would gladly – as he says in the last scene – lose if he could.

It may be worth pointing out that the sharpest inner contradictions in Faustus's thinking are manifest in the passage that we have just discussed. Faustus is so much terrified by Mephistopheles's threat to tear his flesh piecemeal that he hysterically courts the favour of Mephistopheles by begging him to tear the flesh of the Old Man. Yet Mephistopheles in his reply actually deflates the terror by remarking of the Old Man that "His faith is great, I cannot touch his soul". He promises to try to afflict the Old Man's body, but he observes with business-like candour that this kind of affliction amounts to little – it "is but little worth".

Perhaps the most powerful testimony in the play against any shallow legalistic interpretation of Faustus's damnation occurs in one of the earlier speeches of Mephistopheles. If Mephistopheles later in the play sees to it, by using distractions, by appealing to Faustus's sense of justice, by invoking terror, that Faustus shall not escape, it is notable that early in the play he testifies to the folly of what Faustus is proposing to do with his life.

When Faustus asks Mephistopheles why it was that Lucifer fell, Mephistopheles replies with complete orthodoxy and with even Christian eloquence: "Oh, by aspiring pride and insolence," When Faustus asks him "What are you that live with Lucifer?" Mephistopheles answers that he is one of the "unhappy spirits that fell with Lucifer", and that with Lucifer he is damned forever. It is at this point that Faustus, obsessed with the notion that hell is a place, expresses his astonishment that Mephistopheles can be said at this very moment to be in hell. Mephistophele's answer deserves to be quoted in full:

> Why, this is hell, nor am I out of it:
> Think'st thou that I who saw the face of God,
> And tasted the eternal joys of Heaven,
> Am not tormented with ten thousand hells,
> In being deprived of everlasting bliss?
> Oh Faustus, leave these frivolous demands,
> Which strike a terror to my fainting soul.

Faustus is surprised that great Mephistopheles should be, as he puts it, "so passionate" on this subject, and the reader of the play may himself wonder that Mephistopheles can be so eloquent on the side of the angels – of the good angels, that is. But Marlowe has not been careless nor is he absent-minded. The psychology is ultimately sound. In this connection, two points ought to be observed. Though there is good reason to believe that Marlowe expected his audience to accept his devils as actual beings with an objective reality of their own and not merely as projections of Faustus's state of mind, in this play – as in any other sound and believable use of ghosts, spirits, and other such supernatural beings – the devils do have a very real relation to the minds of the persons to whom they appear. Though not necessarily merely projections of the characters' emotions, they are always in some sense mirrors of the inner states of the persons to whom they appear.

The second point to be observed is this: Faustus does learn something in the course of the play, and in learning it suffers change and becomes a different man. At the beginning of the play, he does seem somewhat naïve and jejune. He is fascinated by the new possibilities that his traffic with magic may open to him. Mephistopheles's use of the phrase "these frivolous demands" is quite justified. But in a sense, the very jauntiness with which he talks to Mephistopheles is proof that he is not yet fully damned, has not involved himself completely with the agents of evil. As the play goes on, he will lose his frivolousness: he will learn to take more and more seriously the loss of heaven. Yet at the same time, this very experience of deeper involvement in evil will make more and more difficult any return to the joys of heaven.

At any rate, there is a tremendous honesty as the play is worked out. Faustus may appear at times frivolous, but he is honest with himself. With all of his yearning for the state of grace that he has lost, he always acknowledges the strength of his desire for illicit pleasures and powers. At one point in the play, before he signed the fatal bond. Faustus says to himself that he will turn to God again. But immediately he dismisses the notion: "To God?" he asks incredulously, and then replies to himself: "He loves thee not, / The God thou servest is thine own appetite."

Most of all, however, Faustus is the prisoner of his own conceptions and indeed preconceptions. It is not so much that God has damned him as that he has damned himself. Faustus is trapped in his own legalism. The emphasis on such legalism seems to be a constant element in all treatments of the Faustian compact. It occurs in Yeats's *The Countess Cathleen*, when the devils, trusting in the letter of the law, are defeated and at the end find they have no power over the soul of the Countess. Legalism is also a feature of one of the most brilliant recent treatments of the story, that given by William Faulkner in *The Hamlet*.

Faustus's entrapment in legalism is easily illustrated. If the devils insist that a promise is a promise and a bond is a bond that has to be honoured – though it is plain that they are far from sure that the mere signing of the bond has effectively put Faustus's soul in their possession – Faustus himself is all too easily convinced that this is true. Apparently, he can believe in and understand a God of justice, but not a God of mercy. If Faustus's self-knowledge makes him say in Scene vi: "My heart's so hardened, I cannot repent," his sense of legal obligation makes him say in Scene xiii: "Hell calls for right, and with a roaring voice / Says, Faustus come, thine hour is come / And Faustus will come to do thee right." Even at this point the Old Man thinks that Faustus can still be saved. The good angel has reiterated that he might be saved. The devils themselves would seem to fear that Faustus even at the last might escape them: but Faustus himself is convinced that he cannot be saved and his despair effectually prevents any action which would allow him a way out.

In one sense, then, this play is a study in despair. But the despair does not paralyze the imagination of Faustus. He knows constantly what is happening to him. He reports on his state of mind with relentless honesty. And at the end of the play, in tremendous poetry, he dramatizes for us what it is to feel the inexorable movement toward the abyss, not numbed, not dulled with apathy, but with every sense quickened and alert. (Kurtz, in Conrad's *Heart of Darkness*, shows these qualities. He is damned, knows that he's damned, indeed flees from redemption, but never deceives himself about what is happening, and mutters, "The horror, the horror.")

One may still ask, however, whether these changes that occur in Faustus's soul are sufficient to constitute a middle. Does Faustus act? Is there a sufficient conflict? Is Faustus so incapacitated for choice that he is a helpless victim and not a conscious re-agent with circumstance?

Yet, one must not be doctrinaire and pedantic in considering this concept of decisive action. As T. S. Eliot put it in *Murder in the Cathedral*, suffering is action and action is suffering. Faustus's suffering is not merely passive: he is constantly reaffirming at deeper and deeper levels his original rash tender of his soul to Lucifer. Moreover, if Faustus's action amounts in the end to suffering, the suffering is not meaningless. It leads to knowledge – knowledge of very much the same sort as that which Milton's Adam acquired in *Paradise Lost* – "Knowledge of good bought dear by knowing ill" – and through something of the same process. Early in the play, Mephistopheles told him: "Think so still till experience change thy mind." Perhaps this is the best way in which to describe the "middle" of the play: the middle consists of the experiences that do change Faustus's mind so that in the end he knows what hell is and has become accommodated to it, now truly damned.

My own view is that the play does have a sufficient middle, but this is not to say that it is not a play of a rather special sort – and that its dependence upon its poetry – though a legitimate dependence, I would insist – is very great.

There is no need to praise the poetry of the wonderful last scene, but I should like to make one or two brief observations about it. The drama depends, of course, upon Faustus's obsession with the clock and his sense of time's moving on inexorably, pushing him so swiftly to the final event. But this final scene really grows integrally out of the play. The agonized and eloquent clock-watching matches perfectly the legalism which has dominated Faustus from the beginning of the play. What Faustus in effect tries to do is to hold back the hand of the clock, not to change his relation to God. Incidentally, what Faustus does not notice is that like Mephistopheles earlier, he himself is now already in hell. The coming of the hour of twelve can hardly bring him into greater torment than that which now possesses him and which the poetry he utters so powerfully bodies forth.

Everybody has commented on Marlowe's brilliant use of the quotation from Ovid: "O lente, lente, currite noctis equi," in the *Amores* words murmured by the lover to his mistress in his wish that the night of passion might be prolonged, in this context so jarringly ironic. But the irony is not at all factitious. The scholar who now quotes the lines from Ovid in so different a context is the same man who a little earlier had begged the phantasm of Helen to make his soul immortal with a kiss. Now, in his agony, he demands of himself: "Why wert thou not a creature wanting soul? / Or, why is this immortal that thou hast?"

Again, the great line, "See, see where Christ's blood streams in the firmament," echoes a significant passage much earlier in the play. (I do not insist that the reader has to notice it, or that Marlowe's audience would have necessarily been aware of the echo, but I see no reason why we should not admire it if we happen upon it ourselves or if someone calls it to our attention.) When Faustus prepares to sign the document that will consign his soul to the devil, he finds that he must sign in blood, and he pierces his arm to procure the sanguine ink. But his blood will hardly trickle from his arm, and he interprets his blood's unwillingness to flow as follows: "What might the staying of my blood portend? / Is it unwilling I should write this bill? / Why streams it not, that I might write afresh?" His own blood, in an instinctive horror, refuses to stream for his damnation. Now, as he waits for the clock to strike twelve, he has a vision of Christ's blood *streaming* in the firmament for man's salvation. But in his despair he is certain that Christ's blood does not stream for his salvation.

In short, the magnificent passage in the final scene bodies forth the experience of Faustus in a kind of personal *dies irae*, but it is not a purple patch tacked on to the end of a rather amorphous play. Rather, the great outburst of poetry finds in the play a supporting context. It sums up the knowledge that Faustus has bought at so dear a price, and if it is the expression of a creature fascinated with, and made eloquent by, horror, it is still the speech of a man who, for all of his terror, somehow preserves his dignity. Faustus at the end is still a man, not a cringing wretch. The poetry saves him from abjectness. If he wishes to escape from himself, to be changed into little water drops, to be swallowed up in the great ocean of being, he maintains to the end – in spite of himself, in spite of his desire to blot out his personal being – his individuality of mind, the special quality of the restless spirit that aspired. This retention of his individuality is at once his glory and his damnation.

Index

Index